VOID of
Davidson College

THE DIRECTORY OF
ATHLETIC SCHOLARSHIPS

THE DIRECTORY OF ATHLETIC SCHOLARSHIPS

BARRY AND ALAN GREEN

G. P. PUTNAM'S SONS
NEW YORK

Copyright © 1981 by Barry Green and Alan Green
All rights reserved. This book, or parts thereof,
may not be reproduced in any form without permission.
Published simultaneously in Canada by Academic Press
Canada Limited, Toronto.

Library of Congress Cataloging in Publication Data

Green, Alan, date.
The directory of athletic scholarships.

Summary: A complete, up-to-date listing of
colleges and universities that offer scholarships
to athletes, and of the sports for which scholarships
are offered.
1. Sports—United States—Scholarships, fellowships,
etc.—Directories. 2. Universities and
colleges—United States—Directories. [1. Sports—
scholarships, fellowships, etc.—Directories.
2. Universities and colleges—Directories]
I. Green, Barry, date. II. Title.
GV583.G73   1981   796'.079   81-4498

ISBN 0-399-12620-1 AACR2

PRINTED IN THE UNITED STATES OF AMERICA

To Ruth and Roy first of all,
and to April most of all

ACKNOWLEDGMENTS

We would like to thank all the coaches, athletic directors and sports information directors who provided us with all the essential information that went into the making of this book. We'd also like to thank Jennifer Green and Abby Green, who helped in the research and preparation of the manuscript. In addition, special thanks go to April Green, whose time and effort on the manuscript make even the dedication insufficient.

AUTHOR'S NOTE

To insure that the material contained in this book remains current, we plan to update subsequent editions, including all changes in a school's athletic program. To that end, we invite correspondence from colleges and universities on the status of their programs and their scholarship policies. We can be contacted at P.O. Box 25162, Tamarac, FL, 33320.

B.G./A.G.

CONTENTS

Introduction	13
Part I: The Ins and Outs of the Recruiting Process	17
Warming Up	19
The Rule Book	27
The Game Plan	37
The Ticket to Financial Aid	48
One More Chance	57
Time Out	60
Part II: School-by-School Index	63
Getting Started	65
Conference Listing	65
School-by-School Listing	69
Part III: Sport-by-Sport Index	265
Getting Started	267
State Abbreviations	267
Sport-by-Sport Listing	269

THE DIRECTORY OF
ATHLETIC SCHOLARSHIPS

INTRODUCTION

You no longer have to be a football hero to win an athletic scholarship: proficiency in rodeo, archery, badminton, weightlifting, and, yes, even synchronized swimming, is good enough these days for a four-year free ride to college.

Each year, the nation's colleges and universities award millions of dollars in grants-in-aid to student-athletes. And each year, a significant percentage of available assistance is not awarded—partly because recruiters and coaches, with limited budgets, are unable to locate qualified students, and partly because qualified students are either unaware of all the potential opportunities or uncertain about how to go after them.

Undoubtedly, the easiest way to win an athletic scholarship is to be a star—particularly in "major" sports like football or basketball, which get considerable coverage in local newspapers. The word on top talent is never kept secret, and an outstanding high school or junior college athlete will find the mailbox overflowing, the telephone ringing off the hook, the stands loaded with interested coaches, and, where permitted by association rules, a long line of recruiters waiting to ring the doorbell.

But if you're not a star, if you're an average or above-average athlete, you may never see or hear from a recruiter, despite the fact that you may be scholarship material. As such, you may have to go looking actively for financial aid. The problem, though, is that most prospective student-athletes don't know how to go about it, and the majority of campaigns end up haphazard at best, and unproductive at worst.

This is unfortunate, because with skyrocketing college costs most students need some sort of financial assistance to help pay the bills. For qualified talent, an athletic scholarship can be that ticket to an education—whether it be a "full ride" or partial assistance—and with the great emphasis placed on sports today, the opportunities are enormous.

The task, then, is to learn just how to go about looking for an athletic scholarship. If you go about it the right way, with an understanding of the rules of the game, your chances of success will increase. On the other hand, if you go about it the wrong way, you may end up with little aid, or, more likely, you may have to pay your own way.

This book can help with your search in a number of ways. For one thing, it makes available a comprehensive listing of where the sports are being played, and who is offering scholarships. Without such a list, a good deal of otherwise valuable time, energy, and money can be spent just making inquiries about whether a school has an intercollegiate team in a particular sport, and whether aid is available. But with the list, you can quickly pinpoint the schools in which you may be interested.

In addition, the book outlines a workable strategy that will hopefully end with a grant-in-aid.

This strategy includes an explanation of all the rules you'll need to know—which should eliminate the possibility of being declared ineligible because of some oversight. It gives you an explanation of the types of aid available at different schools, including outright scholarships or awards based on financial need, and what you may be entitled to. It shows you how to establish contact with a coach and offers suggestions on the best way of getting seen in action—which is the bottom line when it comes to winning an athletic scholarship. It outlines the process involved if you miss the first time around and explores ways of moving up to a better situation. Most importantly, it establishes a realistic picture of exactly how colleges and universities operate, and whether you should really be spending time tracking down an athletic scholarship.

This last point is particularly significant because, while there are thousands of opportunities for aid for college athletes, not everyone, of course, is qualified. In fact, there are more than six million students participating in interscholastic athletics today, with more than one million young men playing football, and more than a half-million young women playing basketball. But on the intercollegiate level, where the competition is keener, the number of players is a small fraction of that total.

This does not mean, however, that you have to be a superstar or play a major sport to end up with an athletic scholarship. But it may mean that, in order to win a scholarship, you will have to do some extra work off the field in the form of research, letter writing, and telephone calls, and it may also mean expanding your search for a school.

Many students, it seems, make the mistake of looking for an athletic scholarship independent of their search for a college to attend—as if it were an afterthought. That is poor strategy. The search for an athletic scholarship should instead be coordinated with the overall process of picking a school. Just as you prepare for Scholastic Aptitude Tests, research academic scholarship and loan possibilities, and gather general information about colleges and their academic requirements, so, too, should you be collecting information about various athletic programs and the possibilities of an athletic scholarship.

Similarly, you should have the lines of communication open with your high school coaches, because more so than anyone else, a coach can open the door for you to a college recruiter.

Naturally, merely having a foot in the door is not enough. In the long run, the true test is talent, and, without that, all the planning and strategy won't mean a thing. But if you really do have the necessary talent, then use it for what it's worth. In this case, it may be worth thousands of dollars in tuition, room and board, and other education-related expenses. In short, it may be worth the cost of an education, which can be quite a large benefit for sinking putts or hitting a bull's-eye.

PART I

The Ins and Outs of the Recruiting Process

PART I

The Ins and Outs
of the Recruiting Process

WARMING UP

Most coaches seem to subscribe to different sorts of philosophies, but they all have one thing in common: they're always on the lookout for talented athletes, and they'll go to great lengths to attract that talent to their school.

Similarly, high school and junior college athletes are forever looking for a free ride, hoping to catch the eye of a recruiter or coach.

But even with both groups looking for one another, the twain just does not always meet. And, on close examination, there is good reason for this.

Take, for example, the athletic department at a typical four-year school. With more students than ever before playing interscholastic sports, there is increasing competition for athletic scholarships. Many students, uncertain about how to look for a grant-in-aid, send off stacks of newspaper clippings to college coaches, then sit back and wait for something to happen. Depending on the sport you play, and depending on where you've been playing it, clips may be a valuable tool, and a possible first step in the recruiting process. A coach who likes what he or she sees in the clips may follow up, talking to high school coaches and perhaps watching an athlete in action—all in preparation for what may be a firm offer of financial assistance. In the end, however, coaches often find that the talent they've taken an interest in can't meet the institution's admissions requirements, meaning time wasted for them and no scholarship for the student.

Sometimes schools don't award their available aid because, believe it or not, they can't find anyone to give it to. This is often the case when an institution either adds a new sport to its program or offers scholarships in a sport for the first time. The word doesn't always get out quickly, and coaches are usually reluctant to grant scholarships simply because the money is available.

There are other reasons, as well. Not every school has a substantial recruiting budget, and their efforts may be limited to random mailings to coaches, clubs, and prospective students, and in-person recruiting in the surrounding area. If the school plays a number of "minor" sports, which don't traditionally get extensive media coverage on the high school level, it may have particular trouble finding talented athletes. And if the college does not have a good reputation for its athletic program, potential student-athletes in the area may look elsewhere, while out-of-state students may not even be aware that the school has a team in a particular sport with scholarships to give away.

But even larger schools tend to concentrate their recruiting efforts in a limited geographical area. Usually, this is the result of financial and staff limitations, although sometimes it is the result of conference rules. For instance, the Athletic Association of Community Colleges limits scholarships to residents of Idaho, Washington, Oregon, and British Columbia. Thus, a coach at a member school in Oregon, who has a number of scholarships to award, has no reason to go looking for talent in neighboring northern California.

Actually, most recruiting, except that done by the National Collegiate Athletic Association Division I schools, is usually accomplished within an area of relatively close proximity to the school. This is done for obvious reasons: coaches can spend time looking at the talent, possibly watching all of a prospective athlete's games both in interscholastic play and summer leagues. In addition, college and high school coaches in an area usually get to know one another, and information about athletes is exchanged.

This, of course, is not always the case. Some coaches look to other parts of the country for talent, and frequently return to the same high schools or junior colleges year after year where they know the competition is good. Or, coaches moving from one part of the country to another may keep their old contacts intact and recruit students from that region for their program.

Unfortunately, some cities and counties develop reputations for being less competitive than others, and recruiters tend to stay away. This obviously makes it hard for prospective athletes, who will have less chance of being seen in action.

Many coaches rely on statewide directories or recruiting services that give statistics or scouting reports on high school athletes. The directory numbers can't tell the whole story about a player, but coaches look for ways to narrow down the field, and if your numbers aren't impressive, you could easily be passed over. And the way high school sports have been growing, a good athlete can easily get lost in the shuffle.

As such, it's often necessary to aggressively go after financial aid, and make sure that you at least receive the appropriate consideration. But it is also necessary that you understand exactly what you may encounter as a prospective student-athlete.

In the past, athletic scholarships at many institutions were given to athletes who rarely saw anything other than the athletic dormitory and the playing field. Student-athletes frequently had little to do with being students, and schools made certain their course load in no way interfered with their play. In short, a lot of athletes left school with a degree, but no education. Others never even finished.

In addition, the recruiting practices at some schools were anything but legitimate, and a prospective star was lured to a college with everything from clothing, to money, to a new car, to a promise of a new home for the athlete's parents. Exactly how widespread these violations have been is uncertain, but they have been serious enough to attract attention all the way to the United States Congress.

Only the most naive person would say that the recruiting abuses have stopped. But if the abuses were once widespread, many believe they are now on the decline, and media attention to the problem will probably help reduce instances of rules violation even further in the future.

Historically, the abuses have been a problem almost solely in men's sports. One reason for this is that, until recently, women's sports on most campuses were more or less an afterthought. But that has certainly changed.

At the beginning of the 1970s, only one out of thirteen participants in interscholastic sports were women; a decade later, that figure jumped to one out of three. And as participation in high school athletics has grown, it also has grown in colleges, meaning a significant rise in the number of athletic scholarships available for women.

These changes came as a result of federal law, and there is general agreement that the opportunities for women will continue to increase. The reason for the upsurge is Title IX of the Education Amendments of 1972, which says that no one can be denied the benefits of any program receiving federal money on the basis of their sex. Congress passed the law in 1972, and, three years later, the Department of Health, Education, and Welfare adopted a regulation to implement it. HEW gave schools until July 21, 1978, to bring their athletic programs into compliance.

Basically, Title IX says that schools have to give male and female athletes equal benefits and opportunities, including coaches, equipment and supplies, games and practice, publicity and recruiting. In addition, it states that scholarship dollars must be divided equally, in proportion to the numbers of male and female athletes.

So far, participation rates for men and women are not yet equal, and the money allotted to women's programs is still disproportionately small, even though schools have made efforts to achieve a balance. What this means is that women's programs will continue to see significant growth. (Incidentally, while the budgets for women's programs have been on the rise, the result has not been a decrease in the budgets for men. In fact, the money allotted to men's programs, on the average, also has been on the rise.)

Although they are governed by different rules, both men and women can approach the search for financial aid in pretty much the same way. This involves patience, planning, and persistence. Perhaps the only real shortcut to the process is being named to a high school All-America team.

Indeed, being a high school All-American is a real plus. Each year, the National High School Athletic Coaches Association publishes its All-America picks, and, each year, coaches call, trying to get a leg up on the competition and find out who the winners are.

High school All-Americans are not the only ones sought after, however.

Recruiting services put together All-State, All-County, and All-Conference lists, as well, which will help spread your name—assuming you're included in one of those categories. If you're not, don't despair: you can still obtain financial assistance. But it will be up to you to disseminate word of your talents.

Before you start indiscriminately sending off letters, clips, and photographs, you ought to ask yourself some of the questions that coaches will be asking you. First of all, coaches want to know if you'll be able to meet the school's admission requirements. They'll want to know your academic interests, your SAT scores, and your class rank. In other words, they'll want to know whether they should spend time and effort recruiting you.

Your first step is to investigate the schools which interest you. If you have your sights set on being a veterinarian, there is no point applying to a school that doesn't have a pre-vet program—even if it has a dozen available scholarships in your sport. Some coaches may want you solely because of your speed, strength, and size—regardless of what you might gain academically—but most want to know if you'll fit in at the school. A talented athlete who transfers after one year because the school fails to fit his needs is no good to a coach trying to build a team.

Obviously, not everyone in high school knows what career they want to pursue. But there are definite characteristics that may be important to you when choosing a school: is it coed?; are there fraternities and sororities?; is it in a city or a suburb?; how large is the school?

Most information about a school is quickly available from a catalogue. Since the rules in intercollegiate athletics usually require a one-year loss of eligibility for scholarships for transfer students, you must choose potential schools carefully.

The athletic program is definitely going to be of central importance, but it shouldn't be the only factor. Approach the athletic scholarship as one more variable in an overall choice of schools. And with the large number of scholarships available, it is usually feasible to do this. If you can't find a school with the facilities you like that also offers athletic scholarships, you'll have to make up your mind as to what is really more important—a scholarship or an institution totally to your liking.

Preferably, you'll want to involve your coach in the process—and don't wait until your senior year to do it. A coach can put you on the right path and can use established contacts to pave the way. If you're not certain exactly what school you want to attend, then at least try to narrow down your choices in terms of region, size, etc. In other words, don't start off your search for an athletic scholarship by looking only at athletic programs. Instead, check the lists of schools that give scholarships in Part II of this book—in conjunction with other materials.

This means exploring fully the type of financial aid a school offers, and what you may be eligible for. Remember, aid can be either an outright scholarship or an award based on financial need. It also means exploring alternative routes to receiving aid based on your athletic ability, and it may be that the place to look, depending on your sport, is outside of an institution.

For example, while parachuting has not yet become a bona fide intercollegiate sport, there are, nonetheless, a number of schools around the country with parachuting clubs. Each year, the National Collegiate Parachuting League awards a scholarship to the winner of the national championships.

Similarly, each year the All-American Collegiate Golf Foundation selects one woman for the $10,000 Colgate Woman's Golf Scholarship, a four-year award based on financial need, academic excellence, and golfing ability.

There are other such scholarships given independently of educational institutions, and they should be included in the overall search for financial aid. All appropriate material about a sport should be collected, so you'll know, for example, how to get ranked, where the major amateur tournaments are being held, where clinics are being offered, where the best summer camps are, and if there are any awards given each year for college students.

If your coach or guidance counselor doesn't have the necessary information, you might try contacting the associations listed below, many of which publish newsletters or magazines that may be of help. In addition, the associations can probably answer most questions you may have, and their resource material could prove valuable in your campaign.

GENERAL INTEREST

Amateur Athletic Union of the
  United States
3400 West 86th Street
Indianapolis, IN 46268
(317) 872-2900

National Field Archery
  Association
Route Two, Box 514
Redlands, CA 92373
(714) 794-2133

ARCHERY

National Archery Association of
  the United States
1951 Geraldson Drive
Lancaster, PA 17601
(717) 569-6900

BADMINTON

United States Badminton
  Association
P.O. Box 237
Swartz Creek, MI 48473
(313) 655-4502

BASEBALL

American Legion Baseball
1100 North Pennsylvania
Indianapolis, IN 46204
(317) 635-8411

BOWLING

American Junior Bowling
  Congress
5301 South 76th Street
Greendale, WI 53129
(414) 421-4700

National Bowling Council
1919 Pennsylvania Ave., NW
Washington, DC 20006
(202) 659-9070

FENCING

Amateur Fencers League of
  America
601 Curtis Street
Albany, CA 94706
(415) 525-8282

FIELD HOCKEY

Field Hockey Association of
  America
17 Indian Spring Road
Rowayton, CT 06853
(203) 853-0033

United States Field Hockey
  Association
4415 Buffalo Road
North Chili, NY 14514
(716) 594-4300

GOLF

Professional Golfers' Association
  of America
Box 12458
Lake Park, FL 33403
(305) 626-3600

GYMNASTICS

United States Gymnastics
  Federation
5025 East Baker
Tucson, AZ 85711
(602) 327-6201

HANDBALL

United States Handball
  Association
4101 Dempster Street
Skokie, IL 60076
(312) 673-4000

HOCKEY

Amateur Hockey Association of
  the United States
2997 Broadmoor Valley Road
Colorado Springs, CO 80906
(303) 576-4990

LACROSSE

United States Intercollegiate
  Lacrosse Association
Washington College
Chestertown, MD 21620
(301) 778-2800

RACQUETBALL

United States Racquetball
  Association
4101 Dempster Street
Skokie, IL 60076
(312) 673-4000

RIDING

Professional Horsemen's
  Association of America
301 North Union Street
Kennett Square, PA 19348

American Horse Shows
  Association
598 Madison Avenue
New York, NY 10022
(212) 759-3070

RIFLERY

National Rifle Association of
  America
1600 Rhode Island Avenue, NW
Washington, DC 20036
(202) 828-6000

RODEO

National Intercollegiate Rodeo
  Association
c/o Shaun Davis
Rt. 1
Filer, ID 83328
(208) 734-4651

National High School Rodeo
  Association
Box 35
Edgar, MT 59026
(406) 962-3411

ROWING

National Association of Amateur
  Oarsmen
4 Boat House Row
Philadelphia, PA 19130
(215) 769-2068

RUGBY

Eastern Rugby Union of America
c/o Kevin Kitto
3216 Fowler St.
Ft. Myers, FL 33901

SAILING

Inter-collegiate Yacht Racing
  Association of North America
8893 Melinda Court
Milan, MI 48160
(313) 434-0746

SKIING

United States Ski Association
1726 Champa Street, Suite 300
Denver, CO 80202
(303) 825-9183

SOCCER

United States Soccer Federation
350 Fifth Avenue, Room 4010
New York, NY 10001
(212) 736-0915

SOFTBALL

Amateur Softball Association of
   America
P.O. Box 11437
Oklahoma City, OK 73136
(405) 424-5266

SQUASH

United States Squash Racquets
   Association
211 Ford Road
Bala-Cynwyd, PA 19004
(215) 667-4006

TENNIS

United States Tennis Association
51 East 42nd Street
New York, NY 10017
(212) 949-9112

TRACK & FIELD

Track & Field Association of the
   United States of America
10920 Ambassador Drive
Suite 322
Kansas City, MO 64153
(816) 891-1077

VOLLEYBALL

United States Volleyball
   Association
1750 East Boulder
Colorado Springs, CO 80909
(303) 632-5551

WRESTLING

United States Amateur Wrestling
   Foundation
Wrestling Division
Amateur Athletic Union
3400 West 86th Street
Indianapolis, IN 46268
(317) 872-2900

THE RULE BOOK

Understanding the rules that govern recruiting practices is essential to winning, and keeping, an athletic scholarship. Unlike the sports you play, where an infraction may result in a five-yard penalty or loss of serve, breaking the recruiting rules may mean trouble for the school involved and an end to your financial assistance.

As already noted, abuses do occur—some of which are quite serious. Intercollegiate athletics, particularly for NCAA Division I teams, is often a major source of revenue. A good team can mean lucrative television contracts, national exposure, and gifts from alumni. As such, recruiters go after talent in a serious way, and sometimes they offer far more than the cost of an education to make their school attractive.

But other types of violations—whether they be conscious or not—may occur. These less-serious infractions may be your fault or the fault of the recruiter, but the end result could be the same: loss of your scholarship. Therefore, it is imperative that you understand the rules governing recruiting and the awarding of financial aid.

There is, however, no standard set of rules that everyone follows. In fact, the rules governing the Association for Intercollegiate Athletics for Women barely resemble those laid down by the National Collegiate Athletic Association. The National Association of Intercollegiate Athletics, with more than 500 members, has its own bylaws, as does the National Junior College Athletic Association, which has close to 600 members. But an understanding of the rules prescribed by these four groups will, in most cases, give you all the necessary information, since a large percentage of the schools that offer financial aid to student-athletes belong to at least one of the organizations.

Other groups, such as that governing the more than 100 community colleges in California, have their own standards. When in doubt, ask. The organization can provide you with an interpretation on recruiting questions, and a simple phone call or letter may save a lot of trouble in the long run.

The basic rule to follow, though, is that you can't receive anything more than aid for the cost of your education. This aid can include books, tuition, room and board, or it can include employment to help defray your expenses, but it can't include gifts of any sort, no matter what league, conference, or association the school belongs to.

THE NATIONAL JUNIOR COLLEGE ATHLETIC ASSOCIATION

The NJCAA, whose members traditionally do not recruit as heavily as four-year schools, have few specific rules relating to the awarding of scholarships. In a nutshell, the association limits athletic grants-in-aid to tuition and fees, room and board, and course-related material, including books.

A member school can pay for you to visit the campus one time, providing you don't stay more than two days, and providing that the visit is completed at least ten days prior to the opening day of classes. If they do offer you aid, the terms of that assistance must be given to you, in writing, no later than two weeks after the beginning of classes.

And once a school has agreed to give you that assistance, it can't change its mind because of your caliber of play. If your performance isn't up to par, or you're injured and unable to play, the school can't cancel the grant. It can be cancelled, however, if you become ineligible because of academic and/or disciplinary reasons, or because of general misconduct that results in permanent suspension or dismissal from the athletic program.

THE NATIONAL ASSOCIATION OF INTERCOLLEGIATE ATHLETICS

Like the NJCAA, the NAIA's membership consists primarily of smaller schools. Also like the NJCAA, the association limits grants-in-aid to the cost of tuition, room and board, and books and supplies.

Unlike the junior college association, however, the NAIA does not allow members to pay for a prospective student-athlete's visit to the campus. The only exception involves schools that have a general institutional policy of paying for visits by students in general, which eliminates most schools.

The NAIA also prohibits individual or group tryouts—on- or off-campus—by prospective applicants. But this doesn't prohibit tryouts by students enrolled at the university. So if you find yourself at an NAIA school without a scholarship, you can still end up receiving aid as a walk-on.

In addition, the NAIA has specific policies regarding the eligibility of transfer students for financial aid. For example, if you transfer from a four-year school to an NAIA member institution, you're not eligible for intercollegiate competition for sixteen weeks. If the sixteen-week period is completed at the end of the spring term, you then become eligible for the following fall term. Summer school attendance does not count toward satisfying the residence requirement.

There are instances when this provision can be waived, however. A junior college transfer who has not previously attended a four-year school is eligible for a waiver, as is a junior college graduate who goes directly to a four-year institution.

There are other exemptions, as well, covering such areas as students returning from the military or studying abroad. If there are special circumstances, specific inquiries, with any pertinent details, should be presented to a member school or the NAIA for a ruling on eligibility.

THE NATIONAL COLLEGIATE ATHLETIC ASSOCIATION

The NCAA, founded in 1906, is the oldest and best known collegiate sports organization, although it is second in size to the Association for Intercollegiate Athletics for Women (AIAW).

Unlike the other associations that govern men's sports, the NCAA does not lump all schools into one class. Instead, it maintains three separate divisions, with specific rules for each.

Undoubtedly, the strongest teams are found in Division I, which includes slightly more than one-third of the NCAA's members. This is where the nation's big-time athletic programs are found, and the athletic scholarship budgets at these schools may run as high as one million dollars per year.

Division II schools also maintain competitive programs, although the squads are sometimes smaller and fewer scholarships are awarded each year. The real difference in the NCAA, though, is with Division III schools.

Under NCAA rules, Division III institutions are not permitted to award financial aid based on athletic ability, but rather only on the basis of financial need. This rule became effective on August 1, 1979; prior to that, Division III schools, like their Division I and II counterparts, were allowed to award financial aid without regard to need, but instead based on athletic prowess.

But there are other rules that distinguish the three divisions, and the NCAA spells out in great detail what is (and is not) acceptable.

To begin with, you become a prospective student-athlete as soon as a member of an athletic staff, or someone representing the staff, such as an alumnus, contacts you or your family for the purpose of recruiting. This can include a telephone call, an in-person visit at your home, or a visit you make to the campus for which they provide transportation.

For Division I and II schools, only six in-person contacts with you or your parents can be made, and the initial contact can't come until you finish your junior year in high school. For football and basketball, no contact can be made after May 15 of your senior year. Once you sign a National Letter of Intent with one of these schools, however (and the signing counts as one contact), there is then no limit on the number of off-campus recruiting contacts a school can make.

Division III schools don't have the three-contact rule, but they also require that no in-person off-campus contacts be made until you finish your junior year.

In addition, all three divisions have rules about what sort of contact can be made at your school. To begin with, a recruiter can't contact you on your campus without first receiving permission from the school. A recruiter also is barred from talking to you at the site of a game in which you participate. So, although they may be in the stands, and although you may have a great day on the field, don't expect them to come looking for you after the game. No such meetings are allowed to occur until after you have left the school grounds.

Of course, a school that's interested in you is going to try to sell you on its program, but the rules simply don't allow the school to bring all prospective athletes—at least in football and basketball—to the campus. Nor do the rules allow you to fly off each weekend to another school.

In fact, as a prospective student-athlete, you're allowed to receive only one expense-paid visit to an NCAA member school's campus, and the visit can't last more than forty-eight hours. Furthermore, no such trips can be made until you begin your senior year in high school, and you're not allowed to accept more than six expense-paid visits to Division I and Division II institutions. And if you're counting on the red carpet treatment on these trips, that won't be the case for the entire journey: the rules stipulate that your seat on the airplane be tourist class.

Once on campus, the treatment may indeed be first class, although the purpose of the trip can only be for seeing the facilities; the coaching staff cannot test your abilities. No actual tryouts are permitted, but that doesn't mean leave your sneakers at home: developmental clinics or contests involving prospective student-athletes are permitted, and you're certainly allowed to spend time on the courts and playing fields.

If a school doesn't invite you for a look around, or you didn't have ample opportunity to see the campus on your two-day expense-paid tour, there is nothing stopping you from visiting the school on your own. As long as you're paying, you're allowed to visit a campus as often as you want.

And even on these trips, the athletic department can provide you with a meal in an on-campus dining room, as well as three complimentary tickets to a campus athletic event for you and those accompanying you. But keep in mind that if you accept anything more than the meal and the tickets, the trip then becomes an official expense-paid visit, only one of which is allowable at each school.

There are exceptions, however. A prospective student can receive only one expense-paid visit to a school if it is athletically related, but that same student can receive another expense-paid trip to the school if it's for a reason other than athletic recruitment—such as a fraternity weekend—and provided that the school's athletic department is not involved in the arrangements.

While on campus, or while speaking with a recruiter, it is acceptable to discuss the prospects of financial aid, so ask specific questions. Although it is a school's financial aid officer that actually awards the aid, a member of the athletic staff can describe their program and recommend you for an award. If an award is to be made, it is the responsibility of the financial aid officer to provide you with a written statement outlining terms and conditions of the grant.

But in order to be eligible for aid at an NCAA school, high school and junior college transfer students must meet certain academic requirements. In fact, the requirements must be met in order to be eligible just to practice with the team.

A high school student entering a Division I school must have graduated with a minimum grade-point average of 2.0, based on a 4.0 maximum for your high school career. For a junior college transfer to be eligible during the first academic year at a Division I school, the athlete must have graduated from high school with the same 2.0 average, and be able to meet the requirements of the new school and its athletic conference. Junior college students with less than a 2.0 average in high school are required to graduate from junior college before becoming eligible for varsity sports at an NCAA school.

The NCAA also has specific rules relating to professional competition, and any violation of these rules makes you ineligible for intercollegiate play.

Essentially, you can't compete in a particular sport if you have ever accepted any pay, or promise of any pay, for participating in that sport. You should be aware, though, that being payed to play in one sport doesn't affect your eligibility for competition in another sport.

If, for example, you tried out for a professional baseball team prior to enrolling at college, and subsequently signed a contract, you would be ineligible for intercollegiate baseball, although you could still play basketball. If your baseball tryout did not result in a signed contract, however, you would still be eligible for intercollegiate baseball. The rule further states that you can accept only one paid visit with each organization, lasting not more than forty-eight hours, to remain eligible for competition in that sport. Nor can you be disqualified for being employed as an instructor in a sport. You are also entitled to compensation from the United States Olympic Committee to cover financial losses resulting from lost job time to prepare for the Olympics without jeopardizing your standing.

But you do give up your eligibility in a particular sport if, at any time, you request that your name be put on the draft list of a professional team, or you negotiate a contract to play pro sports. Playing on a professional team disqualifies you, as does using your athletic skill for pay in any form. And trying out for a professional team during the school year also renders you ineligible.

In addition, there are situations that may make you ineligible for competition in all intercollegiate sports. The first involves your entering into an agreement with an agent who is looking to market your athletic ability or reputation; the second prohibits you from endorsing a commercial product for pay while still in school. So if you have ideas about doing a panty hose commercial, wait until you sign with the New York Jets.

THE ASSOCIATION FOR INTERCOLLEGIATE ATHLETICS FOR WOMEN

Since its founding in 1971, the AIAW has grown from 280 members to its current position as the nation's largest intercollegiate governing body. During this time, the AIAW rules have changed considerably, and coupled with changes in federal regulations, women's sports programs have increased dramatically in size.

While the rule changes have contributed to the growth of women's sports, the AIAW bylaws are in many ways significantly different than those of the NCAA, with regulations that many believe make recruiting for women a lot harder than for men.

Although the AIAW specifies that, like the NCAA, a coach can't recruit a prospective student-athlete until after her junior year, the similarities generally stop there. Under AIAW rules, coaches can recruit via telephone calls or letters, but off-campus contact of any sort is prohibited. In fact, if a chance meeting occurs between a coach and you or your parents, the coach must explain that the regulations don't allow for such contact, and put an end to the conversation.

The only recruiting contact that can occur if you're not a senior is limited to brochures about the school's program, which a coach is free to send to anyone. But if you're still a junior and you write or phone an athletic department for information, the athletic department is required to inform you of the rules, thereby putting an end to the matter.

A college coach is free, however, to speak to high school coaches about prospective students, even if they haven't finished their junior year. Similarly, athletic department personnel can't request you to supply them with information about your abilities if you haven't finished your junior year, but neither do they have to ignore the material. So, realizing the limitations that coaches are under, the correspondence can be a one-way affair until you reach your senior year, by which time you hopefully will have caught someone's attention and will be free to talk with them at length.

If you have completed your junior year in high school, a coach can initiate contact with you—either by letter or phone. Recruiters will actively go looking for talent, but, once again, they are prohibited from making personal off-campus contact with you or your parents.

You are free, however, to visit a campus, along with your parents if you wish, where coaches are allowed to talk with you. But unlike the NCAA, which allows schools to pay the way of the athlete for a visit, the AIAW prohibits paying for such trips. Schools can, if they wish, subsidize part of one visit, including on-campus meals, overnight lodging in a dormitory, complimentary tickets to on-campus events, and transportation to and from an airport, train station, or bus depot.

This prohibition against paying for an on-campus visit obviously puts women at a disadvantage—particularly those women whose families are not well off financially. But those who can pay their way to a campus have one advantage over the men: a chance for an audition. An audition is not a tryout, but rather a way to assess a person's talent. If the school agrees, the audition can be counted as the one on-campus visit for which limited subsidies are permitted.

An audition can be a ticket to financial aid, and since you're allowed to participate in only one audition at each school per academic year, which must be completed within one day, try to make the most of it. Although a coach can agree to hold an audition at any time, he or she is under no obligation to do so.

So set up a definite appointment, and come prepared to play. You can't participate in an actual intercollegiate event during an audition, but you can practice with a team, giving you a chance to really show your talent. A word of caution, though: check first with your high school to make certain that the state association permits such auditions. Rendering yourself ineligible for an interscholastic season—where you may be seen by dozens of recruiters—could be too big a price to pay for one or two auditions.

If you're already enrolled in a college, a coach from another school isn't allowed to contact you for the purpose of recruiting unless you're in the process of completing your studies. This applies whether or not you're playing a sport, so you must make the initial contact. And if you're not completing your studies at a school, auditioning at another institution is tabu.

Under AIAW rules, you're given four years of eligibility. Beginning in September 1981, a woman not receiving an athletic scholarship can transfer to another school and play immediately. If her original college agrees, she can also receive an athletic scholarship immediately. A scholarship athlete changing schools can participate right away at the new school only if she gave the original institution sufficient advance notice of the transfer. To be eligible for a scholarship at the new school, her original college must sign a written release; otherwise, she must wait one year.

In general, the AIAW says that, to be eligible for intercollegiate athletics, you have to be a full-time student, make normal progress toward a degree (if you're a transfer or returning athlete), and maintain the required academic average as stipulated by the school.

In addition, you have to have amateur status in the sport in which you're participating, which means that you've never played the sport professionally. If you have played a sport professionally, however, you can be restored to amateur status by appealing to the AIAW Ethics and Eligibility Committee after attending a class at the institution in which you've enrolled. But even if your amateur status is restored, you're not eligible for financial aid until you've completed one year at the school.

Maintaining your amateur status means you can't accept payment or cash prizes for activities in that sport or for commercial ventures. You can receive merchandise awards without affecting your amateur status, provided they don't exceed $250 in value per year. It is also acceptable to receive money to cover the cost of food, lodging, transportation, and entry fees for open events, as well as money for officiating and coaching.

Once you graduate from high school and are admitted to a college, you're allowed to practice with that school's team. You can compete with the college team when classes for the term preceding your enrollment at that school have ended.

A key to ensuring your scholarship, which should be paid great attention, is the AIAW letter of intent. The letter is a formal statement that you intend to enroll in a member school and that financial aid based on athletic ability has been offered. Signing a letter of intent means that other schools may no longer try to recruit you; if someone does approach you for recruiting purposes, you're obliged to tell them that you've already signed a letter.

Under AIAW rules, a prospective student-athlete may sign one letter of intent. The letter can't be issued by a college before the first Monday in March, in your senior year, and accompanying the letter must be a statement detailing the specific conditions under which financial aid is being offered. The school is required to mail your letter, rather than give it to you after an audition, for example, and you, in turn, are not permitted to sign it on a college campus. It must, instead, be signed at home and mailed back to the school.

Before you do sign a letter of intent, think seriously about whether you really want to go to that school. Although you're always free to attend another institution, signing a letter of intent for a college means you can receive financial aid based on your athletic ability from that school only. In order to receive aid at another school, you'd have to first complete one year of classes there. If you sign a letter of intent, however, and then decide not to go to any school that year, you're free to sign another letter the following March as a prospective student-athlete. But be aware that there are special circumstances under which you can be released from the obligation incurred by signing the letter of intent. This release must be approved by the Ethics and Eligibility Committee, and, until such a release is granted, you're not free to discuss attendance at another school with a coach, even if you're not looking for financial aid.

When a school sends you a letter of intent, you have fourteen days to sign it. (That means fourteen days from the date the athletic director signed it, not fourteen days from the time you received it.) Accompanying the letter of intent will be the agreement outlining the financial aid being offered. If the letter of intent isn't signed within fourteen days, it expires, and another one would have to be issued. The school may or may not have the same fourteen-day deadline for signing the financial aid agreement, but the form will clearly show a deadline date. If the letter of intent is not signed by the designated date, the school can renew its offer by sending you another letter. You can then decide again whether to accept the offer and sign and return both forms.

One important point to remember about the rules of all the governing associations is that they change. Each year, at their annual meetings, policy changes are discussed and voted on.

The NCAA has far and away the most regulations, while the greatest changes have been coming from the AIAW, which has continued to liberalize its policies. It is doubtful that the AIAW rules will mirror those of the NCAA anytime soon, if ever, but it is expected that, as women's sports grow and all the implications of Title IX are understood, the AIAW will continue to refine its policies.

Also keep in mind that individual conferences may have additional rules of their own, as may individual schools, although members of these associations have to abide by the regulations outlined here. A lot of these regulations—for both the men and the women—are sometimes difficult to decipher. And if you're affected by special circumstances, you'll want to get a ruling on your eligibility. The association offices, listed below, will be able to answer any questions you have if your coaches are unable to.

The National Collegiate Athletic Association
P.O. Box 1906
Shawnee Mission, KS 66222
(913) 384-3220

The Association for Intercollegiate Athletics for Women
1201 16th Street, NW
Washington, DC 20036
(202) 833-5485

The National Association of Intercollegiate Athletics
1221 Baltimore
Kansas City, MO 64105
(816) 842-5050

The National Junior College Athletic Association
P.O. Box 1586
Hutchinson, KS 67501
(316) 663-5445

THE GAME PLAN

SCOUTING THE SCOUTS

Perhaps the best way to go about forming a strategy for winning an athletic scholarship is to first understand how recruiters operate. When you have a line on their moves, you can pattern your own offense accordingly.

Take, as an example, the men's basketball program at a Division I Eastern university. As a state school, the coaches are always getting reports about local talent—from high school coaches, alumni, newspapers, and that good old established standby: the grapevine.

The general cycle begins in the spring, when the coaches pore through the recruiting services scouting reports and the files they have been keeping on young talent. In March or April, the school will send out questionnaires to potential prospects, asking them general questions about their physical attributes and their athletic background.

During the summer, the coaches will head for some of the basketball camps, where they'll have a chance to evaluate, first-hand, talent from all over the country. In addition to the camps, they'll spend time sizing up players at summer league competition, keeping notes on prospective talent.

By the end of the summer, the staff might have a list of 400 names that questionnaires were sent to. Those people that didn't respond will receive telephone calls to see what their situation is, and whether they might be interested in the school. In September, the field will be narrowed down to include those students that could possibly fit into the program, and arrangements will be made to start visiting them at their schools.

When this list is complete, the coaches will begin their travels, which last until mid-October. They'll visit with students and make a presentation about the university and its basketball program. Generally, the students that receive visits are those that the coaches believe they might be able to attract to the institution.

But once that visit is over, the student isn't forgotten. Periodic mailings are sent out about the program and how the team seems to be shaping up.

During the last three weeks in December, the coaches are out on the road again, this time watching the talent in action. A transcript request form may be sent to an athlete's high school, so the coaches can decide whether it's feasible to continue with the recruitment process.

As the season progresses, the field will be narrowed down, and the coaches will begin trying to figure out exactly who may give them a commitment. If the coaches are especially interested in certain players, they'll try to get to all their games—even those 150 or 200 miles away.

If they like what they see, they'll try to assess what an athlete is thinking, perhaps by talking to friends or high school coaches. If they think the student may be leaning in their direction, they'll invite him up to the school for a two-day visit.

In February, the situation will probably become a lot clearer, and they'll have a better idea about a student's grades and how interested he really is in the school. The coaches' offices become field generals' headquarters: a large board sits in one corner with names of prospective student-athletes on it. Names are moved around or dropped off, depending on how the coaches assess the situation for each student.

The coaches will try to develop a rapport with the student and/or anyone who might be able to influence his decision. At the same time, they'll be trying to establish exactly what their needs are, and what sorts of players they would most like to have.

As the school year draws to a close, the coaches will try to influence the athletes they're interested in to sign letters of intent. Offers of financial aid are made, and the letters of intent can be signed.

The coaches, with an idea of what the team will look like the following season, start the process all over, sending out questionnaires, reading through scouting reports, and adding new names to the book. In other words, the recruiting process never ends.

Not every school works exactly this way, but this is typical of a big-time program. Coaches at smaller schools, which generally put less of an emphasis on sports, may visit less camps each summer, talk to fewer high school coaches about their talent, and watch fewer interscholastic games, but the methods are essentially the same. In the end, all roads lead in the same direction: where possible, go out and see the talent in action.

At smaller schools, the recruiting budgets may not allow coaches to cover much territory. Nevertheless, these are the places where the average athlete has a good chance of getting an athletic scholarship. So, if you're interested in the school, it's your job to make sure they know about you.

NOW IT'S YOUR TURN

Collaborating with Your Coach

The point can't be overemphasized that a high school coach is crucial to the whole process of winning a scholarship. Many times, a college coach will go directly to your high school coach for information about your ability and interests, without you ever knowing about it. A call to your coach could come as a result of your initial contact, an alumni suggestion, or a scouting report. If a coach is aware of your ambitions and interests, it will make matters easier for all concerned. Eventually, college coaches are going to get to your high school coach for information, so it's wise to work with that coach from the very beginning of your search.

A respected high school coach can also adequately assess the competition in your area as compared with other parts of the country. Some states or regions are known for a high level of play in certain sports. In women's sports, the Philadelphia area is known to produce good field hockey players, because the game is played from grade school to high school. California, meanwhile, is volleyball country.

Some women in the Philadelphia area may not even consider applying for a scholarship because there might be a number of players on their own team with more talent. But that could be a mistake. Even the second-level players on such a team might be able to perform better than the top talent in other parts of the country, where field hockey is just starting to come into its own. If those players are willing to go to school outside the area, there may indeed be an attractive scholarship waiting for them.

The average student can't assess the level of play in his or her area, compared to other parts of the country. A coach may be able to, however, so don't automatically rule yourself out because you weren't tops on your team. Instead, talk it over with your coach and try to get an accurate reading on your abilities.

Correspondence

Some high school coaches say that it is difficult for students to get scholarships on their own; instead, they should be leading the way for their students and making contacts. In many cases, this is true. But it is also true that coaches can't do everything for you, and you're going to have to do your own investigation of where you might like to go, and narrow down choices, independent of your coach's assistance.

Most college athletic departments have general literature available about their programs, which can be a good first step in the selection process. Schools may send this information to anyone who calls or writes, but you'll want your initial contact to be more than just a simple request for a brochure. A letter is probably better than a call for the first contact, because a coach is likely to ask you to send along specifics about yourself anyway, and what's said in a conversation may be quickly forgotten, while a letter will probably go right into a permanent file. An initial letter to a college coach will tell a lot about you, so make certain you get off on the right foot.

A good idea is to include a brief résumé with your first letter. A one-page description of yourself will quickly give a coach an idea of whether you may possibly be the sort of athlete the team needs. This résumé can be photocopied and sent to all the schools in which you're interested. A blanket mailing to every school is of no value, however—not to you or an athletic department. The schools you contact should be ones you have at least some interest in, and schools that could conceivably be interested in you.

The résumé should have all pertinent data, including such things as your grade-point average, SAT scores, the sports you play, awards and honors received, personal statistics, and references. Where appropriate, you should include your times for sprints and longer distances, such as a mile. A field hockey coach, for example, may be impressed to know that you can handle a stick, but that coach may want to know even more how well you move—and how long you can continue moving.

The sample résumé shown here does not have to be followed exactly, but yours should include similar information. The idea behind the résumé is to quickly give coaches an idea of who you are, what you've done, and at least some indication of what your potential may be. If you play a sport such as tennis, by all means include your ranking. A college coach is not likely to be impressed to know that, in your junior year, you won fifteen of sixteen matches. That same coach will be impressed, however, to know that you were highly ranked and made it to the state finals.

This is particularly true if you're looking at schools outside your region, where coaches may not know the caliber of play at your high school.

Along with your résumé should be a cover letter. A form letter will suffice if you have a general interest in the school *(see Sample Letter #1),* but if for some reason you're really enthusiastic about the institution, a personal letter explaining your interest is definitely more appropriate *(see Sample Letter #2).* If your parents are alumni of the school, or you have friends that play sports there, that can be included in the letter. The letter should be addressed to the appropriate coach; if you don't know the coach's name, you can simply address the letter to the coach for a particular sport, such as in Sample Letter #1. If you play more than one sport and haven't decided which sport you want to play in college, you can address the letter to the athletic director.

In addition, it's not a bad idea to include a copy of your upcoming schedule, if available. A coach who is impressed with your numbers will probably want to see you in action. With a schedule of games, a coach who is familiar with your competition can pick the best time to take a look.

SAMPLE LETTER #1

Ralph Seidner
278 Perlov Street
Worcester, MA 01610

June 4, 1981

Soccer Coach
University of Vermont
Patrick Gymnasium
Burlington, VT 05401

Dear Coach,

I am a junior at Birchbrook High School, where I have played soccer for the last three years. I am in the process of investigating colleges and am interested in the University of Vermont. I am particularly interested in exploring the possibility of an athletic scholarship, as I believe I can be an asset to your team.

I have enclosed a brief résumé outlining my accomplishments, along with some newspaper clippings. I would appreciate it if you would provide me with information about your soccer program and scholarship opportunities. Thank you very much.

Sincerely,

Ralph Seidner

SAMPLE LETTER #2

Ralph Seidner
278 Perlov Street
Worcester, MA 01610

June 4, 1981

Mr. Gary Prushansky
Soccer Coach
Gussie State College
San Diego, CA 92109

Dear Coach Prushansky,

I am a junior at Birchbrook High School, where I have played soccer for the last three years. As a freshman, I was the leading scorer on the junior varsity team with 11 goals and 21 assists. In my sophomore year, playing right wing for the varsity, I scored nine goals and had 24 assists, and was named Honorable Mention All-County. This past season, I led the league in scoring with 23 goals and was named second team All-State. Next year, I expect to do even better.

I am in the process of investigating colleges, and am interested in Gussie State. Having grown up in the San Diego area, I am aware of its fine reputation. I am particularly interested in exploring the possibility of an athletic scholarship, since I believe I can be an asset to the Gussie State team.

I should add that I am quite familiar with the athletic program at Gussie State. My brother, Michael, who went to Gussie State on a wrestling scholarship, graduated in 1972. I would appreciate it if you could provide me with information about the soccer program and the opportunities for scholarships.

I have enclosed a brief résumé outlining my career to date, along with some newspaper clippings. I look forward to hearing from you. Thank you very much.

Sincerely,

Ralph Seidner

SAMPLE RÉSUMÉ

Ralph Seidner
278 Perlov Street
Worcester, MA 01610
(617) 675-4321

<u>Academic Information</u>
Birchbrook High School
Darien Terrace
Worcester, MA 01614

Expected graduation: June, 1982
PSAT scores: 519 (V) 611 (M)
GPA: 2.8
Expected field of study: Engineering
Student council treasurer, junior year

Personal Statistics
Date of birth: November 12, 1964
Height: 5'9"
Weight: 164
40-yard time: 4.95
100-yard time: 10.9
mile time: 5:12

Athletic History
Soccer, freshman year: left wing, junior varsity; 11 goals, 21 assists. Team finished second in league, 12–4.
Soccer, sophomore year: right wing, varsity; 9 goals, 24 assists. Team finished first in league; named Honorable Mention All-County.
Track, sophomore year: quarter mile, best time 52.8.
All-American Soccer camp, North Sutton, N.H., summer of sophomore year.
Soccer, junior year: right wing, varsity; 23 goals, 19 assists. Team made it to state quarter finals; named to second team All-State. Elected team captain for senior year.

References
Charlie Russo, varsity soccer coach, Birchbrook High, (617) 675-1234.
Jerrold Schoenholtz, jv soccer coach, Birchbrook High, (617) 675-1234.
Peter Goldwater, director, Murrayville Soccer Camp (603) 234-1000.

If you want general information about a school's athletic program, which you'd like in advance of writing to a coach, contact the sports information director, c/o the athletic department.

Keep a list of every school you write to. When discussing possibilities with your coach, let him know who you've contacted and who has responded. Before you send any letters, though, you might want to discuss your choices with your coach and decide whether they're appropriate.

Some people also send newspaper clippings along with letters. This can be valuable to a coach, depending on the sport you play. For instance, a newspaper account of one basketball game you played will tell a coach virtually nothing—even if your name is in the headline and you were fifteen of fifteen from the floor. If a coach is unfamiliar with the competition in your area, such clips are meaningless. A high-scoring center in one league could end up sitting the bench in another league, and coaches are very aware of this. On the other hand, a sprinter who does a nine-point-five-second hundred-yard dash can run that same time anywhere. Or a high jumper who clears six-feet-five-inches is in a similar situation. In short, when your performance is measured with a tape measure or based on what the stopwatch says, there is no subjective interpretation possible: you're fast or you're not, you can jump high or you can't, and clips about such performances will give coaches information they want.

A number of athletic departments operate on the premise that if they haven't heard of you, they probably don't care to. As such, letters to a college coach touting your abilities may be immediately placed in the circular file. Their recruiters, they believe, are paid to recruit, and their expertise, coupled with the aid of outside services, makes them more than qualified to track down enough talent. So don't be totally put off if you never hear from a school you contact, since you can never be absolutely certain about their needs and what sorts of athletes they're looking for.

Getting Seen in Action

If a coach likes what he sees, he'll want to follow up. The process, as noted, may start with a questionnaire, and then may go to the point of wanting to see you in action. But before spending time traveling, a coach may ask for films instead. College coaches rely heavily on films, and therefore it is imperative once again that you work closely with your high school coach, who can see that a college receives any available footage of you in action.

Not all sports are filmed, but there are other opportunities for coaches to get to see you play. One way is at a summer camp, which recruiters rely on for spotting talent. Camps are an excellent chance not only for you to be seen, but also to help you improve your skills. Each summer, there are dozens of camps in operation—for all sports—that recruiters routinely spend time at. Many camps are run on college campuses by college coaches, who obviously have an interest in the athletes attending. And just as there are scholarships for schools, there are also scholarships for camps. Each year, for example, the Women's Sports Foundation awards a large number of scholarships to women. Some camps are coed, while others are all-male or all-female. High school and college coaches are usually up on both established and new camps, so it is wise to check on where the best ones for your particular purposes are located. And if you've attended a camp, say so on your résumé.

A camp might be a particularly good idea if you play in a weak league. Private school leagues often have levels of competition that aren't as strong as public school leagues. Therefore, a standout player at a private school is at a disadvantage, because recruiters are uncertain how well that player might do in a more competitive situation. A camp can give you that opportunity to play against top athletes and hopefully prove your ability.

Similarly, recruiters keep a close eye on summer leagues, so by all means get involved with one if possible. Once again, your coach can probably steer you in the right direction.

Even if a college coach can't get to see you in person, there are ways that he can get to assess your talent. Many coaches rely on alumni; others rely on high school or junior college coaches they trust. And no matter where you are, if you're a good player, they'll want to know about you.

In fact, coaches will use their contacts to try to pursue athletes from Canada or Europe if they believe those athletes can contribute to the team. So don't think for one minute they won't go after you because you're on the other side of the Mississippi River.

Smaller schools in particular are on the lookout for athletes who initiate first contact, because it saves them the work—with a limited staff—of trying to hunt down prospects. The top talent often looks to schools with reputations for first-rate programs, making it difficult for smaller schools to compete for an athlete's attention. Similarly, it is the top athletes who attract all the media attention, overshadowing competitive teammates who may fit in at a smaller school. It is those second-level athletes who smaller schools are often looking for, yet have trouble finding, simply because the players don't receive much press.

A Closer Look

Making contact with a college coach can mean a lot in your search for a college, helping you to decide not only if you're interested in the athletic program, but the school in general. Athletic departments frequently have receptions for prospective student-athletes in an area, hosted, perhaps, by the local alumni association. These functions should be taken for what they are: they're basically held to sell you on the school. But they're not always hard sell, and you can walk away with a general feeling about the institution.

These presentations typically include films of the school, and here, too, you can get at least somewhat of a picture of the campus and its facilities. Naturally, an in-person visit to the school will give you an even better idea of what may be in store.

A word of caution, however. Some universities paint a distorted picture for visiting athletes, rolling out the red carpet and giving them the royal treatment. College is more than fraternity parties and steak dinners. An on-campus visit is a good time to ask questions about the school, not only from the student who's assigned to show you around, but from anyone and everyone.

In order to get an invitation to visit a school, you have to first impress a coach sufficiently. The NCAA puts a limit on the number of prospective athletes a team can invite to the school if it's paying their way, and coaches want to be certain those invited are athletes with real potential.

Women, of course, have to pay their own way to a campus, but the visit should accomplish the same thing. It's a chance to find out about the facilities, the competition, the competence of the coaches, and aspects of the academic environment.

OUTSIDE AID

One available option to assist you in your search is placement services that match athletes and colleges—an option that we recommend you approach with a good deal of caution. Some coaches complain about these "flesh peddlers," arguing that these services rarely care anything about placing students in schools they'll be happy at. Instead, they say, the services do nothing more than get a student a scholarship—or at least try to—anywhere one can be found.

The other major gripe coaches have with these services is that they're usually not necessary. All these services do, they say, is what a student is capable of doing on his own: work. Most coaches see little reason why a student should spend hundreds of dollars to have someone find them a scholarship, when they can write the same letters and make the same phone calls.

KEY POINTS

Coaches say they get a steady stream of letters from athletes looking for scholarships, so your job is to make a good impression. This is particularly important for women, because while the men's grapevine is fully established, the women's grapevine is still growing. This means that women athletes are less likely to be scouted and more likely to have to go looking on their own.

When you do go looking—and this applies to men and to women—keep in mind some of the hidden costs of going to various schools. A Florida tennis player may be thrilled to win a $1,500 tennis scholarship at a California school, but the value of the scholarship may be spent on airfare during the year. A $1,000 scholarship at a local school may be worth considerably more—at least in dollar value—than the $1,500 scholarship. So weigh carefully your options, and don't just jump at any opportunity. The whole point of winning an athletic scholarship is that it will help pay the bills that you might not have been able to otherwise pay. Therefore, a careful analysis of what you're being offered is essential. Also essential is a thorough understanding of the different types of financial aid and what different schools are allowed to offer.

Before you go exploring in that area, though, make certain you understand the key points in the search for aid:

• *Don't wait until your senior year to get the process going.* Coaches want to know where the talent is as early as possible, so they can build a file on an athlete and watch him or her in action. With spring sports, it is especially crucial that you make contact in your sophomore or junior year. A college baseball coach may never get to see you play if it doesn't happen in your junior year. If the coach does get to see you, it may be once or twice, and if you happen to be having an off-day, your chances of a scholarship obviously won't be helped.

• *Work closely with your coach.* It is no accident that recruiters find talented athletes. College and high school coaches work closely together, and if a high school coach has an athlete he thinks might be suitable for a particular college, he'll tell that coach. But a coach can't read your mind. If you're interested in a school, let your coach know, and find out if he thinks the choice is a good one. As the pressures of recruiting have built over the years, many coaches have stepped in and taken the responsibility for working as a go-between with their students and college coaches. This can only help, because it will take some of the pressure off and let you play up to par.

• *Be seen as often as possible.* Although some coaches offer scholarships on the recommendation of someone they trust—without ever seeing the student in action—they prefer not to. This happens more often in women's sports, where the opportunities for coaches to travel are limited, and women are required to pay their own way to a campus. But most coaches agree that the bottom line in winning a scholarship is to be seen in competition. This means interscholastic competition, summer leagues, camps, or wherever a recruiter is likely to look. And they're likely to look anywhere and everywhere for talent.

• *Explore all your options.* If you think you may have an interest in a school, take a closer look. Making an initial inquiry about a program takes little time, and the follow-up information you receive should help you to decide whether a closer look is warranted. It will also give the coaches an idea whether they want to take a closer look at you. By filling out a simple questionnaire, a coach may know immediately whether there might be a spot for you on the team. If there isn't any interest on the school's behalf, you can pursue those avenues that are still open.

• *Be realistic.* Coaches are always eager to see and hear from talented athletes, but you have to realize your limits. If you know a school is out of your league, then don't waste your time pursuing a scholarship there. Set your sights instead on schools that you have an honest shot at. You can't go looking everywhere, so try to look only to those schools that may eventually produce positive results.

THE TICKET TO FINANCIAL AID

When it comes to the awarding of financial aid for college athletes, there is a lot more than meets the eye. And understanding the intricacies of the awards process could very well mean the difference between a hefty aid package or paying your own way.

Perhaps the biggest misconception is that all aid for student-athletes is in the form of outright scholarships, with schools budgeting a specific amount of money each year for a specific number of free rides in each sport. Nothing could be further from the truth. In fact, the majority of money given student-athletes each year is based on financial need, rather than athletic ability. But need doesn't necessarily mean poverty: in fact, one student we know received a need-based grant even though his father is a successful dentist practicing in Westchester County, New York.

NCAA Division III schools, for example, as well as Ivy League schools, are prohibited from giving outright athletic scholarships. Instead, these institutions award aid based only on financial need, using the same needs assessment systems used for all students. Basically, need is defined as the difference between your educational expenses—tuition, fees, room and board, books and supplies, and miscellaneous expenses—and the amount you and your family can afford to pay.

There have been some arguments in the past few years for the abolishment of outright scholarships based on athletic ability, limiting, instead, grants to student-athletes strictly on a need basis. The biggest resistance to this plan has come from the major schools, where sports are big-time. But even these schools—like the smaller institutions—have limits on the number of scholarships they can award, and understanding just what types of aid schools are allowed to give will help you determine your eligibility. And like specifics involving recruiting, the financial aid picture for men and women is in many ways different.

NCAA

As noted, Division III schools award financial aid to student-athletes only on a showing of financial need. Divisions I and II, however, are able to give students athletic scholarships provided that: a) the award covers only the cost of tuition and fees, room and board, and required course-related books; and b) the award is offered for only one year at a time, with the understanding that it can be renewed for additional one-year periods as long as you remain eligible.

Whereas Division I and Division II schools used to limit aid awarded to athletes to scholarships only, the NCAA now allows a school to give a student-athlete a combination of funds, including an outright scholarship and money from government sources, such as the Basic Educational Opportunity Grants programs, which accounts for billions of dollars in assistance annually. In addition, part of the package can include money from employment during the school year, as long as the total earned, once again, combined with other assistance, doesn't exceed the allowable amount for educational expenses.

Although there are thousands of scholarships available each year from private sources—from companies, associations, and a variety of organizations—the NCAA says you can only accept a scholarship based on your athletic ability from the institution you're attending. Accepting financial aid from an outside source in recognition of your athletic accomplishments would make you ineligible for all intercollegiate sports.

Division I schools, which traditionally have the most powerful athletic programs, are able to maintain superior teams, in part, because each year they're allowed to give out more scholarships than smaller schools. Take football, for example. In this sport only, there are Divisions I–A and I–AA, with the former being the top-notch grouping. Under NCAA rules, Division I–A schools can give up to thirty scholarships each year to new students, and can have no more than ninety-five financial aid awards in effect in any one year. Division I–AA schools, meanwhile, can also give up to thirty football scholarships to new students, but they have a limit of seventy-five that can be in effect each year.

With basketball, all Division I teams have a limit of fifteen on the number of financial aid awards that may be in effect each year.

But beyond Division I football and basketball, schools not only have to limit the total number of scholarships they give, but they also have a limit on the value of the financial aid awards in effect. For example, Division I schools can't have more than eighty financial aid awards in effect at any one time for all sports combined, while Division II schools can't have more than fifty-five, and, by the 1982–83 academic year, they can only have forty-five. And of these totals, schools are allowed the following maximum awards in effect at any one time:

DIVISION I

Baseball	13	Skiing	7
Cross Country/Track	14	Soccer	11
Fencing	5	Swimming	11
Golf	5	Tennis	5
Gymnastics	7	Volleyball	5
Ice Hockey	20	Water Polo	5
Lacrosse	14	Wrestling	11

DIVISION II

Baseball	10	Lacrosse	12
Basketball	12	Skiing	7
Cross Country/Track	14	Soccer	10
Fencing	5	Swimming	9
Football	45	Tennis	5
Golf	4	Volleyball	5
Gymnastics	6	Water Polo	5
Ice Hockey	15	Wrestling	10

These are maximum awards; if a school chooses, it could give either five full scholarships to volleyball players or it could spread the value of the five scholarships among more students, offering, perhaps, ten half-rides. As such, it would be deceiving to merely look at the total amount of money a school may have available for scholarships, or the number of scholarships it awarded previously in individual sports. Depending on how the athletic director wants to apportion the money, a school could shift its emphasis to certain sports—as long as the number of maximum awards doesn't exceed the total prescribed by the NCAA. Or an individual coach could either give full scholarships to a select few, or spread the available aid out among a greater number of players.

Although a school can offer you financial aid only for one academic year, it can renew your scholarship even if you're injured and unable to play—a practice which many schools adhere to, and one you should inquire about when discussing terms of an aid package with a recruiter. By the same token, you can't be penalized if your performance is poor, nor can your aid be increased if you have an outstanding season.

Part of your financial aid package can include employment, but the total received from the job, when added to other assistance, can't exceed the maximum permissible institutional financial aid—covering educational expenses only. Any such employment included in the package, however, is work done during the school term. Therefore, you're free to work at another job between semesters or during the spring break without requiring any adjustment to your grant-in-aid. So if the athletic department can help you find a job during vacations—which many departments do—it only adds to your bank account, rather than affecting your scholarship.

The same is true for summer jobs, and coaches will go out of their way to help find a good job for their talent. This is often accomplished with the help of alumni, and while it obviously can't be included as an official part of a financial-aid package, it is, nonetheless, a benefit that can significantly help to pay your expenses. Often, the promise of helping to find you a good summer job is extended by schools that give only need-based assistance. The opportunity to work in a good job in your field of study, for example, may be more important and lucrative in the long run than perhaps more aid during your undergraduate career. Therefore, when weighing the options about which school to attend—if you have more than one offer—consider all parts of the package.

With schools that give need-based assistance, the composition of the financial aid package is especially important. These schools are often at a disadvantage because they can't offer you an outright scholarship, but they actively recruit talented athletes and they often put together packages for student-athletes that keep their costs to a minimum. Part of this package can be an academic honor award, which can be given without consideration of your financial need.

At these institutions, the athletic department does not make arrangements for aid; the package is instead put together by the financial aid officer, who determines assistance for all students. But the rules governing the decisions on aid are not uniform: your situation could be assessed differently by the five schools you apply to, with each putting together a different financial aid package. Some schools have more money than others, and your aid package may therefore end up larger. A student with top grades is likely to win a merit or honors scholarship, no matter what his family income, and a competent athlete is likely to end up with a good financial aid package that will close the gap between his resources and the cost of college.

AIAW

The financial aid picture for women is considerably different than that for men, the major difference being that while the NCAA does not allow Division III schools to award aid based on athletic ability, all AIAW schools do use that criterion for their awards process.

The AIAW limits the value of financial aid based on athletic ability to tuition, fees, and room and board, while books are not covered. In addition, an AIAW member school can award an athlete aid that is not based on athletic ability—combining the two for a total package. So the difference between a partial scholarship and the full cost of an education can be made up by any sort of package that a school puts together for you, including money from grants, loans, or employment, if you have established need.

According to the rules, the amount of financial aid for a returning athlete has to be at least equal to that given the previous year. And a school has to renew the aid—by July 1—if you're maintaining academic eligibility and if you made the team the previous year. Your part of the bargain states that, in order to have your aid renewed, you have to try out for the sport you participated in the previous year—and play if selected. If you take a year off from school, the institution is not required to automatically renew your aid.

But the school can't withdraw your aid because of illness or injury, nor can it change the terms of the agreement because of your performance. And since you're eligible for aid for four years, you ought to look closely at the financial aid agreement that accompanies the letter of intent.

Like the NCAA, the AIAW also places limits on the number of student-athletes allowed to receive aid based on athletic ability in each sport.

Archery	6	Riflery	5
Badminton	8	Sailing	6
Basketball	12	Skiing	12
Bowling	6	Slowpitch Softball	13
Crew	16	Soccer	14
Cross Country	8	Softball	15
Fencing	5	Squash	9
Field Hockey	14	Swimming	15
Golf	8	Synchronized Swimming	12
Gymnastics	10	Tennis	8
Ice Hockey	15	Track & Field	20
Lacrosse	14	Volleyball	12

Schools are free to offer financial aid in other sports, but the limit on the number of awards has to be ruled on by the AIAW.

These maximum awards are a little deceiving, however, because they reflect the number of awards that can be made, but not the amount of money that can be offered. Under a formula devised by the AIAW, a school that plays a sport in Division I can offer considerably more aid than schools that play the same sport in Division II or Division III, even though all three divisions can have the same number of students on scholarship. (A school is not necessarily affiliated with only one division; instead, individual sports at a school are aligned with one of the three divisions.)

Take Track & Field, for example. Using the AIAW formula, the maximum number of student-athletes receiving aid based on athletic ability can be twenty. A school in Division I competition is permitted to sponsor awards up to the maximum amount of money, which is the equivalent of twenty full scholarships. But Division II schools, while also permitted to give aid to as many as twenty athletes, can only offer up to fifty percent of the total maximum dollar amount, while Division III schools can award only ten percent of the maximum permissible limits. This means that, for Division II schools, only ten "equivalencies" of full scholarships can be offered, and Division III schools can offer only two "equivalencies" of full scholarships.

This money can be divided any way an athletic department sees fit, provided it stays within the limit of twenty students receiving aid.

Obviously, spreading two full scholarships out among twenty students is not a way to attract good athletes. So the final result is that schools in Division I competition end up with more talent, because they're able to give out so much more aid. But keep in mind that schools don't have to maintain these maximum limits—they just can't exceed them.

Don't automatically assume, though, that a school playing Division III competition won't have a good team or you won't be able to get substantial aid. Remember: in addition to financial aid based on athletic ability, schools are able to make other awards as well, meaning they may be able to put together a very attractive financial aid package. Therefore, make sure to fill out the appropriate forms to determine financial need, and inquire about the possibility of receiving such assistance.

NEED-BASED AWARDS

Establishing financial need is the key to a substantial aid package for most students. In fact, at many schools, financial need is the only criterion by which students are awarded aid, so make certain that careful attention is paid to this facet of the search process.

Undoubtedly, the ideal situation for a student—at least, financially speaking—is to be awarded an outright full-ride scholarship. But with the tremendous cost of an education today, and with costs on the rise, few schools are willing (or able) to pay the entire way for their athletes. As such, a combination of various types of aid is increasingly becoming the rule, and your actual need is the standard to which schools adhere.

When colleges put together an aid package, they draw the money from a variety of sources, including federal and state money. A financial aid officer will sit down with your record and, after determining the maximum you can receive, he'll decide how much to give you, based on what the school has available.

This could be a risky proposition, since there is no guarantee that a school will find the money to completely fill the gap between actual cost and your need. With promising student-athletes, however, the gap is often closed completely.

When you look at an entry in Part II of this book and see that a school does not award outright scholarships, your first impulse may be to go on to another school. Don't. Schools that offer only need-based aid often have very competitive athletic programs, and are very aggressive in their recruiting efforts. And although they won't promise you a scholarship, they will usually see to it that the financial gap is filled in full. Since many fine private schools—including the Ivy League—operate this way, the money you receive could be greater than the amount you would have received at a school that gives athletic scholarships. So explore all possibilities, and take the necessary steps to insure your eligibility for need-based aid. This means filling out all the necessary forms—on time.

There are a number of forms that you may be required to complete, depending on the college you're planning to attend and the state in which you live. Most financial aid offices have brochures that describe the types of aid available, the forms that have to be completed, deadline dates for filing, and the estimated cost of attending the school.

When you complete an application, it is forwarded to one of the need analysis services, such as the American College Testing Program or the College Scholarship Service, where your need is determined. Although the applications are slightly different, they consider the contribution that both you and your parents will be able to make to the cost of your education, taking into account such factors as available income, assets, debts, and family size.

Completing the necessary forms requires some time and effort, and you will have to attach copies of your parents' most recent federal income tax return, along with your own if you filed one. It may take four to six weeks for the analysis to be completed and returned to the school, so plan ahead. A typical deadline for entering freshmen to have all forms completed and in the hands of the financial aid office is March 1, but there is no standard deadline and a school may want the forms a month earlier.

College catalogues will tell you exactly when the material must be received, along with the estimated costs of attending the school. But remember, the cost of the institution does not in any way affect the amount you can afford to pay. Your expected contribution is constant, based on the analysis of your family's financial situation. Need is determined by subtracting that contribution from the cost of attending a particular institution.

Say, for example, your total family contribution is projected to be $4,000, and you are considering three schools, all of which have recruited you and would like you to sign a letter of intent. The cost of attending the first school is $5,000 per year, the cost of the second school is $7,000 per year, and the cost of the third school is $9,000 per year. School number one, a state university in the Southwest, offers you a $3,000 scholarship, based on your ability as a miler. School number two, a private university in Washington, D.C., which is considerably farther from your home in Kansas, offers you a $4,000 scholarship, also based on your ability as a miler. School number three, a Division III school in Illinois, cannot offer you an athletic scholarship, but is impressed with your times and says it will make up the difference between your expected contribution and your need.

What now? Some students jump at the second offer, which at first glance appears to be the most lucrative. But depending on your situation, there may be better offers.

School number one offered you $3,000 per year, meaning that your cost will be $2,000 per year, which isn't a bad deal. School number two offered $4,000 a year, which seems like a better deal. But this school costs $7,000 per year, meaning you'll have to pay $3,000 on your own. And since your expected family contribution is $4,000, you won't be able to add any further aid to this award to cut your costs. In addition, the school is halfway across the country, which means you can add significant transportation costs. All of a sudden, a $4,000 scholarship is worth a lot less than a $3,000 scholarship.

School number three, by contrast, offers to fill in your financial gaps. With a cost of $9,000 per year, and an expected family contribution of $4,000, the value of your aid is $5,000, which is more than the other two schools. Besides, your transportation costs from Kansas to Illinois will not be as great as they would be to Washington, making the value of the aid even greater.

But examine this closely. The value of your aid is more, but you're also paying more. School number one offered $3,000 per year, but you would only have to pay $2,000 per year; school number two offered $4,000 per year, but you would have to pay $3,000 per year, plus large transportation costs; school number three offered $5,000 in aid, but you would have to pay $4,000 of your own, which is twice what you'd have to pay at school number one and $1,000 more than you'd be paying in educational expenses at school number two.

In the end, however, when you account for transportation, you might be spending the same amounts to go to schools two and three. Obviously, school number one is cheaper, but it is a state school and may not have academic programs that can compete with school number three, which is a prestigious university. That should certainly be a consideration, as should size, coaching staff, facilities, etc.

In short, assistance based solely on financial need may be a better deal than an outright athletic scholarship. And since the majority of money given to athletes is based on financial need, it is imperative that you fully explore your options and understand how the need analysis system works. It is also imperative that you weigh all factors about a school carefully when considering a final decision.

Although aid may come from a number of sources, schools rely heavily on the federal government, with the maximum amount of aid available for students determined by the Congress. Other sources of aid include state funds and private gifts. If a school does not give athletic scholarships, but rather aid based on need, your financial aid package can take any number of forms. It may not only include grants, however. It may also include work-study, and a portion of it might even be in the form of a loan.

Therefore, ask questions and read any financial aid agreement carefully. Make certain you understand exactly what the value of the aid is and what you will be required to contribute during a year. Above all, be aware of deadlines. If you end up being recruited only by schools that award aid based on need, you could be out of luck if all the proper forms are not filled out and received by the financial aid office by the appropriate date.

In addition to the information provided by college catalogues and brochures from financial aid offices, there are two pamphlets that will also give you a better understanding of how to proceed. Single copies of the pamphlets are available at no cost by writing to the addresses below:

Meeting College Costs
College Board Publications Orders
Box 2815
Princeton, NJ 08541

The Student Consumer's Guide
Bureau of Student Financial Assistance
7th & D Streets, SW
Washington, DC 20202

ONE MORE CHANCE

Not everyone who tries to win an athletic scholarship does so. Some give up and never try again. Others do give it another shot—sometimes with success.

Although it is not easy, it is possible to end up with a scholarship after not having been recruited in high school. One way of accomplishing this is by being a walk-on. The chances of this happening at a smaller school are better, because major institutions, where athletics are big-time, look long and hard for talent, and often come up with exactly the type of players they want.

At smaller schools, though, there may be an opportunity for an athletic scholarship the second time around. Once again, coaches are always looking for solid talent, and anyone is free to try out for a team. If a coach likes what he sees, you may end up with a scholarship, although chances are it won't be the first year. But if you prove yourself during the first season and show that your services are valuable, you could very well receive aid the following year.

Another possibility is to win a scholarship as a transfer student. Not every school gives scholarships in every sport. And if you play a minor sport, the opportunities for assistance are especially limited. But if a coach did not offer you aid the first time around, he may be willing to do so after you've proven yourself on the college level.

Take a golfer, for example. If no offer was made during high school, you may want to attend a state school where golf is played but no scholarships are offered. If you have an exceptional year, you may be able to transfer to a private university that emphasizes golf with a promise of aid when you become eligible.

This, of course, is risky, and choosing a school simply because it has a golf program is contrary to what many coaches would advise. But if your financial situation is such that a state school is perhaps your only option, then taking this road makes sense.

The easiest way to move up, though, is via a junior college. Most junior colleges recruit close to home, but they often do so aggressively, and their programs are usually competitive.

Just as with four-year schools, it is possible at most two-year schools to win a scholarship as a walk-on, although the preferable route is to be recruited in high school. And the procedure for dealing with junior college coaches is really no different.

But keep in mind some of the thoughts that may go through the mind of a coach at a two-year school. If you're from the area, a coach probably won't have any suspicions about why you're applying to that school. If you're from out of the area, however, a coach may want to know why you haven't been recruited by schools close to home. In short, if there are schools in your area—particularly two-year schools—that offer the same academic program, a coach may want to know why you're not looking to play with the local school. With that in mind, the coach may get on the phone to coaches of schools in your region to find out what sort of athlete you are. Coaches have developed a good network among themselves, and if your caliber of play is not what it should be for a scholarship, that fact will be reported.

So don't think that a two-year school is going to snatch you up because you have good clips. Many of these schools look long and hard at athletes before they give out scholarships. But even if you don't receive aid to play at a junior college (not all of them offer such assistance), these schools are good training grounds for four-year schools, and they offer a chance to develop your skills.

Some schools have reputations for having particularly good programs, and four-year schools look to them year after year for talent. The grapevine is in place here, too, and it works both ways. Not only will coaches at four-year schools come looking for talent at junior colleges, but junior college coaches can also open doors for you with a phone call.

Therefore, the lines of communication with your junior college or community college coach should also be kept open. Keeping your former high school coaches apprised of your progress also isn't a bad idea, because a recruiter may go back to that coach for a conversation about your ability.

Another possible way to move up is via club sports, although this is a long shot. Some schools that don't have intercollegiate teams in certain sports give club scholarships, but these are rare. It is possible, though, to use your experience in a club sport to move up to an athletic scholarship at another school. The chances of this happening in sports like football or basketball are next to none, but a sport like riflery or track, where precision and numbers tell the tale, may give you the necessary ammunition to end up with a grant-in-aid.

All of these second-chance methods can work, and while the junior college route is undoubtedly the best, the others are strictly long shots. Often, a top-quality athlete—who may, in fact, be scholarship material—decides to forego athletics to concentrate solely on academics. A year away from the playing field may produce withdrawal symptoms too serious to ignore, and the student shows up at tryouts the following year. This student may be a potential star, but remember, schools just can't give out an unlimited number of scholarships. Depending on what division the school plays in, its scholarship money for that year may have already been committed. A coach may be glad to see you, but don't expect a check for tuition to be in the mail the following day.

Therefore, the best way to go about it is to give it an honest effort the first time around. Make sure you contact all the schools in which you have an interest, and exhaust all possibilities. But if you really believe you have the talent that's worthy of a scholarship, and you can back that up with your play, by all means go after it a second time. Just be careful not to expect too much, as the odds in round two are considerably steeper.

TIME OUT

If you've fully digested the basics, then you're halfway there. Now it's time for the selection process, which, as you've hopefully learned, requires more than simply sending off a letter to every school that awards aid in the sport you play.

What follows is a school-by-school listing of nearly every institution that has an athletic program, along with the sports they play and their scholarship policies. We say "nearly" every school because, as noted, circumstances change. A school that has only club baseball one year may have an intercollegiate team the following year. Or a school may decide to drop an intercollegiate sport. So don't take anything for granted. If you're interested in a school that doesn't presently play your sport, check to see if there are any plans for that sport down the road. And similarly, if a school does not now give scholarships in a sport, it doesn't mean that it won't someday. Here again, it's worth an inquiry if you're particularly interested in a certain institution.

Also omitted were some of the smaller schools with limited scholarship opportunities. If you're considering applying to a school that isn't listed, you ought to inquire about their program anyway, and pursue any leads you come up with.

There are a number of ways to proceed, but your best bet is to work with the lists that follow—in concert with other sources of information on colleges. If you've already decided on a geographical area you want to confine yourself to, your task will be that much easier. Check the sport-by-sport index for colleges in a region by moving your eyes down the right side of the column. From there, the individual school entries will give you all the basic sports information about a school, including whether scholarships are, in fact, available.

Be aware, however, that while a scholarship can mean a significant amount of money, it can also mean significant problems for you if you're not prepared. An athletic scholarship for you means that a coach has a high regard for your talent, and expects you to contribute quite a lot to the team. Meeting those expectations is often difficult for student-athletes, especially freshmen, who sometimes have all they can handle adapting to college life in general. The added pressure to perform can be too much for students, and they end up either failing their courses, quitting school, or giving up athletics altogether.

So, before you go searching frantically for an athletic scholarship, try to understand exactly what you may be getting yourself into. If, for example, your long-range goals are to be a doctor, the time you'll have to spend practicing and playing may hinder your academic progress to the point of affecting your grades, and possibly jeopardize your chances of getting into medical school. Of course, depending on your capabilities, athletics may not affect your studies. The point is, you have to know yourself, know your abilities and aspirations, and decide what your priorities are.

You should also know that a number of coaches are not particularly happy about the situation today concerning the awarding of athletic scholarships. These coaches are acutely aware of the added pressures put on their athletes, and they feel that it may be too high a price to pay.

This is especially true in women's sports, which have been undergoing radical changes the last few years and will likely experience major growing pains for many years to come. The problem, basically, is that while women want parity with the men, they're not sure they want their programs to end up like those of some of the men's which have a win-at-any-cost philosophy. The women want the same amount of money as the men for scholarships, facilities, coaches, and recruiting, but they don't want their programs to grow too big, too fast. This ends up putting coaches in an odd position: they want to stay low-key, but they also want to see their sports receive their due recognition and grow.

It's not just the women who worry, though. Many men's coaches are aware of the almost professional nature that some college sports have taken on, and they would like to see more emphasis placed on raising academic standards for athletes, so their college career encompasses more than just sports. Some of the suggestions put forth include a limit on face-to-face off-campus recruiting and reducing the number of a prospect's allowable college-paid visits.

Whether these suggestions will become established rules is uncertain, but they are indicative of the mood in various quarters. Some would actually like to see athletic scholarships eliminated completely, with all awards based instead on financial need only.

That, however, is not likely to happen. Athletic scholarships, like academic scholarships, or music scholarships, or art scholarships, or any number of other types of scholarships, offer valuable assistance to students, and eliminating them would raise an enormous furor on campuses.

But that doesn't mean there may not be a cutback in the number of athletic scholarships offered. With the high cost of maintaining teams, a number of universities have already been forced to eliminate some of their varsity teams. Just as inflation hits every other facet of the economy, intercollegiate athletics are affected as well. This will probably mean less money budgeted for recruiting in the future, and the cutbacks will most likely have the greatest effect on the "minor" sports.

With that in mind, the methods you use to search out an athletic scholarship become even more important. For those students who don't approach the search the proper way, athletic scholarships might as well be eliminated, because chances are they'll go to someone else anyway. This search will require time and effort, but it can pay off handsomely in the end.

The final test, however, which should not be forgotten, is athletic ability. Winning a scholarship means you've displayed sufficient talent to have a school pay your way—or part of your way. If the talent isn't there, don't expect miracles.

If you do have the talent, make sure you know how to display it. Keep all your newspaper clippings and be aware of any films that may be available of you in action. Any contacts you've made should be used, including coaches, alumni, relatives, and friends. Since the key to winning a scholarship is being seen in action, your job is to somehow attract enough attention so a coach will follow a hunch and take a look.

If your talent has already been recognized in the media, you may not have to be as aggressive in your search for a scholarship. But the same sort of search techniques—collecting all the available information about a school and what it has to offer—should be used. Find out everything you can about an institution, and try to determine if you'll feel at home there. In short, just don't pick an attractive scholarship offer, but instead pick a school and weigh the benefits of the scholarship.

If you haven't received media recognition, but you believe you're good enough to receive serious consideration, you're going to have your work cut out for you. But remember, the recruiters are out there looking for you. So make sure they find you.

PART II

School-by-School Index

GETTING STARTED

What follows is a school-by-school listing, giving all the pertinent information about an institution to help you in your search for an athletic scholarship. The schools are arranged alphabetically, and the entries are easy to follow. The data each contains, in order, includes:
- The school name;
- The address;
- The phone number of both the men's (M) and women's (W) athletic departments;
- The school's enrollment size, which corresponds to the following code: A = less than 2,500; B = 2;500 to 5,000; and C = over 5,000;
- Whether the school is a two-year or four-year institution, and whether funding is public or private;
- The athletic conferences that the men (M) and women (W) belong to. A list of the conferences named in the individual entries is listed below;
- A complete list of the sports played by both men (M) and women (W). In this list, the sports for which scholarships are available are underlined;
- Additional notes about a school, giving information about special circumstances regarding the awarding of athletic scholarships, such as if a school awards aid only on the basis of financial need.

CONFERENCE LISTING

Alabama Junior College Conference — AJCC
Arizona Community College Athletic Conference — ACCAC

Arkansas Intercollegiate Conference	AIC
Arkansas Women's Intercollegiate Sports Association	AWISA
Arrowhead Athletic Conference	AAC
Associated Colleges of the Midwest	ACM
Association of the Intercollegiate Athletics for Women	AIAW
Athletic Association of Community Colleges	AACC
California Collegiate Athletic Association	CCAC
Central Illinois Athletic Conference	CIAC
Central Intercollegiate Athletic Association	CIAA
Central States Intercollegiate Conference	CSIC
Chicagoland Collegiate Athletic Conference	CCAC
City University New York	CUNY
College Conference of Illinois and Wisconsin	CCIW
Collegiate Athletic Conference	CAC
Connecticut Community College Athletic Association	CCCAA
Dixie Intercollegiate Athletic Conference	DIAC
East Coast Conference	ECC
Eastern Athletic Association	EAS
Eastern College Athletic Conference	ECAC
Eastern Iowa Junior College Conference	EIJCC
Eastern Pennsylvania Community College Conference	EPCCC
Florida Community College Activities Association	FCCAA
Georgia Intercollegiate Athletic Conference	GIAC
Georgia Junior College Athletic Association	GJCAA
Great Lakes Intercollegiate Athletic Conference	GLIAC
Great Lakes Valley Conference	GLVC
Heart of America Athletic Conference	HAAC
Hoosier Buckeye Collegiate Conference	HBCC
Intermountain Collegiate Athletic Conference	ICAC
Interregional Athletic Conference	IAC
Iowa Intercollegiate Athletic Conference	IIAC
Kansas Collegiate Athletic Conference	KCAC
Kansas Jayhawk Community College Conference	KJCCC
Kentucky Intercollegiate Athletic Conference	KIAC
Kentucky Junior College Athletic Conference	KJCAC
Kentucky Women's Intercollegiate Athletic Association	KWIAA
Massachusetts Community College Athletic Conference	MCCAC
Michigan Community College Athletic Association	MCCAA
Michigan Intercollegiate Athletic Association	MIAA

Mid-America Community College Conference	MACCC
Mid-America Conference	MAC
Mid-Ohio Conference	MOC
Midwest Collegiate Athletic Conference	MCAC
Midwest Conference of Christian Colleges	MCCC
Midwest Junior Collegiate Athletic Conference	MJCAC
Minnesota Intercollegiate Athletic Conference	MIAC
Minnesota State Community College Conference	MSCCC
Mississippi Junior College Association	MJCA
Missouri Intercollegiate Athletic Association	MIAA
Missouri Valley Conference	MVC
National Association of Intercollegiate Athletics	NAIA
National Christian College Athletic Association	NCCAA
National Collegiate Athletic Association	NCAA
National Junior College Athletic Association	NJCAA
Nebraska College Conference	NCC
Nebraska Community College Conference	NCCC
Nebraska Intercollegiate Athletic Conference	NIAC
New England Intercollegiate Amateur Athletic Association	NEIAAA
New England Small College Athletic Conference	NESCAC
New Jersey College Athletic Conference	NJCAC
North Atlantic Christian Conference	NACC
North Central Christian Athletic Conference	NNCAC
North Central Community College Conference	NCCCC
North Dakota College Athletic Conference	NDCAC
Northern Intercollegiate Christian Conference	NICC
Ohio Athletic Conference	OAC
Ohio Valley Conference	OVC
Old Dominion Athletic Conference	ODAC
Oklahoma Intercollegiate Conference	OIC
Oklahoma Junior College Conference	OJCC
Oregon Community College Athletic Association	OCCAA
Pacific Coast Athletic Conference	PCAC
Pacific Northwest College Conference	PNCC
Pacific 10 Conference	PAC–10
Pennsylvania State College Athletic Conference	PSCAC
President's Athletic Conference	PAC
Rocky Mountain Athletic Conference	RMAC
South Atlantic Conference	SAC
South Dakota Intercollegiate Conference	SAIC
Southeastern Conference	SEC
Southern California Intercollegiate Athletic Conference	SCIAC
Southern Christian Athletic Conference	SCAC

Southern Intercollegiate Athletic Conference	SIAC
State University of New York Athletic Conference	SUNYAC
Sunshine State Conference	SSC
Tennessee Junior College Athletic Association	TJCAA
Texas Christian College Athletic Conference	TCCAC
Texas Intercollegiate Athletic Association	TIAA
Texas Junior College Athletic Conference	TJCAC
Trans America Athletic Conference	TAAC
Twin Rivers Collegiate Conference	TRCC
Volunteer State Athletic Conference	VSAC
West Coast Athletic Conference	WCAC
West Virginia Intercollegiate Athletic Conference	WVIAC
Western Athletic Conference	WAC
Western Carolina Coastal	WCC
Western Junior College Athletic Conference	WJCAC
Wisconsin Junior College Athletic Association	WJCAA
Wisconsin State University Conference	WSUC
Wisconsin Technical College Conference	WTCC

Although the above list represents the major conferences, there are some smaller conferences appearing in the individual entries that have not been included. To ascertain the meaning of their initials, use the following guide: first one or two letters—state or region

        CC—Community College
        JC—Junior College
        AA—Athletic Association
        AC—Athletic Conference
        SA—Sports Association
        AW—Athletics for Women

Thus, WJCAA stands for Wisconsin Junior College Athletics Association. Also note that many women's programs are members of the Association for Intercollegiate Athletics for Women (AIAW) for an individual state. For example, NJAIAW is the New Jersey Association for Intercollegiate Athletics for Women. Other unlisted conferences use their initials as their official names.

SCHOOL-BY-SCHOOL LISTING

Abilene Christian University
Abilene, TX 79601
M: (915) 677–1911
W: (915) 677–1911
Enrollment: B
4-year private
M: Lone Star, NAIA
W: TAIAW
M: Golf, Tennis, Basketball, Cross Country, Football, Track & Field
W: Tennis, Basketball, Cross Country, Track & Field, Volleyball

Adams State College
Alamosa, CO 81101
M: (303) 589–7401
W: (303) 589–7401
Enrollment: A
4-year public funding
M: RMAC
W: RMAC
M: Basketball, Cross Country, Football, Golf, Tennis, Track & Field, Wrestling
W: Basketball, Cross Country, Gymnastics, Softball, Track & Field, Volleyball

Adrian College
110 South Madison Street
Adrian, MI 49221
M: (213) 265–5161 X. 245
W: (213) 265–5161 X. 213
Enrollment: A
4-year private
M: MIAA
W: MIAA
M: Baseball, Basketball, Cross Country, Football, Golf, Soccer, Swimming-Diving, Tennis, Track & Field, Wrestling
W: Basketball, Field Hockey, Softball, Swimming-Diving, Tennis, Track & Field, Volleyball

University of Akron
Akron, OH 44325
M: (216) 375–7080
W: (216) 375–7080
Enrollment: C
4-year public funding
M: OVC
W: Independent
M: Riflery, Swimming-Diving, Wrestling, Baseball, Basketball, Cross Country, Football, Golf, Soccer, Track & Field

W: Volleyball, Basketball,
   Softball, Tennis

University of Alabama
Birmingham, AL 35294
M: (205) 934-3402
W: (205) 934-3824
Enrollment: C
4-year public funding
M: Sun Belt
W: AAIAW
M: Baseball, Basketball, Cross
   Country, Golf, Soccer, Tennis
W: Basketball, Cross Country,
   Tennis, Volleyball

University of Alabama
Huntsville, AL 35807
M: (205) 895-6144
W: (205) 895-6144
Enrollment: B
4-year public funding
M: Southern States
W: Northern Athletic
M: Basketball, Crew, Soccer
W: Basketball, Crew, Tennis

University of Alabama
University, AL 35486
M: (205) 348-6161
W: (205) 348-7077
Enrollment: C
4-year public funding
M: Southeastern
W: Independent
M: Baseball, Basketball, Cross
   Country, Football, Golf,
   Swimming-Diving, Tennis,
   Track & Field
W: Basketball, Golf, Gymnastics,
   Swimming-Diving, Tennis,
   Track & Field, Volleyball

Alabama A & M University
Normal, AL 35762
M: (205) 859-7362
W: (205) 859-7361
Enrollment: B
4-year public funding
M: SIAC
W: SIAC, AIAW
M: Golf, Swimming-Diving,
   Baseball, Basketball, Cross
   Country, Football, Soccer,
   Tennis, Track & Field
W: Basketball, Cross Country,
   Golf, Swimming-Diving,
   Tennis, Track & Field,
   Volleyball

Alabama Christian Junior College
5345 Atlanta Highway
Montgomery, AL 36109
M: (205) 272-5820 X. 49
W: (205) 272-5820 X. 49
Enrollment: A
2-year private
M: Alabama JCAC, NLC
W: Alabama JCAC, NLC
M: Tennis, Baseball, Basketball
W: Basketball, Tennis

Alabama State University
915 South Jackson Street
Montgomery, AL 36101
M: (205) 832-6072
W: (205) 832-6072
Enrollment: B
4-year public funding
M: Independent
W: AAIAW
M: Baseball, Basketball, Football,
   Tennis, Track & Field
W: Basketball, Tennis, Track &
   Field, Volleyball

University of Alaska
Anchorage, AK 99504
M: (907) 263-1230
W: (907) 263-1230
Enrollment: C
4-year public funding
M: NCAA
W: AIAW
M: Riflery, Swimming-Diving, Basketball, Cross Country, Hockey, Skiing (cross country & alpine)
W: Riflery, Swimming-Diving, Basketball, Cross Country, Skiing (cross country & alpine), Volleyball

University of Alaska
Fairbanks, AK 99701
M: (907) 479-7205
W: (907) 479-7205
Enrollment: A
4-year public funding
M: NCAA
W: AIAW
M: Cross Country, Basketball, Ice Hockey, Riflery, Skiing (cross country only)
W: Cross Country, Basketball, Riflery, Skiing (cross country), Volleyball

Junior College of Albany
140 New Scotland Avenue
Albany, NY 12208
M: (518) 445-1711
W: (518) 445-1757
Enrollment: A
2-year private
M: NJCAA
W: NJCAA
M: Bowling, Basketball, Volleyball
W: Bowling, Basketball, Volleyball

Albany State College
504 College Drive
Albany, GA 31705
M: (912) 439-4040
W: (912) 439-4040
Enrollment: A
4-year public funding
M: SIAC
W: SIAC, GAIAW
M: Tennis, Baseball, Basketball, Cross Country, Football, Track & Field
W: Tennis, Basketball, Track & Field

Albion College
Albion, MI 49224
M: (517) 629-5511
W: (517) 629-5511
Enrollment: B
4-year private
M: MIAA
W: MIAA
M: Baseball, Basketball, Cross Country, Football, Golf, Lacrosse, Soccer, Swimming-Diving, Tennis, Track & Field
W: Archery, Basketball, Field Hockey, Softball, Swimming-Diving, Tennis, Track & Field, Volleyball

Division III: all aid awarded on the basis of financial need.

Albright College
North 13th Street
Reading, PA 19604
M: (215) 921-2381 X. 210

W: (215) 921–2381 X. 210
Enrollment: A
4-year private
M: NCAA, ECAC, MAC
W: Independent
M: Baseball, Basketball, Cross Country, Football, Golf, Soccer, Tennis, Track & Field, Wrestling
W: Badminton, Basketball, Field Hockey, Softball, Tennis, Track & Field, Volleyball

Division III: all aid awarded on the basis of financial need.

Alcorn State University
Lorman, MS 39096
M: (601) 877–3762
W: (601) 877–3762
Enrollment: B
4-year public funding
M: Southwestern
W: SWAC
M: <u>Baseball</u>, <u>Basketball</u>, <u>Cross Country</u>, <u>Football</u>, <u>Golf</u>, <u>Tennis</u>, <u>Track & Field</u>
W: <u>Basketball</u>, <u>Cross Country</u>, <u>Tennis</u>, <u>Track & Field</u>

Alfred University
Alfred, NY 14802
M: (607) 871–2144
W: (607) 871–2144
Enrollment: A
4-year private
M: Independent
W: Independent
M: Basketball, Football, Lacrosse, Skiing, Soccer, Swimming-Diving, Tennis, Track & Field
W: Basketball, Skiing, Soccer, Swimming-Diving, Tennis, Track & Field, Volleyball

Division III: all aid awarded on the basis of financial need.

Alice Lloyd College
Pippa Passes, KY 41844
M: (606) 368–2101 X. 211
W: (606) 368–2101 X. 212
Enrollment: A
2-year private
M: KWIAA
W: KWIC
M: Basketball
W: Basketball

Allegheny College
Meadville, PA 16335
M: (814) 724–5372
W: (814) 724–3351
Enrollment: A
4-year private
M: President's
W: Keystone
M: Baseball, Basketball, Cross Country, Football, Golf, Soccer, Swimming-Diving, Tennis, Track & Field, Volleyball, Wrestling
W: Basketball, Cross Country, Softball, Swimming-Diving, Tennis, Track & Field, Volleyball

Allen County Community College
1801 North Cottonwood
Iola, KS 66749
M: (316) 365–5116
W: (316) 365–5116
Enrollment: A
2-year public funding
M: Jayhawk
W: Jayhawk
M: Golf, <u>Baseball</u>, <u>Basketball</u>,

Cross Country, Tennis, Track
  & Field
W: Golf, Basketball, Cross
  Country, Tennis, Track &
  Field, Volleyball

**Allentown College of St. Francis
  De Sales**
Center Valley, PA 18034
M: (215) 283–1100 X. 218
W: (215) 283–1100 X. 218
Enrollment: A
4-year private
M: ECAC, Independent
W: EAIAW, PAIAW
M: Baseball, Basketball, Cross
  Country, Soccer, Tennis
W: Basketball, Cross Country,
  Softball, Tennis, Volleyball

Alma College
Alma, MI 48801
M: (517) 463–2141 X. 394
W: (517) 463–2141 X. 394
Enrollment: A
4-year private
M: MIAA
W: MIAA
M: Baseball, Basketball, Cross
  Country, Football, Golf,
  Soccer, Swimming-Diving,
  Tennis, Track & Field,
  Wrestling
W: Archery, Basketball, Cross
  Country, Field Hockey,
  Softball, Swimming-Diving,
  Tennis, Track & Field,
  Volleyball

Alpena Community College
Alpena, MI 49707
M: (517) 356–9021 X. 274
W: (517) 356–9021 X. 274
Enrollment: A
2-year public funding
M: MCCAA
W: MCCAA
M: Basketball, Bowling, Golf
W: Basketball

Alvin Community College
3110 Mustang Road
Alvin, TX 77511
M: (713) 331–6111 X. 219
W: (713) 331–6111 X. 219
Enrollment: A
2-year public funding
M: NJCAA
W: NJCAA
M: Baseball, Basketball, Golf,
  Tennis
W: Tennis, Volleyball

American International College
170 Wilbraham Road
Springfield, MA 01109
M: (413) 737–5331
W: (413) 737–5331
Enrollment: A
4-year private
M: Northeast-7
W: Northeast-7
M: Golf, Soccer, Tennis, Baseball,
  Basketball, Football
W: Basketball, Softball, Volleyball

The American University
Massachusetts and Nebraska
  Avenues, NW
Washington, DC 20016
M: (202) 686–2560
W: (202) 686–2560
Enrollment: C
4-year private

M: East Coast, ECAC
W: EAIAW, AIAW
M: Golf, Tennis, Baseball, Basketball, Soccer, Swimming-Diving, Wrestling
W: Field Hockey, Basketball, Swimming-Diving, Tennis, Volleyball

Amherst College
Amherst, MA 01002
M: (413) 542-2273
W: (413) 542-2273
Enrollment: A
4-year private
M: NESCAC
W: AIAW
M: Baseball, Basketball, Crew, Cross Country, Golf, Hockey, Lacrosse, Skiing, Soccer, Squash, Swimming-Diving, Tennis, Track & Field, Wrestling
W: Basketball, Cross Country, Field Hockey, Golf, Lacrosse, Skiing, Soccer, Swimming-Diving, Tennis, Track & Field

No athletic scholarships are available at Amherst. Assistance is given through financial aid programs encompassing the whole school.

Anderson College
1100 East Fifth Street
Anderson, IN 46011
M: (317) 649-9071 X. 2119
W: (317) 649-9071 X. 2119
Enrollment: A
4-year private
M: HBCC
W: AIAW
M: Baseball, Basketball, Cross Country, Football, Golf, Tennis, Track & Field, Wrestling
W: Basketball, Softball, Tennis, Track & Field, Water Polo

Anderson Junior College
Anderson, SC 29621
M: (803) 226-6181
W: (803) 226-6181
Enrollment: A
2-year private
M: NJCWCC
W: NJCWCC
M: Basketball, Tennis
W: Basketball, Tennis

Angelina College
Lufkin, TX 75901
M: (713) 639-1301
W: (713) 639-1301
Enrollment: A
2-year private
M: Texas Eastern
W: Texas Eastern
M: Baseball, Basketball, Tennis
W: Basketball, Tennis

Angelo State University
2001 West Avenue N
San Angelo, TX 76901
M: (915) 942-2264
W: (915) 942-2271
Enrollment: C
4-year public funding
M: Lone Star, NAIA, NCAA
W: TAIAW, AIAW
M: Basketball, Cross Country, Football, Golf, Tennis, Track & Field

W: Basketball, Cross Country, Softball, Tennis, Track & Field, Volleyball

Anne Arundel Community College
101 College Parkway
Arnald, MD 21012
M: (301) 269–7302
W: (301) 269–7302
Enrollment: C
2-year public funding
M: JUCO
W: JUCO
M: Baseball, Basketball, Cross Country, Football, Golf, Lacrosse, Soccer, Swimming-Diving, Tennis, Track & Field, Wrestling
W: Basketball, Cross Country, Field Hockey, Lacrosse, Softball, Swimming-Diving, Tennis, Track & Field

Appalachian State University
Boone, NC 28607
M: (704) 262–3080
W: (704) 262–3080
Enrollment: C
4-year public funding
M: Southern
W: NCAIAW
M: Baseball, Basketball, Cross Country, Football, Golf, Riflery, Soccer, Swimming-Diving, Tennis, Track & Field, Wrestling
W: Field Hockey, Golf, Riflery, Softball, Swimming-Diving, Tennis, Track & Field, Volleyball

Aquinas College
1607 Robinson Road, SE
Grand Rapids, MI 49506
M: (616) 459–8281
W: (616) 459–8281
Enrollment: A
4-year private
M: Independent
W: Independent
M: Baseball, Basketball, Cross Country, Golf, Soccer, Tennis, Track & Field
W: Basketball, Softball, Tennis, Track & Field, Volleyball

All aid for men and women is based on financial need.

University of Arizona
Tucson, AZ 85721
M: (602) 626–1101
W: (602) 626–2473
Enrollment: C
4-year public funding
M: Pacific-10
W: WCAA
M: Baseball, Basketball, Cross Country, Football, Golf, Gymnastics, Swimming-Diving, Tennis, Track & Field
W: Basketball, Cross Country, Field Hockey, Golf, Gymnastics, Swimming-Diving, Synchronized Swimming, Tennis, Track & Field, Volleyball

Arizona State University
Tempe, AZ 85281
M: (602) 965–6592
W: (602) 965–6592
Enrollment: C
4-year public funding

M: Pacific-10
W: AIAW
M: Archery, Badminton, Baseball,
	Basketball, Cross Country,
	Football, Golf, Gymnastics,
	Swimming-Diving, Tennis,
	Track & Field, Volleyball,
	Wrestling
W: Archery, Badminton,
	Basketball, Golf, Gymnastics,
	Softball, Swimming-Diving,
	Tennis, Track & Field,
	Volleyball

Arizona Western College
Yuma, AZ 85364
M: (602) 726-1000 X. 235
W: (602) 726-1000 X. 240
Enrollment: B
2-year public funding
M: ACCAC
W: ACCAC
M: Baseball, Basketball, Football,
	Golf, Tennis, Wrestling
W: Basketball, Softball, Tennis,
	Volleyball

University of Arkansas
Fayetteville, AR 72701
M: (501) 575-2751
W: (501) 575-3707
Enrollment: C
4-year public funding
M: Southwest
W: Southwest
M: Baseball, Basketball, Cross
	Country, Football, Golf,
	Swimming-Diving, Tennis,
	Track & Field
W: Basketball, Cross Country,
	Swimming-Diving, Tennis,
	Track & Field

University of Arkansas
Little Rock, AR 72204
M: (501) 569-3304
W: (501) 569-3305
Enrollment: C
4-year public funding
M: TAA
W: AWISA
M: Baseball, Basketball, Golf,
	Swimming-Diving, Tennis,
	Water Polo
W: Basketball, Swimming-Diving,
	Tennis, Volleyball

University of Arkansas
Highway 83
Monticello, AR 71655
M: (501) 367-6811 X. 58
W: (501) 367-6811 X. 58
Enrollment: A
4-year public funding
M: AIC
W: AWISA
M: Baseball, Bowling, Cross
	Country, Golf, Tennis, Track
	& Field, Basketball, Football
W: Tennis, Basketball

University of Arkansas
Highway 79 North
Pine Bluff, AR 71601
M: (501) 541-6589
W: (501) 541-6589
Enrollment: B
4-year public funding
M: Independent
W: AWISA
M: Basketball, Football, Tennis,
	Track & Field
W: Basketball, Volleyball

Arkansas State University
State University, AR 72467
M: (501) 972-2082
W: (501) 972-2077
Enrollment: C
4-year public funding
M: Southland
W: AWISA
M: Fencing, Riflery, Swimming-
   Diving, Volleyball, Baseball,
   Basketball, Cross Country,
   Football, Golf, Tennis, Track
   & Field (indoor & outdoor)
W: Basketball, Tennis, Volleyball

Arkansas Tech University
Highway 7
Russelville, AR 72801
M: (501) 968-0345
W: (501) 968-0285
Enrollment: B
4-year public funding
M: AIC
W: AWISA
M: Baseball, Cross Country, Golf,
   Swimming-Diving, Tennis,
   Track & Field, Basketball,
   Football
W: Basketball, Tennis, Volleyball

Armstrong State College
1195 Abercorn Express
Savannah, GA 31406
M: (912) 927-5336
W: (912) 927-5336
Enrollment: B
4-year public funding
M: South Atlantic
W: South Atlantic
M: Bowling, Cross Country, Golf,
   Baseball, Basketball, Tennis
W: Bowling, Tennis, Basketball,
   Softball

Asbury College
North Lexington Avenue
Wilmore, KY 40390
M: (606) 858-3511
W: (606) 858-3511
Enrollment: A
4-year private
M: KIAC
W: KIAC
M: Basketball, Cross Country,
   Golf, Soccer, Track & Field
W: Field Hockey, Tennis, Track &
   Field, Volleyball

**Asheville-Buncombe Technical
College**
340 Victoria Road
Asheville, NC 28801
M: (704) 254-1921
W: (704) 254-1921
Enrollment: A
2-year public funding
M: NJCAA, Western Tarheel
W: NJCAA, Western Tarheel
M: Basketball, Cross Country,
   Golf, Tennis
W: Basketball, Cross Country,
   Golf, Tennis

Ashland College
Ashland, OH 44805
M: (419) 289-4019
W: (419) 289-4019
Enrollment: A
4-year private
M: Great Lakes, Heartland
W: AIAW
M: Baseball, Basketball, Cross
   Country, Football, Lacrosse,
   Soccer, Swimming-Diving,
   Track & Field, Wrestling
W: Basketball, Field Hockey,
   Softball, Swimming-Diving,

Tennis, Track & Field,
Volleyball

W: Softball, Volleyball,
Basketball, Tennis

Assumption College
Worcester, MA 01609
M: (617) 752-5615 X. 279
W: (617) 752-5615 X. 416
Enrollment: A
4-year private
M: Northeast-7
W: Northeast-7
M: Baseball, Crew, Cross
  Country, Football, Golf,
  Lacrosse, Soccer, Tennis,
  Track & Field, Basketball
W: Basketball, Crew, Cross
  Country, Field Hockey,
  Softball, Tennis, Track &
  Field, Volleyball

Athens State College
Athens, AL 35611
M: (205) 232-1802
W: (205) 232-1802
Enrollment: A
4-year public funding
M: Southern States
W: Independent
M: Baseball, Basketball
W: Basketball

Atlantic Christian College
West Lee Street
Wilson, NC 27893
M: (919) 237-3161
W: (919) 237-3161
Enrollment: A
4-year private
M: Carolinas, NAIA
W: Carolinas, NAIA
M: Baseball, Basketball, Golf,
  Soccer, Tennis, Track & Field

Auburn University
Auburn, AL 36830
M: (205) 826-4750
W: (205) 826-4750
Enrollment: C
4-year public funding
M: Southeastern, NCAA
W: Southeastern, AIAW
M: Baseball, Basketball, Cross
  Country, Football, Golf,
  Swimming-Diving, Tennis,
  Track & Field, Wrestling
W: Softball, Basketball, Cross
  Country, Golf, Gymnastics,
  Swimming-Diving, Tennis,
  Track & Field, Volleyball

Auburn University
Montgomery, AL 36109
M: (205) 279-9110 X. 541
Enrollment: B
4-year public funding
M: NAIA, Southern States
M: Basketball, Tennis

Augusta College
2500 Walton Way
Augusta, GA 30904
M: (404) 828-3606
W: (404) 828-3606
Enrollment: B
4-year public funding
M: South Atlantic, NCAA
W: GAIAW, AIAW
M: Soccer, Baseball, Basketball,
  Cross Country, Golf,
  Swimming-Diving, Tennis
W: Basketball, Swimming-Diving,
  Tennis, Volleyball

Augustana College
Rock Island, IL 61201
M: (309) 794–7923
W: (309) 794–7254
Enrollment: A
4-year private
M: CCIW
W: AIAW
M: Baseball, Basketball, Cross Country, Football, Golf, Soccer, Swimming-Diving, Tennis, Track & Field, Wrestling
W: Basketball, Cross Country, Softball, Swimming-Diving, Tennis, Track & Field, Volleyball

All aid for men and women is based on financial need.

Augustana College
Sioux Falls, SD 57102
M: (605) 336–4311
W: (605) 336–4311
Enrollment: A
4-year private
M: North Central
W: AIAW
M: Baseball, Golf, Tennis, <u>Basketball</u>, <u>Cross Country</u>, <u>Football</u>, <u>Track & Field</u>, <u>Wrestling</u>
W: <u>Basketball</u>, <u>Cross Country</u>, <u>Golf</u>, <u>Softball</u>, <u>Tennis</u>, <u>Track & Field</u>, <u>Volleyball</u>

Aurora College
347 South Gladstone
Aurora, IL 60507
M: (312) 892–6431 X. 70
W: (312) 892–6431 X. 70
Enrollment: A
4-year private
M: Baseball, Basketball, Golf, Soccer, Tennis, Wrestling
W: Basketball, Softball, Tennis, Volleyball
All aid for men and women is based on financial need.

Averett College
420 Main Street
Danville, VA 24541
M: (804) 793–7811 X. 281
W: (804) 793–7811 X. 257
Enrollment: A
4-year private
M: NCAA, DICC
W: AIAW
M: Basketball, Cross Country, Golf, Soccer, Tennis, Track & Field
W: Basketball, Field Hockey, Golf, Softball, Tennis

Azusa Pacific College
Azusa, CA 91702
M: (213) 969–3434
W: (213) 969–3434
Enrollment: A
4-year private
M: Southern League
W: Southern League
M: <u>Baseball</u>, <u>Basketball</u>, <u>Cross Country</u>, <u>Football</u>, <u>Soccer</u>, <u>Tennis</u>, <u>Track & Field</u>
W: <u>Basketball</u>, <u>Cross Country</u>, <u>Track & Field</u>, <u>Volleyball</u>

Babson College
Babson Park, MA 02157
M: (617) 235–1200 X. 250
W: (617) 235–1200 X. 250
Enrollment: A

4-year private
M: NCAA, ECAC
W: Independent
M: Baseball, Basketball, Cross
   Country, Golf, Hockey,
   Lacrosse, Sailing, Skiing,
   Soccer, Squash, Swimming-
   Diving
W: Basketball, Tennis, Volleyball

Baker University
Baldwin, KS 66006
M: (913) 594–6451
W: (913) 594–6451
Enrollment: A
4-year private
M: HAAC
W: HAAC, AIAW, NAIA
M: Baseball, Basketball, Bowling,
   Cross Country, Football,
   Golf, Tennis, Track & Field
W: Basketball, Bowling, Cross
   Country, Softball, Tennis,
   Track & Field, Volleyball

Ball State University
2000 University Avenue
Muncie, IN 47306
M: (317) 285–1249
W: (317) 285–1671
Enrollment: C
4-year public funding
M: Mid-American
W: IAIAW
M: Baseball, Basketball, Cross
   Country, Football, Golf,
   Gymnastics, Soccer,
   Swimming-Diving, Tennis,
   Track & Field, Volleyball,
   Wrestling
W: Badminton, Basketball, Cross
   Country, Field Hockey, Golf,
   Gymnastics, Lacrosse,
   Softball, Swimming-Diving,
   Tennis, Track & Field,
   Volleyball

Community College of Baltimore
2901 Liberty Heights Avenue
Baltimore, MD 21215
M: (301) 396–0993
W: (301) 396–0993
Enrollment: C
2-year public funding
M: JUCO, NJCAA
W: JUCO, NJCAA
M: Badminton, Baseball,
   Basketball, Bowling, Cross
   Country, Soccer, Tennis,
   Track & Field
W: Badminton, Basketball,
   Bowling, Cross Country,
   Softball, Tennis, Track &
   Field, Volleyball

University of Baltimore
1420 North Charles Street
Baltimore, MD 21201
M: (301) 727–6350
Enrollment: C
4-year public funding
M: NCAA, ECAC
M: Baseball, Basketball, Cross
   Country, Golf, Lacrosse,
   Soccer, Tennis

Baptist Bible College
628 East Kearney
Springfield, MO 65802
M: (417) 869–9811 X. 258
Enrollment: A
4-year private
M: Ozark, NAIA
M: Baseball, Basketball, Cross
   Country, Golf, Soccer

Baptist Bible College
538 Venard Road
Clarks Summit, PA 18411
M: (717) 587–1172
W: (717) 587–1172
Enrollment: A
4-year private
M: NACC
W: NACC
M: Baseball, Basketball, Cross Country, Soccer, Tennis, Track & Field, Wrestling
W: Basketball, Cross Country, Softball, Tennis, Track & Field, Volleyball

Baptist College of Charleston
Charleston, SC 29411
M: (803) 797–4117
W: (803) 797–4117
Enrollment: A
4-year private
M: NCAA, Independent
W: AIAW
M: Baseball, Basketball, Cross Country, Golf, Soccer, Tennis, Track & Field
W: Basketball, Tennis, Track & Field, Volleyball

Barat College
700 East Westleigh Road
Lake Forest, IL 60045
W: (312) 234–3000 X. 320
Enrollment: A
4-year private
W: IAIAW
W: Basketball, Volleyball

Barber-Scotia College
145 Cabarrus Avenue
Concord, NC 28025
M: (704) 786–5171
W: (704) 786–5171
Enrollment: A
4-year private
M: NAIA
W: NAIA
M: Soccer, Swimming-Diving, Tennis, Track & Field, Volleyball, Basketball, Wrestling
W: Soccer, Softball, Swimming-Diving, Tennis, Track & Field, Volleyball, Basketball

Barnard College
606 West 120th Street
New York, NY 10027
W: (212) 280–2233
Enrollment: B
4-year private
W: Ivy League
W: Archery, Basketball, Cross Country, Fencing, Swimming-Diving, Tennis, Track & Field, Volleyball

Barton County Community College
Route 3
Great Bend, KS 67530
M: (316) 792–2701 X. 178
W: (316) 792–2701 X. 178
Enrollment: A
2-year public funding
M: Jayhawk
W: Jayhawk
M: Baseball, Basketball, Cross Country, Golf, Tennis, Track & Field
W: Basketball, Cross Country, Golf, Tennis, Track & Field, Volleyball

81

Bates College
Lewiston, ME 04240
M: (207) 784–9336
W: (207) 784–9336
Enrollment: A
4-year private
M: ECAC, CBB, NCAA
W: AIAW, EAIAW, MAIAW
M: Baseball, Basketball, Cross Country, Football, Golf, Lacrosse, Skiing, Soccer, Tennis, Track & Field
W: Basketball, Cross Country, Field Hockey, Lacrosse, Skiing, Soccer, Softball, Tennis, Track & Field, Volleyball

All aid for men and women is based on financial need.

Baylor University
Waco, TX 76706
M: (817) 754–4648
W: (817) 754–4648
Enrollment: C
4-year private
M: Southwest
W: AIAW
M: Tennis, Baseball, Basketball, Cross Country, Football, Golf, Track & Field
W: Tennis, Basketball, Softball, Track & Field, Volleyball

Beaver College
Glenside, PA 19038
M: (215) 884–3500 X. 370
W: (215) 884–3500 X. 339
Enrollment: A
4-year private
M: Keystone
W: PAIAW
M: Baseball, Basketball, Cross Country, Equestrian, Soccer, Tennis, Track & Field
W: Basketball, Cross Country, Equestrian, Field Hockey, Lacrosse, Soccer, Softball, Tennis, Track & Field

Belhaven College
1500 Peachtree Street
Jackson, MS 39202
M: (601) 944–1454
W: (601) 948–3172
Enrollment: A
4-year private
M: Southern States
W: MAIAW
M: Baseball, Basketball, Soccer, Tennis
W: Basketball, Softball

Bellarmine College
Newburg Road
Louisville, KY 40205
M: (502) 452–8380
W: (502) 452–8380
Enrollment: A
4-year private
M: Great Lakes Valley
W: KWIC
M: Baseball, Basketball, Cross Country, Golf, Soccer, Tennis, Track & Field
W: Basketball, Softball, Volleyball

Bellevue College
Bellevue, NE 68005
M: (402) 291–8100 X. 49
W: (402) 291–8100 X. 49
Enrollment: A
4-year private
M: NAIA, NCC

W: AIAW
M: Baseball, Basketball
W: Softball, Volleyball

Belmont College
Nashville, TN 37203
M: (615) 383–7001 X. 306
W: (615) 383–7001 X. 306
Enrollment: A
4-year private
M: VSAC
W: VSAC
M: Cross Country, Baseball,
　　Basketball, Tennis
W: Basketball, Tennis

Beloit College
Beloit, WI 53511
M: (608) 365–3391 X. 238
W: (608) 365–3391 X. 238
Enrollment: A
4-year private
M: Midwest
W: WIC, WAC
M: Basketball, Cross Country,
　　Football, Golf, Soccer,
　　Swimming-Diving, Tennis,
　　Track & Field
W: Basketball, Cross Country,
　　Golf, Softball, Swimming-
　　Diving, Tennis, Track &
　　Field, Volleyball

Bemidji State University
Bemidji, MN 56601
M: (218) 755–2940
W: (218) 755–2940
Enrollment: B
4-year public funding
M: NIC
W: Northern Sun
M: Baseball, Cross Country, Golf,
　　Swimming-Diving, Tennis,
　　Wrestling, Basketball,
　　Football, Ice Hockey, Track
　　& Field
W: Basketball, Field Hockey,
　　Gymnastics, Swimming-
　　Diving, Tennis, Track &
　　Field, Volleyball

The Benedictine College
Atchison, KS 66002
M: (913) 367–5340 X. 542
W: (913) 367–5340 X. 542
Enrollment: A
4-year private
M: Independent
W: KIC
M: Bowling, Cross Country, Golf,
　　Tennis, Track & Field,
　　Baseball, Basketball,
　　Football, Soccer
W: Bowling, Cross Country, Track
　　& Field, Basketball, Softball,
　　Tennis, Volleyball

Bennett College
Greensboro, NC 27420
W: (919) 273–4431
Enrollment: A
4-year private
W: AIAW
W: Basketball, Volleyball

Bentley College
450 Beaver Street
Waltham, MA 02154
M: (617) 891–2256
W: (617) 891–2256
Enrollment: B
4-year private
M: NCAA, ECAC, NECAC,
　　Northeast-7

W: AIAW, EAIAW, MAIAW,
   Northeast-7
M: Baseball, Cross Country, Golf,
   Ice Hockey, Soccer, Tennis,
   Track & Field, <u>Basketball</u>
W: Field Hockey, Softball,
   Tennis, <u>Basketball</u>

Berea College
Berea, KY 40403
M: (606) 986–9341 X. 423/519
W: (606) 986–9341 X. 524
Enrollment: A
4-year private
M: KIAC
W: KWIC
M: Baseball, Basketball, Cross
   Country, Golf, Soccer,
   Swimming-Diving, Tennis,
   Track & Field
W: Basketball, Field Hockey,
   Golf, Softball, Swimming-
   Diving, Tennis, Track &
   Field, Volleyball

Berea College offers no outright athletic scholarships. However, Berea offers much aid and grants for athletes.

Berry College
Mount Berry, GA 30149
M: (404) 232–5374 X. 334
W: (404) 232–5374 X. 334
Enrollment: A
4-year private
M: GIAC
W: GAIAW
M: <u>Basketball</u>, <u>Cross Country</u>,
   <u>Soccer</u>, <u>Tennis</u>, <u>Track & Field</u>
W: <u>Basketball</u>, <u>Cross Country</u>,
   <u>Tennis</u>, <u>Track & Field</u>

Bethany College
Lindsborg, KS 67456
M: (913) 227–3311
W: (913) 227–3311
Enrollment: A
4-year private
M: KCAC
W: KCAC
M: Baseball, Basketball, Cross
   Country, Golf, Tennis, Track
   & Field
W: Basketball, Golf, Softball,
   Tennis, Track & Field,
   Volleyball

Although Bethany gives no outright athletic scholarships, the school does give much aid to student athletes.

Bethany Lutheran College
734 Marsh Street
Mankato, MN 56001
M: (507) 625–2977
W: (507) 625–2977
Enrollment: A
2-year private
M: MSCCC
W: MSCCC
M: Tennis, <u>Basketball</u>, <u>Soccer</u>,
   Wrestling
W: Tennis, <u>Basketball</u>, <u>Volleyball</u>

Bethel College
3900 Bethel Drive
St. Paul, MN 55112
M: (612) 638–6397
W: (612) 638–6397
Enrollment: A
4-year private
M: MIAC
W: MAIAW
M: Baseball, Basketball, Cross

Country, Football, Golf, Ice
Hockey, Soccer, Tennis,
Track & Field, Wrestling
W: Basketball, Cross Country,
Softball, Tennis, Track &
Field, Volleyball

Bethune-Cookman College
640 Second Avenue
Daytona, Beach, FL 32015
M: (904) 255–1401
W: (904) 255–1401
Enrollment: A
4-year private
M: MEAC
W: MEAC
M: Baseball, Basketball, Cross
Country, Football, Golf,
Indoor Track, Tennis, Track
& Field
W: Track & Field, Basketball

Biola College
13800 Biola Avenue
La Mirada, CA 90638
M: (213) 944–0351
W: (213) 944–0351
Enrollment: A
4-year private
M: NAIA, NCCAA
W: AIAW
M: Baseball, Basketball, Cross
Country, Soccer, Tennis,
Track & Field, Wrestling
W: Basketball, Tennis, Volleyball

Biscayne College
16400 NW 32nd Avenue
Miami, FL 33054
M: (305) 625–6000
W: (305) 625–6000
Enrollment: A
4-year private
M: Sunshine State
W: Sunshine State
M: Golf, Soccer, Tennis, Baseball,
Basketball
W: Cross Country, Tennis

Bishop College
3837 Simpson-Stuart Road
Dallas, TX 75241
M: (214) 372–8089
W: (214) 372–8089
Enrollment: A
4-year private
M: Independent
W: Independent
M: Baseball, Basketball, Football,
Track & Field, Volleyball
W: Basketball, Track & Field,
Volleyball

Bismarck Junior College
Bismarck, ND 58501
M: (701) 255–3934
W: (701) 255–3934
Enrollment: B
2-year public funding
M: NDCAC
W: Sakakawea
M: Baseball, Basketball, Cross
Country, Football, Golf,
Tennis, Track & Field,
Wrestling
W: Basketball, Cross Country,
Golf, Tennis, Track & Field,
Volleyball

Blackburn College
700 College Avenue
Carlinville, IL 62626
M: (217) 854–3231
W: (217) 854–3231

Enrollment: A
4-year private
M: Independent
W: AIAW
M: Basketball, Golf, Soccer,
    Tennis, Track & Field
W: Basketball, Tennis, Track &
    Field, Volleyball

Blinn College
902 College Avenue
Brenham, TX 77833
M: (713) 836–6603
W: (713) 836–6603
Enrollment: A
2-year public funding
M: TJCFC, TJCAC, NJCAA
W: TJCFC, TJCAC, NJCAA
M: Baseball, Basketball, Football,
    Tennis, Track & Field
W: Basketball, Tennis

Blue Mountain College
Blue Mountain, MS 38610
W: (601) 685–5711
Enrollment: A
4-year private
W: AIAW
W: Softball, Basketball

Bluefield College
Bluefield, VA 24605
M: (304) 327–7137
W: (304) 327–7137
Enrollment: A
4-year private
M: NLCAA
W: Independent
M: Baseball, Basketball
W: Volleyball

Bluefield State College
Bluefield, WV 24701
M: (304) 325–7102
W: (304) 325–7102
Enrollment: A
4-year public funding
M: WVIAC
W: WVIAA
M: Basketball, Football, Golf
W: Basketball

Bluffton College
College Avenue
Bluffton, OH 45817
M: (419) 358–8015 X. 236
W: (419) 358–8015 X. 245
Enrollment: A
4-year private
M: Hoosier-Buckeye
W: AIAW
M: Baseball, Basketball, Cross
    Country, Football, Golf,
    Soccer, Tennis, Track & Field
W: Basketball, Cross Country,
    Golf, Softball, Tennis, Track
    & Field, Volleyball

Boise State University
1910 University Drive
Boise, ID 83725
M: (208) 385–1503
W: (208) 385–1655
Enrollment: C
4-year public funding
M: Big Sky
W: AIAW, NCWSA
M: Basketball, Cross Country,
    Football, Golf, Tennis, Track
    & Field, Wrestling
W: Cross Country, Basketball,
    Field Hockey, Gymnastics,
    Tennis, Track & Field,
    Volleyball

Boston College
Chestnut Hill, MA 02167
M: (617) 969–0100 X. 3000
W: (617) 969–0100 X. 3031
Enrollment: C
4-year private
M: Big East
W: AIAW
M: Baseball, Golf, Lacrosse, Sailing, Skiing, Soccer, Swimming-Diving, Track & Field, Basketball, Cross Country, Football, Ice Hockey, Tennis
W: Basketball, Cross Country, Fencing, Field Hockey, Golf, Lacrosse, Sailing, Skiing, Soccer, Swimming-Diving, Tennis, Track & Field, Volleyball

Boston State College
625 Huntington Avenue
Boston, MA 02115
M: (617) 731–3300 X. 363
W: (617) 731–3300 X. 363
Enrollment: C
4-year public funding
M: NCAA, ECAC, MASCAC
W: AIAW, EAIAW
M: Baseball, Basketball, Cross Country, Football, Ice Hockey, Lacrosse, Soccer, Softball, Volleyball, Wrestling
W: Basketball, Cross Country, Gymnastics, Tennis

Boston University
Commonwealth Avenue
Boston, MA 02215
M: (617) 353–2872
W: (617) 353–2872
Enrollment: C
4-year private
M: NCAA, Yankee
W: AIAW, EAIAW
M: Basketball, Crew, Cross Country, Football, Ice Hockey, Sailing, Soccer, Swimming-Diving, Tennis, Track & Field, Wrestling
W: Basketball, Crew, Cross Country, Field Hockey, Sailing, Swimming-Diving, Tennis, Track & Field

Bowdoin College
Brunswick, ME 04011
M: (207) 725–8731
Enrollment: A
4-year private
M: NESCAC, NECAC, EBB, NCAA, ECAC
M: Baseball, Basketball, Cross Country, Football, Golf, Ice Hockey, Lacrosse, Sailing, Skiing, Soccer, Squash, Swimming-Diving, Tennis, Track & Field, Wrestling

All aid for men is based on financial need.

Bowie State College
Bowie, MD 20715
M: (301) 464–3244
W: (301) 464–3244
Enrollment: B
4-year public funding
M: CIAA
W: CIAA
M: Baseball, Basketball, Football, Tennis, Track & Field
W: Basketball, Softball, Tennis, Track & Field, Volleyball

Bowling Green State University
Bowling Green, OH 43403
M: (419) 372–2401
W: (419) 372-2401
Enrollment: C
4-year public funding
M: Mid-American
W: Mid-American
M: Soccer, Baseball, Basketball, Cross Country, Football, Golf, Ice Hockey, Swimming-Diving, Tennis, Track & Field, Wrestling
W: Lacrosse, Basketball, Cross Country, Field Hockey, Golf, Gymnastics, Softball, Swimming-Diving, Tennis, Track & Field, Volleyball

Bradley University
1501 West Bradley Avenue
Peoria, IL 61625
M: (309) 676–7611
W: (309) 676–7611
Enrollment: B
4-year private
M: MVC
W: MVC
M: Cross Country, Baseball, Basketball, Golf, Swimming-Diving, Tennis, Track & Field
W: Basketball, Softball, Tennis, Track & Field, Volleyball

Brandeis University
Waltham, MA 02154
M: (617) 647–2972/2967
W: (617) 647–2972/2967
Enrollment: B
4-year private
M: ECAC, NCAA, Greater Boston
W: ECAC, NCAA
M: Baseball, Basketball, Cross Country, Fencing, Lacrosse, Soccer, Swimming-Diving, Tennis, Track & Field
W: Basketball, Cross Country, Fencing, Soccer, Softball, Tennis, Track & Field, Volleyball

Brandywine College
Concord Pike
Wilmington, DE 19803
M: (302) 478–3000
W: (302) 478–3000
Enrollment: A
2-year private
M: NJCAA
W: NJCAA
M: Baseball, Basketball, Golf, Soccer, Tennis
W: Basketball, Field Hockey, Softball, Tennis, Volleyball

Brevard College
Brevard, NC 28712
M: (704) 883–8292 X. 270
W: (704) 883–8292 X. 270
Enrollment: A
2-year public
M: NJCAA, WCJCC
W: Independent
M: Golf, Basketball, Cross Country, Soccer, Tennis, Track & Field
W: Basketball, Tennis, Volleyball

Brevard Junior College
Clearlake Road
Cocoa, FL 32922
M: (305) 632–1111 X. 375/376
W: (305) 632–1111 X. 375/376
Enrollment: C

2-year public funding
M: FCCAA
W: FCCAA
M: Archery, Fencing, Soccer, Baseball, Basketball, Cross Country, Golf, Swimming-Diving, Tennis, Track & Field, Wrestling
W: Archery, Fencing, Soccer, Basketball, Cross Country, Softball, Swimming-Diving, Tennis, Track & Field, Volleyball

Briar Cliff College
3303 Rebecca
Sioux City, IA 51104
M: (712) 279-5441/5405
W: (712) 279-5441/5405
Enrollment: A
4-year private
M: Independent
W: Io-Kota
M: Golf, Tennis, Baseball, Basketball
W: Basketball, Golf, Softball, Tennis, Volleyball

Bridgewater College
East College Street
Bridgewater, VA 22812
M: (703) 828-2501 X. 502
W: (703) 828-2501 X. 503
Enrollment: A
4-year private
M: ODAC
W: ODAC, AIAW
M: Baseball, Basketball, Cross Country, Football, Golf, Tennis, Track & Field, Volleyball
W: Basketball, Field Hockey, Lacrosse, Tennis, Volleyball

Bridgewater State College
Bridgewater, MA 02324
M: (617) 697-8321
W: (617) 697-8321
Enrollment: B
4-year public funding
M: MSCAC, ECAC, NCAA
W: AIAW
M: Baseball, Basketball, Cross Country, Football, Golf, Ice Hockey, Soccer, Swimming-Diving, Tennis, Track & Field, Wrestling
W: Basketball, Cross Country, Field Hockey, Gymnastics, Lacrosse, Softball, Swimming-Diving, Tennis, Track & Field, Volleyball

Brigham Young University
Provo, UT 84602
M: (801) 378-4911
W: (801) 378-4225
Enrollment: C
4-year private
M: WAC
W: Intermountain
M: Baseball, Basketball, Cross Country, Football, Golf, Gymnastics, Soccer, Swimming-Diving, Tennis, Track & Field, Wrestling
W: Basketball, Cross Country, Field Hockey, Golf, Gymnastics, Swimming-Diving, Tennis, Track & Field, Volleyball

Brigham Young University
Laie, HI 96762
M: (808) 293-9211
W: (808) 293-9211
Enrollment: A

4-year private
M: Independent
W: Independent
M: Basketball, Tennis, Volleyball
W: Basketball, Tennis, Volleyball

Bristol College
Bristol College Drive
Bristol, TN 37620
M: (615) 968–1442
Enrollment: A
2-year private
M: NAIA
M: Basketball, Golf, Tennis

Brooklyn College—City University of New York
Brooklyn, NY 11210
M: (212) 780–5367
W: (212) 780–5367
Enrollment: C
4-year public funding
M: NCAA, ECAC
W: AIAW, EAIAW
M: Archery, Baseball, Basketball, Bowling, Cross Country, Fencing, Football, Golf, Riflery, Soccer, Swimming-Diving, Tennis, Track & Field, Wrestling
W: Archery, Baseball, Cross Country, Fencing, Softball, Swimming-Diving, Tennis, Track & Field, Volleyball

Brown University
Providence, RI 02912
M: (401) 863–2211
W: (401) 483–2211
Enrollment: C
4-year private
M: Ivy League, ECAC
W: Ivy League, EAIAW
M: Baseball, Basketball, Crew, Cross Country, Football, Golf, Ice Hockey, Lacrosse, Soccer, Swimming-Diving, Tennis, Track & Field, Water Polo, Wrestling
W: Basketball, Crew, Cross Country, Field Hockey, Gymnastics, Lacrosse, Soccer, Softball, Squash, Swimming-Diving, Tennis, Track & Field, Volleyball

Bryan College
Bryan Hill
Dayton, TN 37321
M: (615) 775–2041 X. 255
W: (615) 775–2041 X. 255
Enrollment: A
4-year private
M: SCAC
W: SCAC
M: Tennis, Baseball, Basketball, Cross Country, Soccer
W: Tennis, Basketball, Softball, Volleyball

Bryant College
Smithfield, RI 02917
M: (401) 231–1200 X. 336
W: (401) 231–1200 X. 336
Enrollment: B
4-year private
M: NCAA
W: NCAA
M: Baseball, Bowling, Cross Country, Golf, Soccer, Tennis, Track & Field, Volleyball, Basketball
W: Cross Country, Soccer, Tennis, Track & Field, Basketball, Softball, Volleyball

Bucknell University
Lewisburg, PA 17837
M: (717) 524-1233
W: (717) 524-1212
Enrollment: B
4-year private
M: ECAC
W: AIAW
M: Baseball, Basketball, Cross Country, Football, Golf, Lacrosse, Soccer, Swimming-Diving, Tennis, Track & Field, Water Polo, Wrestling
W: Basketball, Cross Country, Field Hockey, Lacrosse, Softball, Swimming-Diving, Tennis, Track & Field, Volleyball

All aid for men and women is based on financial need.

Butler County Community Junior College
El Dorado, KS 67042
M: (316) 321-5083
W: (316) 321-5083
Enrollment: A
2-year public funding
M: KSCCC
W: KSCCC
M: Baseball, Basketball, Cross Country, Football, Golf, Tennis, Track & Field
W: Basketball, Cross Country, Softball, Tennis, Track & Field, Volleyball

Butler University
4600 Sunset Avenue
Indianapolis, IN 46208
M: (317) 283-9375
W: (317) 283-9211
Enrollment: A
4-year private
M: Heartland, Midwestern City
W: AIAW
M: Baseball, Basketball, Cross Country, Football, Golf, Swimming-Diving, Tennis, Track & Field
W: Basketball, Swimming-Diving, Tennis, Volleyball

University of California
Davis, CA 95616
M: (916) 752-0511
W: (916) 752-0511
Enrollment: C
4-year public funding
M: Far Western
W: Golden State
M: Baseball, Basketball, Cross Country, Football, Golf, Gymnastics, Soccer, Swimming-Diving, Tennis, Track & Field, Water Polo, Wrestling
W: Basketball, Cross Country, Field Hockey, Gymnastics, Softball, Swimming-Diving, Tennis, Track & Field, Volleyball

University of California
Irvine, CA 92717
M: (714) 844-6931
W: (714) 833-6931
Enrollment: C
4-year public funding
M: PCAA
W: SCAA
M: Crew, Golf, Sailing, Baseball, Basketball, Cross Country, Swimming-Diving, Tennis, Track & Field, Water Polo

W: Sailing, Cross Country, Swimming-Diving, Tennis, Track & Field, Volleyball

University of California (UCLA)
Los Angeles, CA 90024
M: (213) 825-3326
W: (213) 825-9541
Enrollment: C
4-year public funding
M: Pacific-10
W: WCAA
M: Crew, Fencing, Riflery, Badminton, Baseball, Basketball, Cross Country, Football, Golf, Gymnastics, Soccer, Swimming-Diving, Tennis, Track & Field, Volleyball, Water Polo
W: Crew, Fencing, Badminton, Basketball, Cross Country, Golf, Gymnastics, Softball, Swimming-Diving, Tennis, Track & Field, Volleyball

University of California
Riverside, CA 92502
M: (714) 787-5432
W: (714) 787-5432
Enrollment: B
4-year public funding
M: CCAA
W: PCAC
M: Golf, Karate, Soccer, Swimming-Diving, Tennis, Volleyball, Water Polo, Baseball, Basketball, Cross Country, Track & Field
W: Cross Country, Karate, Softball, Swimming-Diving, Tennis, Track & Field, Basketball, Volleyball

University of California (at San Diego)
La Jolla, CA 92093
M: (714) 452-4211
W: (714) 452-4211
Enrollment: C
4-year public funding
M: NCAA, NAIA, CCAA
W: AIAW, CCAC
M: Badminton, Baseball, Basketball, Crew, Cross Country, Fencing, Golf, Sailing, Skiing, Soccer, Swimming-Diving, Tennis, Track & Field, Volleyball, Water Polo
W: Badminton, Basketball, Crew, Cross Country, Fencing, Field Hockey, Sailing, Soccer, Softball, Squash, Swimming-Diving, Tennis, Track & Field, Volleyball

University of California
Santa Barbara, CA 93106
M: (805) 961-3291
W: (805) 961-3291
Enrollment: C
4-year public funding
M: PCAA
W: SCAA
M: Baseball, Basketball, Cross Country, Golf, Gymnastics, Soccer, Swimming-Diving, Tennis, Track & Field, Volleyball, Water Polo
W: Gymnastics, Softball, Swimming-Diving, Tennis, Track & Field, Volleyball

California Institute of Technology
1201 East California Boulevard
Pasadena, CA 91109
M: (213) 795-6811 X. 2146
W: (213) 795-6811 X. 2146

Enrollment: A
4-year private
M: SCIC
W: SCIC
M: Baseball, Basketball, Cross Country, Fencing, Football, Golf, Soccer, Swimming-Diving, Tennis, Track & Field, Water Polo, Wrestling
W: Cross Country, Fencing, Soccer, Swimming-Diving, Track & Field, Volleyball

California Polytechnic State University
San Luis Obispo, CA 93407
M: (805) 546-2923
W: (805) 546-2923
Enrollment: C
4-year public funding
M: CCAA
W: SCAA
M: Soccer, Swimming-Diving, Tennis, Volleyball, Water Polo, Baseball, Basketball, Cross Country, Football, Track & Field, Wrestling
W: Basketball, Cross Country, Gymnastics, Softball, Swimming-Diving, Tennis, Track & Field, Volleyball

California State College
Bakersfield, CA 93309
M: (805) 833-2188
W: (805) 833-2188
Enrollment: B
4-year public funding
M: CCAA
W: PCAC
M: Soccer, Basketball, Cross Country, Tennis, Track & Field, Wrestling
W: Cross Country, Tennis, Track & Field, Volleyball

California State College (Sonoma)
Rohnert Park, CA 94928
M: (707) 664-2357
W: (707) 664-2357
Enrollment: B
4-year public funding
M: NCAA, NAIA
W: Golden State
M: Baseball, Basketball, Cross Country, Fencing, Football, Gymnastics, Sailing, Soccer, Tennis, Track & Field
W: Basketball, Cross Country, Fencing, Gymnastics, Sailing, Softball, Tennis, Track & Field, Volleyball

California State College (Stanislaus)
800 Monte Vista Avenue
Turlock, CA 95380
M: (209) 633-2566
W: (209) 633-2566
Enrollment: B
4-year public funding
M: Far Western
W: Golden State
M: Baseball, Basketball, Cross Country, Golf, Soccer, Tennis, Track & Field, Wrestling
W: Basketball, Softball, Tennis, Track & Field, Volleyball

California State University
Chico, CA 95926
M: (916) 895-6470
W: (916) 895-6470

Enrollment: C
4-year public funding
M: Far Western
W: Golden State
M: Baseball, Basketball, Cross Country, Football, Gymnastics, Soccer, Swimming-Diving, Track & Field, Wrestling
W: Basketball, Cross Country, Field Hockey, Gymnastics, Softball, Swimming-Diving, Tennis, Track & Field, Volleyball

California State University
Fullerton, CA 92634
M: (714) 773-2677
W: (714) 773-2677
Enrollment: C
4-year public funding
M: PCAA
W: WCAA
M: Cross Country, Track & Field, Baseball, Basketball, Fencing, Football, Golf, Gymnastics, Soccer, Tennis, Water Polo, Wrestling
W: Cross Country, Track & Field, Basketball, Fencing, Golf, Gymnastics, Softball, Tennis, Volleyball

California State University
Hayward, CA 94542
M: (415) 881-3038
W: (415) 881-3038
Enrollment: C
4-year public funding
M: Far Western
W: Golden State
M: Badminton, Baseball, Basketball, Cross Country, Football, Soccer, Swimming-Diving, Tennis, Track & Field, Water Polo
W: Badminton, Basketball, Cross Country, Gymnastics, Softball, Swimming-Diving, Tennis, Track & Field, Volleyball

California State University
1250 Bellflower Boulevard
Long Beach, CA 90801
M: (213) 498-4655
W: (213) 498-4655
Enrollment: C
4-year public funding
M: PCAA
W: WCAA
M: Archery, Badminton, Crew, Fencing, Baseball, Basketball, Cross Country, Football, Golf, Gymnastics, Soccer, Swimming-Diving, Tennis, Track & Field, Volleyball, Water Polo, Wrestling
W: Archery, Badminton, Fencing, Basketball, Cross Country, Field Hockey, Golf, Gymnastics, Softball, Swimming-Diving, Tennis, Track & Field, Volleyball

Calvary Bible College
111 West 39th Street
Kansas City, MO 64111
M: (816) 753-4511 X. 201
W: (816) 756-4511 X. 201
Enrollment: A
4-year private
M: MCCC
W: MCCC
M: Basketball, Bowling, Cross

Country, Golf, Soccer, Tennis
W: Basketball, Bowling, Cross
   Country, Tennis, Volleyball

Calvin College
1801 East Beltline
Grand Rapids, MI 49506
M: (616) 949–4000 X. 169
W: (616) 949–4000 X. 169
Enrollment: B
4-year private
M: MIAA
W: MIAA
M: Baseball, Basketball, Cross
   Country, Golf, Ice Hockey,
   Soccer, Swimming-Diving,
   Tennis, Track & Field,
   Wrestling
W: Archery, Basketball, Field
   Hockey, Softball, Swimming-
   Diving, Tennis, Track &
   Field, Volleyball

Cameron University
2800 Gore Boulevard
Lawton, OK 73501
M: (405) 248–2200
W: (405) 248–2200
Enrollment: B
4-year public funding
M: NAIA, Independent
W: NAIA, Independent
M: Baseball, Basketball, Football
W: Basketball, Softball, Tennis,
   Volleyball

Campbell College
Buies Creek, NC 27506
M: (919) 893–4111
W: (919) 893–4111
Enrollment: A
4-year private

M: NCAA
W: AIAW
M: Baseball, Basketball, Cross
   Country, Golf, Soccer,
   Tennis, Track & Field,
   Wrestling
W: Basketball, Softball, Tennis

Campbellsville College
Campbellsville, KY 42718
M: (502) 465–8158 X. 258
W: (502) 465–8158 X. 258
Enrollment: A
4-year public funding
M: KIAC
W: AIAW
M: Baseball, Basketball, Golf,
   Tennis
W: Basketball, Softball, Tennis

Canisius College
2001 Main Street
Buffalo, NY 14208
M: (716) 883–7000 X. 252
W: (716) 883–7000 X. 673
Enrollment: B
4-year private
M: NCAA, ECAC
W: NYSAIAW, EAIAW, AIAW
M: Football, Ice Hockey,
   Baseball, Basketball,
   Bowling, Crew, Cross
   Country, Golf, Riflery,
   Soccer, Swimming-Diving,
   Tennis, Track & Field
W: Bowling, Softball, Basketball,
   Gymnastics, Tennis,
   Volleyball

Cape Cod Community College
Route 132
West Barnstable, MA 02668

M: (617) 362–2131 X. 365
W: (617) 362–2131 X. 365
Enrollment: A
2-year public funding
M: MCCAC
W: MCCAC
M: Baseball, Basketball, Tennis
W: Basketball, Tennis

Carl Sandburg College
Galesburg, IL 61401
M: (309) 344–2518 X. 212
W: (309) 344–2518 X. 212
Enrollment: A
2-year public funding
M: Arrowhead
W: Arrowhead
M: Baseball, Basketball, Cross Country, Golf, Tennis
W: Basketball, Softball, Volleyball

Carlow College
Pittsburgh, PA 15213
W: (412) 578–6002
Enrollment: A
4-year private
W: Pennwood West
W: Basketball, Tennis, Volleyball

Carroll College
Helena, MT 59601
M: (406) 442–3450 X. 281
W: (406) 442–3450 X. 281
Enrollment: A
4-year private
M: Frontier
W: AIAW
M: Basketball, Football
W: Basketball, Volleyball

Carroll College
Waukesha, WI 53186
M: (414) 547–1211 X. 321
W: (414) 547–1211 X. 324
Enrollment: A
4-year private
M: CCIW
W: WIAA
M: Baseball, Basketball, Cross Country, Football, Golf, Swimming-Diving, Tennis, Track & Field, Wrestling
W: Basketball, Cross Country, Swimming-Diving, Tennis, Track & Field, Volleyball

All aid for men and women is based on financial need.

Carson-Newman College
Jefferson City, TN 37760
M: (615) 475–9061
W: (615) 475–9061
Enrollment: A
4-year private
M: SAC, VSAC
W: VSAC
M: Baseball, Basketball, Cross Country, Football, Golf, Tennis, Track & Field, Wrestling
W: Basketball, Tennis, Volleyball

Carthage College
2001 Alford Park Drive
Kenosha, WI 53140
M: (414) 551–8500 X. 301
W: (414) 551–8500 X. 302
Enrollment: A
4-year private
M: CCIW
W: WWIAC
M: Baseball, Basketball, Cross

Country, Football, Golf,
   Swimming-Diving, Tennis,
   Track & Field, Wrestling
W: Badminton, Basketball,
   Softball, Swimming-Diving,
   Tennis, Track & Field,
   Volleyball

Division III: all aid awarded on
   the basis of financial need.

Casper College
125 College Drive
Casper, WY 82601
M: (307) 268–2626
W: (307) 268–2424
Enrollment: B
2-year public funding
M: Empire, WCAA
W: WCAA
M: Basketball, Golf, Tennis
W: Basketball, Golf, Gymnastics,
   Tennis, Volleyball

Castleton State College
Castleton, VT 05735
M: (802) 468–5611
W: (802) 468–5611
Enrollment: A
4-year public funding
M: Mayflower
W: Independent
M: Baseball, Basketball, Cross
   Country, Lacrosse, Skiing,
   Soccer, Tennis
W: Basketball, Cross Country,
   Field Hockey, Lacrosse,
   Skiing, Soccer, Softball,
   Tennis

Catawba College
Salisbury, NC 28144
M: (704) 637–4392
W: (704) 637–4392
Enrollment: A
4-year private
M: SAC, Carolinas
W: Carolinas
M: Soccer, Tennis, Baseball,
   Basketball, Football, Golf,
   Track & Field, Wrestling
W: Field Hockey, Softball,
   Tennis, Volleyball, Basketball

Cathedral College
Douglaston, NY 11362
M: (212) 631–4600
Enrollment: A
4-year private
M: ECAC
M: Basketball, Swimming-Diving

Centenary College
Hackettstown, NJ 07840
W: (201) 852–1400
Enrollment: A
2-year private
W: Independent
W: Badminton, Field Hockey,
   Lacrosse, Riding, Softball,
   Swimming-Diving, Tennis,
   Volleyball

Centenary College
Shreveport, LA 71104
M: (318) 869–5275
W: (318) 869–5275
Enrollment: A
4-year private
M: Trans America
W: LAIAW
M: Soccer, Baseball, Basketball,
   Cross Country, Golf, Tennis
W: Basketball, Gymnastics,
   Tennis

University of Central Arkansas
Conway, AR 72032
M: (501) 329–2802
W: (501) 329–2931
Enrollment: C
4-year public funding
M: AIC
W: AWIC
M: Baseball, Cross Country, Golf, Tennis, Track & Field, Basketball, Football
W: Basketball, Gymnastics, Swimming-Diving, Tennis, Volleyball

Centralia College
Centralia, WA 98531
M: (206) 736–9391 X. 247
W: (206) 736–9391 X. 247
Enrollment: B
2-year public funding
M: AACC
W: AACC
M: Baseball, Basketball, Tennis
W: Basketball, Tennis, Volleyball

Scholarships are awarded to students from Washington, Oregon, Idaho, and British Columbia by conference rule.

Central Junior College
McPherson, KS 67460
M: (316) 241–0723
W: (316) 241–0723
Enrollment: A
2-year private
M: Prairie JC
W: Prairie JC
M: Baseball, Basketball, Cross Country, Soccer, Tennis, Track & Field
W: Basketball, Cross Country, Softball, Tennis, Track & Field, Volleyball

Central Michigan University
Mount Pleasant, MI 48858
M: (517) 774–3041
W: (517) 774–3041
Enrollment: C
4-year public funding
M: Mid-American
W: Mid-American
M: Baseball, Basketball, Cross Country, Football, Golf, Gymnastics, Soccer, Swimming-Diving, Tennis, Track & Field, Wrestling
W: Basketball, Cross Country, Field Hockey, Golf, Gymnastics, Softball, Swimming-Diving, Tennis, Track & Field, Volleyball

Central Missouri State University
Warrensburg, MO 64093
M: (816) 429–4250
W: (816) 429–4250
Enrollment: C
4-year public funding
M: MICAA
W: MAIAW
M: Baseball, Basketball, Cross Country, Football, Golf, Swimming-Diving, Tennis, Track & Field, Wrestling
W: Basketball, Cross Country, Field Hockey, Gymnastics, Softball, Swimming-Diving, Tennis, Track & Field, Volleyball

Central State University
100 North University Drive

Edmond, OK 73034
M: (405) 341-2980 X. 501
W: (405) 341-2980 X. 501
Enrollment: C
4-year public funding
M: Independent
W: Independent
M: Cross Country, Golf, Baseball, Basketball, Football, Tennis, Track & Field, Wrestling
W: Field Hockey, Gymnastics, Track & Field, Basketball, Softball, Tennis, Volleyball

Centre College
Danville, KY 40422
M: (606) 236-5211
W: (606) 236-5211
Enrollment: A
4-year private
M: CAC
W: KWIAA
M: Baseball, Basketball, Cross Country, Football, Golf, Soccer, Swimming-Diving, Tennis, Track & Field
W: Basketball, Field Hockey, Squash, Tennis, Track & Field

Chadron State College
Chadron, NE 69337
M: (308) 432-4451
W: (308) 432-4451
Enrollment: A
4-year public funding
M: NCC
W: Independent
M: Golf, Tennis, Baseball, Basketball, Cross Country, Football, Rodeo, Track & Field, Wrestling
W: Golf, Tennis, Basketball, Rodeo, Softball, Track & Field, Volleyball

Chaminade University
3140 Waialae Avenue
Honolulu, HI 96816
M: (808) 735-4790
Enrollment: A
4-year private
M: Independent
M: Baseball, Cross Country, Golf, Tennis, Track & Field, Basketball

Champlain College
232 South Willard Street
Burlington, VT 05401
M: (802) 658-0800
W: (802) 658-0800
Enrollment: A
2-year private
M: NJCAA
W: NJCAA
M: Skiing, Basketball, Soccer
W: Skiing, Field Hockey, Softball

College of Charleston
Charleston, SC 29401
M: (803) 792-5556
W: (803) 792-5556
Enrollment: C
4-year public funding
M: NAIA
W: AIAW
M: Sailing, Basketball, Golf, Soccer, Swimming-Diving, Tennis
W: Sailing, Basketball, Swimming-Diving, Tennis, Volleyball

University of Charleston
Charleston, WV 25304

M: (304) 346–9471
W: (304) 346–9471
Enrollment: A
4-year public funding
M: NCAA, NAIA, WVIAC
W: AIAW, MAIAW, WVIAA
M: Baseball, Basketball, Crew, Soccer, Tennis
W: Basketball, Softball, Tennis, Volleyball

Chatham College
Woodland Road
Pittsburgh, PA 15232
W: (412) 441–8200
Enrollment: A
4-year private
W: Pennwood West
W: Basketball, Field Hockey, Softball, Tennis, Volleyball

Chattahoochee Valley Community College
2602 Savage Drive
Prenix City, AL 36867
M: (205) 297–4981
W: (205) 297–4981
Enrollment: A
2-year public funding
M: AJCAA
W: AJCAA
M: Baseball, Basketball, Golf, Tennis
W: Basketball, Tennis

University of Chicago
5640 University Avenue
Chicago, IL 60637
M: (312) 753–4683
W: (312) 753–3574
Enrollment: A
4-year private

M: MCAC
W: AIAW, Midwest IAIAW, IAIAW
M: Baseball, Basketball, Cross Country, Fencing, Football, Soccer, Swimming-Diving, Tennis, Track & Field, Wrestling
W: Basketball, Field Hockey, Softball, Swimming-Diving, Tennis, Track & Field, Volleyball

Chicago State University
95th and King Drive
Chicago, IL 60628
M: (312) 995–2290
W: (312) 995–2290
Enrollment: B
4-year public funding
M: CCAC
W: AIAW
M: Baseball, Tennis, Basketball, Swimming-Diving, Wrestling
W: Cross Country, Track & Field, Softball, Volleyball

Chowan College
Murfreesboro, NC 27855
M: (919) 398–4101
W: (919) 398–4101
Enrollment: A
2-year private
M: Independent
W: Independent
M: Football, Golf, Tennis, Wrestling, Baseball, Basketball
W: Golf, Softball, Tennis, Basketball, Volleyball

Christopher Newport College
Newport News, VA 23606
M: (804) 599–7025
W: (804) 599–7025
Enrollment: B
4-year public funding
M: Dixie
W: VAIAW, AIAW
M: Basketball, Cross Country, Golf, Soccer, Tennis, Track & Field
W: Basketball, Tennis, Volleyball

University of Cincinnati
Cincinnati, OH 45221
M: (513) 475–5601
W: (513) 475–6763
Enrollment: C
4-year public funding
M: Metro
W: OAISW, Metro
M: Baseball, Basketball, Cross Country, Football, Golf, Soccer, Swimming-Diving, Tennis, Track & Field, Volleyball
W: Basketball, Golf, Swimming-Diving, Tennis, Volleyball

Cincinnati Bible College
Cincinnati, OH 45204
M: (512) 471–4800
W: (512) 471–4800
Enrollment: A
4-year private
M: SCHC
W: AISW
M: Basketball, Track & Field
W: Basketball, Softball, Volleyball

Cisco Junior College
Cisco, TX 76437
M: (817) 442–3883
W: (817) 442–3883
Enrollment: A
2-year public funding
M: NTJCAA
W: NTJCAA
M: Basketball, Football, Golf
W: Basketball

The Citadel
Charleston, SC 29409
M: (803) 792–5070
Enrollment: A
4-year public funding
M: Southern
M: Baseball, Basketball, Cross Country, Football, Golf, Riflery, Soccer, Swimming-Diving, Tennis, Track & Field, Wrestling

Citrus College
18824 East Foothill Boulevard
Azusa, CA 91702
M: (213) 335–0521
W: (213) 335–0521
Enrollment: A
4-year private
M: Mission
W: Mission
M: Badminton, Baseball, Basketball, Cross Country, Football, Golf, Swimming-Diving, Tennis, Track & Field, Water Polo
W: Badminton, Basketball, Cross Country, Softball, Swimming-Diving, Tennis, Track & Field, Volleyball

Clackamas Community College
19600 South Molalla Avenue

Oregon City, OR 97045
M: (503) 657–8400 X. 291
W: (503) 654–8700 X. 291
Enrollment: B
2-year public funding
M: OCCAA
W: OCCAA
M: Golf, Baseball, Basketball, Cross Country, Soccer, Tennis, Track & Field, Wrestling
W: Basketball, Cross Country, Tennis, Track & Field, Volleyball

Claremore College
Claremore, OK 74017
M: (918) 341–7510
W: (918) 341–7510
Enrollment: A
2-year public funding
M: Bi-State
W: Bi-State
M: Riflery, Baseball, Basketball, Golf, Soccer, Tennis
W: Basketball, Golf, Soccer, Tennis

Clarion State College
Clarion, PA 16214
M: (814) 226–2371
W: (814) 226–2371
Enrollment: B
4-year public funding
M: PAC, ECAC, NCAA, NAIA
W: AIAW, EAIAW
M: Baseball, Cross Country, Golf, Riflery, Track & Field, Basketball, Football, Swimming-Diving, Wrestling
W: Cross Country, Riflery, Softball, Tennis, Track & Field, Basketball, Gymnastics, Swimming-Diving, Volleyball

Clark College
240 Chestnut Street, SW
Atlanta, GA 30314
M: (404) 524–8552
W: (404) 542–2552
Enrollment: A
4-year private
M: SIAC
W: SIAC
M: Baseball, Basketball, Cross Country, Football, Tennis, Track & Field
W: Basketball, Tennis, Track & Field

Clarke College
1550 Clarke Drive
Dubuque, IA 52001
W: (319) 588–0818
Enrollment: A
4-year private
W: Independent
W: Volleyball, Basketball

Clark University
950 Main Street
Worcester, MA 01610
M: (617) 793–7161
W: (617) 793–7161
Enrollment: A
4-year private
M: NEIAA, ECAC, NCAA
W: AIAW, NEAIAW
M: Baseball, Basketball, Crew, Cross Country, Golf, Soccer, Swimming-Diving, Tennis, Track & Field
W: Basketball, Cross Country, Field Hockey, Golf, Softball,

Swimming-Diving, Tennis,
Track & Field, Volleyball

Clemson University
Clemson, SC 29631
M: (803) 656–2101/2114
W: (803) 656–2101/2114
Enrollment: C
4-year public funding
M: Atlantic Coast
W: Atlantic Coast
M: Baseball, Basketball, Cross
 Country, Fencing, Football,
 Golf, Soccer, Swimming-
 Diving, Tennis, Track &
 Field, Wrestling
W: Basketball, Cross Country,
 Fencing, Field Hockey,
 Swimming-Diving, Tennis,
 Volleyball

Cleveland State University
2451 Euclid Avenue
Cleveland, OH 44114
M: (216) 687–4800
W: (216) 687–4800
Enrollment: C
4-year public funding
M: NCAA
W: AIAW, Independent
M: Golf, Sailing, Tennis, Water
 Polo, Baseball, Basketball,
 Cross Country, Fencing,
 Soccer, Swimming-Diving,
 Track & Field, Wrestling
W: Sailing, Softball, Tennis,
 Basketball, Fencing,
 Swimming-Diving, Track &
 Field, Volleyball

Coahoma Junior College
Clarksdale, MS 38614
M: (601) 627–2571 X. 35
W: (601) 627–2571 X. 35
Enrollment: A
4-year public funding
M: MJCA
W: MJCA
M: Baseball, Basketball, Football,
 Track & Field
W: Softball, Basketball

Coastal Carolina College
Conway, SC 29526
M: (803) 347–3161 X. 145
W: (803) 347–3161
Enrollment: A
4-year public funding
M: NAIA
W: SCAIAW
M: Baseball, Basketball, Golf,
 Soccer, Tennis
W: Basketball, Tennis, Volleyball

**Coastal Carolina Community
 College**
Jacksonville, NC 28540
M: (919) 455–1221 X. 260
W: (919) 455–1221 X. 260
Enrollment: A
2-year public funding
M: NJCAA, NCCCAC
W: NJCAA, NCCCAC
M: Soccer, Basketball, Golf,
 Softball, Tennis
W: Golf, Softball, Tennis

**Cochise County Community
 College**
Highway 80 West
Douglas, AZ 85607
M: (602) 364–7943
W: (602) 364–7943
Enrollment: A

2-year public funding
M: ACCAC
W: ACCAC
M: Baseball, Basketball
W: Basketball, Volleyball

Coe College
1220 1st Avenue, NE
Cedar Rapids, IA 52402
M: (319) 399–8599
W: (319) 399–8599
Enrollment: A
4-year private
M: Midwest
W: Midwest
M: Baseball, Basketball, Cross
   Country, Football, Golf,
   Soccer, Swimming-Diving,
   Tennis, Track & Field,
   Wrestling
W: Basketball, Cross Country,
   Softball, Swimming-Diving,
   Tennis, Track & Field,
   Volleyball

Coffeyville Community College
Coffeyville, KS 67337
M: (316) 251–7700 X. 62
W: (316) 251–7700 X. 62
Enrollment: A
2-year public funding
M: Kansas Jayhawk
W: Kansas Jayhawk
M: Baseball, Basketball, Football,
   Golf, Tennis, Track & Field
W: Basketball, Tennis, Track &
   Field, Volleyball

Colby College
Waterville, ME 04901
M: (207) 873–1131 X. 250
W: (207) 873–1131 X. 253

Enrollment: A
4-year private
M: ECAC, NCAA, NESCAC
W: MAIAW, AIAW, EAIAW
M: Baseball, Basketball, Cross
   Country, Football, Golf, Ice
   Hockey, Lacrosse, Sailing,
   Soccer, Squash, Swimming-
   Diving, Tennis, Track & Field
W: Basketball, Cross Country,
   Field Hockey, Lacrosse,
   Sailing, Soccer, Softball,
   Squash, Swimming-Diving,
   Tennis, Track & Field

Colgate University
Hamilton, NY 13346
M: (315) 824–1000
W: (315) 824–1000
Enrollment: A
4-year private
M: NCAA, ECAC
W: AIAW
M: Baseball, Basketball, Cross
   Country, Football, Golf, Ice
   Hockey, Lacrosse, Soccer,
   Swimming-Diving, Tennis,
   Track & Field, Wrestling
W: Basketball, Field Hockey,
   Lacrosse, Softball, Swimming-
   Diving, Tennis, Volleyball

University of Colorado
Boulder, CO 80302
M: (303) 492–7931
W: (303) 492–8860
Enrollment: C
4-year public funding
M: Big Eight
W: Big Eight
M: Basketball, Cross Country,
   Football, Golf, Skiing,
   Tennis, Track & Field

W: Basketball, Cross Country,
  Skiing, Tennis, Track & Field

Colorado College
Colorado Springs, CO 80903
M: (303) 473–2233
W: (303) 473–2233
Enrollment: A
4-year private
M: WCHA, NCAA Independent
W: AIWA
M: Baseball, Basketball, Cross
  Country, Football, Golf,
  Lacrosse, Skiing, Soccer,
  Swimming-Diving, Tennis,
  Track & Field, Volleyball,
  Hockey
W: Cross Country, Field Hockey,
  Golf, Skiing, Soccer, Softball,
  Swimming-Diving, Tennis,
  Track & Field, Volleyball,
  Basketball

**Colorado Northwestern
  Community College**
Rangely, CO 81648
M: (303) 675–2261
W: (303) 675–2261
Enrollment: A
2-year public funding
M: ICAC
W: ICAC
M: Archery, Baseball, Basketball,
  Wrestling
W: Archery, Basketball, Softball,
  Volleyball

Colorado School of Mines
Golden, CO 80401
M: (303) 279–0300 X. 360
W: (303) 279–0300 X. 360
Enrollment: A

4-year public funding
M: Rocky Mountain
W: Rocky Mountain
M: Cross Country, Golf, Skiing,
  Baseball, Basketball,
  Football, Lacrosse, Soccer,
  Swimming-Diving, Tennis,
  Track & Field, Wrestling
W: Skiing, Basketball, Volleyball

Colorado State University
Fort Collins, CO 80521
M: (303) 491–5067
W: (303) 491–5067
Enrollment: C
4-year public funding
M: Western Athletic
W: AIAW
M: Golf, Tennis, Baseball,
  Basketball, Cross Country,
  Football, Track & Field,
  Wrestling
W: Field Hockey, Golf, Tennis,
  Basketball, Cross Country,
  Softball, Swimming-Diving,
  Track & Field, Volleyball

**Columbia Basin Community
  College**
2600 North 20th Avenue
Pasco, WA 99301
M: (509) 547–0511
W: (509) 547–0511
Enrollment: B
2-year public funding
M: AACC
W: AACC
M: Basketball, Football, Golf,
  Tennis, Wrestling
W: Basketball, Tennis, Volleyball

Scholarships are awarded to
  students from Washington,

Oregon, Idaho, and British Columbia by conference rule.

Columbia Christian College
200 NE 91st
Portland, OR 97220
M: (503) 255–7060
W: (503) 255–7060
Enrollment: A
4-year private
M: PNCC
W: PNCC
M: Soccer, Tennis, Basketball
W: Tennis, Volleyball

Columbia College
Columbia, SC 29203
W: (803) 786–3778
Enrollment: A
4-year private
W: AIAW
W: Basketball, Tennis, Volleyball

Columbia University
116th Street and Broadway
New York, NY 10027
M: (212) 280–2548
Enrollment: C
4-year private
M: Ivy League
M: Baseball, Basketball, Crew, Cross Country, Fencing, Football, Golf, Soccer, Swimming-Diving, Tennis, Track & Field, Wrestling

Columbus College
Algonquin Drive
Columbus, GA 31907
M: (404) 568–2046
W: (404) 568–2046

Enrollment: C
4-year public funding
M: South Atlantic
W: GAIAW
M: Soccer, Baseball, Basketball, Cross Country, Golf, Tennis
W: Softball, Tennis, Volleyball

Compton Community College
Compton, CA 90221
M: (213) 635–8081 X. 300
W: (213) 635–8081 X. 300
Enrollment: B
2-year public funding
M: Western State
W: Western State
M: Baseball, Basketball, Football, Tennis, Track & Field
W: Basketball, Tennis, Track & Field

Concord College
Athens, WV 24712
M: (304) 384–7283
W: (304) 384–7283
Enrollment: A
4-year public funding
M: WVIAC
W: WVIAA
M: Tennis, Track & Field, Baseball, Basketball, Football, Golf
W: Tennis, Track & Field, Basketball, Softball, Volleyball

Concordia College
7400 Augusta Street
River Forest, IL 60305
M: (312) 771–8300 X. 201
W: (312) 771–8300 X. 201
Enrollment: A

4-year private
M: NIIC
W: NIIC
M: Baseball, Basketball, Cross Country, Football, Tennis, Track & Field, Wrestling
W: Basketball, Field Hockey, Gymnastics, Softball, Tennis, Track & Field, Volleyball

Concordia College
St. Paul, MN 55104
M: (612) 641–8241
W: (612) 641–8241
Enrollment: A
4-year private
M: TRCC
W: MAIAW
M: Basketball, Football, Golf, Soccer, Tennis, Wrestling
W: Basketball, Softball, Tennis, Track & Field, Volleyball

Concordia College
800 North Columbia
Seward, NE 68434
M: (402) 643–3651 X. 328
W: (402) 643–3651 X. 328
Enrollment: A
4-year private
M: NIAC
W: NIAC
M: Baseball, Soccer, Tennis, Basketball, Cross Country, Football, Golf, Swimming-Diving, Track & Field
W: Golf, Tennis, Basketball, Cross Country, Softball, Swimming-Diving, Track & Field, Volleyball

Concordia College
2811 North East Holman
Portland, OR 97211
M: (503) 288–9371 X. 237
W: (503) 288–9371 X. 237
Enrollment: A
2-year private
M: NAIA, NLCAA
W: NCWSA
M: Soccer, Tennis, Baseball, Basketball
W: Soccer, Softball, Tennis, Basketball, Volleyball

Concordia College
3400 North Interregional
Austin, TX 78705
M: (512) 453–1538
W: (512) 453–1538
Enrollment: A
4-year private
M: Independent
W: Independent
M: Baseball, Basketball, Golf, Tennis
W: Basketball, Tennis, Volleyball

University of Connecticut
Storrs, CT 06268
M: (203) 486–3531
W: (203) 486–3531
Enrollment: C
4-year public funding
M: Big East
W: Big East
M: Cross Country, Golf, Lacrosse, Soccer, Swimming-Diving, Tennis, Track & Field, Baseball, Basketball, Football
W: Cross Country, Swimming-Diving, Tennis, Track & Field, Volleyball, Basketball, Field Hockey, Soccer, Softball

Connecticut College
New London, CT 06320
M: (203) 447–1911
W: (203) 447–1911
Enrollment: A
4-year private
M: ECAC, NCAA
W: NCAA, AIAW
M: Crew, Cross Country,
   Lacrosse, Soccer, Tennis
W: Crew, Cross Country, Field
   Hockey, Gymnastics,
   Lacrosse, Swimming-Diving,
   Tennis, Volleyball

Division III: all aid awarded on
   the basis of financial need.

Connors State College
Warner, OK 74469
M: (918) 463–2931 X. 218
W: (918) 463–2931 X. 218
Enrollment: A
2-year public funding
M: Oklahoma Juco
W: Oklahoma Juco
M: <u>Baseball</u>, <u>Basketball</u>, <u>Tennis</u>
W: <u>Basketball</u>, <u>Tennis</u>

Contra Costa College
2600 Mission Bell Drive
San Pablo, CA 94806
M: (415) 235–7800
W: (415) 235–7800
Enrollment: C
2-year public funding
M: Camino Norte
W: Camino Norte
M: <u>Baseball</u>, <u>Basketball</u>, <u>Football</u>,
   <u>Golf</u>, <u>Soccer</u>, <u>Swimming-
   Diving</u>, <u>Tennis</u>, <u>Track &
   Field</u>, <u>Water Polo</u>

W: <u>Basketball</u>, <u>Golf</u>, <u>Softball</u>,
   <u>Swimming-Diving</u>, <u>Tennis</u>,
   <u>Track & Field</u>, <u>Volleyball</u>

Converse College
Spartanburg, SC 29301
W: (803) 585–6421 X. 275
Enrollment: A
4-year private
W: SCAIAW
W: Basketball, Field Hockey,
   Synchronized Swimming,
   Tennis, Volleyball

Cooke County Junior College
Gainesville, TX 76240
M: (817) 668–7731 X. 254
W: (817) 668–7731 X. 254
Enrollment: A
2-year public funding
M: Northern Texas
W: Northern Texas
M: <u>Basketball</u>, <u>Tennis</u>
W: <u>Basketball</u>, <u>Tennis</u>

Copiah-Lincoln Junior College
Wesson, MS 39191
M: (601) 643–5101
W: (601) 643–5101
Enrollment: A
4-year public funding
M: MJCAA
W: MJCAA
M: Baseball, Golf, Tennis, Track
   & Field, <u>Basketball</u>, <u>Football</u>
W: Golf, Softball, Tennis,
   <u>Basketball</u>

Cornell College
Mount Vernon, IA 52314
M: (319) 895–8811

W: (319) 895-8811
Enrollment: A
4-year private
M: Midwest
W: MACW
M: Baseball, Basketball, Cross
   Country, Football, Golf,
   Soccer, Swimming-Diving,
   Tennis, Track & Field,
   Wrestling
W: Basketball, Cross Country,
   Softball, Swimming-Diving,
   Tennis, Track & Field,
   Volleyball

Cornell University
Ithaca, NY 14853
M: (607) 256-7440
W: (607) 256-5133
Enrollment: C
4-year private
M: Ivy League
W: Ivy League
M: Baseball, Basketball, Crew,
   Cross Country, Fencing,
   Football, Golf, Gymnastics,
   Ice Hockey, Lacrosse, Riflery,
   Sailing, Skiing, Soccer,
   Squash, Swimming-Diving,
   Tennis, Track & Field, Water
   Polo, Wrestling
W: Basketball, Bowling, Crew,
   Cross Country, Fencing, Field
   Hockey, Gymnastics,
   Lacrosse, Sailing, Skiing,
   Soccer, Swimming-Diving,
   Tennis, Track & Field,
   Volleyball

Cosumnes River College
8401 Center Parkway
Sacramento, CA 95823
M: (916) 421-1000 X. 261

W: (916) 421-1000 X. 261
Enrollment: B
2-year public funding
M: Camino Norte
W: Camino Norte
M: Baseball, Basketball, Cross
   Country, Golf, Soccer,
   Tennis, Track & Field
W: Cross Country, Softball,
   Tennis, Track & Field,
   Volleyball

Cottey College
Nevada, MO 64772
W: (417) 667-7310
Enrollment: A
2-year private
W: Independent
W: Archery, Basketball, Cross
   Country, Gymnastics,
   Softball, Swimming-Diving,
   Track & Field, Volleyball

Covenant College
Lookout Mountain, TN 37350
M: (404) 820-1560
W: (404) 820-1560
Enrollment: A
4-year private
M: NAIA
W: AIAW
M: Cross Country, Golf, <u>Baseball</u>,
   <u>Basketball</u>, <u>Soccer</u>
W: <u>Basketball</u>, <u>Volleyball</u>

**Cowley County Community Junior
   College**
125 South Second
Arkansas City, KS 67005
M: (316) 442-0430
W: (316) 442-0430
Enrollment: A

2-year public funding
M: KJCC
W: KJCC
M: Baseball, Basketball, Football,
   Tennis
W: Basketball, Softball, Volleyball

Creighton University
2500 California
Omaha, NE 68178
M: (402) 449–2720
W: (402) 449–2720
Enrollment: B
4-year private
M: Missouri Valley, NCAA
W: AIAW, Independent
M: Soccer, Tennis, Baseball,
   Basketball
W: Tennis, Basketball, Softball,
   Volleyball

Crowder College
Neosho, MO 64850
M: (417) 451–5530
W: (417) 451–5530
Enrollment: A
2-year public funding
M: NJCAA
W: NJCAA
M: Baseball, Basketball, Wrestling
W: Basketball, Softball

Culver-Stockton College
Canton, MO 63435
M: (314) 288–5221 X. 37
W: (314) 288–5221 X. 37
Enrollment: A
4-year private
M: NAIA
W: Independent
M: Baseball, Golf, Basketball,
   Football

W: Softball, Tennis, Basketball,
   Volleyball

Cumberland College
Williamsburg, KY 40769
M: (606) 549–0366
W: (606) 549–0366
Enrollment: A
4-year private
M: KIAC
W: KWIAA
M: Soccer, Baseball, Basketball,
   Cross Country, Golf, Judo,
   Tennis, Track & Field
W: Basketball

Cuyahoga Community College
11000 Pleasant Valley Road
Parma, OH 44130
M: (216) 845–4000
W: (216) 845–4000
Enrollment: C
2-year public funding
M: Independent
W: Independent
M: Baseball, Basketball, Bowling,
   Golf, Soccer, Tennis,
   Wrestling
W: Basketball, Bowling, Tennis,
   Volleyball

Cuyahoga Community College
Metro Campus
Cleveland, OH 44115
M: (216) 241–5966
W: (216) 241–5966
Enrollment: C
2-year public funding
M: NJCAA
W: NJCAA
M: Baseball, Basketball, Bowling,

Soccer, Track & Field,
    Wrestling
W: Basketball, Bowling, Softball,
    Track & Field, Volleyball

C. W. Post College
Greenvale, NY 11548
M: (516) 299–2289
W: (516) 299–2288
Enrollment: C
4-year private
M: NCAA
W: NYSAIAW
M: Golf, Baseball, Basketball,
    Cross Country, Football,
    Lacrosse, Soccer, Tennis,
    Track & Field, Wrestling
W: Basketball, Field Hockey,
    Softball, Tennis, Volleyball

Cypress College
Cypress, CA 90630
M: (714) 826–2220 X. 352
W: (714) 826–2220 X. 352
Enrollment: C
2-year public funding
M: Southern California
W: Southern California
M: Archery, Baseball, Basketball,
    Cross Country, Golf,
    Swimming-Diving, Tennis,
    Track & Field, Water Polo,
    Wrestling
W: Archery, Basketball, Cross
    Country, Softball, Tennis,
    Track & Field, Volleyball

Daemen College
Amherst, NY 14226
M: (716) 839–3600 X. 300
W: (716) 839–3600 X. 300
Enrollment: A

4-year private
M: NAIA
W: NYSAIAW
M: Basketball, Soccer
W: Basketball, Softball

Dakota Wesleyan University
Mitchell, SD 57301
M: (605) 996–6511
W: (605) 996–6511
Enrollment: B
4-year private
M: SDIC
W: Independent
M: Tennis, Basketball, Cross
    Country, Football, Track &
    Field
W: Basketball, Cross Country,
    Softball, Track & Field,
    Volleyball

Dartmouth College
Hanover, NH 03755
M: (603) 646–2465
W: (603) 646–2871
Enrollment: B
4-year private
M: Ivy League
W: Ivy League
M: Baseball, Basketball, Crew,
    Cross Country, Football,
    Golf, Gymnastics, Lacrosse,
    Riflery, Sailing, Skiing,
    Soccer, Squash, Swimming-
    Diving, Tennis, Track &
    Field, Water Polo
W: Basketball, Cross Country,
    Field Hockey, Gymnastics,
    Lacrosse, Sailing, Soccer,
    Squash, Swimming-Diving,
    Tennis, Water Polo

David Lipscomb College
Granny White Pike
Nashville, TN 37203
M: (615) 385–3855 X. 418
W: (615) 385–3855 X. 418
Enrollment: A
4-year private
M: VSAC
W: VSAC
M: Baseball, Basketball, Cross
  Country, Golf, Tennis, Track
  & Field
W: Basketball, Tennis

Davidson College
Davidson, NC 28036
M: (704) 892–2000
W: (704) 892–2000
Enrollment: A
4-year private
M: Southern, NCAA
W: AIAW, NCAIAW
M: Baseball, Cross Country,
  Football, Golf, Riflery,
  Sailing, Soccer, Swimming-
  Diving, Tennis, Track &
  Field, Wrestling, Basketball
W: Basketball, Cross Country,
  Field Hockey, Riflery, Sailing,
  Tennis, Track & Field

Dawson Community College
Glendive, MT 59330
M: (406) 365–3396
W: (406) 365–3396
Enrollment: A
2-year public funding
M: Mon-Dak, Empire, NJCAA,
  Big Sky
W: Big Sky, NJCAA, Empire
M: Basketball, Rodeo
W: Basketball, Rodeo

University of Dayton
300 College Park
Dayton, Ohio 45469
M: (513) 229–4421
W: (513) 229–4421
Enrollment: C
4-year private
M: Independent
W: Independent
M: Basketball
W: Basketball, Volleyball

Daytona Beach Community College
Daytona Beach, FL 32015
M: (904) 255–8131 X. 301
W: (904) 255–8131 X. 301
Enrollment: C
2-year public funding
M: FCCAA
W: FCCAA
M: Basketball, Swimming-Diving,
  Tennis
W: Swimming-Diving, Tennis,
  Volleyball

**DeKalb Community College
(Central)**
555 North Indian Creek Drive
Clarkston, GA 30021
M: (404) 292–1520
W: (404) 292–1520
Enrollment: C
2-year public funding
M: GJCAA
W: GJCAA
M: Basketball, Golf, Soccer,
  Tennis, Track & Field
W: Basketball, Tennis, Track &
  Field

University of Delaware
Newark, DE 19711

M: (302) 738–2256
W: (302) 738–2496
Enrollment: C
4-year public funding
M: NCAA, ECC, ECAC, ICAAAA, USILA
W: AIAW, EAIAW, USWILA
M: Baseball, Cross County, Golf, Lacrosse, Soccer, Swimming-Diving, Tennis, Track & Field, Wrestling, Basketball, Football
W: Cross Country, Lacrosse, Softball, Swimming-Diving, Tennis, Track & Field, Volleyball, Basketball, Field Hockey

All aid for men and women is based on financial need.

Delaware State College
Dover, DE 19901
M: (302) 736–4928
W: (302) 736–4928
Enrollment: A
4-year public funding
M: MEAC
W: MEAC
M: Golf, Baseball, Basketball, Cross Country, Football, Track & Field, Wrestling
W: Golf, Basketball, Cross Country, Track & Field

Delaware Valley College
Doylestown, PA 18901
M: (215) 345–1500
W: (215) 345–1500
Enrollment: A
4-year private
M: MAC, ECAC
W: Independent

M: Baseball, Basketball, Cross Country, Football, Golf, Soccer, Track & Field, Wrestling
W: Basketball, Cross Country, Field Hockey, Softball, Volleyball

Delta State University
Cleveland, MS 38732
M: (601) 843–2640
W: (601) 843–2640
Enrollment: B
4-year public funding
M: Gulf South
W: AIAW
M: Baseball, Basketball, Cross Country, Football, Golf, Tennis, Track & Field
W: Cross Country, Softball, Basketball, Tennis

University of Denver
Denver, CO 80210
M: (303) 753–2275
W: (303) 753–2275
Enrollment: C
4-year private
M: WCHA
W: IAC
M: Skiing, Tennis, Baseball, Basketball, Ice Hockey, Soccer, Swimming-Diving
W: Swimming-Diving, Basketball, Field Hockey, Gymnastics, Skiing, Tennis

DePauw University
Greencastle, IN 46135
M: (312) 321–8010
W: (312) 321–8010
Enrollment: B

4-year private
M: Independent
W: Independent
M: Basketball, Cross Country, Golf, Soccer, Tennis, Track & Field
W: Basketball, Softball, Tennis, Volleyball

College of the Desert
43–500 Monterey Avenue
Palm Desert, CA 92260
M: (714) 346–8041
W: (714) 346–8041
Enrollment: A
2-year public funding
M: Desert, Mission
W: Desert, Mission
M: Baseball, Basketball, Cross Country, Football, Golf, Soccer, Tennis, Track & Field, Volleyball
W: Basketball, Cross Country, Soccer, Softball, Tennis, Track & Field, Volleyball

University of Detroit
4001 West McNichols
Detroit, MI 48221
M: (313) 927–1155
W: (313) 927–1155
Enrollment: C
4-year private
M: Midwestern City
W: AIAW
M: Baseball, Basketball, Cross Country, Fencing, Golf, Tennis
W: Basketball, Softball

Dickinson State College
Dickinson, ND 58601
M: (701) 227–2181
W: (701) 227–2719
Enrollment: A
4-year public funding
M: NDCAC
W: WACND
M: Tennis, Baseball, Basketball, Cross Country, Football, Golf, Track & Field, Wrestling
W: Tennis, Basketball, Cross Country, Track & Field, Volleyball

Dillard University
2601 Gentilly Boulevard
New Orleans, LA 70122
M: (504) 949–2123 X. 218
W: (504) 949–2123 X. 218
Enrollment: A
4-year private
M: Independent, NAIA
W: AIAW
M: Basketball
W: Basketball

University of District of Columbia
1529 16th Street, NW
Washington, DC 20036
M: (202) 727–2052/53/54
W: (202) 727–2052/53/54
Enrollment: C
4-year public funding
M: NCAA, NAIA, Independent
W: AIAW, NCAA, Independent
M: Baseball, Crew, Football, Golf, Soccer, Tennis, Track & Field, Volleyball
W: Basketball, Cross Country, Golf, Softball, Tennis, Track & Field, Volleyball

Doane College
Crete, NE 68333
M: (402) 826–2161
W: (402) 826–2161
Enrollment: A
4-year private
M: NIAC
W: NIAC
M: Cross Country, Golf, Tennis, Basketball, Football, Track & Field
W: Cross Country, Tennis, Basketball, Track & Field, Volleyball

Dominican College
Western Highway
Orangeburg, NY 10962
M: (914) 359–7800
W: (914) 359–7800
Enrollment: A
4-year private
M: NAIA
W: HWVAC
M: Baseball, Basketball, Soccer
W: Basketball, Softball, Volleyball

Drew University
Madison, NJ 07940
M: (201) 377–3000 X. 441
W: (201) 377–3000 X. 441
Enrollment: A
4-year private
M: IAC, MASC, ECAC, NCAA
W: NJAIAW, MASC
M: Basketball, Cross Country, Fencing, Lacrosse, Soccer, Tennis
W: Basketball, Cross Country, Fencing, Lacrosse, Tennis

All aid for men and women is based on financial need.

Drury College
900 North Benton
Springfield, MO 65802
M: (417) 865–8731 X. 294
W: (417) 865–8731 X. 294
Enrollment: A
4-year private
M: NAIA
W: NAIA
M: Basketball, Golf, Swimming-Diving, Tennis
W: Tennis, Volleyball

University of Dubuque
Dubuque, IA 52001
M: (319) 589–3225
W: (319) 589–3225
Enrollment: A
4-year private
M: IIAC
W: Independent
M: Baseball, Basketball, Cross Country, Football, Golf, Soccer, Tennis, Track & Field, Wrestling
W: Cross Country, Basketball, Softball, Track & Field, Volleyball

Duke University
Durham, NC 27706
M: (919) 684–2120
W: (919) 684–2120
Enrollment: C
4-year private
M: Atlantic Coast
W: NCAIAW
M: Cross Country, Fencing, Lacrosse, Swimming-Diving, Track & Field, Baseball, Basketball, Football, Golf, Soccer, Tennis, Wrestling
W: Fencing, Lacrosse, Swimming-

Diving, Volleyball, Basketball, Field Hockey, Golf, Gymnastics, Tennis

Dundalk Community College
7200 Sollers Point Road
Baltimore, MD 21222
M: (301) 282–6700 X. 250
W: (301) 282–6700 X. 250
Enrollment: A
2-year public funding
M: JUCO
W: JUCO
M: Baseball, Basketball, Soccer, Tennis
W: Basketball, Softball, Tennis, Volleyball

Duquesne University
600 Forbes Avenue
Pittsburgh, PA 15219
M: (412) 434–6565
W: (412) 434–6566
Enrollment: C
4-year private
M: NCAA, EAA
W: AIAW, Pennwood West
M: Bowling, Football, Swimming-Diving, Baseball, Basketball, Cross Country, Golf, Riflery, Tennis
W: Bowling, Swimming-Diving, Basketball, Cross Country, Riflery, Tennis, Volleyball

D'Youville College
Buffalo, NY 14201
M: (716) 886–8100 X. 249
W: (716) 886–8100 X. 249
Enrollment: A
4-year private
M: NCCAA

W: NYSAIAW
M: Basketball, Bowling, Tennis
W: Basketball, Bowling, Tennis, Volleyball

East Carolina University
Greenville, NC 27834
M: (919) 757–6448
W: (919) 757–6448
Enrollment: C
4-year public funding
M: Independent
W: Independent
M: Baseball, Basketball, Football, Golf, Soccer, Swimming-Diving, Tennis, Track & Field, Wrestling
W: Basketball, Field Hockey, Gymnastics, Softball, Swimming-Diving, Tennis, Track & Field, Volleyball

East Central Junior College
Union, MO 63084
M: (314) 583–5193 X. 225
W: (314) 583–5193 X. 225
Enrollment: A
2-year private
M: MJCAC
W: MJCAC
M: Baseball, Basketball, Tennis
W: Basketball, Softball, Tennis, Volleyball

East Central University
East 14th Street
Ada, OK 74820
M: (405) 332–8000
W: (405) 332–8000
Enrollment: B
4-year public funding
M: Oklahoma Intercollegiate

W: OAIAW
M: Baseball, Golf, Tennis, Track
    & Field, Basketball, Football
W: Basketball, Tennis

Eastern College
Fairview Drive
St. Davids, PA 19087
M: (215) 688–3300 X. 250
W: (215) 688–3300 X. 251
Enrollment: A
4-year private
M: Seaboard
W: Independent
M: Baseball, Basketball, Cross
    Country, Soccer, Tennis
W: Basketball, Field Hockey,
    Softball, Tennis, Volleyball

Eastern Illinois University
Charleston, IL 61920
M: (217) 581–2319/2310
W: (217) 581–2106
Enrollment: C
4-year public funding
M: Mid-Continent
W: AIWA
M: Golf, Tennis, Baseball,
    Basketball, Cross Country,
    Football, Soccer, Swimming-
    Diving, Track & Field,
    Wrestling
W: Badminton, Basketball, Cross
    Country, Field Hockey,
    Softball, Swimming-Diving,
    Tennis, Track & Field,
    Volleyball

Eastern Kentucky University
Richmond, KY 40475
M: (606) 622–3654
W: (606) 622–3654
Enrollment: C
4-year public funding
M: Ohio Valley
W: Ohio Valley, Kentucky
    Women's
M: Baseball, Basketball, Cross
    Country, Football, Golf,
    Gymnastics, Riflery,
    Swimming-Diving, Tennis,
    Track & Field
W: Basketball, Cross Country,
    Field Hockey, Gymnastics,
    Riflery, Swimming-Diving,
    Tennis, Track & Field,
    Volleyball

Eastern Michigan University
Ypsilanti, MI 48197
M: (313) 487–1050
W: (313) 487–0351
Enrollment: C
4-year public funding
M: Mid-American
W: Mid-American
M: Baseball, Basketball, Cross
    Country, Football, Golf,
    Gymnastics, Soccer,
    Swimming-Diving, Tennis,
    Track & Field, Wrestling
W: Basketball, Cross Country,
    Field Hockey, Gymnastics,
    Softball, Swimming-Diving,
    Tennis, Track & Field,
    Volleyball

Eastern Montana College
1500 North 27th
Billings, MT 59101
M: (406) 657–2369
W: (406) 657–2369
Enrollment: B
4-year public funding
M: Independent

W: Frontier
M: Golf, Tennis, Basketball, Cross Country, Gymnastics, Track & Field
W: Golf, Tennis, Basketball, Cross Country, Gymnastics, Track & Field, Volleyball

Eastern Nazarene College
Quincy, MA 02170
M: (617) 773–6350 X. 345
W: (617) 773–6350 X. 345
Enrollment: A
4-year private
M: ECAC, NAIA, NCCAA
W: AIAW, WCIA
M: Baseball, Basketball, Cross Country, Soccer, Tennis
W: Softball, Basketball, Tennis, Volleyball

Eastern Oklahoma State College
Wilburton, OK 74578
M: (918) 465–2361 X. 273
W: (918) 465–2361 X. 273
Enrollment: A
2-year public funding
M: OKJC
W: OKJC
M: Golf, Baseball, Basketball, Cross Country, Tennis, Track & Field
W: Golf, Basketball, Cross Country, Tennis, Track & Field

College of Eastern Utah
Price, UT 84501
M: (801) 637–2120 X. 248
W: (801) 637–2120 X. 248
Enrollment: A
2-year public funding

M: ICAC
W: ICAC
M: Baseball, Basketball, Football, Tennis, Track & Field, Wrestling
W: Basketball, Gymnastics, Softball, Volleyball

Eastern Wyoming College
3200 West C Street
Torrington, WY 82240
M: (307) 532–7111 X. 244
W: (307) 532–7111 X. 244
Enrollment: A
2-year public funding
M: WCCAC, NJCAA
W: WCCAC, NJCAA
M: Basketball, Tennis, Track & Field
W: Basketball, Tennis, Track & Field, Volleyball

East Stroudsburg State College
East Stroudsburg, PA 18301
M: (717) 424–3642
W: (717) 424–3309
Enrollment: B
4-year public funding
M: ECAC, NCAA
W: EAIAW, AIAW
M: Archery, Baseball, Basketball, Cross Country, Football, Golf, Gymnastics, Soccer, Swimming-Diving, Tennis, Track & Field, Volleyball, Wrestling
W: Archery, Basketball, Field Hockey, Gymnastics, Lacrosse, Softball, Swimming-Diving, Tennis, Track & Field, Volleyball

All aid for men and women is based on financial need.

East Tennessee State University
Johnson City, TN 37601
M: (615) 929–4220
W: (615) 929–4220
Enrollment: C
4-year public funding
M: Southern
W: AIAW
M: Baseball, Basketball, Cross
   Country, Football, Golf,
   Riflery, Tennis, Track & Field
W: Basketball, Cross Country,
   Gymnastics, Riflery, Tennis,
   Track & Field

East Texas State University
Commerce, TX 75428
M: (214) 886–5549
W: (214) 886–5572
Enrollment: C
4-year public funding
M: Lone Star
W: TAIAW
M: Basketball, Football, Golf,
   Tennis, Track & Field
W: Basketball, Tennis, Track &
   Field, Volleyball

Eckerd College
5400 34th Street South
St. Petersburg, FL 33733
M: (813) 867–1166 X. 251
W: (813) 867–1166 X. 295
Enrollment: A
4-year private
M: NCAA
W: AIAW
M: Baseball, Basketball, Cross
   Country, Golf, Sailing,
   Soccer, Tennis, Water Skiing
W: Basketball, Softball, Tennis,
   Track & Field

Edgewood College
855 Woodrow Street
Madison, WI 53711
M: (608) 257–4861 X. 256
W: (608) 257–4861 X. 289
Enrollment: A
4-year private
M: WCIC
W: WIC, WAC
M: Baseball, Basketball
W: Basketball, Softball,
   Swimming-Diving

All aid for men and women is
based on financial need.

Edinboro State College
Edinboro, PA 16444
M: (814) 732–2776
W: (814) 732–2776
Enrollment: C
4-year public funding
M: PSCAC
W: AIAW
M: Baseball, Basketball, Cross
   Country, Football, Soccer,
   Swimming-Diving, Tennis,
   Track & Field, Wrestling
W: Basketball, Gymnastics,
   Softball, Tennis, Track &
   Field, Volleyball

Edmonds Community College
2000 68th Avenue West
Lynnwood, WA 98036
M: (206) 771–1520
W: (206) 771–1520
Enrollment: B
2-year public funding
M: AACC
W: AACC
M: Baseball, Basketball, Soccer
W: Basketball, Softball, Volleyball

Scholarships are awarded to students from Washington, Oregon, Idaho, and British Columbia by conference rule.

Edward Williams Junior College
Hackensack, NJ 07061
M: (201) 836–6300 X. 331
Enrollment: A
2-year private
M: WJCAA
M: Basketball

Eisenhower College
Seneca Falls, NY 13148
M: (315) 568–7129
W: (315) 568–7129
Enrollment: A
4-year private
M: PCAC
W: PCAC
M: Baseball, Basketball, Bowling, Cross Country, Fencing, Golf, Lacrosse, Soccer, Swimming-Diving, Tennis, Track & Field
W: Basketball, Bowling, Cross Country, Fencing, Golf, Softball, Swimming-Diving, Tennis, Track & Field, Volleyball

El Camino College
Torrance, CA 90506
M: (213) 532–3670 X. 524
W: (213) 532–3670 X. 524
Enrollment: C
2-year public funding
M: Metropolitan
W: Metropolitan
M: Badminton, Baseball, Basketball, Cross Country, Football, Golf, Soccer, Swimming-Diving, Tennis, Track & Field, Volleyball, Water Polo, Wrestling
W: Badminton, Basketball, Cross Country, Gymnastics, Softball, Swimming-Diving, Tennis, Track & Field, Volleyball

Elizabethtown College
Elizabethtown, PA 17022
M: (717) 367–1151
W: (717) 367–1151
Enrollment: A
4-year private
M: Middle Atlantic, NCAA
W: Penn-Mar, Middle Atlantic
M: Baseball, Basketball, Soccer, Swimming-Diving, Tennis, Track & Field, Wrestling
W: Basketball, Field Hockey, Softball, Swimming-Diving, Tennis, Track & Field, Volleyball

Division III: all aid awarded on the basis of financial need.

Elmhurst College
190 Prospect
Elmhurst, IL 60126
M: (312) 279–4100 X. 455
W: (312) 279–4100 X. 455
Enrollment: A
4-year public funding
M: CCIW
W: AIAW
M: Baseball, Basketball, Football, Golf, Tennis, Track & Field, Wrestling
W: Basketball, Softball, Tennis, Volleyball

Division III: all aid awarded on the basis of financial need.

Elmira College
Elmira, NY 14901
M: (607) 734-3911
W: (607) 739-8786
Enrollment: A
4-year private
M: NCAA, ECAC, NYCHA, PCAC
W: NCAA, ECAC, NYCHA, PCAC
M: Basketball, Bowling, Fencing, Golf, Soccer, Swimming-Diving, Tennis
W: Basketball, Bowling, Fencing, Softball, Swimming-Diving, Tennis, Volleyball

All aid for men and women is based on financial need.

Elon College
Haggard Avenue
Elon College, NC 27244
M: (919) 584-9711
W: (919) 584-9711
Enrollment: A
4-year private
M: Carolinas, SAC
W: Carolinas, SAC
M: Baseball, Basketball, Football, Golf, Soccer, Tennis, Track & Field, Wrestling
W: Basketball, Softball, Tennis, Volleyball

Emory and Henry College
Emory, VA 24327
M: (703) 944-3121
W: (703) 944-3121

Enrollment: A
4-year private
M: ODAC
W: AIAW
M: Baseball, Basketball, Cross Country, Football, Golf, Lacrosse, Tennis, Track & Field
W: Basketball, Softball, Tennis, Track & Field, Volleyball

Emory University
1380 Oxford Road
Atlanta, GA 30322
M: (404) 329-6545
W: (404) 329-6545
Enrollment: C
4-year private
M: NCAA, Independent
W: NCAA, Independent
M: Cross Country, Soccer, Swimming-Diving, Tennis
W: Swimming-Diving, Tennis

Division III: all aid awarded on the basis of financial need.

Emporia State University
Emporia, KS 66801
M: (316) 343-1200 X. 354
W: (316) 343-1200 X. 354
Enrollment: C
4-year public funding
M: CSIC
W: AIAW
M: Baseball, Basketball, Cross Country, Football, Golf, Tennis, Track & Field
W: Basketball, Cross Country, Gymnastics, Softball, Swimming-Diving, Tennis, Track & Field, Volleyball

Erskine College
Due West, SC 29639
M: (803) 379-8858
W: (803) 379-8858
Enrollment: A
4-year private
M: NAIA
W: AIAW
M: Baseball, Basketball, Golf,
  Soccer, Tennis
W: Basketball, Softball, Tennis,
  Volleyball

Essex Community College
7201 Rossville Boulevard
Baltimore, MD 21237
M: (301) 682-6000 X. 394
W: (301) 682-6000 X. 394
Enrollment: C
2-year public funding
M: JUCO
W: JUCO
M: Baseball, Basketball, Bowling,
  Cross Country, Golf,
  Gymnastics, Lacrosse, Soccer,
  Swimming-Diving, Tennis,
  Track & Field
W: Basketball, Bowling, Cross
  Country, Field Hockey,
  Gymnastics, Lacrosse,
  Softball, Swimming-Diving,
  Tennis, Track & Field,
  Volleyball

University of Evansville
Evansville, IN 47702
M: (812) 479-2350
W: (812) 479-2849
Enrollment: B
4-year private
M: Heartland, Midwestern City
W: Independent
M: Cross Country, Baseball,
  Basketball, Football, Golf,
  Soccer, Swimming-Diving,
  Tennis, Track & Field,
  Wrestling
W: Basketball, Golf, Softball,
  Tennis, Track & Field

Everett Community College
801 Wetmore Avenue
Everett, WA 98201
M: (206) 259-7151
W: (206) 259-7151
Enrollment: B
2-year public funding
M: AACC
W: AACC
M: Baseball, Basketball, Cross
  Country, Golf, Soccer,
  Tennis, Track & Field
W: Basketball, Cross Country,
  Tennis, Track & Field,
  Volleyball

Scholarships are awarded to
  students from Washington,
  Oregon, Idaho, and British
  Columbia by conference rule.

Fairleigh Dickinson University
1000 River Road
Teaneck, NJ 07666
M: (201) 692-2245
W: (201) 692-2245
Enrollment: C
4-year private
M: ECAC
W: NJAIAW, AIAW
M: Baseball, Cross Country, Golf,
  Lacrosse, Tennis, Wrestling,
  Basketball, Soccer, Track &
  Field
W: Fencing, Softball, Tennis,
  Basketball, Volleyball

Fairmont State College
Locust Avenue
Fairmont, WV 26554
M: (304) 367–4220
W: (304) 367–4220
Enrollment: C
4-year public funding
M: WVIAC
W: WVIAA
M: Baseball, Cross Country, Track & Field, Basketball, Football, Golf, Swimming-Diving, Tennis
W: Basketball, Cross Country, Swimming-Diving, Tennis, Track & Field, Volleyball

Fergus Falls Community College
Fergus Falls, MN 56537
M: (218) 736–7544 X. 36
W: (218) 736–7544 X. 36
Enrollment: A
4-year public funding
M: MCCC
W: MCCC
M: Baseball, Basketball, Football, Golf, Tennis, Track & Field
W: Basketball, Golf, Softball, Tennis, Volleyball

Ferris State College
Big Rapids, MI 49307
M: (616) 796–0461 X. 3525
W: (616) 796–0461 X. 3525
Enrollment: C
4-year public funding
M: Great Lakes
W: AIAW
M: Baseball, Basketball, Cross Country, Football, Hockey, Swimming-Diving, Tennis, Track & Field, Wrestling
W: Softball, Tennis, Volleyball

Ferrum College
Ferrum, VA 24088
M: (703) 365–2121 X. 179
W: (703) 365–2121 X. 179
Enrollment: A
2-year private
M: NJCAA
W: AIAW
M: Baseball, Basketball, Cross Country, Football, Golf, Swimming-Diving, Tennis, Track & Field
W: Basketball, Tennis, Volleyball

Findlay College
Findlay, OH 45840
M: (419) 422–8313 X. 363
W: (419) 422–8313 X. 363
Enrollment: A
4-year private
M: HBCC
W: Independent
M: Baseball, Basketball, Cross Country, Football, Golf, Soccer, Tennis, Track & Field, Wrestling
W: Basketball, Softball, Tennis, Track & Field, Volleyball

Fitchburg State College
Fitchburg, MA 01420
M: (617) 345–2151 X. 226
W: (617) 345–2151 X. 226
Enrollment: B
4-year public funding
M: NCAA, MASCAS
W: MASCAC, MAIAW
M: Baseball, Cross Country, Football, Soccer, Tennis, Track & Field
W: Cross Country, Field Hockey, Softball, Tennis, Track & Field, Volleyball

Flagler College
King Street
St. Augustine, FL 32084
M: (904) 829–6481
W: (904) 829–6481
Enrollment: A
4-year private
M: NAIA, Independent
W: FAIAW, Independent
M: Baseball, Basketball, Cross
  Country, Golf, Soccer, Tennis
W: Basketball, Softball, Tennis,
  Volleyball

University of Florida
Gainesville, FL 32611
M: (904) 392–0664
W: (904) 392–0664
Enrollment: C
4-year public funding
M: SEC
W: AIAW
M: Baseball, Basketball, Cross
  Country, Football, Golf,
  Swimming-Diving, Tennis,
  Track & Field
W: Basketball, Golf, Gymnastics,
  Softball, Swimming-Diving,
  Tennis, Track & Field

Florida A & M University
Tallahassee, FL 32307
M: (904) 599–3868
W: (904) 599–3272
Enrollment: C
4-year public funding
M: NCAA, MEAC
W: AIAW
M: Bowling, Baseball, Basketball,
  Cross Country, Football,
  Golf, Swimming-Diving,
  Tennis, Track & Field
W: Bowling, Basketball, Cross
  Country, Golf, Softball,
  Swimming-Diving, Tennis,
  Track & Field, Volleyball

Florida Atlantic University
Boca Raton, FL 33431
M: (305) 395–5100 X. 2581
W: (305) 395–5100 X. 2581
Enrollment: B
4-year public funding
M: NAIA
W: AIAW
M: Baseball, Golf, Soccer, Tennis
W: Golf, Softball, Tennis

Florida Institute of Technology
720 South Indian River Drive
Jensen Beach, FL 33457
M: (305) 334–4200 X. 42
Enrollment: A
4-year private
M: NCAA
M: Crew, Soccer

Florida International University
Miami, FL 33199
M: (305) 552–2756
W: (305) 552–2756
Enrollment: C
4-year public funding
M: NCAA, Independent
W: AIAW, Independent
M: Baseball, Cross Country, Golf,
  Soccer, Tennis, Wrestling
W: Basketball, Cross Country,
  Golf, Softball, Tennis,
  Volleyball

Florida Junior College
Cumberland Road
Jacksonville, FL 32205

M: (904) 965–1616
W: (904) 965–1616
Enrollment: C
2-year public funding
M: FCCAA
W: FCCAA
M: Baseball, Basketball, Cross
   Country, Golf, Tennis, Track
   & Field
W: Cross Country, Softball,
   Tennis, Track & Field,
   Volleyball

Florida Southern College
Lakeland, FL 33802
M: (813) 683–5521
W: (813) 683–5521
Enrollment: A
4-year private
M: NCAA, Sunshine State
W: AIAW
M: Cross Country, Soccer,
   Baseball, Basketball, Golf,
   Tennis
W: Softball, Basketball, Tennis,
   Volleyball

Florida State University
Tallahassee, FL 32306
M: (904) 644–4038
W: (904) 644–4038
Enrollment: C
4-year public funding
M: Independent, Metro
W: AIAW
M: Baseball, Basketball, Cross
   Country, Football, Golf,
   Swimming-Diving, Tennis,
   Track & Field
W: Golf, Basketball, Cross
   Country, Softball, Swimming-
   Diving, Tennis, Track &
   Field, Volleyball

Florida Technological University
Orlando, FL 32816
M: (305) 275–2256
W: (305) 275–2256
Enrollment: C
4-year public funding
M: Sunshine State
W: AIAW
M: Cross Country, Football,
   Baseball, Basketball, Golf,
   Soccer, Tennis, Wrestling
W: Cross Country, Basketball,
   Golf, Soccer, Softball, Tennis,
   Volleyball

Fontbonne College
6800 Wyderun
St. Louis, MO 63105
W: (314) 889–1432
Enrollment: A
4-year private
W: Independent
W: Bowling, Softball, Tennis,
   Basketball, Volleyball

Fordham University
Bronx, NY 10458
M: (212) 933–2233
W: (212) 933–2233
Enrollment: C
4-year private
M: NCAA, ECAC
W: AIAW
M: Football, Baseball, Basketball,
   Cross Country, Soccer,
   Squash, Swimming-Diving,
   Tennis, Track & Field, Water
   Polo
W: Basketball, Cross Country,
   Swimming-Diving, Tennis,
   Track & Field, Volleyball

Fort Hayes State College
Hayes, KS 67601
M: (913) 628–4420
W: (913) 628–4420
Enrollment: C
4-year public funding
M: Central States
W: Central States
M: Baseball, Basketball, Cross Country, Football, Golf, Gymnastics, Tennis, Track & Field, Wrestling
W: Basketball, Cross Country, Gymnastics, Softball, Tennis, Track & Field, Volleyball

Fort Steilacoom Community College
9401 Far West Drive, SW
Tacoma, WA 98498
M: (206) 964–6614
W: (206) 964–6614
Enrollment: C
2-year public funding
M: AACC
W: AACC
M: Baseball, Basketball, Soccer, Tennis
W: Basketball, Tennis, Volleyball

Scholarships are awarded to students from Washington, Oregon, Idaho, and British Columbia by conference rule.

Fort Valley State College
State College Drive
Fort Valley, GA 31030
M: (912) 825–6389
W: (912) 825–6319
Enrollment: A
4-year public funding
M: SIAC
W: AIAW, GAIAW
M: Cross Country, Football, Tennis, Baseball, Basketball, Track & Field
W: Basketball, Cross Country, Track & Field

Fort Wayne Bible College
1025 West Rudisill Boulevard
Fort Wayne, IN 46807
M: (219) 456–2111
W: (219) 456–2111
Enrollment: A
4-year private
M: NCCAC
W: NCCAC
M: Basketball, Soccer, Tennis
W: Basketball, Volleyball

Framingham State College
100 State Street
Framingham, MA 01701
M: (617) 620–1220 X. 277
W: (617) 620–1220 X. 277
Enrollment: B
4-year public funding
M: MSCC
W: MSCC
M: Baseball, Basketball, Cross Country, Football, Hockey, Soccer, Tennis
W: Field Hockey, Soccer, Softball, Tennis, Volleyball

Francis Marion College
Florence, SC 29501
M: (803) 669–4121 X. 256
W: (803) 669–4121 X. 256
Enrollment: B
4-year public funding
M: NAIA
W: SCAIAW

M: Baseball, Basketball, Cross
   Country, Soccer, Tennis,
   Track & Field
W: Basketball, Softball, Tennis,
   Volleyball

Frank Phillips College
Borger, TX 79007
M: (806) 274-5311
W: (806) 274-5311
Enrollment: A
2-year public funding
M: Independent
W: Independent
M: Basketball
W: Basketball

Franklin Pierce College
Rindge, NH 03461
M: (603) 899-5111
W: (603) 899-5111
Enrollment: A
4-year private
M: NAIA
W: AIAW
M: Baseball, Basketball, Cross
   Country, Golf, Sailing,
   Skiing, Soccer, Tennis
W: Basketball, Field Hockey,
   Softball, Volleyball

Freed-Hardeman College
Henderson, TN 38340
M: (901) 989-4611
W: (901) 989-4611
Enrollment: A
4-year private
M: VSAC
W: VSAC
M: Baseball, Basketball, Cross
   Country, Golf, Tennis

W: Basketball, Cross Country,
   Tennis

Fresno State University
Fresno, CA 93704
M: (209) 487-2509
W: (209) 487-2509
Enrollment: C
4-year public funding
M: PCAA
W: NCAC
M: Baseball, Basketball, Cross
   Country, Football, Golf,
   Soccer, Swimming-Diving,
   Tennis, Track & Field, Water
   Polo, Wrestling
W: Badminton, Basketball,
   Gymnastics, Softball,
   Swimming-Diving, Tennis,
   Volleyball

Friendship Junior College
Rock Hill, SC 29730
M: (803) 327-1186
W: (803) 327-1186
Enrollment: A
2-year private
M: Independent
W: SEAC
M: Baseball, Basketball
W: Basketball, Track & Field

Friends University
2100 University
Wichita, KS 67213
M: (316) 261-5853
W: (316) 261-5853
Enrollment: A
4-year private
M: KCAC
W: AIAW, KCAC
M: Baseball, Basketball, Football,

Golf, Tennis, Track & Field
W: Basketball, Softball, Tennis, Track & Field, Volleyball

Frostburg State College
Frostburg, MD 21532
M: (301) 689–4461
W: (301) 689–4461
Enrollment: B
4-year public funding
M: NCAA
W: AIAW
M: Baseball, Basketball, Cross Country, Football, Gymnastics, Soccer, Swimming-Diving, Tennis, Track & Field
W: Field Hockey, Gymnastics, Lacrosse, Swimming-Diving, Tennis, Track & Field

Furman University
Greenville, SC 29613
M: (803) 294–2151
W: (803) 294–2118
Enrollment: A
4-year private
M: Southern
W: AIAW
M: Riflery, Volleyball, Wrestling, Baseball, Basketball, Cross Country, Football, Golf, Soccer, Swimming-Diving, Tennis
W: Basketball, Field Hockey, Golf, Gymnastics, Softball, Swimming-Diving, Tennis, Volleyball

Gadsden State Junior College
Gadsden, AL 35903
M: (205) 546–0484
W: (205) 546–0484
Enrollment: B
2-year public funding
M: Alabama JCAC
W: Alabama JCAC
M: Baseball, Basketball, Golf, Tennis
W: Basketball

Gainesville Junior College
Gainesville, GA 30501
M: (404) 536–5226
W: (404) 536–5226
Enrollment: A
2-year public funding
M: NJCAA
W: NJCAA
M: Basketball, Golf, Tennis
W: Basketball, Tennis

Gannon College
Perry Square
Erie, PA 16501
M: (814) 871–7307
W: (814) 871–7307
Enrollment: B
4-year private
M: Independent
W: AIAW
M: Baseball, Basketball, Cross Country, Golf, Soccer, Tennis
W: Basketball, Softball, Tennis, Volleyball

Gardner-Webb College
Boiling Springs, NC 28017
M: (704) 434–2361
W: (704) 434–2361
Enrollment: A
4-year private
M: NAIA
W: AIAW, NCAIAW

M: Cross Country, Golf, Baseball,
   Basketball, Football, Tennis,
   Track & Field
W: Basketball, Tennis, Volleyball
   Softball, Track & Field,
   Volleyball

Garrett Community College
McHenry, MD 21541
M: (301) 387-6666
W: (301) 387-6666
Enrollment: A
2-year public funding
M: JUCO
W: JUCO
M: Baseball, Basketball
W: Basketball, Volleyball

Gateway Technical Institute
3520 30th Avenue
Kenosha, WI 53140
M: (414) 631-7373
W: (414) 631-7373
Enrollment: A
2-year public funding
M: WTCC
W: WTCC
M: Basketball, Bowling, Cross
   Country, Golf, Tennis
W: Basketball, Bowling, Cross
   Country, Tennis, Volleyball

George Fox College
Newberg, OR 97132
M: (503) 538-8383
W: (503) 538-8383
Enrollment: A
4-year private
M: Independent, NAIA
W: Independent, NAIA
M: Soccer, Baseball, Basketball,
   Cross Country, Track & Field
W: Cross Country, Basketball,

Georgetown University
37th and "O" Streets
Washington, DC 20057
M: (202) 625-4182
W: (202) 625-4182
Enrollment: C
4-year private
M: Big East
W: AIAW
M: Baseball, Crew, Football,
   Golf, Lacrosse, Sailing,
   Soccer, Swimming-Diving,
   Tennis, Basketball, Cross
   Country, Track & Field
W: Crew, Field Hockey,
   Gymnastics, Lacrosse, Sailing,
   Swimming-Diving, Basketball,
   Cross Country, Tennis, Track
   & Field, Volleyball

George Washington University
600 22nd Street, NW
Washington, DC 20052
M: (202) 676-6650
W: (202) 676-6283
Enrollment: C
4-year private
M: Eastern 8, NCAA
W: AIAW
M: Crew, Golf, Baseball,
   Basketball, Soccer,
   Swimming-Diving, Tennis,
   Wrestling
W: Badminton, Basketball, Crew,
   Gymnastics, Squash,
   Swimming-Diving, Tennis,
   Volleyball

University of Georgia
Athens, GA 30602
M: (404) 542-1307
W: (404) 542-5817
Enrollment: C
4-year public funding
M: Southeastern
W: Southeastern
M: Baseball, Basketball, Cross Country, Football, Golf, Gymnastics, Riflery, Swimming-Diving, Tennis, Track & Field
W: Basketball, Cross Country, Golf, Gymnastics, Riflery, Swimming-Diving, Tennis, Track & Field, Volleyball

Georgia College
Milledgeville, GA 31061
M: (912) 453-5319
W: (912) 453-5319
Enrollment: B
4-year public funding
M: GIAC, NAIA
W: AIAW, GAIAW
M: Baseball, Basketball, Soccer, Tennis
W: Gymnastics, Softball

Georgia Institute of Technology
190 Third Street, NW
Atlanta, GA 30332
M: (404) 894-5445
W: (404) 894-5445
Enrollment: C
4-year public funding
M: ACC
W: ACC
M: Baseball, Basketball, Football, Golf, Gymnastics, Swimming-Diving, Tennis, Track & Field, Wrestling
W: Basketball

Georgian Court College
Lakewood, NJ 08701
M: (201) 364-2200 X. 38
Enrollment: A
4-year private
W: NJAIAW
W: Softball, Volleyball, Basketball

Georgia Southern College
Statesboro, GA 30458
M: (912) 681-5522
W: (912) 681-5222
Enrollment: C
4-year public funding
M: TAAC
W: GAIAW
M: Baseball, Basketball, Golf, Soccer, Swimming-Diving, Tennis, Water Polo
W: Basketball, Softball, Swimming-Diving, Tennis

Georgia Southwestern College
Americus, GA 31709
M: (912) 928-1262
W: (912) 928-1262
Enrollment: A
4-year public funding
M: GAIC
W: GAIAW
M: Track & Field, Baseball, Basketball, Tennis
W: Basketball, Softball, Tennis

Georgia State University
University Plaza
Atlanta, GA 30303
M: (404) 658-2772
W: (404) 658-2772
Enrollment: C
4-year public funding
M: Sun Belt

W: GAIAW
M: Baseball, Basketball, Cross
   Country, Golf, Soccer,
   Swimming-Diving, Tennis
W: Basketball, Cross Country,
   Golf, Softball, Swimming-
   Diving, Tennis

Gettysburg College
Gettysburg, PA 17325
M: (717) 334–3131
W: (717) 334–3131
Enrollment: A
4-year private
M: MAC, NCAA
W: MAC, AIAW
M: Baseball, Basketball, Bowling,
   Cross Country, Football,
   Golf, Lacrosse, Riflery,
   Soccer, Swimming-Diving,
   Tennis, Track & Field,
   Wrestling
W: Basketball, Bowling, Cross
   Country, Field Hockey,
   Lacrosse, Riflery, Softball,
   Swimming-Diving, Tennis,
   Volleyball

Division III: all aid awarded on
   the basis of financial need.

Glassboro State College
Route 322
Glassboro, NJ 08028
M: (609) 445–5206
W: (609) 445–5206
Enrollment: C
4-year public funding
M: NJSCAC
W: AIAW
M: Archery, Baseball, Basketball,
   Cross Country, Football,
   Golf, Gymnastics, Ice
   Hockey, Soccer, Swimming-
   Diving, Tennis, Track &
   Field, Wrestling
W: Archery, Basketball, Cross
   Country, Field Hockey,
   Gymnastics, Lacrosse,
   Softball, Swimming-Diving,
   Tennis, Track & Field,
   Volleyball

Glen Oaks Community College
109 Shimmel Road
Centreville, MI 49032
M: (616) 467–9945
W: (616) 467–9945
Enrollment: A
4-year public funding
M: Western
W: Western
M: Baseball, Basketball, Golf
W: Basketball, Volleyball

Golden Valley Lutheran College
6125 Olson Highway
Minneapolis, MN 55422
M: (612) 542–1240
W: (612) 542–1263
Enrollment: A
2-year private
M: MJAC
W: MJAC
M: Baseball, Basketball, Cross
   Country, Football, Soccer,
   Track & Field, Wrestling
W: Basketball, Cross Country,
   Softball, Track & Field,
   Volleyball

Gonzaga University
East 502 Boone Avenue
Spokane, WA 99202
M: (509) 328–4220

W: (509) 328–4220
Enrollment: B
4-year private
M: WCAC, Nor Pac
W: Inland Valley
M: Cross Country, Golf, Soccer,
   Tennis, Baseball, Basketball
W: Basketball, Cross Country,
   Tennis, Volleyball

Gordon College
Wenham, MA 01984
M: (617) 927–2300 X. 307
W: (617) 927–2300 X. 307
Enrollment: A
4-year private
M: NAIA
W: MAIAW
M: Basketball, Cross Country, Ice
   Hockey, Soccer, Tennis
W: Basketball, Field Hockey,
   Softball, Tennis, Volleyball

Gordon Junior College
Barnesville, GA 30204
M: (404) 358–1700
W: (404) 358–1700
Enrollment: A
2-year public funding
M: NJCAA
W: GJCAA
M: Baseball
W: Basketball

Grace College
Winona Lake, IN 46590
M: (219) 267–8191 X. 175
W: (219) 267–8191 X. 142
Enrollment: A
4-year private
M: Independent
W: Independent

M: Baseball, Basketball, Cross
   Country, Golf, Soccer,
   Tennis, Track & Field
W: Basketball, Softball, Volleyball

Graceland College
Lamoni, IA 50140
M: (515) 784–5311
W: (515) 784–5311
Enrollment: A
4-year private
M: Heart of America
W: Heart of America
M: Baseball, Cross Country, Golf,
   Swimming-Diving, Tennis,
   Track & Field, Volleyball,
   Wrestling, Basketball,
   Football
W: Field Hockey, Softball,
   Swimming-Diving, Tennis,
   Track & Field, Basketball,
   Volleyball

Grand Canyon State College
3300 West Camelback
Phoenix, AZ 85017
M: (602) 249–3300
W: (602) 249–3300
Enrollment: A
4-year private
M: NAIA, Independent
W: NAIA, Independent
M: Baseball, Basketball, Golf,
   Tennis
W: Volleyball, Tennis

Grand Rapids Baptist College
Grand Rapids, MI 49505
M: (616) 949–5300 X. 213
W: (616) 949–5300 X. 213
Enrollment: A
4-year private

M: NCCA
W: NCCA
M: Crew, Tennis, Track & Field,
   Baseball, Basketball, Soccer,
   Wrestling
W: Basketball, Softball, Volleyball

Grand Rapids Junior College
143 Bostwick, NE
Grand Rapids, MI 49502
M: (616) 456–4229
W: (616) 456–4229
Enrollment: C
2-year public funding
M: MCCAA
W: MCCAA
M: Baseball, Basketball, Cross
   Country, Football, Golf,
   Swimming-Diving, Tennis,
   Track & Field, Wrestling
W: Basketball, Softball,
   Swimming-Diving, Tennis,
   Volleyball

Grand Valley State College
Allendale, MI 49401
M: (616) 895–6611 X. 250
W: (616) 895–6611 X. 250
Enrollment: C
4-year public funding
M: Great Lakes
W: Great Lakes
M: Crew, Baseball, Basketball,
   Cross Country, Football,
   Golf, Tennis, Track & Field,
   Wrestling
W: Crew, Basketball, Field
   Hockey, Softball, Tennis,
   Volleyball

College of Great Falls
1301 20th Street South
Great Falls, MT 59405
M: (406) 761–8210
W: (406) 761–8210
Enrollment: A
4-year private
M: Frontier, NAIA
W: Frontier, AIAW
M: Basketball
W: Basketball

Green River Community College
12401 SE 320th Street
Auburn, WA 98002
M: (206) 833–9111 X. 337
W: (206) 833–9111 X. 337
Enrollment: C
2-year public funding
M: AACC
W: AACC
M: Baseball, Basketball, Cross
   Country, Golf, Soccer,
   Tennis, Track & Field
W: Basketball, Cross Country,
   Golf, Soccer, Softball, Tennis,
   Track & Field, Volleyball

Scholarships are awarded to
   students from Washington,
   Oregon, Idaho, and British
   Columbia by conference rule.

Greensboro College
Greensboro, NC 27402
M: (919) 275–1109
W: (919) 275–1109
Enrollment: A
4-year private
M: DIAC
W: NCAIAW
M: Basketball, Golf, Soccer,
   Swimming-Diving, Tennis
W: Basketball, Swimming-Diving,
   Tennis, Volleyball

Greenville College
Greenville, IL 62246
M: (618) 664–1840 X. 300
W: (618) 664–1840 X. 305
Enrollment: A
4-year private
M: NAIA
W: AIAW
M: Baseball, Basketball, Cross Country, Golf, Soccer, Tennis, Track & Field
W: Basketball, Softball, Tennis, Track & Field, Volleyball

Grinnell College
Grinnell, IA 50112
M: (515) 236–6181 X. 316
W: (515) 236–6181 X. 316
Enrollment: A
4-year private
M: Midwest
W: Midwest
M: Baseball, Basketball, Cross Country, Football, Golf, Soccer, Swimming-Diving, Tennis, Track & Field, Wrestling
W: Basketball, Cross Country, Field Hockey, Softball, Swimming-Diving, Tennis, Track & Field, Volleyball

Grove City College
Grove City, PA 16127
M: (412) 458–6600 X. 264
W: (412) 458–6600 X. 264
Enrollment: A
4-year private
M: NCAA
W: AIAW
M: Baseball, Basketball, Cross Country, Football, Golf, Soccer, Swimming-Diving, Tennis, Track & Field
W: Basketball, Cross Country, Softball, Tennis, Volleyball

Division III: all aid awarded on the basis of financial need.

Guilford College
Greensboro, NC 27410
M: (919) 292–5511
W: (919) 292–5511
Enrollment: A
4-year private
M: Carolinas
W: Carolinas
M: Baseball, Basketball, Football, Golf, Lacrosse, Soccer, Tennis
W: Basketball, Softball, Tennis, Volleyball

Gustavus Adolphus College
St. Peter, MN 56082
M: (507) 931–4300
W: (507) 931–4300
Enrollment: A
4-year private
M: MIAC
W: MIAC
M: Baseball, Basketball, Bowling, Cross Country, Football, Golf, Ice Hockey, Soccer, Swimming-Diving, Tennis, Track & Field, Wrestling
W: Basketball, Bowling, Cross Country, Golf, Gymnastics, Softball, Swimming-Diving, Tennis, Track & Field, Volleyball

Division III: all aid awarded on the basis of financial need.

Hagerstown Junior College
751 Robinwood Drive
Hagerstown, MD 21740
M: (301) 790–2800
W: (301) 790–2800
Enrollment: A
4-year public funding
M: JUCO
W: Independent
M: Baseball, Basketball, Cross Country, Golf, Track & Field
W: Basketball, Volleyball

Hamilton College
Clinton, NY 13323
M: (315) 859–4115
W: (315) 859–4115
Enrollment: A
4-year private
M: NCAA, ECAC, NESCAC
W: NCAA, ECAC, NESCAC
M: Baseball, Basketball, Cross Country, Football, Golf, Lacrosse, Soccer, Squash, Swimming-Diving, Tennis, Track & Field
W: Basketball, Cross Country, Field Hockey, Lacrosse, Swimming-Diving, Track & Field

Hamline University
1536 Hewitt
St. Paul, MN 55104
M: (612) 641–2326
W: (612) 641–2326
Enrollment: A
4-year private
M: MIAC
W: MIAC
M: Baseball, Basketball, Cross Country, Football, Soccer, Swimming-Diving, Tennis, Track & Field, Wrestling
W: Basketball, Cross Country, Gymnastics, Swimming-Diving, Tennis, Track & Field, Volleyball

Hampton Institute
Hampton, VA 23668
M: (804) 727–5641
W: (804) 727–5354
Enrollment: C
4-year private
M: CIAA, NAIA, NCAA
W: CIAA, VAIAW
M: Riflery, Basketball, Cross Country, Football, Tennis, Track & Field, Wrestling
W: Softball, Volleyball, Basketball, Cross Country, Track & Field

Hannibal-La Grange College
Hannibal, MO 63401
M: (314) 221–3675
Enrollment: A
2-year private
M: Independent
M: Golf, Baseball, Basketball

Hanover College
Hanover, IN 47243
M: (812) 866–2151 X. 302
W: (812) 866–2151 X. 216
Enrollment: A
4-year private
M: Hoosier-Buckeye
W: AIAW
M: Baseball, Basketball, Cross Country, Football, Golf, Tennis, Track & Field, Wrestling
W: Field Hockey, Tennis, Volleyball

Harding University
Searcy, AR 72143
M: (501) 268–6161 X. 344
Enrollment: B
4-year private
M: AIC
M: Baseball, Bowling, Cross
Country, Golf, Swimming-
Diving, Tennis, Track &
Field, <u>Basketball</u>, <u>Football</u>

Hardin-Simmons University
Abilene, TX 79601
M: (915) 677–7281
W: (915) 677–7281
Enrollment: A
4-year private
M: TAAC, NCAA
W: TAIAW
M: Cross Country, Soccer,
<u>Baseball</u>, <u>Basketball</u>, <u>Golf</u>,
<u>Tennis</u>
W: Cross Country, <u>Basketball</u>,
<u>Tennis</u>, <u>Volleyball</u>

University of Hartford
200 Bloomfield Avenue
West Hartford, CT 06117
M: (203) 243–4658
W: (203) 243–4658
Enrollment: B
4-year private
M: Northeast-7
W: Northeast-7
M: Baseball, Lacrosse, Soccer,
Tennis, Wrestling, <u>Basketball</u>,
<u>Golf</u>
W: <u>Basketball</u>, <u>Softball</u>, <u>Tennis</u>,
<u>Volleyball</u>

Harvard University
60 Boylston Street
Cambridge, MA 02138
M: (617) 495–2202
W: (617) 495–2202
Enrollment: C
4-year private
M: Ivy League
W: Ivy League
M: Baseball, Basketball, Crew,
Cross Country, Fencing,
Football, Golf, Ice Hockey,
Lacrosse, Sailing, Skiing,
Soccer, Squash, Swimming-
Diving, Tennis, Track &
Field, Volleyball, Water Polo,
Wrestling
W: Basketball, Crew, Cross
Country, Fencing, Field
Hockey, Lacrosse, Sailing,
Skiing, Soccer, Softball,
Squash, Swimming-Diving,
Tennis, Track & Field

Hastings College
Hastings, NE 68901
M: (402) 463–2402 X. 218
W: (402) 463–2402 X. 258
Enrollment: A
4-year private
M: NIAC
W: NIAC
M: Golf, Tennis, <u>Basketball</u>,
<u>Cross Country</u>, <u>Football</u>,
<u>Track & Field</u>
W: Golf, Tennis, <u>Basketball</u>,
<u>Track & Field</u>, <u>Volleyball</u>

University of Hawaii
Hilo, HI 96720
M: (808) 961–9520
W: (808) 961–9520
Enrollment: B
4-year public funding
M: NAIA

W: AIAW
M: Baseball, Basketball, Golf,
   Tennis
W: Tennis, Volleyball

University of Hawaii
1337 Lower Campus Road
Honolulu, HI 96822
M: (808) 948–7301
W: (808) 948–7347
Enrollment: C
4-year public funding
M: WAC
W: AIAW
M: Baseball, Basketball, Football,
   Golf, Sailing, Swimming-
   Diving, Tennis, Volleyball
W: Basketball, Cross Country,
   Golf, Swimming-Diving,
   Tennis, Track & Field,
   Volleyball

Hawaii Pacific College
1060 Bishop Street
Honolulu, HI 96813
M: (808) 521–3881
W: (808) 521–3881
Enrollment: A
4-year private
M: NAIA
W: NAIA
M: Basketball, Golf, Volleyball
W: Golf, Volleyball

Heidelberg College
Tiffin, OH 44883
M: (419) 448–2981
W: (419) 448–2981
Enrollment: A
4-year private
M: OAC
W: Independent

M: Baseball, Basketball, Football,
   Golf, Soccer, Swimming-
   Diving, Tennis, Track &
   Field, Wrestling
W: Basketball, Swimming-Diving,
   Tennis, Track & Field,
   Volleyball

Henderson State University
Arkadelphia, AR 71923
M: (501) 246–5511
W: (501) 246–5511
Enrollment: B
4-year public funding
M: AIC
W: AWISA
M: Baseball, Cross Country, Golf,
   Swimming-Diving, Tennis,
   Track & Field, Basketball,
   Football
W: Basketball, Swimming-Diving,
   Tennis, Volleyball

Hendrix College
Conway, AR 72032
M: (501) 450–1313
W: (501) 450–1313
Enrollment: A
4-year private
M: NAIA, AIC
W: AIAW
M: Cross Country, Golf, Soccer,
   Swimming-Diving, Tennis,
   Track & Field, Water Polo,
   Basketball
W: Swimming-Diving, Tennis,
   Volleyball

Herbert H. Lehman College
Bronx, NY 10468
M: (212) 960–8101
W: (212) 960–8101

Enrollment: C
4-year public funding
M: ECAC, NCAA
W: AIAW
M: Baseball, Basketball, Cross Country, Ice Hockey, Swimming-Diving, Tennis, Track & Field
W: Basketball, Cross Country, Softball, Swimming-Diving, Tennis, Track & Field, Volleyball

Hesston College
Hesston, KS 67062
M: (316) 327–4221
W: (316) 327–4221
Enrollment: A
2-year private
M: PJCC
W: PJCC
M: Baseball, Basketball, Soccer
W: Basketball, Softball, Volleyball

High Point College
933 Montlieu Avenue
High Point, NC 27262
M: (919) 885–5101
W: (919) 885–5101
Enrollment: A
4-year private
M: Carolinas, NAIA
W: Carolinas, AIAW
M: Baseball, Basketball, Golf, Soccer, Tennis, Track & Field
W: Basketball, Field Hockey, Tennis, Volleyball

Highland Community Junior College
Highland, KS 66035
M: (913) 442–3238
W: (913) 442–3238
Enrollment: A
2-year public funding
M: MACC
W: MACC
M: Baseball, Basketball, Football, Track & Field
W: Basketball, Softball, Track & Field, Volleyball

Highland Community Junior College pays in-state tuition for some athletes.

Highland Park Community College
Third at Glendale
Highland Park, MI 48203
M: (313) 956–0589
W: (313) 956–0589
Enrollment: B
2-year public funding
M: MCCAC
W: MCCAC
M: Baseball, Basketball, Cross Country, Swimming-Diving, Tennis, Track & Field
W: Basketball, Cross Country, Swimming-Diving, Track & Field

Hilbert College
Hamburg, NY 14075
M: (716) 649–7900
W: (716) 649–7900
Enrollment: A
2-year private
M: Penn-York, NJCAA
W: Penn-York, NJCAA
M: Baseball, Basketball
W: Basketball, Softball, Volleyball

Hillsborough Community College
Tampa, FL 33622
M: (813) 879–7222 X. 582/583
W: (813) 879–7222 X. 582/583
Enrollment: C
2-year public funding
M: NJCAA, FCCAA
W: NJCAA, FCCAA
M: Baseball, Basketball, Golf
W: Softball, Tennis, Volleyball

Hillsdale College
201 Oak Street
Hillsdale, MI 49242
M: (517) 437–7364
W: (517) 437–7364
Enrollment: A
4-year private
M: Great Lakes
W: AIAW
M: Baseball, Basketball, Cross Country, Football, Golf, Tennis, Track & Field
W: Basketball, Cross Country, Softball, Tennis, Track & Field, Volleyball

Hiram College
Hiram, OH 44234
M: (216) 569–3211 X. 233
W: (216) 569–3211 X. 215
Enrollment: A
4-year private
M: PAC
W: NEOS
M: Baseball, Basketball, Cross Country, Football, Golf, Soccer, Swimming-Diving, Tennis, Track & Field, Wrestling
W: Basketball, Cross Country, Field Hockey, Golf, Softball, Swimming-Diving, Tennis, Track & Field, Volleyball

Hofstra University
Hempstead, NY 11550
M: (516) 560–3578
W: (516) 560–3578
Enrollment: C
4-year private
M: NCAA, ECAC
W: AIAW, EAIAW, NYSAIAW
M: Basketball, Lacrosse, Soccer, Wrestling
W: Basketball, Fencing, Field Hockey, Gymnastics, Lacrosse, Softball, Volleyball

Holy Cross College
Worcester, MA 01610
M: (617) 793–2571
W: (617) 793–2629
Enrollment: A
4-year private
M: ECAC
W: AIAW
M: Baseball, Crew, Cross Country, Fencing, Golf, Lacrosse, Soccer, Swimming-Diving, Tennis, Track & Field, Basketball, Football
W: Crew, Cross Country, Fencing, Field Hockey, Lacrosse, Softball, Swimming-Diving, Tennis, Track & Field, Volleyball, Basketball

Holy Family College
Philadelphia, PA 19114
M: (215) 637–7700
W: (215) 637–7700
Enrollment: A
4-year private
M: Independent
W: Independent
M: Basketball
W: Basketball, Softball

Hood College
Frederick, MD 21701
W: (301) 663-3131
Enrollment: A
4-year private
W: AIAW
W: Basketball, Field Hockey,
    Swimming-Diving, Tennis,
    Volleyball

Hope College
Holland, MI 49423
M: (616) 392-5111 X. 3270
W: (616) 392-5111 X. 3270
Enrollment: A
4-year private
M: MIAA
W: MIAA
M: Baseball, Basketball, Cross
    Country, Football, Golf,
    Soccer, Swimming-Diving,
    Tennis, Track & Field,
    Wrestling
W: Archery, Basketball, Field
    Hockey, Softball, Swimming-
    Diving, Tennis, Track &
    Field, Volleyball

Houghton College
Houghton, NY 14744
M: (716) 567-2211 X. 360
W: (716) 567-2211 X. 360
Enrollment: A
4-year private
M: NAIA, PCAC
W: NCCAA
M: Baseball, Basketball, Cross
    Country, Soccer, Tennis,
    Track & Field
W: Basketball, Cross Country,
    Field Hockey, Soccer, Tennis,
    Track & Field, Volleyball

Housatonic Community College
510 Barnum Avenue
Bridgeport, CT 06608
M: (203) 579-6488
W: (203) 579-6488
Enrollment: A
2-year public funding
M: CCCAA
W: CCCAA
M: Baseball, Basketball, Golf
W: Basketball, Golf, Softball

University of Houston
4800 Calhoun Boulevard
Houston, TX 77004
M: (713) 749-7105
W: (713) 749-7105
Enrollment: C
4-year public funding
M: Southwest
W: TAIAW
M: Baseball, Basketball, Cross
    Country, Football, Golf,
    Swimming-Diving, Tennis,
    Track & Field
W: Basketball, Cross Country,
    Swimming-Diving, Tennis,
    Track & Field, Volleyball

Houston Baptist University
7502 Fondern Road
Houston, TX 77036
M: (713) 774-7661
W: (713) 774-7661
Enrollment: A
4-year private
M: NCAA, Trans America
W: AIAW
M: Basketball, Cross Country,
    Golf, Gymnastics, Soccer,
    Tennis, Track & Field
W: Golf, Tennis

Howard Payne University
Brownwood, TX 76801
M: (915) 646–2502 X. 234
W: (915) 646–2502 X. 354
Enrollment: A
4-year private
M: Lone Star
W: TAIAW
M: Basketball, Cross Country, Football, Golf, Track & Field
W: Basketball, Volleyball

Humboldt State University
Arcata, CA 95521
M: (707) 826–3666
W: (707) 826–4538
Enrollment: C
4-year public funding
M: Far Western
W: Golden State
M: Baseball, Basketball, Cross Country, Football, Golf, Soccer, Track & Field, Wrestling
W: Basketball, Cross Country, Softball, Swimming-Diving, Tennis, Track & Field, Volleyball

Hunter College
695 Park Avenue
New York, NY 10021
M: (212) 570–5202
W: (212) 570–5240
Enrollment: C
4-year public funding
M: CUNY
W: CUNY
M: Baseball, Basketball, Cross Country, Fencing, Gymnastics, Soccer, Swimming-Diving, Tennis, Track & Field, Wrestling
W: Basketball, Cross Country, Fencing, Gymnastics, Swimming-Diving, Tennis, Track & Field

Huntington College
Huntington, IN 46750
M: (219) 356–6000 X. 39
W: (219) 356–6000 X. 76
Enrollment: A
4-year private
M: Mid-Central
W: AIAW
M: Baseball, Basketball, Cross Country, Golf, Soccer, Tennis, Track & Field, Wrestling
W: Basketball, Tennis, Track & Field, Volleyball

Husson College
Bangor, ME 04401
M: (207) 945–5641 X. 334
W: (207) 945–5641 X. 333
Enrollment: A
4-year private
M: Independent
W: MAIAW
M: Baseball, Basketball, Golf, Soccer
W: Basketball, Softball, Volleyball

Hutchinson Community Junior College
1300 North Plum
Hutchinson, KS 67501
M: (316) 663–5781
W: (316) 663–5781
Enrollment: A
2-year public funding

M: Jayhawk
W: Jayhawk
M: Baseball, Basketball, Cross Country, Football, Golf, Tennis, Track & Field
W: Basketball, Tennis, Track & Field, Volleyball

The College of Idaho
Caldwell, ID 83605
M: (208) 459–5512
W: (208) 459–5512
Enrollment: A
4-year private
M: Independent
W: Independent
M: Basketball, Skiing, Tennis
W: Skiing, Tennis, Volleyball

University of Idaho
Moscow, ID 83843
M: (208) 885–7031
W: (208) 885–6384
Enrollment: C
4-year public funding
M: Big Sky
W: NCWSA
M: Basketball, Cross Country, Football, Golf, Swimming-Diving, Tennis, Track & Field
W: Basketball, Cross Country, Field Hockey, Golf, Gymnastics, Swimming-Diving, Tennis, Track & Field, Volleyball

Idaho State University
Pocatello, ID 83209
M: (208) 236–2771
W: (208) 236–2771
Enrollment: C
4-year public funding

M: Big Sky
W: IAIAW
M: Basketball, Cross Country, Football, Golf, Indoor Track, Tennis, Track & Field, Wrestling
W: Basketball, Cross Country, Softball, Tennis, Track & Field, Volleyball

University of Illinois
112 Assembly Hall
Urbana, IL 61801
M: (217) 333–1390
W: (217) 333–0171
Enrollment: C
4-year public funding
M: Big Ten
W: Big Ten
M: Baseball, Basketball, Cross Country, Fencing, Football, Golf, Gymnastics, Swimming-Diving, Tennis, Track & Field, Wrestling
W: Basketball, Cross Country, Golf, Gymnastics, Swimming-Diving, Tennis, Track & Field, Volleyball

University of Illinois at Chicago Circle
Chicago, IL 60680
M: (312) 996–2772
W: (312) 996–2772
Enrollment: C
4-year public funding
M: Independent
W: Independent
M: Golf, Baseball, Basketball, Cross Country, Gymnastics, Soccer, Swimming-Diving, Tennis, Track & Field
W: Basketball, Cross Country,

Gymnastics, Softball,
Swimming-Diving, Tennis,
Track & Field, Volleyball

Illinois Benedictine College
5700 College Road
Lisle, IL 60532
M: (312) 968-7270
W: (312) 968-7270
Enrollment: A
4-year private
M: NIIC
W: AIAW
M: Baseball, Basketball, Cross
   Country, Football, Golf,
   Swimming-Diving, Tennis,
   Track & Field
W: Basketball, Cross Country,
   Golf, Softball, Swimming-
   Diving, Track & Field,
   Volleyball

Illinois College
1101 West College Avenue
Jacksonville, IL 62650
M: (217) 245-7510
W: (217) 245-7510
Enrollment: A
4-year private
M: Collegiate Athletic
W: AIAW
M: Baseball, Basketball, Football,
   Golf, Tennis, Track & Field,
   Wrestling
W: Basketball, Softball, Tennis,
   Track & Field, Volleyball

Illinois State University
Normal, IL 61761
M: (309) 438-5631
W: (309) 438-5631
Enrollment: C

4-year public funding
M: Independent
W: AIAW
M: Baseball, Basketball, Cross
   Country, Football, Golf,
   Gymnastics, Soccer,
   Swimming-Diving, Tennis,
   Track & Field, Wrestling
W: Badminton, Basketball, Cross
   Country, Field Hockey, Golf,
   Gymnastics, Softball,
   Swimming-Diving, Tennis,
   Track & Field, Volleyball

Illinois Valley Community College
Oglesby, IL 61348
M: (815) 224-2720 X. 472
W: (815) 224-2720 X. 472
Enrollment: B
2-year public funding
M: NCCCC
W: NCCCC
M: Baseball, Basketball, Cross
   Country, Football, Golf,
   Tennis, Track & Field
W: Basketball, Cross Country,
   Softball, Tennis, Track &
   Field, Volleyball

Illinois Wesleyan University
Bloomington, IL 61701
M: (309) 556-3181
W: (309) 556-3141
Enrollment: A
4-year private
M: CCIW
W: AIAW
M: Baseball, Basketball, Cross
   Country, Football, Golf,
   Tennis, Track & Field,
   Wrestling
W: Basketball, Softball, Tennis,
   Track & Field, Volleyball

All aid for men and women is
based on financial need.

Indian Hills Community College
Centerville, IA 52544
M: (515) 856-2143
W: (515) 856-2143
Enrollment: A
2-year public funding
M: Iowa JUCO
W: Iowa JUCO
M: Golf, Baseball, Basketball
W: Golf, Basketball, Softball

Indian River Community College
Fort Pierce, FL 33450
M: (305) 469-2000
W: (305) 469-2000
Enrollment: B
2-year public funding
M: NJCAA
W: NJCAA
M: Baseball, Basketball,
    Swimming-Diving, Tennis
W: Basketball, Swimming-Diving,
    Tennis, Volleyball

Indiana Central University
1400 East Hanna Avenue
Indianapolis, IN 46227
M: (317) 788-3246
W: (317) 788-3246
Enrollment: A
4-year private
M: Heartland, Great Lakes
    Valley, NCAA
W: AIAW
M: Baseball, Basketball, Cross
    Country, Football, Golf,
    Tennis, Track & Field,
    Wrestling
W: Basketball, Softball, Tennis,
    Track & Field, Volleyball

Indiana Institute of Technology
1600 East Washington Boulevard
Fort Wayne, IN 46803
M: (219) 422-5561
W: (219) 422-5561
Enrollment: A
4-year private
M: Independent, NAIA
W: Independent, NAIA
M: Basketball, Soccer
W: Basketball, Volleyball

Indiana State University
8600 University Boulevard
Evansville, IN 47712
M: (812) 464-1846
W: (812) 464-1846
Enrollment: C
4-year public funding
M: Great Lakes Valley
W: Great Lakes Valley, AIAW
M: Baseball, Basketball, Cross
    Country, Golf, Soccer, Tennis
W: Basketball, Softball, Tennis,
    Volleyball

Indiana University
Bloomington, IN 47401
M: (812) 337-2421
W: (812) 337-8261
Enrollment: C
4-year public funding
M: Big Ten
W: Big Ten
M: Baseball, Basketball, Cross
    Country, Football, Golf,
    Gymnastics, Soccer,
    Swimming-Diving, Tennis,
    Track & Field, Wrestling
W: Basketball, Cross Country,
    Field Hockey, Golf,
    Gymnastics, Softball,
    Swimming-Diving, Tennis,
    Track & Field

Indiana University of Pennsylvania
Indiana, PA 15701
M: (412) 357-2747
W: (412) 357-2747
Enrollment: C
4-year public funding
M: NCAA, NAIA, ECAC
W: AIAW, EAIAW
M: Baseball, Cross Country, Fencing, Golf, Riflery, Soccer, Swimming-Diving, Tennis, Track & Field, Wrestling, <u>Basketball</u>, <u>Football</u>
W: Basketball, Cross Country, Fencing, Field Hockey, Gymnastics, Softball, Swimming-Diving, Tennis, Track & Field, Volleyball

Indiana University-Purdue University
1010 West 64th Street
Indianapolis, IN 46260
M: (317) 264-2725
W: (317) 267-2725
Enrollment: C
4-year public funding
M: NAIA
W: AIAW
M: <u>Baseball</u>, <u>Basketball</u>, <u>Tennis</u>
W: <u>Basketball</u>, <u>Softball</u>, <u>Volleyball</u>

Indiana University-Purdue University
2101 Coliseum Boulevard East
Fort Wayne, IN 46805
M: (219) 482-5351
W: (219) 482-5351
Enrollment: C
4-year public funding
M: Independent
W: AIAW
M: Baseball, Basketball, Soccer, Tennis, Volleyball
W: Basketball, Tennis, Track & Field, Volleyball

Inver Hills College
8445 College Trail
Inver Grove Heights, MN 55075
M: (612) 455-9621
W: (612) 455-9621
Enrollment: B
2-year public funding
M: MCCC
W: MCCC
M: Baseball, Basketball, Football, Golf, Tennis
W: Basketball, Softball, Tennis, Volleyball

University of Iowa
Iowa City, IA 52242
M: (319) 353-3038
W: (319) 353-4354
Enrollment: C
4-year public funding
M: Big Ten
W: Big Ten
M: <u>Baseball</u>, <u>Basketball</u>, <u>Cross Country</u>, <u>Football</u>, <u>Golf</u>, <u>Gymnastics</u>, <u>Swimming-Diving</u>, <u>Tennis</u>, <u>Track & Field</u>, <u>Wrestling</u>
W: <u>Basketball</u>, <u>Cross Country</u>, <u>Field Hockey</u>, <u>Golf</u>, <u>Gymnastics</u>, <u>Softball</u>, <u>Swimming-Diving</u>, <u>Tennis</u>, <u>Track & Field</u>, <u>Volleyball</u>

Iowa Lakes Community College
300 South 18th Street
Estherville, IA 51334
M: (712) 362-2604

W: (712) 362–2604
Enrollment: A
2-year public funding
M: NJCAA, Northern Iowa JUCO
W: NJCAA, Northern Iowa JUCO
M: Baseball, Basketball, Football, Golf
W: Basketball, Softball, Volleyball

Iowa State University
Ames, IA 50010
M: (515) 294–3723
W: (515) 294–3404
Enrollment: C
4-year public funding
M: Big Eight
W: Big Eight
M: Baseball, Basketball, Cross Country, Football, Golf, Gymnastics, Swimming-Diving, Tennis, Track & Field, Wrestling
W: Basketball, Cross Country, Golf, Gymnastics, Softball, Swimming-Diving, Tennis, Track & Field, Volleyball

Iowa Wesleyan College
Mount Pleasant, IA 52641
M: (319) 385–8021
W: (319) 385–8021
Enrollment: A
4-year private
M: Independent
W: Independent
M: Baseball, Basketball, Football, Golf, Swimming-Diving, Tennis, Track & Field
W: Basketball, Field Hockey, Golf, Softball, Swimming-Diving, Tennis, Track & Field, Volleyball

Ithaca College
Ithaca, NY 14850
M: (607) 274–3209
W: (607) 274–3219
Enrollment: B
4-year private
M: ICAC, ECAC, NCAA
W: NYSAIAW, EAIAW, AIAW
M: Baseball, Basketball, Crew, Cross Country, Football, Golf, Ice Hockey, Lacrosse, Soccer, Swimming-Diving, Tennis, Track & Field, Wrestling
W: Basketball, Bowling, Field Hockey, Gymnastics, Lacrosse, Softball, Swimming-Diving, Tennis, Track & Field, Volleyball

Jacksonville State University
Pelham Road
Jacksonville, AL 36265
M: (205) 435–9820
W: (205) 435–9820
Enrollment: C
4-year public funding
M: Gulf South
W: AAIAW
M: Baseball, Basketball, Cross Country, Football, Golf, Gymnastics, Tennis, Water Polo
W: Basketball, Cross Country, Gymnastics, Softball, Tennis, Track & Field, Volleyball

James Madison University
Harrisonburg, VA 22801

M: (703) 433–6164
W: (703) 433–6248
Enrollment: C
4-year public funding
M: ECAC
W: VAIAW
M: Archery, Equestrian, Baseball, Basketball, Cross Country, Football, Golf, Gymnastics, Soccer, Swimming-Diving, Tennis, Track & Field, Wrestling
W: Archery, Equestrian, Basketball, Cross Country, Fencing, Field Hockey, Golf, Gymnastics, Lacrosse, Swimming-Diving, Tennis, Track & Field, Volleyball

Jamestown College
Jamestown, ND 58401
M: (701) 253–2532
W: (701) 253–2562
Enrollment: A
4-year private
M: NDCAC
W: WACND
M: Golf, Tennis, Baseball, Basketball, Cross Country, Football, Track & Field, Wrestling
W: Softball, Tennis, Basketball, Cross Country, Track & Field, Volleyball

Jarvis Christian College
Hawkins, TX 75765
M: (214) 769–2174 X. 105
W: (214) 769–2174 X. 105
Enrollment: A
4-year public funding
M: IAC
W: IAC

M: Baseball, Basketball, Gymnastics, Track & Field, Volleyball
W: Basketball, Gymnastics, Softball, Track & Field, Volleyball

Jefferson Davis Junior College
Brewton, AL 36426
M: (205) 867–4832
W: (205) 867–4832
Enrollment: A
2-year public funding
M: Alabama JCAC
W: Alabama JCAC
M: Basketball, Golf, Tennis
W: Softball, Tennis

Jefferson State Junior College
2601 Carson Road
Birmingham, AL 35215
M: (205) 853–1200
W: (205) 853–1200
Enrollment: B
2-year public funding
M: Alabama JCAC, NJCAA
W: Alabama JCAC, NJCAA
M: Baseball, Basketball, Tennis, Track & Field
W: Gymnastics, Tennis

Jersey City State College
Jersey City, NJ 07305
M: (201) 547–3317
W: (201) 547–3317
Enrollment: B
4-year public funding
M: NJCAC
W: AIAW
M: Baseball, Basketball, Cross Country, Fencing, Football, Soccer, Swimming-Diving, Tennis, Track & Field

W: Basketball, Fencing, Gymnastics, Softball, Swimming-Diving, Tennis

Division III: all aid awarded on the basis of financial need.

John Carroll University
20700 North Park Boulevard
University Heights, OH 44118
M: (216) 491–4416
W: (216) 491–4416
Enrollment: B
4-year private
M: PAC
W: AIAW
M: Baseball, Basketball, Cross Country, Football, Golf, Riflery, Soccer, Swimming-Diving, Tennis, Track & Field, Wrestling
W: Basketball, Swimming-Diving, Tennis, Volleyball

John C. Calhoun Community College
Decatur, AL 35601
M: (205) 353–3102
W: (205) 353–3102
Enrollment: B
2-year public funding
M: NJCAA, Alabama JCAC
W: NJCAC, Alabama JCAC
M: Baseball, Basketball, Golf, Tennis
W: Basketball, Tennis

Johnson C. Smith University
100 Beatties Ford Road
Charlotte, NC 28216
M: (704) 372–2370 X. 238
W: (704) 372–2370 X. 238
Enrollment: A
4-year private
M: CIAA
W: CIAA
M: Basketball, Cross Country, Football, Golf, Swimming-Diving, Tennis, Track & Field
W: Softball, Basketball, Swimming-Diving, Track & Field

Jones County Junior College
Ellisville, MS 39437
M: (601) 477–9311 X. 310
W: (601) 477–9311 X. 310
Enrollment: B
2-year public funding
M: NJCAA, MJCAA
W: NJCAA, MJCAA
M: Archery, Baseball, Golf, Handball, Tennis, Track & Field, Basketball, Football
W: Archery, Golf, Handball, Tennis, Track & Field, Basketball

Jordan College
360 West Pine Street
Cedar Springs, MI 49319
M: (616) 696–1180
W: (616) 696–1180
Enrollment: A
4-year private
M: NLCAA
W: Independent
M: Basketball, Cross Country
W: Cross Country

Josephenum College
7625 North High Street
Columbus, OH 43085
M: (614) 436–1523

Enrollment: A
4-year private
M: Central Ohio
M: Basketball, Cross Country, Golf, Soccer, Tennis

Judson College
Marion, AL 36756
W: (205) 683–6161
Enrollment: A
4-year private
W: AAIAW
W: Basketball, Field Hockey, Tennis, Volleyball

Juniata College
Huntingdon, PA 16652
M: (814) 643–4310 X. 511
W: (814) 643–4310 X. 511
Enrollment: A
4-year private
M: MAC, ECAC, NCAA
W: MAC, EAIAW, AIAW
M: Baseball, Basketball, Cross Country, Football, Golf, Soccer, Tennis, Track & Field, Wrestling
W: Basketball, Cross Country, Field Hockey, Softball, Tennis, Volleyball

All aid for men and women is based on financial need.

Kalamazoo Valley Community College
6767 West "O" Avenue
Kalamazoo, MI 49007
M: (616) 372–5395
W: (616) 372–5395
Enrollment: C
2-year public funding

M: MCCAA, NJCAA
W: MCCAA, NJCAA
M: Baseball, Basketball, Golf, Tennis
W: Basketball, Softball, Tennis, Volleyball

Kankakee Community College
Kankakee, IL 60901
M: (815) 933–0234
W: (815) 933–0234
Enrollment: A
2-year public funding
M: CIAC
W: CIAC
M: Baseball, Basketball
W: Basketball, Softball, Volleyball

University of Kansas
Lawrence, KS 66044
M: (913) 864–3143
4-year public funding
M: Big Eight
W: Big Eight
M: Baseball, Basketball, Cross Country, Football, Golf, Swimming-Diving, Tennis, Track & Field
W: Basketball, Cross Country, Golf, Softball, Swimming-Diving, Tennis, Track & Field, Volleyball

Kansas State University
Manhattan, KS 66502
M: (913) 532–6910
W: (913) 532–6910
Enrollment: C
4-year public funding
M: Big Eight
W: Big Eight
M: Baseball, Basketball, Cross

Country, Football, Golf,
Tennis, Track & Field
W: Basketball, Cross Country,
Golf, Softball, Tennis, Track
& Field, Volleyball

Kansas Wesleyan College
Salina, KS 67401
M: (913) 827–5541
W: (913) 827–5541
Enrollment: A
4-year private
M: KCAC
W: KCAC
M: Basketball, Cross Country,
Football, Track & Field
W: Basketball, Cross Country,
Softball, Track & Field,
Volleyball

Kean College of New Jersey
Union, NJ 07083
M: (201) 527–2435
W: (201) 527–2435
Enrollment: C
4-year public funding
M: NCAA, NJSCAC, ECAC
W: AIAW, NJAIAW, EAIAW
M: Baseball, Basketball, Football,
Golf, Lacrosse, Soccer,
Swimming-Diving, Tennis,
Wrestling
W: Basketball, Field Hockey,
Gymnastics, Softball,
Swimming-Diving, Tennis,
Volleyball

Kearney State College
Kearney, NE 68847
M: (308) 236–4283
W: (308) 236–4283
Enrollment: C
4-year public funding
M: CSIC
W: CSIC
M: Baseball, Basketball, Cross
Country, Football, Tennis,
Track & Field, Wrestling
W: Basketball, Cross Country,
Softball, Swimming-Diving,
Tennis, Track & Field,
Volleyball

Kent State University
Kent, OH 44240
M: (216) 672–3120
W: (216) 672–3717
Enrollment: C
4-year public funding
M: Mid-American
W: OAISW, Mid-American
M: Baseball, Basketball, Cross
Country, Football, Golf,
Gymnastics, Ice Hockey,
Soccer, Swimming-Diving,
Tennis, Track & Field (indoor
and outdoor), Wrestling
W: Basketball, Cross Country,
Field Hockey, Gymnastics,
Softball, Swimming-Diving,
Tennis, Track & Field,
Volleyball

University of Kentucky
Lexington, KY 40506
M: (606) 257–3838
W: (606) 257–3838
Enrollment: C
4-year public funding
M: Southeastern
W: Southeastern, KWIC
M: Baseball, Basketball, Cross
Country, Football, Golf,
Swimming, Tennis, Track &
Field (indoor and outdoor),

Water Polo, Wrestling
W: Basketball, Cross Country, Golf, Gymnastics, Tennis, Track & Field (indoor and outdoor), Volleyball

Kentucky State University
East Main Street
Frankfort, KY 40601
M: (502) 564–6011
W: (502) 564–5971
Enrollment: B
4-year public funding
M: Independent
W: Independent
M: Tennis, Baseball, Basketball, Football, Track & Field
W: Basketball, Softball, Volleyball

Kentucky Wesleyan College
Owensboro, KY 42301
M: (502) 683–4795
W: (502) 683–4795
Enrollment: A
4-year private
M: Great Lakes Valley
W: Independent
M: Baseball, Basketball, Golf, Soccer, Tennis
W: Softball, Volleyball, Basketball, Golf, Tennis

Kenyon College
Gambier, OH 43022
M: (614) 427–2244
W: (614) 427–2244
Enrollment: A
4-year private
M: OAC
W: OAIAW, OAISW
M: Baseball, Basketball, Cross Country, Football, Golf, Lacrosse, Soccer, Swimming-Diving, Tennis, Track & Field
W: Basketball, Cross Country, Field Hockey, Golf, Lacrosse, Swimming-Diving, Tennis, Track & Field, Volleyball

The Kings College
Lodge Road
Briarcliff Manor, NY 10510
M: (914) 941–7200 X. 254
W: (914) 941–7200 X. 254
Enrollment: A
4-year private
M: CACC, SAC
W: Independent
M: Baseball, Basketball, Cross Country, Soccer, Tennis, Track & Field, Wrestling
W: Basketball, Field Hockey, Gymnastics, Softball, Tennis, Volleyball

Kirkwood Community College
Cedar Rapids, IA 52406
M: (319) 398–5462
W: (319) 398–5462
Enrollment: B
2-year public funding
M: EIJC
W: EIJC
M: Baseball, Basketball
W: Basketball, Softball

Kishwaukee College
Malta, IL 60150
M: (815) 825–2086
W: (815) 825–2086
Enrollment: A
2-year public funding
M: Arrowhead
W: Arrowhead

M: Baseball, Basketball, Golf,
    Soccer
W: Basketball, Gymnastics,
    Softball, Volleyball

Kutztown State College
Kutztown, PA 19530
M: (215) 683–4113
W: (215) 683–4113
Enrollment: B
4-year public funding
M: PSAC
W: AIAW
M: Baseball, Basketball, Cross
    Country, Football, Golf,
    Lacrosse, Riflery, Soccer,
    Swimming-Diving, Tennis,
    Track & Field, Wrestling
W: Basketball, Cross Country,
    Field Hockey, Lacrosse,
    Riflery, Softball, Tennis,
    Track & Field, Volleyball

Lackawanna Junior College
Scranton, PA 18503
M: (307) 382–2121
W: (307) 382–2121
Enrollment: A
2-year private
M: Wyoming CC
W: Wyoming CC
M: Basketball, Golf, Tennis
W: Basketball, Tennis, Volleyball

Lafayette College
Easton, PA 18042
M: (215) 253–6281
W: (215) 253–6281
Enrollment: A
4-year private
M: ECC
W: ECC

M: Baseball, Basketball, Cross
    Country, Fencing, Football,
    Golf, Lacrosse, Soccer,
    Swimming-Diving, Tennis,
    Track & Field, Wrestling
W: Basketball, Cross Country,
    Fencing, Field Hockey,
    Lacrosse, Softball, Swimming-
    Diving, Tennis, Volleyball

All aid for men and women is
    based on financial need.

LaGrange College
LaGrange, GA 30240
M: (404) 882–2911 X. 62
Enrollment: A
4-year private
M: GIAC
M: Basketball

Lake Erie College
Painesville, OH 44077
W: (216) 352–3361 X. 286
Enrollment: A
4-year private
W: OAISW, MAIAW, AIAW
W: Basketball, Field Hockey,
    Softball, Tennis, Volleyball

Lake Region Junior College
Devils Lake, ND 58301
M: (701) 662–4951 X. 57
W: (701) 662–4951 X. 57
Enrollment: A
2-year public funding
M: Mon-Dak
W: Mon-Dak
M: Basketball, Golf, Tennis,
    Track & Field
W: Basketball, Golf, Tennis,
    Track & Field

Lake Superior State College
Sault Ste. Marie, MI 49783
M: (906) 632–6841 X. 365
W: (906) 632–6841 X. 365
Enrollment: A
4-year public funding
M: Great Lakes
W: Great Lakes
M: Fencing, Riflery, Skiing,
   Basketball, Cross Country,
   Tennis, Wrestling
W: Fencing, Riflery, Basketball,
   Softball, Tennis, Volleyball

Lamar University
Beaumont, TX 77710
M: (713) 838–8615
W: (713) 838–7127
Enrollment: C
4-year public funding
M: Southland
W: Independent
M: Fencing, Sailing, Soccer,
   Volleyball, Baseball,
   Basketball, Cross Country,
   Football, Golf, Indoor Track,
   Tennis, Track & Field
W: Basketball, Cross Country,
   Golf, Swimming-Diving,
   Tennis, Track & Field,
   Volleyball

Lambuth College
Lambuth Boulevard
Jackson, TN 38301
M: (901) 427–6743 X. 11
W: (901) 427–6743 X. 11
Enrollment: A
4-year private
M: VSAC
W: VSAC
M: Baseball, Basketball, Tennis
W: Basketball, Tennis, Volleyball

Lancaster Bible College
901 Eden Road
Lancaster, PA 17601
M: (717) 569–7071 X. 67
W: (717) 569–7071 X. 67
Enrollment: A
4-year private
M: NACC
W: NACC
M: Baseball, Basketball, Soccer,
   Tennis, Wrestling
W: Basketball, Field Hockey,
   Softball, Tennis

Lander College
Greenwood, SC 29646
M: (803) 229–8314
W: (803) 229–8314
Enrollment: A
4-year public funding
M: NAIA
W: AIAW
M: Basketball, Tennis
W: Basketball, Tennis, Volleyball

Lane Community College
4000 East 30th Avenue
Eugene, OR 97405
M: (503) 726–2215
W: (503) 726–2215
Enrollment: C
2-year public funding
M: OCCAA
W: OCCAA
M: Soccer, Tennis, Baseball,
   Basketball, Cross Country,
   Track & Field, Wrestling
W: Tennis, Basketball, Cross
   Country, Track & Field,
   Volleyball

Laredo Junior College
Laredo, TX 78040
M: (512) 722-7481
W: (512) 722-7481
Enrollment: B
2-year public funding
M: TJCAC
W: TJCAC
M: Golf, Track & Field,
   Basketball, Tennis
W: Tennis, Volleyball

La Salle College
20th Street and Olmey Avenue
Philadelphia, PA 19141
M: (215) 951-1515
W: (215) 951-1523
Enrollment: B
4-year private
M: ECC
W: PAIAW
M: Crew, Riflery, Wrestling,
   Baseball, Basketball, Cross
   Country, Golf, Soccer,
   Swimming-Diving, Tennis,
   Track & Field
W: Crew, Basketball, Cross
   Country, Field Hockey,
   Softball, Swimming-Diving,
   Tennis, Track & Field,
   Volleyball

La Verne College
La Verne, CA 91750
M: (714) 593-3511 X. 221
W: (714) 593-3511 X. 221
Enrollment: A
4-year private
M: SCIAC
W: SCIAC
M: Badminton, Baseball,
   Basketball, Cross Country,
   Football, Golf, Soccer,
   Tennis, Track & Field,
   Volleyball, Wrestling
W: Basketball, Softball, Tennis,
   Track & Field, Volleyball

Lawrence University
Appleton, WI 54911
M: (414) 739-3681 X. 219
W: (414) 739-3681 X. 211
Enrollment: A
4-year private
M: Midwest
W: WIC, WAC
M: Baseball, Basketball, Cross
   Country, Fencing, Football,
   Golf, Soccer, Swimming-
   Diving, Tennis, Track &
   Field, Wrestling
W: Basketball, Cross Country,
   Fencing, Softball, Swimming-
   Diving, Tennis, Track &
   Field, Volleyball

Lebanon Valley College
Annville, PA 17003
M: (717) 867-4411 X. 261
W: (717) 867-4411 X. 261
Enrollment: A
4-year private
M: Independent
W: Independent
M: Baseball, Basketball, Cross
   Country, Football, Golf,
   Lacrosse, Soccer, Tennis,
   Track & Field, Wrestling
W: Basketball, Field Hockey,
   Lacrosse

Lees-McRae College
Banner Elk, NC 28604
M: (704) 898-4929
W: (704) 898-5241

Enrollment: A
2-year private
M: Western Caroline, Coastal
W: Independent
M: Skiing, Tennis, Track & Field, Basketball, Football
W: Skiing, Tennis, Volleyball, Basketball

Lehigh University
Bethlehem, PA 18015
M: (215) 861–4320
W: (215) 861–4317
Enrollment: B
4-year private
M: NCAA, ECAC, ECC
W: AIAW
M: Baseball, Basketball, Cross Country, Football, Lacrosse, Riflery, Soccer, Squash, Swimming-Diving, Tennis, Track & Field, Wrestling
W: Basketball, Field Hockey, Lacrosse, Softball, Swimming-Diving, Volleyball

All aid for men and women is based on financial need.

Le Moyne College
Syracuse, NY 13214
M: (315) 446–2882 X. 206
W: (315) 446–2882 X. 206
Enrollment: A
4-year private
M: ECAC, NCAA
W: ECAC, NCAA
M: Baseball, Basketball, Cross Country, Golf, Soccer, Tennis
W: Basketball, Softball, Tennis, Volleyball

Lenoir Community College
Kinston, NC 28501
M: (919) 527–6223 X. 273
W: (919) 527–6223 X. 273
Enrollment: A
2-year public funding
M: Eastern Tarheel
W: Independent
M: Baseball, Basketball, Golf
W: Basketball, Softball

Lenoir-Rhyne College
Hickory, NC 28601
M: (704) 328–1741 X. 264
W: (704) 328–1741 X. 377
Enrollment: A
4-year private
M: SAC, NAIA
W: AIAW
M: Baseball, Golf, Tennis, Track & Field, Basketball, Football
W: Basketball, Softball, Tennis, Volleyball

Lewis and Clark Community College
Godfrey, IL 62035
M: (618) 466–3411
W: (618) 466–3411
Enrollment: C
2-year public funding
M: Midwest JCAC
W: Midwest JCAC
M: Baseball, Basketball, Soccer, Tennis
W: Basketball, Tennis, Volleyball

Lewis-Clark State College
Lewiston, ID 83501
M: (208) 746–2341
W: (208) 746–2341
Enrollment: A

4-year public funding
M: NAIA
W: AIAW
M: Baseball, Basketball, Tennis
W: Basketball, Tennis, Volleyball

Lewis University
Lockport, IL 60441
M: (815) 838–0500
W: (815) 838–0500
Enrollment: B
4-year private
M: GLVC
W: AIAW
M: Baseball, Basketball, Cross
   Country, Golf, Soccer, Tennis
W: Basketball, Softball, Tennis,
   Volleyball

Liberty Baptist College
3765 Chandlers Mountain Road
Lynchburg, VA 24505
M: (804) 237–5961
W: (804) 237–5961
Enrollment: A
4-year private
M: NCAA, NAIA, NCCAA,
   Independent
W: AIAW, VAIAW
M: Baseball, Basketball, Cross
   Country, Football, Soccer,
   Track & Field, Wrestling
W: Cross Country, Track & Field,
   Basketball, Softball,
   Volleyball

Lincoln Christian College
Lincoln, IL 62656
M: (217) 732–3168 X. 241
W: (217) 732–3168 X. 241
Enrollment: A
4-year private

M: Independent
W: Independent
M: Baseball, Basketball, Soccer
W: Basketball, Softball, Volleyball

Lincoln Land Community College
Shepherd Road
Springfield, IL 62703
M: (217) 786–2423
W: (217) 786–2423
Enrollment: C
2-year public funding
M: CIAC
W: CIAC
M: Baseball, Basketball, Cross
   Country, Golf, Soccer,
   Tennis, Track & Field
W: Basketball, Softball, Tennis,
   Volleyball

Scholarships are restricted to
   graduates of the Junior
   College district.

Lincoln Trail College
Robinson, IL 62454
M: (618) 544–8657
W: (618) 544–8657
Enrollment: A
2-year private
M: Independent
W: Independent
M: Basketball, Golf, Tennis
W: Basketball, Softball, Volleyball

Lincoln University
Jefferson City, MO 65101
M: (314) 751–2325 X. 334
W: (314) 751–2325 X. 337
Enrollment: A
4-year public funding
M: MIAA

W: MAIAW
M: Baseball, Basketball, Cross
   Country, Football, Golf,
   Track & Field, Wrestling
W: Basketball, Softball, Track &
   Field, Volleyball

Lindenwood College
St. Charles, MO 63301
M: (314) 723–7152 X. 346
W: (314) 723–7152 X. 346
Enrollment: A
4-year private
M: SLACAA, NAIA
W: SLACAA, NAIA
M: Golf, Tennis, Baseball,
   Basketball, Soccer
W: Golf, Tennis, Basketball,
   Soccer, Softball, Volleyball

Linfield College
McMinnville, OR 97128
M: (503) 472–4121
W: (503) 472–4121
Enrollment: A
4-year private
M: NAIA
W: NCWSA
M: Soccer, Swimming-Diving,
   Baseball, Basketball, Cross
   Country, Football, Golf,
   Tennis, Track & Field,
   Wrestling
W: Basketball, Cross Country,
   Soccer, Softball, Swimming-
   Diving, Tennis, Track &
   Field, Volleyball

Livingstone College
Salisbury, NC 28144
M: (704) 633–7960
W: (704) 633–7960

Enrollment: A
4-year private
M: NAIA, CIAA
W: CIAA, AIAW
M: Basketball, Football, Golf,
   Tennis, Track & Field,
   Wrestling
W: Basketball, Cross Country,
   Golf, Softball, Tennis, Track
   & Field, Volleyball

Livingston University
Livingston, AL 35470
M: (205) 652–9661
W: (205) 652–9661
Enrollment: A
4-year public funding
M: Gulf South
W: AAIAW
M: Baseball, Basketball, Football,
   Tennis
W: Softball, Basketball, Volleyball

Lock Haven State College
Lock Haven, PA 17745
M: (717) 893–2102
W: (717) 893–2093
Enrollment: A
4-year public funding
M: ECAC, NCAA
W: EAIAW, AIAW
M: Baseball, Cross Country,
   Football, Golf, Soccer,
   Tennis, Track & Field,
   Basketball, Wrestling
W: Basketball, Cross Country,
   Field Hockey, Gymnastics,
   Lacrosse, Softball, Swimming-
   Diving, Tennis, Track & Field

Long Island University
University Plaza

Brooklyn, NY 11201
M: (212) 834–6237
W: (212) 834–6359
Enrollment: C
4-year private
M: ECAC, NCAA
W: NYSAIAW, EAIAW, AIAW
M: Baseball, Basketball,
  Gymnastics, Soccer,
  Swimming-Diving, Tennis
W: Basketball, Cross Country,
  Gymnastics, Tennis, Track &
  Field

Longwood College
Farmville, VA 23901
M: (804) 392–9243
W: (804) 392–9243
Enrollment: A
4-year public funding
M: NCAA
W: AIAW
M: Baseball, Golf, Soccer, Tennis,
  Wrestling, Basketball
W: Lacrosse, Softball, Tennis,
  Volleyball, Basketball, Field
  Hockey, Golf, Gymnastics

Loras College
1450 Alta Vista
Dubuque, IA 52001
M: (319) 588–7112
W: (319) 588–7241
Enrollment: A
4-year private
M: Independent
W: AIAW
M: Football, Golf, Baseball,
  Basketball, Cross Country,
  Swimming-Diving, Tennis,
  Track & Field, Water Polo
W: Basketball, Cross Country,
  Golf, Tennis, Track & Field,
  Softball Swimming-Diving
  Volleyball

Los Angeles Baptist College
Newhall, CA 91321
M: (805) 259–3540 X. 13
W: (805) 259–3540 X. 13
Enrollment: A
4-year private
M: NAIA, NCCAA
W: NAIA
M: Baseball, Cross Country,
  Basketball, Soccer
W: Cross Country, Softball,
  Basketball, Volleyball

Los Angeles City College
855 North Vermont Avenue
Los Angeles, CA 90029
M: (213) 663–9141 X. 244
Enrollment: C
2-year public funding
M: Southern California
M: Baseball, Basketball, Cross
  Country, Football, Judo,
  Soccer, Tennis, Track & Field

Los Angeles Pierce Junior College
Woodland Hills, CA 91364
M: (213) 347–0551
W: (213) 347–0551
Enrollment: C
2-year public funding
M: Metropolitan
W: Metropolitan
M: Baseball, Basketball, Cross
  Country, Football, Golf,
  Soccer, Swimming-Diving,
  Tennis, Track & Field,
  Volleyball, Water Polo,
  Wrestling

W: Badminton, Basketball, Cross
   Country, Gymnastics,
   Softball, Swimming-Diving,
   Tennis, Track & Field,
   Volleyball

Los Angeles Southwest College
1600 West Imperial Highway
Los Angeles, CA 90047
M: (213) 777-2225 X. 275
W: (213) 777-2225 X. 209
Enrollment: C
2-year private
M: Southern California
W: Southern California
M: Baseball, Basketball, Cross
   Country, Football, Tennis,
   Track & Field
W: Cross Country, Track & Field,
   Volleyball

Louisiana College
Pineville, LA 71360
M: (318) 487-7322
W: (318) 487-7502
Enrollment: A
4-year private
M: NAIA
W: AIAW
M: Baseball, Basketball, Tennis
W: Basketball, Tennis

Louisiana State University
Baton Rouge, LA 70803
M: (504) 388-2187
W: (504) 388-8212
Enrollment: C
4-year public funding
M: SEC
W: AIAW
M: Baseball, Basketball, Cross
   Country, Football, Golf,

Gymnastics, Swimming-
Diving, Tennis, Track &
Field, Wrestling
W: Basketball, Cross Country,
   Golf, Gymnastics, Softball,
   Swimming-Diving, Track &
   Field, Volleyball

Louisiana Tech University
Ruston, LA 71270
M: (318) 257-3144
W: (318) 257-2404
Enrollment: C
4-year public funding
M: Southland
W: AIAW
M: Power Lifting, Soccer,
   Baseball, Basketball, Cross
   Country, Football, Golf,
   Riflery, Tennis, Track &
   Field, Volleyball
W: Basketball, Softball, Tennis

University of Louisville
Louisville, KY 40208
M: (502) 588-5732
W: (502) 588-5577
Enrollment: C
4-year public funding
M: Metro
W: KWIC
M: Soccer, Baseball, Basketball,
   Cross Country, Football,
   Golf, Swimming-Diving,
   Tennis, Track & Field
W: Basketball, Cross Country,
   Field Hockey, Gymnastics,
   Softball, Tennis, Track &
   Field, Volleyball

University of Lowell
Lowell, MA 01854

M: (617) 452–5000 X. 2370
W: (617) 452–5000 X. 2461
Enrollment: C
4-year public funding
M: Independent
W: EIAW, MAIAW
M: Bowling, Crew, Football, Golf, Skiing, Squash, Tennis, Baseball, Basketball, Cross Country, Gymnastics, Ice Hockey, Lacrosse, Soccer, Swimming-Diving, Track & Field, Wrestling
W: Bowling, Crew, Swimming-Diving, Track & Field, Basketball, Cross Country, Field Hockey, Softball, Tennis, Volleyball

Lower Columbia College
1600 Maple
Longview, WA 98632
M: (206) 577–2306
W: (206) 577–2306
Enrollment: A
2-year public funding
M: AACC
W: AACC
M: Baseball, Basketball, Golf
W: Basketball, Tennis, Volleyball

Scholarships are awarded to students from Washington, Oregon, Idaho, and British Columbia by conference rule.

Loyola Marymount University
Los Angeles, CA 90045
M: (213) 642–3328
W: (213) 642–2765
Enrollment: B
4-year private
M: West Coast
W: Pacific Coast
M: Crew, Cross Country, Golf, Rugby, Soccer, Swimming-Diving, Tennis, Volleyball, Water Polo, Baseball, Basketball
W: Cross Country, Swimming-Diving, Basketball, Crew, Softball, Tennis, Volleyball

Lubbock Christian College
5601 West 19th
Lubbock, TX 79407
M: (806) 792–3221
W: (806) 792–3221
Enrollment: A
4-year private
M: TIAA
W: TIAA
M: Basketball, Football, Tennis, Baseball
W: Basketball, Tennis, Volleyball

Luther College
Decorah, IA 52101
M: (319) 387–1245
W: (319) 387–1245
Enrollment: A
4-year private
M: Iowa Conference
W: Iowa Conference
M: Baseball, Basketball, Cross Country, Football, Golf, Swimming-Diving, Tennis, Track & Field, Wrestling
W: Basketball, Cross Country, Field Hockey, Softball, Swimming-Diving, Tennis, Track & Field, Volleyball

Lycoming College
Williamsport, PA 17701

M: (717) 326–1951
W: (717) 326–1951
Enrollment: A
4-year private
M: MAC, ECAC, NCAA
W: MAC
M: Archery, Basketball, Football, Golf, Soccer, Swimming-Diving, Tennis, Track & Field, Wrestling
W: Archery, Basketball, Field Hockey, Golf, Swimming-Diving, Tennis, Track & Field

All aid for men and women is based on financial need.

Lynchburg College
Lynchburg, VA 24504
M: (804) 845–9071 X. 234
W: (804) 845–9071 X. 234
Enrollment: A
4-year private
M: ODAC, NCAA
W: AIAW
M: Baseball, Basketball, Cross Country, Golf, Lacrosse, Soccer, Tennis, Track & Field, Wrestling
W: Basketball, Cross Country, Fencing, Field Hockey, Lacrosse, Tennis, Track & Field, Volleyball

Lyndon State College
Lyndonville, VT 05851
M: (802) 626–9371
W: (802) 626–9371
Enrollment: A
4-year public funding
M: May Flower, NCAA, NAIA
W: AIAW
M: Baseball, Basketball, Cross Country, Lacrosse, Skiing, Soccer, Tennis
W: Basketball, Cross Country, Field Hockey, Skiing, Soccer, Softball

Macalester College
St. Paul, MI 55105
M: (612) 647–6267
W: (612) 647–6167
Enrollment: A
4-year private
M: MIAC
W: MAIAW
M: Baseball, Basketball, Cross Country, Football, Golf, Soccer, Swimming-Diving, Tennis, Track & Field
W: Basketball, Cross Country, Softball, Swimming-Diving, Tennis, Track & Field, Volleyball

McKendree College
701 College Road
Lebanon, IL 62254
M: (618) 537–4184
W: (618) 537–4184
Enrollment: A
4-year public funding
M: Independent
W: Independent
M: <u>Baseball</u>, <u>Basketball</u>, <u>Golf</u>, <u>Soccer</u>
W: <u>Basketball</u>, <u>Softball</u>, <u>Volleyball</u>

McMurry College
South 14th and Sayles
Abilene, TX 79605
M: (915) 692–4130 X. 274
W: (915) 692–4130 X. 274
Enrollment: A

4-year private
M: TIAA
W: TIAA
M: Basketball, Football, Golf, Tennis, Track & Field
W: Basketball, Golf, Tennis, Track & Field, Volleyball

McNeese State University
Lake Charles, LA 70601
M: (318) 477–2520
W: (318) 477–2520
Enrollment: C
4-year public funding
M: Southland
W: LAIAW
M: Baseball, Basketball, Cross Country, Football, Golf, Tennis, Track & Field
W: Basketball, Softball, Tennis, Volleyball

McPherson College
McPherson, KS 67460
M: (316) 241–0731 X. 70
W: (316) 241–0731 X. 70
Enrollment: A
4-year private
M: KCAC
W: KCAC
M: Basketball, Cross Country, Football, Golf, Tennis, Track & Field
W: Basketball, Cross Country, Golf, Tennis, Track & Field, Volleyball

University of Maine
Farmington, ME 04938
M: (207) 778–3501
W: (207) 778–3501
Enrollment: A

4-year public funding
M: Western Maine
W: MAIAW
M: Baseball, Basketball, Golf, Skiing, Soccer
W: Basketball, Field Hockey, Gymnastics, Skiing, Volleyball

University of Maine
Fort Kent, ME 04743
M: (207) 834–3162
W: (207) 834–3162
Enrollment: A
4-year public funding
M: NAIA
W: MAIAW
M: Basketball, Soccer
W: Basketball, Volleyball

University of Maine
Presque Isle, ME 04769
M: (207) 764–0311
W: (207) 764–0311
Enrollment: A
4-year public funding
M: NCC, NECC
W: MAIAW
M: Baseball, Basketball, Cross County, Soccer, Wrestling
W: Basketball, Cross Country, Field Hockey, Gymnastics, Tennis, Volleyball

Maine Maritime Academy
Castine, ME 04421
M: (207) 326–4311
Enrollment: A
4-year public funding
M: NEFC, NCC, NCAA, NAIA
M: Cross Country, Football, Golf, Sailing, Soccer

Malone College
515 25th Street, NW
Canton, OH 44709
M: (216) 489-0800 X. 398
W: (216) 489-0800 X. 398
Enrollment: A
4-year private
M: MOC
W: MOC
M: Baseball, Basketball, Cross Country, Golf, Soccer, Tennis, Track & Field, Wrestling
W: Basketball, Tennis, Track & Field, Volleyball

Manchester College
North Manchester, IN 46962
M: (219) 982-2141 X. 285
Enrollment: A
4-year private
M: HBCC
M: Baseball, Basketball, Cross Country, Football, Golf, Soccer, Tennis, Track & Field, Volleyball, Wrestling

Manhattan College
Bronx, NY 10471
M: (212) 548-1400
W: (212) 548-1400
Enrollment: B
4-year private
M: NCAA, ECAC
W: AIAW, EAIAW, NYSAIAW
M: Baseball, Crew, Football, Golf, Soccer, Swimming-Diving, Tennis, Wrestling, Basketball, Cross Country, Track & Field
W: Softball, Volleyball, Basketball

Mankato State University
Mankato, MN 56001
M: (507) 389-6111
W: (507) 389-2018
Enrollment: C
4-year public funding
M: Northern Intercollegiate
W: Northern Sun
M: Baseball, Basketball, Cross Country, Football, Golf, Ice Hockey, Swimming-Diving, Tennis, Track & Field, Wrestling
W: Basketball, Cross Country, Golf, Gymnastics, Softball, Swimming-Diving, Tennis, Track & Field, Volleyball

Mansfield State College
Mansfield, PA 16933
M: (717) 662-4116
W: (717) 662-4293
Enrollment: A
4-year public funding
M: PSAC
W: PSAC
M: Baseball, Basketball, Cross Country, Football, Track & Field, Wrestling
W: Basketball, Field Hockey, Softball

Marietta College
Marietta, OH 45750
M: (614) 373-4643 X. 297
W: (614) 373-4643 X. 297
Enrollment: A
4-year private
M: OAC
W: OAC
M: Baseball, Basketball, Crew, Cross Country, Football,

Golf, Soccer, Tennis, Track & Field
W: Basketball, Crew, Cross Country, Field Hockey, Softball, Tennis, Track & Field, Volleyball

College of Marin
Kentfield, CA 94904
M: (415) 485–9580
W: (415) 485–9580
Enrollment: C
2-year public funding
M: Camino Norte
W: Camino Norte
M: Baseball, Basketball, Cross Country, Football, Golf, Soccer, Swimming-Diving, Tennis, Track & Field, Water Polo
W: Basketball, Cross Country, Softball, Swimming-Diving, Tennis, Track & Field, Volleyball, Water Polo

All aid for men and women is based on financial need.

Marion College
4201 South Washington
Marion, IN 46952
M: (317) 674–6901
W: (317) 674–6901
Enrollment: A
4-year private
M: NAIA, Mid-Central
W: AIAW
M: Baseball, Basketball, Cross Country, Golf, Soccer, Tennis, Track & Field
W: Baseball, Field Hockey, Track & Field, Volleyball

Marion Military Institute
Marion, AL 36756
M: (205) 683–9533
Enrollment: A
2-year private
M: Independent
M: Riflery, Baseball, Football, Golf, Tennis

Marist College
Poughkeepsie, NY 12601
M: (914) 471–3240 X. 302
W: (914) 471–3240 X. 302
Enrollment: A
4-year private
M: Big Apple, NCAA, ECAC
W: EAIAW, Hudson Valley
M: Crew, Cross Country, Football, Lacrosse, Soccer, Swimming-Diving, Tennis, Track & Field, Basketball
W: Crew, Swimming-Diving, Tennis, Track & Field, Volleyball, Basketball

Marquette University
1834 West Wisconsin Avenue
Milwaukee, WI 53233
M: (414) 224–7130
W: (414) 224–7707
Enrollment: C
4-year private
M: Independent
W: Independent
M: Golf, Basketball, Cross Country, Soccer, Tennis, Track & Field, Wrestling
W: Basketball, Cross Country, Tennis, Track & Field, Volleyball

Marshalltown Community College
Marshalltown, IA 50158
M: (515) 752-7106
W: (515) 752-7106
Enrollment: A
2-year public funding
M: Northern JUCO
W: Northern JUCO
M: Baseball, Basketball, Golf, Tennis
W: Basketball, Golf, Softball, Tennis

Marshall University
Huntington, WV 25701
M: (304) 696-5403
W: (304) 696-5403
Enrollment: C
4-year public funding
M: Southern
W: AIAW
M: Baseball, Basketball, Cross Country, Football, Golf, Riflery, Soccer, Swimming-Diving, Tennis, Track & Field, Wrestling
W: Basketball, Golf, Riflery, Softball, Tennis, Track & Field, Volleyball

Mars Hill College
Mars Hill, NC 28754
M: (704) 689-1219
W: (704) 689-1212
Enrollment: A
4-year private
M: South Atlantic Coast
W: AIAW
M: Baseball, Cross Country, Tennis, Track & Field, Basketball, Football
W: Softball, Track & Field, Basketball, Tennis, Volleyball

Martin College
Pulaski, TN 38478
M: (615) 363-7456
W: (615) 363-7456
Enrollment: A
2-year private
M: TJCAA
W: TJCAA
M: Baseball, Basketball, Golf, Tennis
W: Basketball, Golf, Softball, Tennis

Mary Baldwin College
Staunton, VA 24401
W: (703) 885-0811
Enrollment: A
4-year private
W: AIAW, VAIAW
W: Fencing, Golf, Riding, Swimming-Diving

Mary Hardin-Baylor College
Belton, TX 76513
M: (817) 939-5811 X. 238
W: (817) 939-5811 X. 239
Enrollment: A
4-year private
M: Big State
W: Big State
M: Baseball, Basketball, Golf, Tennis
W: Basketball, Tennis, Volleyball

Mary Holmes College
West Point, MS 39773
M: (601) 494-6820
W: (601) 494-6820
Enrollment: A
4-year private
M: NJCAA, NLCAA
W: NJCAA, NLCAA

M: Baseball, Basketball, Track &
   Field
W: Softball, Basketball, Track &
   Field

University of Maryland
Catonsville, MD 21228
M: (301) 455–2126
W: (301) 455–2126
Enrollment: C
4-year public funding
M: ECAC, NCAA
W: MAIAW, AIAW
M: Baseball, Cross Country,
   Soccer, Tennis, Track &
   Field, Basketball, Lacrosse
W: Cross Country, Field Hockey,
   Lacrosse, Tennis, Track &
   Field, Volleyball, Basketball,
   Gymnastics

University of Maryland
College Park, MD 20742
M: (301) 454–4705
W: (301) 454–4705
Enrollment: C
4-year public funding
M: Atlantic Coast
W: Atlantic Coast
M: Baseball, Basketball, Cross
   Country, Fencing, Football,
   Golf, Lacrosse, Soccer,
   Swimming-Diving, Tennis,
   Track & Field, Wrestling
W: Basketball, Cross Country,
   Field Hockey, Gymnastics,
   Lacrosse, Swimming-Diving,
   Tennis, Track & Field,
   Volleyball

Maryville College
Maryville, TN 37801
M: (615) 983–0640
W: (615) 983–0640
Enrollment: A
4-year private
M: ODAC
W: ODAC
M: Baseball, Basketball, Football,
   Soccer, Tennis, Track & Field
W: Basketball, Softball, Tennis,
   Volleyball

Mary Washington College
Fredericksburg, VA 22401
M: (703) 899–4327
W: (703) 899–4327
Enrollment: A
4-year public funding
M: NCAA, Independent
W: AIAW
M: Basketball, Cross Country,
   Golf, Soccer, Tennis, Track &
   Field
W: Basketball, Cross Country,
   Field Hockey, Golf, Lacrosse,
   Riding, Swimming-Diving,
   Tennis, Track & Field,
   Volleyball

Marywood College
Adams Ave.
Scranton, PA 18509
W: (717) 343–6521
Enrollment: A
4-year private
W: NPWIAA, EAIAW, AIAW
W: Basketball, Field Hockey,
   Softball, Tennis

University of Massachusetts
Amherst, MA 01002
M: (413) 545–2460
W: (413) 548–2460

Enrollment: C
4-year public funding
M: ECAC
W: ECAC, AIAW
M: Baseball, Cross Country, Golf, Gymnastics, Lacrosse, Skiing, Soccer, Swimming-Diving, Tennis, Track & Field, Wrestling, <u>Basketball, Football</u>
W: Cross Country, Field Hockey, Golf, Lacrosse, Skiing, Soccer, Softball, Swimming-Diving, Tennis, Track & Field, <u>Basketball, Gymnastics</u>

Massachusetts Institute of Technology
77 Massachusetts Avenue
Cambridge, MA 02139
M: (617) 253-4498
W: (617) 253-4498
Enrollment: C
4-year private
M: NCAA, ECAC, Greater Boston
W: AIAW, EAIAW, MAIAW
M: Baseball, Basketball, Crew, Cross Country, Fencing, Golf, Gymnastics, Lacrosse, Riflery, Sailing, Skiing, Soccer, Squash, Swimming-Diving, Tennis, Track & Field, Water Polo, Wrestling
W: Field Hockey, Softball, Volleyball

Massasoit Community College
290 Thatcher Street
Brockton, MA 02402
M: (617) 588-9100 X. 344
W: (617) 588-9100 X. 344
Enrollment: A

2-year public funding
M: MCCAC, NJCAA
W: NJCAA
M: Baseball, Basketball, Soccer, Tennis
W: Basketball, Softball, Tennis

Mattatuck Community College
640 Chase Parkway
Waterbury, CT 06702
M: (203) 757-9661 X. 250/264
W: (203) 757-9661 X. 250/264
Enrollment: A
2-year public funding
M: NJCAA, CCCAA
W: NJCAA, CCCAA
W: Baseball, Basketball, Cross Country, Golf, Tennis
W: Basketball, Golf, Softball, Tennis, Volleyball

Medger Evers College
1150 Carroll Street
Brooklyn, NY 11225
M: (212) 735-1930
W: (212) 735-1930
Enrollment: B
4-year public funding
M: NCAA, ECAC, CUNY
W: NYSAIAW
M: Basketball, Cross Country, Soccer, Track & Field
W: Cross Country, Track & Field, Volleyball

Memphis State University
Memphis, TN 38152
M: (901) 454-2331
W: (901) 454-2315
Enrollment: C
4-year public funding
M: Metro-7

W: AIAW
M: Handball, Racquetball,
   Weightlifting, Baseball,
   Basketball, Cross Country,
   Football, Golf, Gymnastics,
   Tennis, Track & Field
W: Handball, Racquetball,
   Basketball, Cross Country,
   Golf, Gymnastics, Tennis,
   Track & Field, Volleyball

Menlo College
Menlo Park, CA 94025
M: (415) 323-6141
W: (415) 323-6141
Enrollment: A
2-year private
M: Coast
W: Coast
M: Baseball, Basketball, Cross
   Country, Football, Golf,
   Soccer, Swimming-Diving,
   Tennis, Track & Field,
   Volleyball
W: Cross Country, Swimming-
   Diving, Tennis, Track &
   Field, Volleyball

Mercer University
1400 Coleman Avenue
Macon, GA 31207
M: (912) 745-6811 X. 335
W: (912) 745-6811 X. 335
Enrollment: A
4-year private
M: TAAC
W: AIAW, GAIAW
M: Golf, Soccer, Tennis, Baseball,
   Basketball
W: Tennis, Basketball

Mercer University
3000 Flowers Road South
Atlanta, GA 30341
M: (404) 451-0331
W: (404) 451-0331
Enrollment: A
4-year private
M: NAIA
W: AIAW
M: Baseball, Soccer
W: Track & Field

Mercy College
Dobbs Ferry, NY 10522
M: (914) 693-4500 X. 303
W: (914) 693-4500 X. 303
Enrollment: B
4-year private
M: NCAA
W: AIAW
M: Cross Country, Baseball,
   Basketball, Golf, Soccer,
   Tennis
W: Softball, Basketball, Volleyball

Meredith College
Hillsborough Street
Raleigh, NC 27611
W: (919) 833-6461 X. 309
Enrollment: A
4-year private
W: AIAW
W: Basketball, Golf, Softball,
   Tennis, Volleyball

Merrimack College
North Andover, MA 01845
M: (617) 683-7111 X. 251
W: (617) 683-7111 X. 252
Enrollment: A
4-year private
M: NCAA, ECAC

W: MAIAW
M: Baseball, Golf, Lacrosse,
   Tennis, Basketball, Ice
   Hockey
W: Golf, Tennis, Basketball

Metropolitan State College
1006 11th Street
Denver, CO 80204
M: (303) 629–8300 X. 3145
W: (303) 629–8300 X. 3145
Enrollment: C
4-year public funding
M: Independent NAIA
W: Independent NAIA
M: Baseball, Cross Country,
   Gymnastics, Soccer,
   Swimming-Diving, Tennis,
   Track & Field*
W: Basketball, Softball, Tennis,
   Volleyball*
*Tuition scholarships for instate
residents only

University of Miami
Coral Gables, FL 33124
M: (305) 284–3822
W: (305) 284–3244
Enrollment: C
4-year private
M: Independent
W: AIAW
M: Soccer, Baseball, Football,
   Golf, Swimming-Diving,
   Tennis
W: Softball, Basketball, Golf,
   Swimming-Diving, Tennis,
   Volleyball

Miami Christian University
2300 NW 135th Street
Miami, FL 33167
M: (305) 685–7431
W: (305) 685–7431
Enrollment: A
4-year private
M: NCCAA, FCCC
W: Independent
M: Basketball, Soccer, Tennis
W: Basketball, Softball, Volleyball

**Miami-Dade Community College
(New World Center)**
300 NE 2nd Avenue
Miami, FL 33132
M: (305) 577–6839
W: (305) 577–6839
Enrollment: C
2-year public funding
M: FCCAA
W: FCCAA
M: Baseball, Basketball, Cross
   Country, Golf, Soccer, Tennis
W: Basketball, Softball, Tennis,
   Volleyball

**Miami-Dade Community College
(South Campus)**
11011 SW 104th Street
Miami, FL 33176
M: (305) 596–1151
W: (305) 596–1151
Enrollment: C
2-year public funding
M: NJCAA, FCCAA
W: NJCAA, FCCAA
M: Baseball, Basketball, Golf,
   Soccer, Swimming-Diving,
   Tennis
W: Softball, Swimming-Diving,
   Tennis, Volleyball

Miami University
4200 East University Boulevard

Middletown, OH 45042
M: (513) 424-4444
W: (513) 424-4444
Enrollment: A
2-year public funding
M: ORCC
W: ORCC
M: Basketball, Golf, Tennis
W: Basketball, Tennis, Volleyball

Miami University
Oxford, OH 45056
M: (513) 529-3510
W: (513) 529-3300
Enrollment: C
4-year public funding
M: MAC
W: AIAW, MAIAW, OAISW, MAC
M: Baseball, Basketball, Cross Country, Football, Golf, Soccer, Swimming-Diving, Tennis, Track & Field, Volleyball, Wrestling
W: Basketball, Field Hockey, Softball, Swimming-Diving, Tennis, Track & Field, Volleyball

University of Michigan
1000 South State Street
Ann Arbor, MI 48104
M: (313) 763-1381
W: (313) 763-5399
Enrollment: C
4-year public funding
M: Big Ten
W: Big Ten
M: Baseball, Basketball, Cross Country, Football, Golf, Gymnastics, Ice Hockey, Swimming-Diving, Tennis, Track & Field, Wrestling
W: Basketball, Cross Country, Field Hockey, Golf, Gymnastics, Softball, Swimming-Diving, Synchronized Swimming, Tennis, Track & Field, Volleyball

Michigan Christian Junior College
800 West Avon Road
Rochester, MI 48063
M: (313) 656-1924
W: (313) 656-1924
Enrollment: A
2-year private
M: NCCAC
W: NCCAC
M: Baseball, Basketball, Cross Country, Tennis
W: Basketball, Cross Country, Softball, Tennis

Michigan State University
East Lansing, MI 48824
M: (517) 355-2271
W: (517) 355-2271
Enrollment: C
4-year public funding
M: Big Ten
W: AIAW
M: Fencing, Baseball, Basketball, Cross Country, Football, Golf, Gymnastics, Ice Hockey, Lacrosse, Soccer, Swimming-Diving, Tennis, Track & Field, Wrestling
W: Basketball, Cross Country, Field Hockey, Golf, Gymnastics, Softball, Swimming-Diving, Tennis, Track & Field, Volleyball

Middlebury College
Middlebury, VT 05753
M: (802) 388-7923
W: (802) 388-7751
Enrollment: A
4-year private
M: ECAC, NESCAC
W: NESCAC
M: Baseball, Basketball, Cross Country, Football, Golf, Ice Hockey, Lacrosse, Skiing, Soccer, Tennis, Track & Field
W: Basketball, Cross Country, Field Hockey, Lacrosse, Skiing, Soccer, Squash, Swimming-Diving, Tennis, Track & Field

Middle Tennessee State University
Murfreesboro, TN 37132
M: (615) 898-2450
W: (615) 898-2450
Enrollment: C
4-year public funding
M: Ohio Valley
W: AIAW
M: Baseball, Basketball, Cross Country, Football, Golf, Tennis, Track & Field
W: Basketball, Cross Country, Tennis, Track & Field, Volleyball

Mid-Plains Community College
North Platte, NE 69101
M: (308) 532-8980
W: (308) 532-8980
Enrollment: A
2-year public funding
M: NCJC
W: NCJC
M: Basketball
W: Basketball, Volleyball

Mid-State Technical Institute
500 32nd Street North
Wisconsin Rapids, WI 54494
M: (715) 423-5650 X. 267
W: (715) 423-5650 X. 267
Enrollment: A
2-year public funding
M: WTCC, WSCAA
W: WTCC, WSCAA
M: Basketball, Bowling, Golf, Tennis
W: Basketball, Bowling, Golf, Tennis, Volleyball

Midwest Christian College
6600 North Kelley
Oklahoma City, OK 73111
M: (405) 478-1326 X. 10
W: (405) 478-1326 X. 10
Enrollment: A
4-year private
M: TCCAC
W: TCCAC
M: Baseball, Basketball
W: Basketball, Softball

Midwestern State University
Wichita Falls, TX 76308
M: (817) 692-6611
W: (817) 692-6611
Enrollment: B
4-year public funding
M: TAC, NAIA
W: TAC, NAIA
M: Baseball, Basketball, Soccer, Tennis
W: Basketball, Tennis, Volleyball

Miles Community College
Miles City, MT 59301
M: (406) 232-3031
W: (406) 232-3031

Enrollment: A
4-year public funding
M: Mon-Dak, Empire
W: Mon-Dak, Empire
M: Basketball
W: Basketball

Milligan College
Milligan College, TN 37682
M: (615) 929–0116 X. 16
W: (615) 929–0116 X. 16
Enrollment: A
4-year private
M: NAIA, VSAC
W: TCWSF, AIAW
M: Baseball, Cross Country, Soccer, Tennis, Track & Field, Basketball
W: Softball, Tennis, Volleyball, Basketball

Millikin University
1184 West Main
Decatur, IL 62522
M: (217) 424–6344
W: (217) 424–6344
Enrollment: A
4-year private
M: CCIW
W: AIAW
M: Baseball, Basketball, Cross Country, Football, Golf, Sailing, Swimming-Diving, Tennis, Track & Field, Volleyball, Wrestling
W: Basketball, Tennis, Track and Field, Volleyball

Division III: all aid awarded on the basis of financial need.

Mills College
MacArthur Boulevard
Oakland, CA 94613
W: (415) 632–2700 X. 318
Enrollment: A
4-year private
W: Redwood Coast, AIAW
W: Basketball, Crew, Tennis, Volleyball

Millsaps College
Jackson, MS 39210
M: (601) 354–5201
W: (601) 354–5201
Enrollment: A
4-year private
M: NCAA, Independent
W: AIAW, Independent
M: Baseball, Basketball, Football, Tennis
W: Basketball, Tennis

All aid for men and women is based on financial need.

Milwaukee Area Technical College
1015 North 6th Street
Milwaukee, WI 53203
M: (414) 278–6448
W: (414) 278–6448
Enrollment: C
2-year public funding
M: WTCC, WJCAA, NJCAA
W: WTCC, WJCAA, NJCAA
M: Baseball, Basketball, Bowling, Cross Country, Fencing, Golf, Soccer, Tennis, Track & Field
W: Basketball, Bowling, Cross Country, Fencing, Softball, Tennis, Track & Field, Volleyball

Milwaukee School of Engineering
1025 North Milwaukee Street
Milwaukee, WI 53201

M: (414) 277-7153
W: (414) 277-7153
Enrollment: A
4-year private
M: WICA
W: WICA
M: Baseball, Basketball, Golf
W: Volleyball

Mineral Area Junior College
Flat River, MO 63601
M: (314) 431-4593
W: (314) 431-4593
Enrollment: A
2-year public funding
M: NJCAA
W: NJCAA
M: Baseball, Basketball, Tennis
W: Basketball, Tennis, Volleyball

University of Minnesota
Minneapolis, MN 55455
M: (612) 373-4210
W: (612) 373-2255
Enrollment: C
4-year public funding
M: Big Ten
W: AIAW
M: Baseball, Basketball, Cross Country, Football, Golf, Gymnastics, Ice Hockey, Swimming-Diving, Tennis, Track & Field, Wrestling
W: Basketball, Cross Country, Field Hockey, Golf, Gymnastics, Softball, Swimming-Diving, Tennis, Track & Field, Volleyball

University of Minnesota
Morris, MN 56267
M: (612) 589-2211
W: (612) 589-2211

Enrollment: A
4-year public funding
M: NICC
W: Northern Sun
M: Baseball, Basketball, Football, Golf, Tennis, Track & Field, Wrestling
W: Basketball, Golf, Tennis, Track & Field, Volleyball

Minnesota Bible College
920 Mayowood Road, SW
Rochester, MN 55901
M: (507) 288-4563
W: (507) 288-4563
Enrollment: A
4-year private
M: NICCC
W: NICCC
M: Basketball, Golf, Softball, Tennis, Volleyball
W: Softball, Volleyball

University of Minnesota Technical College
Waseca, MN 56093
M: (507) 835-1000
W: (507) 835-1000
Enrollment: A
2-year public funding
M: MCCAA
W: MCCWAA
M: Basketball, Cross Country, Football, Golf, Track & Field, Wrestling
W: Basketball, Cross Country, Softball, Track & Field, Volleyball

Mira Costa College
Oceanside, CA 92054
M: (714) 757-2121
W: (714) 757-2121

Enrollment: A
2-year public funding
M: Desert-Mission
W: Desert-Mission
M: Baseball, Basketball, Cross Country, Football, Tennis, Track & Field
W: Basketball, Cross Country, Softball, Tennis, Track & Field, Volleyball

Mississippi College
Clinton, MS 39058
M: (601) 924–5131 X. 239
W: (601) 924–5131 X. 356
Enrollment: B
4-year private
M: Gulf South
W: AIAW
M: Baseball, Basketball, Cross Country, Football, Golf, Tennis, Track & Field
W: Basketball, Cross Country, Softball, Tennis, Track & Field

Mississippi State University
Starkville, MS 39762
M: (601) 325–3230
W: (601) 325–3231
Enrollment: C
4-year public funding
M: Southeastern
W: MAIAW
M: Riflery, Baseball, Basketball, Cross Country, Football, Golf, Tennis, Track & Field
W: Riflery, Basketball, Golf, Softball, Tennis, Volleyball

University of Missouri
321 Hearnes
Columbia, MO 65201
M: (314) 882–6501
W: (314) 882–6501
Enrollment: C
4-year public funding
M: Big Eight
W: AIAW
M: Baseball, Basketball, Cross Country, Football, Golf, Swimming-Diving, Tennis, Track & Field, Wrestling
W: Basketball, Cross Country, Golf, Gymnastics, Softball, Swimming-Diving, Tennis, Track & Field, Volleyball

University of Missouri
Rolla, MO 65401
M: (314) 341–4175
W: (314) 341–4175
Enrollment: C
4-year public funding
M: MIAA
W: AIAW
M: Baseball, Cross Country, Riflery, Tennis, Track & Field, Wrestling, Basketball, Football, Soccer, Swimming-Diving
W: Softball, Tennis, Basketball

University of Missouri
8001 Natural Bridge
St. Louis, MO 63121
M: (314) 553–5641
W: (314) 553–5641
Enrollment: C
4-year public funding
M: MIAA
W: Independent
M: Cross Country, Golf, Swimming-Diving, Tennis, Baseball, Basketball, Soccer, Wrestling

W: Basketball, Field Hockey,
   Softball, Swimming-Diving,
   Tennis, Volleyball

Missouri Baptist College
12542 Conway
St. Louis, MO 63141
M: (314) 434–1115 X. 53
W: (314) 434–1115 X. 53
Enrollment: A
4-year private
M: Independent
W: Independent
M: Baseball, Basketball, Soccer
W: Softball, Volleyball

Missouri Southern State College
Joplin, MO 64801
M: (417) 624–8100
W: (417) 624–8100
Enrollment: B
4-year public funding
M: CSIC
W: CSIC
M: Golf, Soccer, Tennis, Baseball,
   Basketball, Football
W: Basketball, Softball, Tennis,
   Track & Field, Volleyball

Missouri Valley College
Marshall, MO 65340
M: (816) 886–6924 X. 118
W: (816) 886–6924 X. 118
Enrollment: A
4-year private
M: HAAC
W: HAAC
M: Baseball, Basketball, Football,
   Golf, Tennis, Track & Field
W: Basketball, Softball, Track &
   Field, Volleyball

Missouri Western College
4525 Downs Drive
St. Joseph, MO 64507
M: (816) 271–4481
W: (816) 271–4481
Enrollment: B
4-year public funding
M: CSIC
W: CSIC
M: Baseball, Basketball, Football,
   Golf, Tennis
W: Basketball, Softball, Tennis,
   Volleyball

Mitchell College
437 Pequot Avenue
New London, CT 06320
M: (203) 443–2811
W: (203) 443–2811
Enrollment: A
2-year private
M: NJCAA
W: NJCAA
M: Tennis, Baseball, Basketball,
   Soccer
W: Tennis, Basketball, Field
   Hockey, Softball

Mitchell Community College
West Broad Street
Statesville, NC 28677
M: (704) 873–2201
W: (704) 873–2201
Enrollment: A
2-year public funding
M: Western Tarheel
W: Western Tarheel
M: Basketball, Golf, Tennis
W: Basketball, Golf, Tennis

Monmouth College
Monmouth, IL 61462

M: (309) 457-2176
W: (309) 457-2176
Enrollment: A
4-year private
M: MCAC
W: MCAC
M: Baseball, Basketball, Cross Country, Football, Golf, Soccer, Swimming-Diving, Tennis, Track & Field, Wrestling
W: Basketball, Softball, Swimming-Diving, Tennis, Volleyball

All aid for men and women is based on financial need.

Monmouth College
West Long Branch, NJ 07764
M: (201) 222-6600 X. 321
W: (201) 222-6600 X. 321
Enrollment: B
4-year private
M: Big Apple
W: AIAW
M: Baseball, Basketball, Cross Country, Soccer, Swimming-Diving, Track & Field, Water Polo
W: Basketball, Field Hockey, Softball, Swimming-Diving

University of Montana
Missoula, MT 59801
M: (406) 243-5331
W: (406) 243-6485
Enrollment: C
4-year public funding
M: Big Sky
W: AIAW
M: Golf, Indoor Track, Tennis, Basketball, Cross Country, Football, Track & Field, Wrestling
W: Basketball, Cross Country, Gymnastics, Indoor Track, Swimming-Diving, Tennis, Track & Field, Volleyball

Montana State University
Bozeman, MT 59715
M: (406) 994-4226
W: (906) 994-3945
Enrollment: C
4-year public funding
M: Big Sky
W: NWAC
M: Basketball, Cross Country, Football, Skiing, Tennis, Track & Field, Wrestling
W: Basketball, Cross Country, Gymnastics, Skiing, Tennis, Track & Field, Volleyball

Montana Tech
Butte, MT 59701
M: (406) 496-4101
W: (406) 496-4101
Enrollment: A
4-year public funding
M: Frontier
W: Frontier
M: Basketball, Football
W: Basketball, Volleyball

Montclair State College
Upper Montclair, NJ 07043
M: (201) 893-5233
W: (201) 893-5251
Enrollment: C
4-year public funding
M: NJSC
W: NJAIAW
M: Baseball, Basketball, Cross

Country, Football, Golf,
Lacrosse, Soccer, Swimming-
Diving, Tennis, Track &
Field, Wrestling
W: Basketball, Cross Country,
Fencing, Field Hockey,
Gymnastics, Lacrosse,
Softball, Swimming-Diving,
Tennis, Track & Field

University of Montevallo
Montevallo, AL 35115
M: (205) 665–2521 X. 410
W: (205) 665–2521 X. 410
Enrollment: A
4-year public funding
M: Southern States, NAIA
W: AAIAW
M: Baseball, Basketball, Golf,
Tennis
W: Basketball, Tennis, Volleyball

Moorhead State University
Moorhead, MN 56560
M: (218) 236–2622
W: (218) 236–2445
Enrollment: C
4-year public funding
M: Independent
W: Northern Sun
M: Baseball, Cross Country, Golf,
Tennis, Wrestling, Basketball,
Football, Track & Field
W: Basketball, Cross Country,
Field Hockey, Golf,
Gymnastics, Softball, Tennis,
Track & Field, Volleyball

Moorpark College
7075 Campus Road
Moorpark, CA 93021
M: (805) 529–2321 X. 220

Enrollment: C
2-year private
M: Independent
M: Baseball, Basketball, Cross
Country, Football, Golf,
Tennis, Track & Field,
Volleyball, Wrestling

Morehead State University
Morehead, KY 40351
M: (606) 783–3335
W: (606) 783–2270
Enrollment: C
4-year public funding
M: OVC
W: KWIC
M: Baseball, Basketball, Cross
Country, Football, Golf,
Tennis, Track & Field
W: Basketball, Cross Country,
Softball, Tennis, Track &
Field, Volleyball

Morehouse College
223 Chestnut Street, SW
Atlanta, GA 30314
M: (404) 681–2800 X. 347
Enrollment: A
4-year private
M: SIAC
M: Football, Baseball, Basketball,
Cross Country, Tennis, Track
& Field

Morgan State University
Coldspring Lane & Hillen Road
Baltimore, MD 21212
M: (301) 444–3050
W: (301) 444–3050
Enrollment: C
4-year public funding
M: Independent

W: Independent
M: Gymnastics, Basketball, Football, Lacrosse, Track & Field, Wrestling
W: Gymnastics, Basketball, Track & Field, Volleyball

Morningside College
1501 Morningside Avenue
Sioux City, IA 51106
M: (712) 277-5192
W: (712) 277-5192
Enrollment: A
4-year private
M: North Central
W: Io-Kota
M: Basketball, Golf, Baseball, Football, Track & Field
W: Golf, Basketball, Softball, Volleyball

Motlow State Community College
Tullahoma, TN 37388
M: (615) 455-8511 X. 300
W: (615) 455-8511 X. 300
Enrollment: A
2-year public funding
M: TJCAA
W: TJCAA
M: Baseball, Basketball
W: Basketball, Softball

Mott Community College
1401 East Court Street
Flint, MI 48503
M: (313) 762-0419
W: (313) 762-0419
Enrollment: C
2-year private
M: NJCAA, MCCAA
W: NJCAA, MCCAA
M: Baseball, Basketball, Golf
W: Basketball, Softball, Volleyball

Mount Ida Junior College
777 Dedham Street
Newton Centre, MA 02159
W: (617) 969-7000 X. 148
Enrollment: A
2-year private
W: NJCAA
W: Basketball, Softball, Tennis, Volleyball

Mount Marty College
Yankton, SD 57078
M: (605) 668-1501
W: (605) 668-1501
Enrollment: A
4-year private
M: Independent
W: Independent
M: Basketball
W: Basketball, Softball, Volleyball

Mount Olive Junior College
Mount Olive, NC 28365
M: (919) 658-2502
W: (919) 658-2502
Enrollment: A
2-year private
M: Eastern Tarheel
W: Independent
M: Baseball, Basketball, Golf, Tennis
W: Basketball, Softball

Mount St. Mary's College
Emmitsburg, MD 21727
M: (301) 447-6122 X. 296
W: (301) 447-6122 X. 296
Enrollment: A
4-year private
M: ECAC, NCAA, Mason-Dixon
W: AIAW, EAIAW, MAIAW
M: Baseball, Golf, Lacrosse, Riflery, Basketball, Cross

Country, Soccer, Tennis,
Track & Field
W: Field Hockey, Golf, Riflery,
Softball, Basketball, Cross
Country, Tennis, Track &
Field

Mount San Jacinto College
San Jacinto, CA 92383
M: (714) 654–7321 X. 251
W: (714) 654–7321 X. 251
Enrollment: A
2-year public funding
M: Desert
W: Desert
M: Baseball, Basketball, Football,
Tennis
W: Basketball, Tennis, Volleyball

College of Mount St. Joseph-on-the-Ohio
Mount St. Joseph, OH 45051
W: (513) 244–4311
Enrollment: A
4-year private
W: AIAW
W: Tennis, Track & Field,
Basketball, Volleyball

Mount Vernon College
Washington, DC 20007
W: (202) 331–3550
Enrollment: A
4-year private
W: Independent
W: Basketball, Field Hockey,
Lacrosse, Tennis

Muhlenberg College
Allentown, PA 18104
M: (215) 433–3191
W: (215) 433–3191

Enrollment: A
4-year private
M: Middle Atlantic
W: Middle Atlantic
M: Baseball, Basketball, Cross
Country, Football, Golf,
Soccer, Tennis, Track &
Field, Wrestling
W: Basketball, Field Hockey,
Softball, Tennis, Volleyball

Murray State University
Murray, KY 42071
M: (502) 762–6184
W: (502) 762–3808
Enrollment: C
4-year public funding
M: Ohio Valley
W: KWIC, Ohio Valley
M: Baseball, Basketball, Cross
Country, Football, Golf,
Riflery, Tennis, Track & Field
W: Volleyball, Basketball, Cross
Country, Riflery, Tennis,
Track & Field

Muskegon Community College
Quartek Line Road
Muskegon, MI 49443
M: (616) 777–0381
W: (616) 777–0381
Enrollment: B
2-year public funding
M: NJCAA, MCCAA
W: NJCAA, MCCAA
M: Basketball, Golf, Wrestling
W: Basketball, Tennis, Volleyball

Napa Community College
2277 Napa-Vallajo Highway
Napa, CA 94558
M: (707) 255–2100 X. 303
W: (707) 255–2100 X. 303

Enrollment: C
2-year public funding
M: Camino Norte
W: Camino Norte
M: Baseball, Basketball, Cross Country, Football, Golf, Swimming-Diving, Tennis, Track & Field
W: Cross Country, Gymnastics, Softball, Swimming-Diving, Tennis, Track & Field, Volleyball

All aid for men and women is based on financial need.

National College
321 Kansas City Street, Box 1780
Rapid City, SD 57709
M: (605) 394–4980
W: (605) 394–4980
Enrollment: A
4-year private
M: NLCAA
W: Independent
M: Basketball, Rodeo
W: Basketball, Volleyball, Rodeo

Nazareth College
Rochester, NY 14610
M: (716) 586–2525
W: (716) 586–2525
Enrollment: A
4-year private
M: PCAC, ECAC, NAIA, NCAA
W: PCAC, NYSAIAW, EAIAW, AIAW
M: Basketball, Cross Country, Golf, Soccer, Swimming-Diving, Tennis
W: Basketball, Cross Country, Golf, Swimming-Diving, Tennis, Volleyball

University of Nebraska
Lincoln, Nebraska 68508
M: (402) 472–2263
W: (402) 472–2263
Enrollment: C
4-year public funding
M: Big 8
W: Big 8
M: Cross Country, Baseball, Basketball, Football, Golf, Gymnastics, Swimming-Diving, Tennis, Track & Field, Wrestling
W: Basketball, Cross Country, Golf, Gymnastics, Softball, Swimming-Diving, Tennis, Track & Field, Volleyball

University of Nebraska
Omaha, NE 68101
M: (402) 554–2305
W: (402) 554–2300
Enrollment: C
4-year public funding
M: North Central
W: North Central
M: Baseball, Basketball, Cross Country, Football, Track & Field, Wrestling
W: Basketball, Cross Country, Softball, Track & Field, Volleyball

Nebraska Wesleyan University
50th and St. Paul Streets
Lincoln, NE 68504
M: (402) 466–2371
W: (402) 466–2371
Enrollment: A
4-year private
M: NIAC
W: NIAC
M: Baseball, Basketball, Cross

Country, Football, Golf,
Tennis, Track & Field,
Wrestling
W: Basketball, Cross Country,
Golf, Softball, Tennis, Track
& Field, Volleyball

Newberry College
Newberry, SC 29108
M: (803) 276-5010
W: (803) 276-5010
Enrollment: A
4-year private
M: NAIA, SAC-8
W: AIAW
M: Golf, Soccer, Tennis, Baseball,
Basketball, Football
W: Tennis, Basketball, Softball,
Volleyball

New Castle Business College
316 Rhodes Place
New Castle, PA 16101
M: (716) 884-9120
Enrollment: A
2-year private
M: NLCAA
M: Basketball

New Hampshire College
Manchester, NH 03104
M: (603) 668-2211 X. 260
W: (603) 668-2211 X. 260
Enrollment: A
4-year private
M: NCAA, ECAC
W: NCAA, AIAW
M: Baseball, Golf, Ice Hockey,
Lacrosse, Skiing, Soccer,
Tennis, Basketball
W: Field Hockey, Skiing, Softball,
Tennis, Volleyball, Basketball

New Hampshire Technical Institute
Concord, NH 03301
M: (603) 271-2531
W: (603) 271-2531
Enrollment: A
2-year public funding
M: NNESCC
W: Independent
M: Baseball, Basketball, Golf,
Skiing, Soccer, Tennis,
Volleyball
W: Basketball, Skiing, Softball,
Tennis, Volleyball

University of New Haven
300 Orange Avenue
West Haven, CT 06516
M: (203) 934-6321 X. 201
W: (203) 934-6321 X. 201
Enrollment: A
4-year private
M: ECAC, NCAA
W: EAIAW, AIAW
M: Tennis, Baseball, Basketball,
Cross Country, Football, Ice
Hockey, Lacrosse, Soccer,
Track & Field
W: Tennis, Basketball, Softball,
Volleyball

New Mexico Highlands University
Las Vegas, NM 87701
M: (505) 425-7511 X. 351
W: (505) 425-7511 X. 287
Enrollment: A
4-year public funding
M: RMAC
W: RMAC, AIAW
M: Baseball, Basketball, Cross
Country, Football, Golf,
Wrestling
W: Basketball, Softball, Tennis,
Volleyball

New Mexico Junior College
Lovington Highway
Hobbs, NM 88240
M: (505) 392-6526
Enrollment: A
2-year public funding
M: WJCAC
M: Basketball, Cross Country,
   Golf, Gymnastics, Rodeo,
   Track & Field

New Mexico Military Institute
Roswell, NM 88201
M: (505) 622-6250 X. 261
Enrollment: A
2-year public funding
M: WJCA, NJCAA
M: Basketball, Football, Golf,
   Tennis

University of New Orleans
Lake Front
New Orleans, LA 70122
M: (504) 283-0230
M: (504) 283-0230
Enrollment: C
4-year public funding
M: Independent
W: Independent
M: Cross Country, Soccer,
   Baseball, Basketball, Golf,
   Tennis
W: Cross Country, Basketball,
   Softball, Tennis, Volleyball

**State University College
   of New York**
Brockport, NY 14420
M: (716) 395-2763
W: (716) 395-2763
Enrollment: C
4-year public funding
M: SUNYAC
W: Independent
M: Basketball, Football, Ice
   Hockey, Soccer, Track &
   Field, Wrestling
W: Basketball, Field Hockey,
   Gymnastics, Softball,
   Swimming-Diving, Track &
   Field, Volleyball

**State University College
   of New York**
Fredonia, NY 14063
M: (716) 673-3102
W: (716) 673-3107
Enrollment: B
4-year public funding
M: SUNYAC, ECAC, NCAA
W: NYSIAW, AAIAW
M: Baseball, Basketball, Cross
   Country, Soccer, Swimming-
   Diving, Tennis, Track & Field
W: Basketball, Tennis, Track &
   Field, Volleyball

**State University College
   of New York**
Genesco, NY 14454
M: (716) 245-5516
W: (716) 245-5516
Enrollment: C
4-year public funding
M: SUNYAC
W: AIAW, NYSAIAW
M: Basketball, Cross Country,
   Lacrosse, Soccer, Swimming-
   Diving, Track & Field
W: Basketball, Cross Country,
   Softball, Swimming-Diving,
   Synchronized Swimming,
   Track & Field

**State University College
of New York**
New Paltz, NY 12561
M: (914) 257-2483
W: (914) 257-2487
Enrollment: C
4-year public funding
M: NCAA, ECAC, CACC
W: NYSAIAW
M: Baseball, Basketball, Cross
  Country, Fencing, Golf,
  Soccer, Swimming-Diving,
  Tennis, Track & Field,
  Volleyball
W: Basketball, Fencing,
  Gymnastics, Softball,
  Swimming-Diving, Tennis,
  Track & Field, Volleyball

Division III: all aid awarded on the basis of financial need.

**State University College
of New York**
Oneonta, NY 13820
M: (607) 431-3594
W: (607) 431-3597
Enrollment: C
4-year public funding
M: SUNYAC, ECAC, NCAA
W: AIAW
M: Baseball, Basketball, Cross
  Country, Gymnastics,
  Lacrosse, Soccer, Tennis,
  Wrestling
W: Basketball, Cross Country,
  Field Hockey, Lacrosse,
  Softball, Swimming-Diving,
  Tennis, Volleyball

**State University College
of New York**
Route 104
Oswego, NY 13126
M: (315) 341-2265
W: (315) 341-2265
Enrollment: C
4-year public funding
M: ECAC, SUNYAC
W: AIAW
M: Basketball, Cross Country,
  Fencing, Golf, Ice Hockey,
  Lacrosse, Soccer, Swimming-
  Diving, Tennis, Track &
  Field, Water Polo, Wrestling
W: Basketball, Bowling, Cross
  Country, Fencing, Field
  Hockey, Softball, Swimming-
  Diving, Track & Field,
  Volleyball

**State University College
of New York**
Plattsburgh, NY 12901
M: (518) 564-3141
W: (518) 564-3140
Enrollment: C
4-year public funding
M: SUNYAC, NCAA, ECAC
W: NYSAIAW
M: Basketball, Cross Country,
  Golf, Ice Hockey, Soccer,
  Tennis, Track & Field
W: Basketball, Field Hockey,
  Soccer, Tennis, Volleyball

**State University College
of New York**
Potsdam, NY 13676
M: (315) 268-3000
W: (315) 268-3000
Enrollment: B
4-year public funding
M: NCAA, ECAC, SUNYAC
W: NYSAIAW, EAIAW, AIAW

M: Basketball, Cross Country,
   Golf, Ice Hockey, Soccer,
   Tennis, Track & Field
W: Basketball, Field Hockey,
   Swimming-Diving, Tennis,
   Volleyball

**State University College
of New York**
Purchase, NY 10577
M: (914) 253–5026
W: (914) 253–5026
Enrollment: A
4-year public funding
M: NCAA
W: NYSAIAW, Hudson Valley
M: Basketball, Fencing, Soccer,
   Tennis, Ultimate Frisbee
W: Basketball, Fencing, Tennis

State University of New York
1400 Washington Avenue
Albany, NY 12222
M: (518) 457–4901
W: (518) 457–4901
Enrollment: C
4-year public funding
M: SUNYAC, NCAA
W: AIAW
M: Baseball, Basketball, Cross
   Country, Football, Lacrosse,
   Soccer, Swimming-Diving,
   Tennis, Track & Field,
   Wrestling
W: Basketball, Cross Country,
   Gymnastics, Softball,
   Swimming-Diving, Tennis,
   Track & Field

State University of New York
Vestal Parkway East
Binghamton, NY 13901
M: (607) 798–3962
W: (607) 798–2113
Enrollment: C
4-year public funding
M: SUNYAC, ECAC, NCAA
W: NYSAIAW, EAIAW, AIAW
M: Baseball, Basketball, Cross
   Country, Soccer, Swimming-
   Diving, Tennis, Track &
   Field, Wrestling
W: Basketball, Cross Country,
   Softball, Swimming-Diving,
   Tennis, Track & Field,
   Volleyball

Division III: all aid awarded on
the basis of financial need.

State University of New York
3435 Main Street
Buffalo, NY 14214
M: (716) 831–2939
W: (716) 831–2939
Enrollment: C
4-year public funding
M: SUNYAC
W: AIAW
M: Baseball, Basketball, Cross
   Country, Football, Golf,
   Soccer, Swimming-Diving,
   Tennis, Track & Field,
   Wrestling
W: Basketball, Bowling, Field
   Hockey, Softball, Swimming-
   Diving, Tennis, Track &
   Field, Volleyball

Division III: all aid awarded on
the basis of financial need.

**State University of New York,
College of Technology**
811 Court Street

Utica, NY 13502
M: (315) 792-3436
W: (315) 792-3436
Enrollment: A
4-year public funding
M: NAIA
W: NYSAIAW
M: Basketball, Soccer
W: Basketball, Softball

New York Institute of Technology
Old Westbury, NY 11568
M: (516) 686-7626
W: (516) 686-7626
Enrollment: B
4-year private
M: ECAC
W: AIAW
M: Football, Baseball, Basketball, Crew, Golf, Soccer, Tennis, Track & Field
W: Basketball, Softball, Track & Field, Volleyball

Niagara University
Niagara University, NY 14109
M: (716) 285-1212 X. 205
W: (716) 285-1212 X. 424
Enrollment: B
4-year private
M: ECAC, North I
W: NYSAIAW, EAIAW, AIAW
M: Golf, Ice Hockey, Martial Arts, Rugby, Tennis, Baseball, Basketball, Cross Country, Soccer, Swimming-Diving, Track & Field
W: Cross Country, Martial Arts, Rugby, Tennis, Track & Field, Basketball, Swimming-Diving, Volleyball

Nicholls State University
Thibodaux, LA 70301
M: (504) 446-8111
W: (504) 446-8111
Enrollment: B
4-year public funding
M: Independent
W: Independent
M: Riflery, Baseball, Basketball, Cross Country, Football, Golf, Tennis, Track & Field
W: Basketball, Softball, Tennis, Volleyball

Nichols College
Dudley, MA 01570
M: (617) 943-1560
W: (617) 943-1560
Enrollment: A
4-year private
M: NCAA, ECAC, NEIAA
W: MAIAW
M: Baseball, Basketball, Football, Golf, Soccer, Tennis, Track & Field
W: Basketball, Field Hockey, Softball, Track & Field

Norfolk State College
2401 Carprew Avenue
Norfolk, VA 23504
M: (804) 623-8373
W: (804) 623-8373
Enrollment: C
4-year public funding
M: CIAA
W: AIAW
M: Baseball, Basketball, Cross Country, Football, Track & Field, Wrestling
W: Basketball

North Adams State College
North Adams, MA 01247
M: (413) 664–4511
W: (413) 664–4511
Enrollment: A
4-year public funding
M: NCAA, ECAC, MSCC
W: Independent
M: Baseball, Basketball, Cross Country, Golf, Soccer, Tennis
W: Basketball, Cross Country, Field Hockey, Golf, Softball, Tennis, Volleyball

Division III: all aid awarded on the basis of financial need.

University of North Alabama
Florence, AL 36530
M: (205) 766–4100 X. 396
W: (205) 766–4100 X. 396
Enrollment: B
4-year public funding
M: Gulf South
W: AAIAW
M: Riflery, Baseball, Basketball, Football, Golf, Tennis
W: Basketball, Tennis, Volleyball

North Carolina Agricultural And Technical State University
312 North Dudley Street
Greensboro, NC 27411
M: (919) 379–7686
W: (919) 379–7687
Enrollment: C
4-year public funding
M: NCAA
W: AIAW
M: Baseball, Basketball, Cross Country, Football, Golf, Tennis, Track & Field, Wrestling

W: Basketball, Softball, Tennis, Track & Field, Volleyball

University of North Carolina
Asheville, NC 28801
M: (704) 253–6440
Enrollment: A
4-year public funding
M: Independent
W: Basketball, Soccer, Tennis

University of North Carolina
Chapel Hill, NC 27514
M: (919) 933–5411
W: (919) 933–5411
Enrollment: C
4-year public funding
M: Atlantic Coast
W: AIAW
M: Baseball, Basketball, Cross Country, Fencing, Football, Golf, Lacrosse, Soccer, Swimming-Diving, Tennis, Track & Field, Wrestling
W: Basketball, Cross Country, Fencing, Field Hockey, Golf, Gymnastics, Soccer, Softball, Swimming-Diving, Tennis, Track & Field, Volleyball

University of North Carolina
Charlotte, NC 28223
M: (704) 597–2354
W: (704) 597–2354
Enrollment: C
4-year public funding
M: Sun Belt
W: AIAW, NCAIAW
M: Baseball, Basketball, Cross Country, Golf, Soccer, Tennis
W: Basketball, Softball, Tennis, Volleyball

University of North Carolina
Greensboro, NC 27412
M: (919) 379–5231
W: (919) 379–5231
Enrollment: C
4-year public funding
M: NCAA, DIXIE
W: NCAIAW
M: Basketball, Golf, Soccer, Swimming-Diving, Tennis, Volleyball
W: Basketball, Field Hockey, Golf, Softball, Swimming-Diving, Tennis, Volleyball

University of North Carolina
Wilmington, NC 28401
M: (919) 791–4330
W: (919) 791–4330
Enrollment: B
4-year public funding
M: Independent
W: Independent
M: Cross Country, Baseball, Basketball, Golf, Soccer, Swimming-Diving, Tennis
W: Cross Country, Basketball, Golf, Softball, Swimming-Diving, Tennis, Volleyball

North Carolina State University
Raleigh, NC 27607
M: (919) 737–2101
W: (919) 737–2101
Enrollment: C
4-year public funding
M: Atlantic Coast
W: Atlantic Coast, NCAIAW
M: Baseball, Basketball, Cross Country, Fencing, Football, Golf, Gymnastics, Lacrosse, Riflery, Soccer, Swimming-Diving, Tennis, Track & Field, Wrestling
W: Basketball, Cross Country, Fencing, Gymnastics, Riflery, Softball, Swimming-Diving, Tennis, Track & Field, Volleyball

North Carolina Wesleyan College
Rocky Mount, NC 27801
M: (919) 442–7121
W: (919) 442–7121
Enrollment: A
4-year private
M: DIAC, NCAA
W: NCAIAW
M: Baseball, Basketball, Golf, Soccer, Tennis
W: Basketball, Softball, Track & Field

North Central College
30 North Brainard
Naperville, IL 60540
M: (312) 420–3470
W: (312) 420–3470
Enrollment: A
4-year private
M: CCIW
W: AIAW
M: Baseball, Basketball, Cross Country, Football, Golf, Soccer, Swimming-Diving, Tennis, Track & Field, Wrestling
W: Basketball, Cross Country, Softball, Swimming-Diving, Tennis, Track & Field, Volleyball

All aid for men and women is based on financial need.

University of North Dakota
Grand Forks, ND 58201
M: (701) 777-2234
W: (701) 777-2234
Enrollment: C
4-year public funding
M: North Central
W: North Central
M: Baseball, Cross Country, Golf, Gymnastics, Swimming-Diving, Tennis, Basketball, Football, Ice Hockey, Track & Field, Wrestling
W: Badminton, Cross Country, Golf, Gymnastics, Softball, Swimming-Diving, Tennis, Basketball, Field Hockey, Track & Field, Volleyball

North Dakota State University
Bottineau, ND 58318
M: (701) 278-2593
W: (701) 278-2593
Enrollment: A
2-year public funding
M: Mon-Dak, NJCAA
W: NJCAA, Sakakawea
M: Baseball, Basketball, Hockey
W: Track & Field, Basketball, Volleyball

North Dakota State University
Fargo, ND 58102
M: (701) 237-8981
W: (701) 237-8981
Enrollment: C
4-year public funding
M: North Central
W: North Central
M: Baseball, Golf, Swimming-Diving, Tennis, Basketball, Cross Country, Football, Track & Field, Wrestling

W: Gymnastics, Tennis, Basketball, Cross Country, Softball, Track & Field, Volleyball

Northeastern Illinois University
Chicago, IL 60625
M: (312) 583-4050 X. 480
W: (312) 583-4050 X. 480
Enrollment: C
4-year public funding
M: CCAC
W: AIAW
M: Baseball, Basketball, Cross Country, Football, Golf, Tennis
W: Basketball, Cross Country, Gymnastics, Softball, Tennis, Volleyball

Northeastern Oklahoma A & M College
Miami, OK 74354
M: (918) 542-8441
W: (918) 542-8441
Enrollment: B
2-year public funding
M: Bi-State
W: Bi-State
M: Baseball, Basketball, Football, Golf, Tennis, Track & Field, Wrestling
W: Basketball, Golf, Softball, Tennis, Track & Field

Northeast Louisiana University
700 University Avenue
Monroe, LA 71201
M: (318) 342-3100
W: (318) 342-3071
Enrollment: C
4-year public funding

M: TAC, Independent
W: AIAW
M: Baseball, Basketball, Cross
   Country, Football, Golf,
   Riflery, Soccer, Swimming-
   Diving, Tennis, Track & Field
W: Basketball, Softball,
   Swimming-Diving, Tennis,
   Track & Field, Volleyball

Northeast Mississippi Junior College
Booneville, MS 38829
M: (601) 728–7751 X. 240
W: (601) 728–7751 X. 240
Enrollment: A
2-year public funding
M: MJCC, NJCAA
W: MJCC, NJCAA
M: Basketball, Football
W: Basketball

Northern Arizona University
Flagstaff, AZ 86001
M: (602) 523–5353
W: (602) 523–5353
Enrollment: C
4-year public funding
M: Big Sky
W: Intermountain
M: Baseball, Basketball, Cross
   Country, Football, Indoor
   Track, Tennis, Track & Field,
   Wrestling
W: Basketball, Cross Country,
   Indoor Track, Softball,
   Tennis, Track & Field,
   Volleyball

University of Northern Colorado
Greeley, CO 80631
M: (303) 351–2522
W: (303) 351–2522
Enrollment: C
4-year public funding
M: Northcentral
W: Intermountain
M: Baseball, Basketball, Cross
   Country, Football, Golf,
   Gymnastics, Swimming-
   Diving, Tennis, Track &
   Field, Wrestling
W: Basketball, Cross Country,
   Field Hockey, Golf,
   Gymnastics, Softball,
   Swimming-Diving, Tennis,
   Track & Field, Volleyball

Northern Illinois University
De Kalb, IL 60115
M: (815) 753–1295
W: (815) 753–1408
Enrollment: C
4-year public funding
M: Mid-American
W: Mid-American
M: Baseball, Basketball, Cross
   Country, Football, Golf,
   Gymnastics, Soccer,
   Swimming-Diving, Tennis,
   Track & Field, Wrestling
W: Badminton, Basketball, Cross
   Country, Field Hockey, Golf,
   Gymnastics, Softball,
   Swimming-Diving, Tennis,
   Track & Field, Volleyball

University of Northern Iowa
Cedar Falls, IA 50613
M: (319) 273–2470
W: (319) 273–2470
Enrollment: C
4-year public funding
M: Mid-Continent
W: AIAW

M: Baseball, Cross Country, Golf,
Gymnastics, Swimming-
Diving, Tennis, Basketball,
Football, Track & Field,
Wrestling
W: Basketball, Cross Country,
Field Hockey, Golf,
Gymnastics, Softball,
Swimming-Diving, Tennis,
Track & Field, Volleyball

Northern Kentucky University
University Drive
Highland Heights, KY 41076
M: (606) 292-5193
W: (606) 292-5193
Enrollment: C
4-year public funding
M: Independent
W: KWIC
M: Baseball, Basketball, Cross
Country, Golf, Soccer, Tennis
W: Basketball, Softball, Tennis,
Volleyball

Northern Michigan University
Marquette, MI 49855
M: (906) 227-2107
W: (906) 227-2109
Enrollment: C
4-year public funding
M: Mid-Continent, CCHA
W: Independent
M: Cross Country, Skiing, Tennis,
Basketball, Football, Ice
Hockey, Wrestling
W: Basketball, Field Hockey,
Gymnastics, Swimming-
Diving, Volleyball

Northern Montana College
Havre, MT 59501

M: (406) 265-7821 X. 3227
W: (406) 265-7821 X. 3227
Enrollment: A
4-year public funding
M: Frontier
W: Frontier
M: Track & Field, Basketball,
Wrestling
W: Track & Field, Basketball,
Volleyball

Northern State College
Aberdeen, SD 57401
M: (605) 622-2488
W: (605) 622-2488
Enrollment: A
4-year public funding
M: NIC
W: Independent
M: Baseball, Basketball, Cross
Country, Football, Golf,
Tennis, Track & Field,
Wrestling
W: Basketball, Golf, Softball,
Tennis, Track & Field,
Volleyball

North Georgia College
Dahlonega, GA 30533
M: (404) 864-3391 X. 289
W: (404) 864-3391 X. 289
Enrollment: A
4-year public funding
M: GIAC
W: GIAC
M: Football, Swimming-Diving,
Track & Field, Volleyball,
Basketball, Riflery, Soccer,
Tennis
W: Swimming-Diving, Track &
Field, Basketball, Riflery,
Softball, Tennis, Volleyball

North Greenville College
Tigerville, SC 29688
M: (803) 895-1410
W: (803) 895-1410
Enrollment: A
2-year private
M: WCJCC
W: WCJCC
M: Baseball, Basketball, Tennis
W: Basketball, Volleyball

North Harris County College
2700 Thorne Drive
Houston, TX 77073
M: (713) 443-6640 X. 375
W: (713) 443-6640 X. 375
Enrollment: C
2-year public funding
M: NJCAA, Independent
W: NJCAA, Independent
M: Basketball, Tennis
W: Basketball, Tennis

North Idaho College
1000 West Garden
Coeur d'Alene, ID 83814
M: (208) 667-7422
W: (208) 667-7422
Enrollment: A
2-year public funding
M: NJCAA
W: NJCAA
M: Baseball, Basketball, Cross
   Country, Tennis, Track &
   Field, Wrestling
W: Basketball, Cross Country,
   Tennis, Track & Field,
   Volleyball

Northland College
Ashland, WI 54806
M: (715) 682-4531

W: (715) 682-4531
Enrollment: A
4-year private
M: NAIA, Independent
W: AIAW
M: Skiing, Soccer, Swimming-
   Diving, Basketball, Wrestling
W: Skiing, Soccer, Swimming-
   Diving, Basketball, Volleyball

Northland Community College
Highway One East
Thief River Falls, MN 56701
M: (218) 681-2181
W: (218) 681-2181
Enrollment: A
2-year public funding
M: Independent
W: Independent
M: Baseball, Basketball, Football,
   Golf, Tennis
W: Basketball, Golf, Softball,
   Tennis, Volleyball

North Texas State University
Denton, TX 76203
M: (817) 788-2278
W: (817) 788-2278
Enrollment: C
4-year public funding
M: Independent
W: AIAW
M: Basketball, Cross Country,
   Football, Golf, Soccer,
   Tennis, Track & Field
W: Basketball, Cross Country,
   Golf, Tennis, Track & Field,
   Volleyball

Northwest Christian College
Eugene, OR 97401
M: (503) 343-1641

191

W: (503) 343–1641
Enrollment: A
4-year private
M: PNCC
W: PNCC
M: Basketball
W: Volleyball

All aid for men and women is based on financial need.

Northwest College
Kirkland, WA 98033
M: (206) 822–8266
W: (206) 822–8266
Enrollment: A
4-year private
M: PNCC
W: PNCC
M: Basketball, Bowling, Golf, Soccer, Tennis
W: Basketball, Bowling, Tennis, Volleyball

Northwestern College
3003 North Snelling Avenue
Roseville, MN 55113
M: (612) 636–4840 X. 238
W: (612) 636–4840 X. 221
Enrollment: A
4-year private
M: TRCC, Upper Midwest
W: AIAW
M: Baseball, Basketball, Cross Country, Football, Golf, Soccer, Tennis, Track & Field, Wrestling
W: Basketball, Softball, Volleyball

Northwestern College
1300 Western Avenue
Watertown, WI 53094
M: (414) 261–0806
Enrollment: A
4-year private
M: Independent
M: Baseball, Basketball, Cross Country, Football, Golf, Tennis, Track & Field, Wrestling

Northwestern State University
Natchitoches, LA 71457
M: (318) 357–6466
Enrollment: C
4-year public funding
M: TAAC
M: Baseball, Basketball, Football, Golf, Tennis, Track & Field

Northwestern University
Evanston, IL 60201
M: (312) 492–3205
W: (312) 492–3204
Enrollment: C
4-year private
M: Big Ten, NCAA
W: AIAW, MAIAW, IAIAW
M: Fencing, Golf, Rugby, Soccer, Water Polo, Baseball, Basketball, Cross Country, Football, Swimming-Diving, Tennis, Track & Field, Wrestling
W: Fencing, Gymnastics, Basketball, Cross Country, Field Hockey, Softball, Swimming-Diving, Tennis, Track & Field, Volleyball

Northwest Missouri State University
Maryville, MO 64468
M: (816) 582–7141 X. 1306

W: (816) 582–7141 X. 1298
Enrollment: B
4-year public funding
M: MIAA
W: MAIA
M: Baseball, Basketball, Cross Country, Football, Track & Field, Wrestling
W: Basketball, Cross Country, Softball, Tennis, Track & Field, Volleyball

Northwest Nazarene College
Nampa, ID 83651
M: (208) 467–8876
W: (208) 467–8876
Enrollment: A
4-year private
M: Independent
W: Inland Valley
M: Baseball, Basketball, Cross Country, Golf, Soccer, Tennis, Track & Field, Wrestling
W: Basketball, Cross Country, Field Hockey, Tennis, Track & Field

Norwich University
Northfield, VT 05663
M: (802) 485–5011 X. 257
W: (805) 485–5011 X. 257
Enrollment: A
4-year private
M: ECAC, NCAA
W: ECAC, NCAA
M: Baseball, Basketball, Cross Country, Football, Gymnastics, Lacrosse, Riflery, Skiing, Soccer, Swimming-Diving, Track & Field, Wrestling
W: Basketball, Cross Country, Field Hockey, Gymnastics, Riflery, Skiing, Softball, Swimming-Diving, Track & Field

College of Notre Dame
4701 North Charles
Baltimore, MD 21210
M: (301) 435–0100 X. 232
Enrollment: A
4-year private
W: MAIAW
W: Lacrosse, Softball, Swimming-Diving, Tennis, Volleyball, Basketball

University of Notre Dame
Notre Dame, IN 46556
M: (219) 283–6107
W: (219) 283–6107
Enrollment: C
4-year private
M: Independent
W: Independent
M: Fencing, Lacrosse, Soccer, Swimming-Diving, Baseball, Basketball, Cross Country, Football, Golf, Tennis, Track & Field, Wrestling
W: Fencing, Basketball, Field Hockey, Swimming-Diving, Tennis, Volleyball

Oakland City College
Oakland City, IN 47660
M: (812) 749–4781 X. 47
W: (812) 749–4781 X. 47
Enrollment: A
4-year private
M: NLCAA, NAIA
W: NAIA
M: Tennis, Baseball, Basketball

W: Tennis, Basketball, Soccer, Volleyball

Oakland University
Rochester, MI 48063
M: (313) 377-3196
W: (313) 377-3196
Enrollment: C
4-year public funding
M: Great Lakes
W: Great Lakes
M: Baseball, Basketball, Cross Country, Golf, Soccer, Swimming-Diving, Tennis, Wrestling
W: Basketball, Golf, Softball, Swimming-Diving, Tennis, Volleyball

Oakton Community College
7900 Nagle
Marton Grove, IL 60053
M: (312) 967-5120
W: (312) 967-5120
Enrollment: C
2-year public funding
M: Skyway
W: Skyway
M: Basketball, Cross Country, Golf, Tennis, Track & Field, Wrestling
W: Cross Country, Gymnastics, Softball, Tennis, Volleyball

Oberlin College
Oberlin, OH 44074
M: (216) 775-8500
W: (216) 775-8500
Enrollment: B
4-year private
M: Ohio Athletic
W: OAISW

M: Baseball, Basketball, Cross Country, Football, Lacrosse, Soccer, Swimming-Diving, Tennis, Track & Field
W: Basketball, Cross Country, Field Hockey, Lacrosse, Swimming-Diving, Tennis, Track & Field, Volleyball

Occidental College
1600 Campus Road
Los Angeles, CA 90041
M: (213) 259-2608
W: (213) 259-2608
Enrollment: A
4-year private
M: SCIAC
W: SCIAC
M: Baseball, Basketball, Cross Country, Football, Golf, Soccer, Swimming-Diving, Tennis, Track & Field, Water Polo
W: Basketball, Cross Country, Swimming-Diving, Tennis, Track & Field, Volleyball

All aid for men and women is based on financial need.

Ohio Northern University
Ada, OH 45810
M: (419) 634-9921 X. 386
W: (419) 634-9921 X. 386
Enrollment: B
4-year private
M: OAC
W: AIAW
M: Baseball, Basketball, Cross Country, Football, Golf, Handball, Soccer, Softball, Squash, Swimming-Diving,

Tennis, Track & Field, Water
Polo, Wrestling
W: Handball, Softball, Squash,
Swimming-Diving, Tennis,
Track & Field, Volleyball,
Water Polo

Division III: all aid awarded on
the basis of financial need.

Ohio State University
410 West Woodruff
Columbus, OH 43210
M: (614) 422-7572
W: (614) 422-0637
Enrollment: C
4-year public funding
M: Big Ten, CCHA, NCAA
W: AIAW
M: Cross Country, Fencing,
Lacrosse, Riflery, Soccer,
Baseball, Basketball,
Football, Golf, Gymnastics,
Ice Hockey, Swimming-
Diving, Tennis, Track &
Field, Volleyball, Wrestling
W: Basketball, Cross Country,
Fencing, Field Hockey, Golf,
Gymnastics, Softball,
Swimming-Diving,
Synchronized Swimming,
Tennis, Track & Field,
Volleyball

Ohio University
Athens, OH 45701
W: (614) 594-5206/5031
Enrollment: C
4-year public funding
W: Ohio State
W: Basketball, Cross Country,
Field Hockey, Softball,
Swimming-Diving, Tennis,
Track & Field

Ohio Valley College
Parkersburg, WV 26101
M: (304) 485-7384
W: (304) 485-7384
Enrollment: A
2-year private
M: NJCAA
W: NJCAA
M: Baseball, Tennis, Basketball
W: Tennis

Ohio Wesleyan University
Delaware, OH 43015
M: (614) 369-4431 X. 500
W: (614) 369-4431 X. 500
Enrollment: A
4-year private
M: OAC
W: OAISW
M: Baseball, Basketball, Cross
Country, Football, Golf,
Lacrosse, Sailing, Soccer,
Swimming-Diving, Tennis,
Track & Field, Wrestling
W: Basketball, Bowling, Field
Hockey, Lacrosse, Sailing,
Softball, Swimming-Diving,
Tennis, Track & Field,
Volleyball

All aid for men and women is
based on financial need.

University of Oklahoma
180 West Brooks
Norman, OK 73019
M: (405) 325-3751
W: (405) 325-3751

Enrollment: C
4-year public funding
M: Big Eight
W: Big Eight
M: Baseball, Basketball, Football, Golf, Gymnastics, Swimming-Diving, Tennis, Track & Field, Wrestling
W: Basketball, Cross Country, Golf, Gymnastics, Softball, Swimming-Diving, Tennis, Track & Field, Volleyball

Oklahoma Baptist University
500 West University
Shawnee, OK 74801
M: (405) 275-2850 X. 2138
W: (405) 275-2850 X. 2138
Enrollment: A
4-year private
M: Sooner Athletic
W: Sooner Athletic
M: Baseball, Basketball, Tennis, Track & Field
W: Basketball, Softball, Volleyball

Oklahoma City University
Oklahoma City, OK 73106
M: (405) 521-5301
W: (405) 521-5301
Enrollment: B
4-year private
M: Midwestern City
W: Midwestern City
M: Baseball, Basketball, Golf, Tennis
W: Basketball, Softball, Tennis, Volleyball

University of Oklahoma College of Science and Arts
Chickasha, OK 73018
M: (405) 224-3140 X. 318
W: (405) 224-3140 X. 318
Enrollment: A
4-year public funding
M: Sooner Athletic
W: Sooner Athletic
M: Basketball, Golf, Tennis
W: Basketball, Golf, Tennis

Oklahoma State University
Stillwater, OK 74074
M: (405) 624-5733
W: (405) 624-5733
Enrollment: C
4-year public funding
M: Big-8
W: Big-8
M: Baseball, Basketball, Cross Country, Football, Golf, Tennis, Track & Field, Wrestling
W: Basketball, Cross Country, Golf, Gymnastics, Softball, Tennis, Track & Field, Volleyball

Old Dominion University
Norfolk, VA 23508
M: (804) 440-3375
W: (804) 44)-3375
Enrollment: C
4-year public funding
M: ECAC
W: AIAW
M: Sailing, Baseball, Basketball, Cross Country, Golf, Soccer, Swimming-Diving, Tennis, Track & Field, Wrestling
W: Basketball, Cross Country, Field Hockey, Lacrosse, Swimming-Diving, Tennis, Track & Field

Olivet College
Olivet, MI 49076
M: (616) 749–7657
W: (616) 749–7657
Enrollment: A
4-year private
M: MIAA
W: MIAA
M: Baseball, Basketball, Cross
   Country, Football, Golf,
   Soccer, Tennis, Track & Field
W: Basketball, Field Hockey,
   Softball, Tennis, Volleyball

All aid for men and women is based on financial need.

Olivet Nazarene College
Kankakee, IL 60901
M: (815) 939–5372
W: (815) 939–5372
Enrollment: A
4-year private
M: Northern Illinois
W: AIAW
M: Baseball, Basketball, Football,
   Soccer, Tennis, Track &
   Field, Wrestling
W: Basketball, Softball, Tennis,
   Volleyball

Olney Central College
Olney, IL 62450
M: (618) 395–4351
W: (618) 395–4351
Enrollment: A
2-year public funding
M: Independent
W: Independent
M: Baseball, Basketball, Golf,
   Tennis
W: Basketball, Softball, Tennis,
   Volleyball

Oral Roberts University
7777 South Lewis Avenue
Tulsa, OK 74102
M: (918) 492–6161 X. 2700
W: (918) 492–6161 X. 2700
Enrollment: B
4-year private
M: Midwestern City
W: AIAW
M: Baseball, Basketball, Cross
   Country, Golf, Tennis, Track
   & Field
W: Basketball, Gymnastics,
   Tennis, Volleyball

University of Oregon
Eugene, OR 97403
M: (503) 686–5464
W: (503) 686–3373
Enrollment: C
4-year public funding
M: PAC-10
W: Independent
M: Golf, Swimming-Diving,
   Tennis, Baseball, Basketball,
   Cross Country, Football,
   Gymnastics, Track & Field,
   Wrestling
W: Basketball, Cross Country,
   Field Hockey, Golf,
   Gymnastics, Softball,
   Swimming-Diving, Tennis,
   Track & Field, Volleyball

Oregon State University
Carvallis, OR 79331
M: (503) 754–2611
W: (503) 754–3015
Enrollment: C
4-year public funding
M: Pacific-10
W: NCWSA

M: Crew, Baseball, Basketball,
   Cross Country, Football,
   Golf, Track & Field,
   Wrestling
W: Crew, Tennis, Basketball,
   Cross Country, Golf,
   Gymnastics, Softball,
   Swimming-Diving, Track &
   Field, Volleyball

Oregon Technical Institute
Klamath Falls, OR 97601
M: (503) 882-6321 X. 233
W: (503) 882-6321 X. 432
Enrollment: A
4-year public funding
M: Evergreen
W: Independent
M: Baseball, Basketball, Football,
   Wrestling
W: Basketball, Softball, Volleyball

Oscar Rose Junior College
6420 SE 15th Street
Midwest City, OK 73110
M: (405) 733-7350
W: (405) 733-7350
Enrollment: C
2-year public funding
M: OJCC
W: OJCC
M: Baseball, Basketball, Tennis,
   Wrestling
W: Basketball, Tennis

Otero Junior College
La Junta, CO 81050
M: (303) 384-8721 X. 231
W: (303) 384-8721 X. 231
Enrollment: A
2-year public funding
M: NJCAA

W: NJCAA
M: Baseball, Basketball, Rodeo
W: Basketball, Rodeo, Volleyball

Ottawa University
Ottawa, KS 66067
M: (913) 242-5200
W: (913) 242-5200
Enrollment: A
4-year private
M: Heart of America
W: Heart of America
M: Basketball, Cross Country,
   Football, Soccer, Tennis,
   Track & Field
W: Basketball, Cross Country,
   Track & Field, Volleyball

Otterbein College
Westerville, OH 43081
M: (614) 890-3000 X. 653
W: (614) 890-3000 X. 653
Enrollment: A
4-year private
M: OAC
W: OAC, AIAW
M: Baseball, Basketball, Cross
   Country, Football, Golf,
   Tennis, Track & Field
W: Basketball, Bowling, Softball,
   Tennis, Track & Field,
   Volleyball

Division III: all aid awarded on
   the basis of financial need.

Ouachita Baptist University
410 Ouachita Street
Arkadelphia, AR 71923
M: (501) 246-4531 X. 181
W: (501) 246-4531 X. 181
Enrollment: A

4-year private
M: AIC
W: AWISA
M: Riflery, Soccer, Baseball,
  Basketball, Cross Country,
  Football, Golf, Swimming-
  Diving, Tennis, Track & Field
W: Basketball, Tennis, Volleyball

Oxford College of Emory University
Oxford, GA 30267
M: (404) 786–7051 X. 250
W: (404) 786–7051 X. 250
Enrollment: A
2-year private
M: GJCAA, NJCAA
W: GJCAA, NJCAA
M: Golf, Soccer, Tennis
W: Golf, Tennis

Oxnard College
Oxnard, CA 93030
M: (805) 488–0911
Enrollment: B
2-year private
M: Western State, SCC
M: Baseball, Basketball, Cross
  Country, Soccer, Tennis,
  Track & Field, Volleyball

College of the Ozarks
Clarksville, AR 72830
M: (501) 754–6544
W: (501) 754–6544
Enrollment: A
4-year private
M: Arkansas Intercollegiate
W: Independent
M: Baseball, Cross Country,
  Tennis, Track & Field,
  Basketball
W: Basketball

School of the Ozarks
Point Lookout, MO 65726
M: (417) 334–6411
W: (417) 334–6411
Enrollment: A
4-year private
M: OCC
W: Independent
M: Baseball, Basketball, Cross
  Country, Track & Field
W: Basketball, Swimming-Diving,
  Track & Field, Volleyball

Pace University
Pleasantville, NY 10570
M: (914) 769–3200
W: (914) 769–3200
Enrollment: B
4-year private
M: Knickerbocker, Big Apple,
  Metropolitan
W: Independent
M: Bowling, Cross Country,
  Fencing, Football, Golf,
  Soccer, Tennis, Baseball,
  Basketball
W: Fencing, Softball, Tennis,
  Volleyball, Basketball

University of the Pacific
Stockton, CA 95211
M: (209) 946–2471
W: (209) 946–2471
Enrollment: C
4-year private
M: PCAA
W: NCAC
M: Baseball, Basketball, Football,
  Golf, Soccer, Swimming-
  Diving, Tennis, Water Polo
W: Basketball, Field Hockey,
  Softball, Swimming-Diving,
  Tennis, Volleyball

Pacific Lutheran University
Tacoma, WA 98447
M: (206) 531–6900
W: (206) 531–6900
Enrollment: B
4-year private
M: Northwest
W: WCIC
M: Baseball, Basketball, Crew, Cross Country, Football, Golf, Skiing, Soccer, Swimming-Diving, Tennis, Track & Field, Water Polo, Wrestling
W: Basketball, Crew, Cross Country, Field Hockey, Skiing, Soccer, Softball, Swimming-Diving, Tennis, Track & Field, Volleyball

Pacific University
Forest Grove, OR 97116
M: (503) 357–6151 X. 376
W: (503) 357–6151 X. 376
Enrollment: A
4-year private
M: Northwest
W: WCIC
M: Baseball, Basketball, Bowling, Cross Country, Football, Golf, Handball, Soccer, Swimming-Diving, Tennis, Track & Field, Wrestling
W: Basketball, Bowling, Cross Country, Handball, Soccer, Softball, Swimming-Diving, Tennis, Track & Field, Volleyball

Paducah Community College
Paducah, KY 42001
M: (502) 442–6131
W: (502) 442–6131
Enrollment: A
2-year public funding
M: KJCAC
W: KJCAC
M: Baseball, Cross Country, Golf, Tennis, Basketball
W: Cross Country, Golf, Softball, Tennis, Basketball

Palm Beach Junior College
4200 Congress Avenue
Lake Worth, FL 33460
M: (305) 965–1616
W: (305) 965–1616
Enrollment: C
2-year public funding
M: NJCAA
W: NJCAA
M: Baseball, Basketball, Golf, Tennis
W: Golf, Softball, Tennis, Volleyball

Palomar Community College
San Marcos, CA 92069
M: (714) 744–1150
W: (714) 757–7550 X. 321
Enrollment: C
2-year public funding
M: Mission
W: Mission
M: Archery, Baseball, Basketball, Cross Country, Football, Golf, Soccer, Swimming-Diving, Tennis, Track & Field, Water Polo, Wrestling
W: Archery, Basketball, Cross Country, Field Hockey, Softball, Swimming-Diving, Tennis, Track & Field, Volleyball

Pan American University
1200 West University

Edinburg, TX 78539
M: (512) 381-2221
W: (512) 381-2221
Enrollment: C
4-year public funding
M: Soccer, Baseball, Basketball, Cross Country, Golf, Gymnastics, Tennis, Track & Field
W: Basketball, Gymnastics, Softball, Volleyball

Paris Junior College
Paris, TX 75460
M: (214) 785-7661
W: (214) 785-7661
Enrollment: A
2-year public funding
M: Texas Eastern
W: Texas Eastern
M: Baseball, Basketball, Golf, Tennis
W: Basketball, Tennis

Park College
Kansas City, MO 64152
M: (816) 741-2000
W: (816) 741-2000
Enrollment: A
4-year private
M: Ozark
W: Ozark
M: Volleyball, Baseball, Basketball, Cross Country, Soccer, Track & Field
W: Tennis, Basketball, Cross Country, Track & Field, Volleyball

Parkland College
2400 West Bradley Avenue
Champaign, IL 61820
M: (217) 351-2297
W: (217) 351-2297
Enrollment: C
2-year public funding
M: CIAC
W: CIAC
M: Baseball, Basketball, Cross Country, Golf, Track & Field
W: Basketball, Cross Country, Softball, Track & Field, Volleyball

Paul Smith's College
Paul Smiths, NY 12970
M: (518) 327-6285
W: (518) 327-6286
Enrollment: A
2-year private
M: NJCAA
W: NJCAA
M: Basketball, Skiing, Soccer, Wrestling
W: Basketball, Skiing, Softball, Volleyball

Peace College
Peace Street
Raleigh, NC 27604
W: (919) 832-2881 X. 242
Enrollment: A
2-year private
W: Independent
W: Basketball, Tennis

Pembroke State University
Pembroke, NC 28372
M: (919) 521-9481
W: (919) 521-9481
Enrollment: A
4-year public funding
M: Carolinas
W: Carolinas
M: Baseball, Basketball, Cross Country, Golf, Soccer,

Tennis, Track & Field,
   Wrestling
W: Basketball, Softball, Tennis,
   Volleyball

University of Pennsylvania
Philadelphia, PA 19104
M: (215) 243-6121
W: (215) 243-7438
Enrollment: C
4-year private
M: Ivy League
W: Ivy League
M: Baseball, Basketball, Crew,
   Cross Country, Fencing,
   Football, Golf, Gymnastics,
   Lacrosse, Sailing, Soccer,
   Squash, Swimming-Diving,
   Tennis, Track & Field,
   Volleyball, Wrestling
W: Badminton, Basketball, Crew,
   Cross Country, Fencing, Field
   Hockey, Gymnastics,
   Lacrosse, Sailing, Softball,
   Squash, Swimming-Diving,
   Tennis, Track & Field,
   Volleyball

Pennsylvania State University
Altoona, PA 16603
M: (814) 946-4321
W: (814) 946-4321
Enrollment: A
2-year public funding
M: SAC, NJCAA, PSC
W: SAC, NJCAA, PSC
M: Baseball, Basketball, Tennis,
   Wrestling
W: Basketball, Tennis, Volleyball

Pennsylvania State University
College Pace
DuBois, PA 15801

M: (716) 896-0700
W: (716) 896-0700
Enrollment: A
2-year public funding
M: Penn-York
W: Penn-York
M: Basketball
W: Softball, Volleyball

Pennsylvania State University
Mc Keesport, PA 15132
M: (412) 678-9501
W: (412) 678-9501
Enrollment: A
2-year public funding
M: CWC
W: CWC
M: Baseball, Basketball
W: Softball, Volleyball

Pennsylvania State University
Middletown, PA 17057
M: (717) 948-6267
W: (717) 948-6267
Enrollment: A
4-year public funding
M: NAIA
W: NAIA
M: Baseball, Bowling, Cross
   Country, Soccer
W: Softball, Volleyball

Penn State University
University Park, PA 16802
M: (814) 865-0413
W: (814) 865-0413
Enrollment: C
4-year public funding
M: Independent
W: Independent
M: Baseball, Basketball, Bowling,
   Cross Country, Fencing,
   Football, Golf, Gymnastics,

Indoor Track, Lacrosse,
Riflery, Soccer, Swimming-
Diving, Tennis, Track &
Field, Volleyball, Wrestling
W: Basketball, Bowling, Cross
Country, Fencing, Field
Hockey, Golf, Gymnastics,
Indoor Track, Lacrosse,
Riflery, Softball, Swimming-
Diving, Tennis, Track &
Field, Volleyball

**Pennsylvania State University
(Beaver Campus)**
Brodhead Road
Monaca, PA 15061
M: (412) 775-8830 X. 41
W: (412) 775-8830 X. 41
Enrollment: A
2-year public funding
M: CCAC, SAC
W: CCAC, SAC
M: Baseball, Basketball, Golf
W: Basketball, Golf, Softball,
Volleyball

**Pennsylvania State University
(Behrend College)**
Station Road
Erie, PA 16563
M: (814) 898-1511
W: (814) 898-1511
Enrollment: A
4-year public funding
M: Independent
W: WKC
M: Baseball, Basketball, Soccer,
Tennis
W: Basketball, Softball, Tennis,
Volleyball

Penn Valley Community College
Westport Road
Kansas City, MO 64111
M: (816) 756-2800 X. 202
W: (816) 756-2800 X. 202
Enrollment: C
2-year public funding
M: MACCC
W: MACCC
M: Basketball, Golf
W: Volleyball

Pensacola Junior College
1000 College Boulevard
Pensacola, FL 32504
M: (904) 476-5410 X. 278
W: (904) 476-5410 X. 278
Enrollment: C
2-year public funding
M: FCCAA
W: FCCAA
M: Baseball, Basketball
W: Basketball, Volleyball

Pepperdine University
Malibu, CA 90265
M: (213) 456-4172
W: (213) 456-4172
Enrollment: C
4-year private
M: WCAC, PCAA
W: Independent
M: Baseball, Basketball,
Swimming-Diving, Tennis,
Volleyball, Water Polo
W: Basketball, Tennis, Volleyball

Pfeiffer College
Misenheimer, NC 28109
M: (704) 463-7343
W: (704) 463-7343
Enrollment: A
4-year private
M: Carolinas, NCAA, NAIA
W: Carolinas, AIAW

M: Baseball, Basketball, Golf,
   Soccer, Tennis, Wrestling
W: Basketball, Field Hockey,
   Golf, Softball (slo-pitch),
   Swimming-Diving, Tennis

Philadelphia Community College
34 South 11th Street
Philadelphia, PA 19107
M: (215) 972-7132
W: (215) 972-7132
Enrollment: C
2-year public funding
M: EPCCAC
W: EPCCAC, PAIAW
M: Baseball, Basketball, Cross
   Country, Soccer, Tennis,
   Track & Field
W: Basketball, Cross Country,
   Softball, Tennis, Track &
   Field, Volleyball

Phillips University
University Station
Enid, OK 73701
M: (405) 237-4433 X. 278
W: (405) 237-4433 X. 278
Enrollment: A
4-year private
M: Sooner Athletic
W: Sooner Athletic
M: Tennis, Baseball, Basketball
W: Basketball

Piedmont Bible College
716 Franklin Street
Winston-Salem, NC 27101
M: (919) 725-8344
W: (919) 725-8344
Enrollment: A
4-year private
M: SCAC

W: SCAC
M: Basketball, Soccer
W: Volleyball

Pikeville College
Pikeville, KY 41501
M: (606) 432-9231
W: (606) 432-9231
Enrollment: A
4-year private
M: KIAC
W: KIAC
M: Baseball, Basketball, Golf,
   Tennis
W: Basketball, Golf, Tennis

Pima Community College
2202 West Anklam Road
Tucson, AZ 85709
M: (602) 884-6005
W: (601) 884-6005
Enrollment: C
2-year public funding
M: ACCAC, NJCAA
W: ACCAC, NJCAA
M: Archery, Baseball, Basketball,
   Cross Country, Golf, Tennis,
   Track & Field, Wrestling
W: Archery, Basketball, Cross
   Country, Softball, Tennis,
   Track & Field, Volleyball

Pittsburg State University
Pittsburg, KS 66762
M: (316) 321-7000 X. 265
W: (316) 231-7000 X. 265
Enrollment: C
4-year public funding
M: CSIC
W: CSIC
M: Basketball, Cross Country,
   Football, Track & Field

W: Basketball, Cross Country,
   Softball, Track & Field

University of Pittsburgh
Johnstown, PA 15904
M: (814) 266-9661
W: (814) 266-9661
Enrollment: A
4-year private
M: NCAA, NAIA
W: EAIAW, AIAW
M: Baseball, Basketball, Cross
   Country, Golf, Soccer, Track
   & Field, Wrestling
W: Basketball, Golf, Gymnastics,
   Volleyball

University of Pittsburgh
Pittsburgh, PA 15213
M: (412) 624-4571
W: (412) 624-4598
Enrollment: C
4-year private
M: Independent
W: Independent
M: Cross Country, Volleyball,
   Baseball, Basketball,
   Football, Gymnastics, Soccer,
   Swimming-Diving, Tennis,
   Track & Field, Wrestling
W: Field Hockey, Basketball,
   Gymnastics, Swimming-
   Diving, Tennis, Track &
   Field, Volleyball

Plymouth State College
Plymouth, NH 03264
M: (603) 536-1550
W: (603) 536-1550
Enrollment: B
4-year public funding
M: NCAA

W: AIAW
M: Baseball, Basketball, Football,
   Golf, Ice Hockey, Lacrosse,
   Skiing, Soccer, Tennis,
   Wrestling
W: Basketball, Field Hockey,
   Lacrosse, Skiing, Soccer,
   Softball, Tennis

Point Loma College
San Diego, CA 92106
M: (714) 222-6474 X. 265
W: (714) 222-6474 X. 265
Enrollment: A
4-year private
M: NAIA
W: AIAW
M: Baseball, Basketball, Cross
   Country, Golf, Soccer,
   Tennis, Track & Field
W: Basketball, Cross Country,
   Softball, Tennis, Track &
   Field, Volleyball

Point Park College
201 Wood Street
Pittsburgh, PA 15522
M: (412) 391-4100 X. 279
W: (412) 391-4100 X. 280
Enrollment: A
4-year private
M: NAIA
W: NAIA
W: Baseball, Basketball
W: Basketball

Porterville College
Porterville, CA 93257
M: (209) 781-3130
Enrollment: A
2-year public funding
M: Central Valley

M: Baseball, Basketball, Cross
Country, Football, Tennis,
Track & Field, Volleyball,
Wrestling

University of Portland
5000 North Williamette Boulevard
Portland, OR 97203
M: (503) 283–7117
W: (503) 283–7117
Enrollment: A
4-year private
M: WCAC, NORPAC
W: WCAC, Independent
M: Baseball, Basketball, Cross
Country, Golf, Soccer,
Tennis, Track & Field
W: Basketball, Tennis, Track &
Field, Volleyball

Portland State University
Portland, OR 97207
M: (503) 229–4400
W: (503) 229–4400
Enrollment: C
4-year public funding
M: Independent
W: NCWA
M: Baseball, Golf, Gymnastics,
Swimming-Diving, Water
Polo, Basketball, Football,
Wrestling
W: Fencing, Swimming-Diving,
Tennis, Basketball,
Gymnastics, Softball,
Volleyball

Pratt Community Junior College
Pratt, KS 67124
M: (316) 672–5641
W: (316) 672–5641
Enrollment: A

2-year public funding
M: KJCC
W: KJCC
M: Baseball, Basketball, Football,
Track & Field
W: Basketball, Track & Field,
Volleyball

Pratt Institute
200 Willoughby Avenue
Brooklyn, NY 11205
M: (212) 636–3771
W: (212) 636–3772/3
Enrollment: B
4-year private
M: ECAC, NCAA
W: ECAC, NCAA
M: Basketball, Cross Country,
Fencing, Golf, Soccer,
Tennis, Track & Field
W: Basketball, Fencing, Tennis,
Track & Field, Volleyball

Presbyterian College
Clinton, SC 29325
M: (803) 833–0705
W: (803) 833–0705
Enrollment: A
4-year private
M: SAC-8
W: AIAW
M: Golf, Riflery, Soccer, Track &
Field, Basketball, Football,
Tennis
W: Basketball, Tennis, Volleyball

Princeton University
Princeton, NJ 08540
M: (609) 452–3568
W: (609) 452–3568
Enrollment: C
4-year private

M: Ivy League
W: Ivy League
M: Baseball, Basketball, Crew, Cross Country, Fencing, Football, Gymnastics, Ice Hockey, Lacrosse, Soccer, Squash, Swimming-Diving, Tennis, Track & Field, Volleyball, Wrestling
W: Basketball, Crew, Cross Country, Fencing, Field Hockey, Golf, Lacrosse, Sailing, Soccer, Softball, Squash, Swimming-Diving, Tennis, Volleyball

Principia College
Elsah, IL 62028
M: (618) 374–2131
W: (618) 374–2131
Enrollment: A
4-year private
M: Independent
W: AIAW
M: Baseball, Basketball, Cross Country, Football, Golf, Soccer, Swimming-Diving, Tennis, Track & Field, Water Polo
W: Basketball, Cross Country, Field Hockey, Softball, Swimming-Diving, Tennis, Track & Field, Volleyball

Providence College
River Avenue
Providence, RI 02918
M: (401) 865–2265
W: (401) 865–2296
Enrollment: B
4-year private
M: Big East
W: AIAW

M: Golf, Lacrosse, Tennis, Volleyball, Baseball, Basketball, Cross Country, Ice Hockey, Soccer, Track & Field
W: Lacrosse, Basketball, Cross Country, Field Hockey, Ice Hockey, Softball, Tennis, Track & Field, Volleyball

Puerto Rico Agricultural and Mechanical University
Mayaquez, PR 00708
M: (809) 832–4040 X. 2565
W: (809) 832–4040 X. 2565
Enrollment: C
4-year public funding
M: Independent
W: Independent
M: Basketball, Cross Country, Judo, Soccer, Swimming-Diving, Tennis, Track & Field, Volleyball, Water Polo, Weightlifting, Wrestling
W: Basketball, Cross Country, Judo, Soccer, Softball, Swimming-Diving, Tennis, Track & Field

Purdue University
West Lafayette, IN 47907
M: (317) 494–8461
W: (317) 494–8561
Enrollment: C
4-year public funding
M: Big Ten
W: AIAW
M: Baseball, Basketball, Cross Country, Football, Golf, Swimming-Diving, Tennis, Track & Field, Wrestling
W: Basketball, Cross Country, Field Hockey, Golf,

Swimming-Diving, Tennis,
Track & Field, Volleyball

Purdue University (Calumet)
2233 171st Street
Hammond, IN 46323
M: (219) 844–6520
W: (219) 844–6520
Enrollment: B
4-year public funding
M: NAIA
W: Independent
M: Golf, Soccer
W: Basketball, Volleyball

Quincy College
1831 College Avenue
Quincy, IL 62301
M: (217) 222–8020 X. 235
W: (217) 222–8020 X. 234
Enrollment: A
4-year private
M: NAIA, Independent
W: IAIAW, MAIAW, AIAW
M: Baseball, Basketball, Soccer,
Tennis
W: Basketball, Softball, Tennis,
Volleyball

Quinnipiac College
Hamden, CT 06518
M: (203) 288–5251 X. 262/263
W: (203) 288–5251 X. 262/263
Enrollment: B
4-year private
M: ECAC, NCAA
W: ECAC, NCAA
M: Baseball, Basketball, Cross
Country, Golf, Soccer, Tennis
W: Basketball, Softball, Tennis

Radford College
Radford, VA 24141
M: (703) 731–5228
W: (703) 731–5228
Enrollment: C
4-year private
M: NCAA, NAIA
W: AIAW, VAIAW
M: Cross Country, Golf, Lacrosse,
Basketball, Soccer, Tennis
W: Cross Country, Basketball,
Gymnastics, Soccer, Tennis,
Volleyball

Randolph-Macon College
Ashland, VA 23005
M: (804) 798–8372
W: (804) 798–8372
Enrollment: A
4-year private
M: ODAC
W: VAIAW
M: Baseball, Football, Golf,
Lacrosse, Tennis, Basketball,
Soccer
W: Basketball, Field Hockey,
Lacrosse, Tennis

University of Redlands
1200 East Colton Avenue
Redlands, CA 92373
M: (714) 793–2121 X. 418
W: (714) 793–2121 X. 418
Enrollment: A
4-year private
M: SCIC
W: SCIC
M: Baseball, Basketball, Cross
Country, Football, Golf,
Soccer, Swimming-Diving,
Tennis, Track & Field, Water
Polo, Wrestling
W: Basketball, Cross Country,

Softball, Swimming-Diving,
Tennis, Track & Field,
Volleyball, Water Polo

All aid for men and women is based on financial need.

College of the Redwoods
Eureka, CA 95501
M: (707) 443–8411 X. 273
W: (707) 443–8411 X. 273
Enrollment: A
2-year public funding
M: Golden Valley
W: Golden Valley
M: Baseball, Basketball, Cross Country, Football, Golf, Tennis, Track & Field, Wrestling
W: Basketball, Golf, Softball, Tennis, Track & Field, Volleyball

Regis College
West 50th and Lowell Boulevard
Denver, CO 80221
M: (303) 458–4070
W: (303) 458–4070
Enrollment: A
4-year private
M: RMAC, NAIA
W: AIAW
M: Baseball, Basketball, Golf, Skiing, Soccer, Swimming-Diving, Tennis
W: Skiing, Swimming-Diving, Basketball, Tennis, Volleyball

Rensselaer Polytechnic Institute
Troy, NY 12181
M: (518) 270–6685
W: (518) 270–6256

Enrollment: B
4-year private
M: NCAA, ECAC
W: AIAW
M: Baseball, Basketball, Cross Country, Football, Golf, Lacrosse, Soccer, Swimming-Diving, Tennis, Track & Field, Wrestling
W: Basketball, Field Hockey, Softball, Tennis

Rice University
6100 South Main
Houston, TX 77001
M: (713) 527–4077
W: (713) 527–9809
Enrollment: B
4-year private
M: Southwest
W: AIAW
M: Swimming-Diving, Baseball, Basketball, Cross Country, Football, Golf, Tennis, Track & Field
W: Basketball, Cross Country, Swimming-Diving, Tennis, Track & Field, Volleyball

Rider College
2033 Lawrenceville Road
Trenton, NJ 08602
M: (609) 896–5054
W: (609) 896–5054
Enrollment: B
4-year private
M: East Coast
W: NJAIAW
M: Golf, Riflery, Baseball, Basketball, Cross Country, Soccer, Swimming-Diving, Tennis, Track & Field, Wrestling

W: Riflery, Basketball, Diving, Field Hockey, Softball, Volleyball

Rio Grande College
Rio Grande, OH 45674
M: (614) 245–5353 X. 249
W: (614) 235–5353 X. 249
Enrollment: A
4-year public funding
M: Mid-Ohio
W: Independent
M: Baseball, Basketball, Track & Field
W: Basketball, Track & Field, Volleyball

Ripon College
Ripon, WI 54971
M: (414) 748–8133
W: (414) 748–8133
Enrollment: A
4-year private
M: MAC
W: WIC, WAC
M: Baseball, Basketball, Football, Golf, Soccer, Swimming-Diving, Tennis, Track & Field, Wrestling
W: Basketball, Softball, Swimming-Diving, Tennis, Track & Field, Volleyball

All aid for men and women is based on financial need.

Riverside City College
4800 Magnolia Avenue
Riverside, CA 92506
M: (714) 684–3240 X. 261
W: (714) 684–3240 X. 261
Enrollment: B

2-year public funding
M: Mission
W: Mission
M: Baseball, Basketball, Cross Country, Football, Golf, Swimming-Diving, Tennis, Track & Field, Water Polo
W: Basketball, Cross Country, Softball, Swimming-Diving, Tennis, Track & Field, Volleyball

Roanoke College
Salem, VA 24153
M: (703) 389–2351
W: (703) 398–2351
Enrollment: A
4-year private
M: ODAC
W: AIAW
M: Basketball, Cross Country, Golf, Lacrosse, Soccer, Tennis, Track & Field
W: Basketball, Cross Country, Field Hockey, Lacrosse, Swimming-Diving, Tennis, Track & Field, Volleyball

Robert Morris College
Narrows Run Road
Coraopolis, PA 15108
M: (412) 264–9300 X. 295
W: (412) 264–9300 X. 297
Enrollment: B
4-year private
M: ECAC, NCAA
W: Pennwood West, EAIAW, AIAW
M: Cross Country, Golf, Baseball, Basketball Tennis
W: Softball, Basketball, Tennis, Volleyball

Roberts Wesleyan College
2301 Westside Drive
Rochester, NY 14624
M: (716) 594–9471
W: (716) 594–9471
Enrollment: A
4-year private
M: PCAC
W: PCAC
M: Basketball, Cross Country, Soccer, Tennis, Track & Field
W: Basketball, Cross Country, Softball, Track & Field, Volleyball

All aid for men and women is based on financial need.

University of Rochester
Rochester, NY 14627
M: (716) 275–4301
W: (716) 275–4281
Enrollment: B
4-year private
M: NCAA, ECAC
W: AIAW
M: Baseball, Basketball, Cross Country, Football, Golf, Lacrosse, Soccer, Squash, Swimming-Diving, Tennis, Track & Field
W: Basketball, Field Hockey, Lacrosse, Soccer, Swimming-Diving, Tennis, Track & Field, Volleyball

Rockhurst College
5225 Troost Avenue
Kansas City, MO 64110
M: (816) 363–4010
W: (816) 363–4010
Enrollment: B
4-year private
M: NAIA
W: NAIA
M: Bowling, Tennis, Basketball, Soccer
W: Bowling, Tennis, Basketball, Volleyball

Rockmont College
8801 West Alameda Avenue
Denver, CO 80226
M: (303) 238–5386
W: (303) 238–5386
Enrollment: A
4-year private
M: Rocky Mountain
W: Rocky Mountain
M: Basketball, Skiing, Soccer
W: Basketball, Skiing

Rollins College
Winter Park, FL 32789
M: (305) 646–2366
W: (305) 646–2366
Enrollment: A
4-year private
M: NCAA, Sunshine
W: AIAW
M: Cross Country, Basketball, Golf, Soccer, Tennis, Water Skiing
W: Basketball, Golf, Tennis, Volleyball, Water Skiing

Rust College
Rust Avenue
Holly Springs, MS 38635
M: (601) 252–4661 X. 223
W: (601) 252–4661 X. 203
Enrollment: A
4-year private
M: NCAA, NAIA
W: MAIAW, NAIA

M Baseball, Basketball, Cross
   Country, Tennis, Track &
   Field
W: Basketball, Cross Country,
   Tennis, Track & Field

Rutgers University
Camden, NJ 08102
M: (609) 757-6193
W: (609) 757-6194
Enrollment: A
4-year public funding
M: NAIA, NCAA
W: NJAIAW
M: Baseball, Basketball, Cross
   Country, Golf, Soccer,
   Tennis, Track & Field,
   Wrestling
W: Basketball, Field Hockey,
   Softball, Tennis

Rutgers University
42 Warren Street
Newark, NJ 07102
M: (201) 648-5474
W: (201) 648-5179
Enrollment: B
4-year public funding
M: NCAA
W: AIAW
M: Baseball, Basketball, Fencing,
   Golf, Soccer, Tennis,
   Wrestling, Volleyball
W: Basketball, Softball, Tennis,
   Volleyball

Rutgers University
New Brunswick, NJ 08903
M: (201) 932-8610
W: (201) 932-8610
Enrollment: C
4-year public funding

M: Independent, EAA
W: Independent
M: Baseball, Basketball, Crew,
   Cross Country, Fencing,
   Football, Golf, Lacrosse,
   Soccer, Swimming-Diving,
   Track & Field, Wrestling
W: Fencing, Basketball, Crew,
   Cross Country, Field Hockey,
   Golf, Gymnastics, Lacrosse,
   Softball, Swimming-Diving,
   Tennis, Track & Field,
   Volleyball

Sacred Heart University
Bridgeport, CT 06604
M: (203) 374-9441 X. 219
W: (203) 374-9441 X. 280
Enrollment: A
4-year private
M: Independent
W: Independent
M: Baseball, Basketball, Cross
   Country, Golf, Soccer,
   Volleyball
W: Basketball, Cross Country,
   Softball, Volleyball

Saginaw Valley College
2250 Pierce Road
University Center, MI 48710
M: (517) 790-4114
W: (517) 790-4114
Enrollment: B
4-year public funding
M: GLIAC
W: GLIAC
M: Golf, Baseball, Basketball,
   Bowling, Cross Country,
   Football, Track & Field,
   Wrestling
W: Tennis, Basketball, Softball,
   Track & Field, Volleyball

212

St. Augustine's College
1315 Oakwood Avenue
Raleigh, NC 27611
M: (919) 828–4451
W: (919) 828–4451
Enrollment: A
4-year private
M: CIAA, NAIA, NCAA
W: CIAA, NAIA, NCAA
M: Bowling, Fencing, Baseball, Basketball, Cross Country, Golf, Soccer, Tennis, Track & Field, Volleyball
W: Bowling, Fencing, Basketball, Cross Country, Golf, Softball, Tennis, Track & Field, Volleyball

St. Bonaventure University
St. Bonaventure, NY 14778
M: (716) 375–2210
W: (716) 375–2210
Enrollment: A
4-year private
M: Eastern-8
W: NYSAIAW, EAIAW
M: Baseball, Cross Country, Golf, Track & Field, Basketball, Soccer, Swimming-Diving, Tennis
W: Field Hockey, Softball, Basketball, Swimming-Diving, Tennis

St. Clair County Community College
323 Erie Street
Port Huron, MI 48060
M: (313) 984–3883
W: (313) 984–3883
Enrollment: B
2-year public funding
M: MCCAA

W: MCCAA
M: Baseball, Basketball, Golf, Tennis
W: Basketball, Softball

St. Cloud State University
St. Cloud, MN 56301
M: (612) 255–3102
W: (612) 255–2182
Enrollment: C
4-year public funding
M: NIC
W: Northern Sun
M: Tennis, Baseball, Basketball, Cross Country, Football, Golf, Gymnastics, Swimming-Diving, Track & Field, Wrestling
W: Cross Country, Golf, Tennis, Basketball, Gymnastics, Softball, Swimming-Diving, Track & Field, Volleyball

St. Edward's University
3001 South Congress Avenue
Austin, TX 78704
M: (512) 444–2621
W: (512) 444–2621
Enrollment: A
4-year private
M: Big State, NAIA
W: AIAW
M: Baseball, Basketball, Golf, Tennis
W: Basketball, Tennis, Volleyball

College of St. Francis
500 Wilcox Street
Joliet, IL 60435
M: (815) 740–3464
W: (815) 740–3464
Enrollment: A

4-year private
M: Chicagoland NAIA
W: AIAW
M: Baseball, Basketball, Golf, Tennis
W: Basketball, Softball, Tennis, Volleyball

St. Francis College
180 Remsen Street
Brooklyn, NY 11201
M: (212) 522-2300
W: (212) 522-2300
Enrollment: B
4-year private
M: NCAA, ECAC
W: AIAW, EIAW, NYSAIAW
M: Bowling, Cross Country, Soccer, Swimming-Diving, Tennis, Baseball, Basketball
W: Basketball, Swimming-Diving, Volleyball

St. Francis College
Loretto, PA 15940
M: (814) 472-7000 X. 276
W: (814) 472-7000 X. 276
Enrollment: A
4-year private
M: ECAC
W: Pennwood West
M: Cross Country, Football, Golf, Tennis, Basketball
W: Basketball, Tennis, Volleyball

St. John Fisher College
2690 East Avenue
Rochester, NY 14618
M: (716) 586-4140
W: (716) 586-4140
Enrollment: A
4-year private

M: ECAC, NAIA, PCAC
W: PCAC, EAIAW, AIAW, NYSAIAW
M: Cross Country, Golf, Tennis, Track & Field, Basketball, Soccer, Wrestling
W: Tennis, Track & Field, Basketball, Soccer, Volleyball

St. John's College
Winfield, KS 67156
M: (316) 221-4000 X. 70
W: (316) 221-4000 X. 69
Enrollment: A
4-year private
M: Independent
W: Independent
M: Baseball, Basketball, Soccer
W: Basketball, Softball, Volleyball

St. John's University
Collegeville, MN 56321
M: (612) 363-2550
Enrollment: A
4-year private
M: MIAC
M: Baseball, Basketball, Cross Country, Football, Golf, Ice Hockey, Soccer, Swimming-Diving, Tennis, Track & Field, Wrestling

All aid is based on financial need.

St. Joseph's College
Rensselear, IN 47978
M: (219) 866-8472
W: (219) 866-8472
Enrollment: A
4-year private
M: Great Lakes Valley, Heartland
W: AIAW

M: Baseball, Cross Country, Golf,
Tennis, Track & Field,
<u>Basketball</u>, <u>Football</u>
W: <u>Basketball</u>, <u>Tennis</u>, <u>Track &
Field</u>, <u>Volleyball</u>

College of St. Joseph the Provider
Rutland, VT 05701
M: (802) 775–0806
W: (802) 775–0806
Enrollment: A
4-year private
M: Mayflower, NAIA
W: Independent
M: <u>Basketball</u>
W: Softball, Volleyball, <u>Basketball</u>

St. Lawrence University
Canton, NY 13617
M: (315) 379–6421
W: (315) 379–6421
Enrollment: A
4-year private
M: Independent
W: NYSAIAW
M: Baseball, Basketball, Cross
Country, Football, Ice
Hockey, Lacrosse, Riding,
Skiing, Soccer, Swimming-
Diving, Tennis, Track &
Field, Wrestling
W: Basketball, Field Hockey,
Lacrosse, Riding, Skiing,
Soccer, Swimming-Diving,
Tennis, Volleyball

All aid for men and women is
based on financial need.

St. Leo College
St. Leo, FL 33574
M: (904) 588–8221
W: (904) 588–8221
Enrollment: A
4-year private
M: Sunshine State
W: AIAW
M: Cross Country, Football, Golf,
Soccer, <u>Baseball</u>, <u>Basketball</u>,
<u>Tennis</u>
W: Cross Country, Softball,
Volleyball, <u>Basketball</u>, <u>Tennis</u>

St. Louis College of Pharmacy
4588 Parkview Place
St. Louis, MO 63110
M: (314) 367–8700 X. 65
W: (314) 367–8700 X. 65
Enrollment: A
4-year private
M: Greater St. Louis
W: Greater St. Louis
M: Basketball, Golf, Tennis
W: Tennis

**St. Louis Community College
(Florissant Valley)**
3400 Pershall Road
St. Louis, MO 63135
M: (314) 595–4275
W: (314) 595–4275
Enrollment: C
2-year public funding
M: Midwest JCAC
W: Midwest JCAC
M: <u>Baseball</u>, <u>Basketball</u>, <u>Bowling</u>,
<u>Cross Country</u>, <u>Soccer</u>,
<u>Swimming-Diving</u>, <u>Tennis</u>,
<u>Track & Field</u>
W: <u>Basketball</u>, <u>Bowling</u>, <u>Cross
Country</u>, <u>Softball</u>, <u>Swimming-
Diving</u>, <u>Tennis</u>, <u>Track &
Field</u>, <u>Volleyball</u>

St. Louis University
3672 West Pine
St. Louis, MO 63103
M: (314) 658–3177
W: (314) 658–3177
Enrollment: C
4-year private
M: Metro
W: AIAW
M: Baseball, Basketball, Cross Country, Golf, Soccer, Swimming-Diving, Tennis, Track & Field
W: Cross Country, Basketball, Field Hockey, Softball, Swimming-Diving, Tennis, Track & Field, Volleyball

College of St. Mary
1901 South 72nd Street
Omaha, NE 68124
W: (402) 393–8800 X. 282
Enrollment: A
4-year private
W: AIAW
W: Basketball, Softball, Volleyball

St. Mary of the Plains College
Dodge City, KS 67801
M: (316) 225–4171 X. 64
W: (316) 225–4171 X. 65
Enrollment: A
4-year private
M: KCAC
W: KCAC
M: Baseball, Basketball, Football, Golf, Tennis
W: Basketball, Golf, Softball, Tennis, Volleyball

St. Mary's College
Moraga, CA 94575
M: (415) 376–4411 X. 383
W: (415) 376–4411 X. 383
Enrollment: A
4-year private
M: West Coast
W: Independent
M: Crew, Cross Country, Golf, Rugby, Tennis, Baseball, Basketball, Football, Soccer
W: Crew, Softball, Basketball, Tennis, Volleyball

St. Mary's College
Orchard Lake, MI 48033
M: (313) 682–1885
Enrollment: A
4-year private
M: NAIA, Independent
M: Basketball

St. Mary's College
Winona, MN 55987
M: (507) 452–4430 X. 374
W: (507) 452–4430 X. 378
Enrollment: A
4-year private
M: MIAC, NAIA
W: AIAW, MAIAW
M: Baseball, Basketball, Cross Country, Ice Hockey, Soccer, Tennis, Wrestling
W: Basketball, Cross Country, Softball, Tennis, Volleyball

St. Mary's University
One Camino Santa Maria
San Antonio, TX 78284
M: (512) 436–3414
W: (512) 436–3414
Enrollment: A
4-year private
M: Big State, NAIA, TCSL

W: TAIAW, AIAW
M: Soccer, Baseball, Basketball, Golf, Tennis
W: Soccer, Basketball, Golf, Softball, Tennis, Volleyball

St. Norbert College
De Pere, WI 54115
M: (414) 337-3030
W: (414) 337-3030
Enrollment: A
4-year private
M: Independent
W: Independent, WIC, WAC
M: Baseball, Basketball, Cross Country, Football, Golf, Riflery, Soccer, Tennis, Track & Field
W: Basketball, Golf, Riflery, Softball, Tennis, Track & Field

St. Olaf College
Northfield, MN 55057
M: (507) 663-3250
W: (507) 663-3250
Enrollment: B
4-year private
M: MIAC
W: MAIAW
M: Baseball, Basketball, Cross Country, Football, Golf, Ice Hockey, Skiing, Soccer, Swimming-Diving, Tennis, Track & Field, Wrestling
W: Basketball, Cross Country, Golf, Skiing, Soccer, Softball, Swimming-Diving, Tennis, Track & Field, Volleyball

St. Paul's College
Lawrenceville, VA 23868
M: (804) 848-2430 X. 238
W: (804) 848-2296 X. 238
Enrollment: A
4-year private
M: CIAA, NCAA
W: CIAA
M: Baseball, Basketball, Football, Golf, Tennis, Track & Field
W: Basketball, Gymnastics, Softball, Tennis, Track & Field, Volleyball

St. Peter's College
2641 Kennedy Boulevard
Jersey City, NJ 07306
M: (201) 333-4400 X. 368
W: (201) 333-4400 X. 368
Enrollment: B
4-year private
M: NCAA, ECAC
W: AIAW, EAIAW, NJAIAW
M: Baseball, Bowling, Cross Country, Fencing, Football, Riflery, Skiing, Soccer, Swimming-Diving, Tennis, Track & Field, Basketball
W: Bowling, Cross Country, Fencing, Riflery, Skiing, Softball, Swimming-Diving, Tennis, Basketball

College of St. Scholastica
1200 Kenwood Ave.
Duluth, MN 55811
W: (218) 723-6199
W: (218) 723-6199
Enrollment: A
4-year private
M: Independent
W: Independent
M: Basketball, Cross Country, Ice Hockey, Soccer, Tennis, Track & Field

W: Basketball, Cross Country,
   Tennis, Track & Field,
   Volleyball

College of St. Teresa
Winona, MN 55987
W: (507) 452-2930
Enrollment: A
4-year private
W: MAIAW
W: Basketball, Softball, Tennis,
   Volleyball

College of St. Thomas
St. Paul, MN 55105
M: (612) 647-5356
W: (612) 647-5356
Enrollment: B
4-year private
M: MIAC
W: MAIAW
M: Baseball, Basketball, Cross
   Country, Football, Golf,
   Soccer, Swimming-Diving,
   Tennis, Track & Field,
   Wrestling
W: Basketball, Cross Country,
   Golf, Softball, Swimming-
   Diving, Tennis, Track &
   Field, Volleyball

St. Vincent College
Latrobe, PA 15650
M: (412) 539-9761
Enrollment: A
4-year private
M: Independent
M: Baseball, Bowling, Cross
   Country, Golf, Soccer,
   Tennis, Basketball

St. Xavier College
3700 West 103rd Street
Chicago, IL 60655
M: (312) 779-3300 X. 230
W: (312) 779-3300 X. 230
Enrollment: A
4-year private
M: Chicagoland
W: AIAW
M: Baseball, Basketball, Cross
   Country
W: Basketball, Softball, Volleyball

Salisbury State College
Salisbury, MD 21801
M: (301) 546-3261
W: (301) 546-3261
Enrollment: B
4-year public funding
M: Independent
W: Independent
M: Baseball, Basketball, Cross
   Country, Football, Golf,
   Lacrosse, Swimming-Diving,
   Tennis, Track & Field,
   Wrestling
W: Basketball, Field Hockey,
   Lacrosse, Softball, Swimming-
   Diving, Tennis, Track &
   Field, Volleyball

Sam Houston State University
Huntsville, TX 77340
M: (713) 295-6211
W: (713) 295-6211
Enrollment: C
4-year public funding
M: Lone Star
W: AIAW, TAIAW
M: Baseball, Basketball, Football,
   Golf, Tennis, Track & Field
W: Basketball, Softball, Tennis,
   Track & Field, Volleyball

University of San Diego
Alcala Park
San Diego, CA 92110
M: (714) 291-6480 X. 4272
W: (714) 291-6480 X. 4272
Enrollment: B
4-year private
M: WCAC, SCBA
W: SCAA
M: Crew, Cross Country, Football, Soccer, Baseball, Basketball, Golf, Tennis
W: Crew, Cross Country, Softball, Basketball, Swimming-Diving, Tennis, Volleyball

San Diego State University
San Diego, CA 92182
M: (714) 265-5163
W: (714) 265-5163
Enrollment: C
4-year public funding
M: Western Athletic
W: WCAA
M: Baseball, Basketball, Cross Country, Football, Golf, Soccer, Swimming-Diving, Tennis, Track & Field, Volleyball
W: Basketball, Cross Country, Golf, Gymnastics, Softball, Swimming-Diving, Tennis, Track & Field, Volleyball

City College of San Francisco
50 Phelan Avenue
San Francisco, CA 94112
M: (415) 239-3412
W: (415) 239-3419
Enrollment: C
2-year public funding
M: Golden Gate
W: Golden Gate
M: Baseball, Basketball, Cross Country, Fencing, Football, Golf, Soccer, Swimming-Diving, Tennis, Track & Field
W: Archery, Badminton, Cross Country, Fencing, Gymnastics, Swimming-Diving, Tennis, Track & Field, Volleyball

University of San Francisco
San Francisco, CA 94117
M: (415) 666-6891
W: (415) 666-6891
Enrollment: C
4-year private
M: WCAC
W: NCWAC
M: Cross Country, Baseball, Basketball, Golf, Soccer, Tennis
W: Cross Country, Basketball, Softball, Tennis, Volleyball

San Francisco State University
San Francisco, CA 94132
M: (415) 469-2218
W: (415) 469-2218
Enrollment: C
4-year public funding
M: Far Western
W: Golden State
M: Badminton, Baseball, Basketball, Cross Country, Fencing, Football, Golf, Soccer, Swimming-Diving, Track & Field, Water Polo, Wrestling
W: Badminton, Basketball, Cross Country, Fencing, Golf, Gymnastics, Softball, Swimming-Diving, Tennis, Track & Field, Volleyball

Sangamon State University
Springfield, IL 62708
M: (217) 786–6674
W: (217) 786–6674
Enrollment: B
4-year public funding
M: Independent
W: Independent
M: Soccer, Tennis
W: Tennis

San Jose State University
San Jose, CA 95192
M: (408) 277-3296
W: (408) 277-3141
Enrollment: C
4-year public funding
M: NCAA, PCAA
W: NCAC
M: Baseball, Basketball, Cross Country, Fencing, Football, Golf, Gymnastics, Soccer, Swimming-Diving, Tennis, Track & Field, Water Polo, Wrestling
W: Basketball, Fencing, Field Hockey, Golf, Gymnastics, Swimming-Diving, Tennis, Volleyball

College of San Mateo
1700 West Hillsdale Boulevard
San Mateo, CA 94402
M: (415) 574–6461
W: (415) 574–6461
Enrollment: C
2-year public funding
M: Golden Gate
W: Golden Gate
M: Baseball, Basketball, Cross Country, Football, Golf, Track & Field, Wrestling
W: Basketball, Cross Country, Softball, Tennis, Track & Field, Volleyball

Santa Ana College
Santa Ana, CA 92706
M: (714) 835–3000 X. 393
W: (714) 835–3000 X. 393
Enrollment: C
2-year public funding
M: South Coast
W: South Coast
M: Baseball, Basketball, Cross Country, Football, Golf, Soccer, Swimming-Diving, Tennis, Track & Field, Water Polo, Wrestling
W: Basketball, Cross Country, Softball, Tennis, Track & Field

Santa Barbara City Junior College
Santa Barbara, California 93109
M: (805) 965–0581 X. 277
W: (805) 965–0581 X. 277
Enrollment: C
2-year public funding
M: Western State
W: Western State
M: Baseball, Basketball, Cross Country, Football, Golf, Tennis, Track & Field, Volleyball
W: Basketball, Cross Country, Tennis, Track & Field, Volleyball

University of Santa Clara
Santa Clara, CA 95053
M: (408) 984–4063
W: (408) 984–4063
Enrollment: B
4-year private

M: West Coast
W: NorCal
M: Crew, Cross Country, Golf,
   Volleyball, Water Polo,
   Baseball, Basketball,
   Football, Soccer, Tennis
W: Crew, Cross Country, Soccer,
   Softball, Basketball, Tennis,
   Volleyball

Schoolcraft College
18600 Haggerty Road
Livonia, MI 48151
M: (313) 591–6400 X. 480
W: (313) 591–6400 X. 480
Enrollment: B
2-year public funding
M: Independent
W: Independent
M: Basketball, Cross Country,
   Golf, Gymnastics, Soccer,
   Tennis
W: Basketball, Cross Country,
   Tennis, Volleyball

Schreiner College
Kerrville, TX 78028
M: (512) 896–5411
W: (512) 896–5411
Enrollment: A
2-year private
M: TJCAC
W: TJCAC
M: Basketball, Golf, Tennis
W: Basketball, Tennis

University of Scranton
Scranton, PA 18510
M: (717) 961–7440
W: (717) 961–7440
Enrollment: A
4-year private

M: NCAA, Middle Atlantic
W: AIAW, Middle Atlantic
M: Baseball, Basketball, Cross
   Country, Golf, Riflery,
   Soccer, Tennis, Wrestling
W: Basketball, Cross Country,
   Field Hockey, Riflery,
   Softball, Tennis, Volleyball

Seminole Community College
Sanford, FL 32771
M: (305) 323–1450 X. 380
W: (305) 321–1450 X. 380
Enrollment: B
2-year public funding
M: NJAA, FCCAA
M: NJAA, FCCAA
M: Baseball, Basketball, Cross
   Country, Tennis, Track &
   Field
W: Basketball, Softball, Tennis,
   Volleyball

College of the Sequoias
915 South Mooney
Visalia, CA 93277
M: (209) 733–5496
W: (209) 733–5496
Enrollment: B
2-year public funding
M: CVC
W: CVC
M: Basketball, Cross Country,
   Football, Golf, Swimming-
   Diving, Tennis, Track &
   Field, Water Polo, Wrestling
W: Basketball, Cross Country,
   Softball, Swimming-Diving,
   Tennis, Track & Field,
   Volleyball

Seward County Community Junior College
Liberal, KS 67901
M: (316) 624–1951 X. 65
W: (316) 624–1951 X. 65
Enrollment: A
2-year public funding
M: Jayhawk
W: Jayhawk
M: Baseball, Basketball, Track & Field, Volleyball
W: Basketball, Track & Field, Volleyball

Shaw College at Detroit
7351 Woodward
Detroit, MI 48202
M: (313) 873–7920
W: (313) 873–7920
Enrollment: A
4-year private
M: Independent
W: Independent
M: Baseball, Basketball, Track & Field
W: Basketball, Softball, Track & Field

Shawnee College
Ullin, IL 62992
M: (618) 634–2242
W: (618) 634–2242
Enrollment: A
2-year private
M: SICC
W: SICC
M: Baseball, Basketball, Golf
W: Basketball, Golf, Softball, Volleyball

Shawnee State College
Portsmouth, OH 45662
M: (614) 354–3205 X. 219
W: (614) 354–3205 X. 219
Enrollment: A
2-year public funding
M: Golf, Tennis, Volleyball, Basketball
W: Golf, Tennis, Volleyball, Basketball

Shelby State Community College
Memphis, TN 38104
M: (901) 528–6754
W: (901) 528–6754
Enrollment: B
2-year public funding
M: TJCAA, NJCAA
W: TJCAA, NJCAA
M: Baseball, Basketball, Golf, Tennis
W: Basketball, Golf, Tennis

Shepherd College
Shepherdstown, WV 25443
M: (304) 876–2511
W: (304) 876–2511
Enrollment: B
4-year public funding
M: WVIAC
W: WVIAA
M: Baseball, Golf, Swimming-Diving, Tennis, Basketball, Football
W: Basketball, Golf, Softball, Swimming-Diving, Tennis, Volleyball

Sheridan College
Sheridan, WY 82801
M: (307) 674–6446
W: (307) 674–6446
Enrollment: A
2-year public funding

M: Empire
W: Independent
M: Basketball, Golf, Tennis
W: Basketball, Golf, Tennis, Volleyball

Shorter College
Rome, GA 30161
M: (404) 291–2121 X. 38
W: (404) 291–2121 X. 38
Enrollment: A
4-year private
M: NAIA
W: AIAW
M: Baseball, Basketball, Golf, Tennis
W: Basketball, Tennis

Siena College
Route Nine
Loudonville, NY 12211
M: (518) 783–2528
W: (518) 783–2528
Enrollment: A
4-year private
M: ECAC
W: NYSAIAW
M: Baseball, Cross Country, Football, Golf, Lacrosse, Soccer, Tennis, Track & Field, Basketball
W: Field Hockey, Soccer, Softball, Tennis, Track & Field, Volleyball, Basketball

Siena Heights College
1247 East Siena Heights Drive
Adrian, MI 49221
M: (517) 263–0731 X. 233
W: (517) 263–0731 X. 286
Enrollment: A
4-year private

M: NAIA, Independent
W: AIAW, Independent
M: Baseball, Basketball, Cross Country, Golf, Soccer, Tennis, Track & Field, Wrestling
W: Basketball, Cross Country, Softball, Tennis, Track & Field

Simmons College
300 The Fenway
Boston, MA 02115
W: (617) 738–2238
Enrollment: A
4-year private
W: AIAW
W: Crew, Sailing, Tennis, Volleyball

College of the Siskiyous
800 College Avenue
Weed, CA 96094
M: (916) 938–4463
W: (916) 938–4463
Enrollment: A
2-year public funding
M: Golden Valley
W: Golden Valley
M: Baseball, Basketball, Cross Country, Football, Skiing, Tennis, Track & Field
W: Basketball, Cross Country, Skiing, Softball, Tennis, Track & Field, Volleyball

Skagit Valley College
2405 College Way
Mount Vernon, WA 98273
M: (206) 428–1240
W: (206) 428–1240
Enrollment: B

2-year public funding
M: AACC
W: AACC
M: Baseball, Basketball, Cross Country, Golf, Soccer, Tennis, Track & Field
W: Basketball, Cross Country, Golf, Softball, Track & Field, Volleyball

Scholarships are awarded to students from Washington, Oregon, Idaho, and British Columbia by conference rule.

Skidmore College
North Broadway
Saratoga, NY 12866
M: (518) 584-5000 X. 337
W: (518) 584-5000 X. 337
Enrollment: A
4-year private
M: Northeastern
W: Northeastern
M: Basketball, Crew, Equestrian, Golf, Lacrosse, Polo, Soccer, Tennis, Volleyball
W: Basketball, Crew, Equestrian, Field Hockey, Golf, Lacrosse, Soccer, Softball, Swimming-Diving, Tennis, Volleyball

Skyline College
3300 College Drive
San Bruno, CA 94066
M: (415) 355-7000
W: (415) 355-7000
Enrollment: B
2-year public funding
M: Coast
W: Coast
M: Baseball, Basketball, Cross Country, Soccer, Tennis, Track & Field, Wrestling
W: Basketball, Cross Country, Softball, Track & Field, Volleyball

All aid for men and women is based on financial need.

Slippery Rock State College
Slippery Rock, PA 16057
M: (412) 794-7336
W: (412) 794-7336
Enrollment: C
4-year public funding
M: NCAA
W: AIAW
M: Baseball, Basketball, Cross Country, Football, Golf, Gymnastics, Judo, Soccer, Swimming-Diving, Tennis, Track & Field, Wrestling
W: Cross Country, Field Hockey, Gymnastics, Judo, Lacrosse, Softball, Swimming-Diving, Tennis, Track & Field, Volleyball

Smith College
Northampton, MA 01060
W: (413) 584-2700 X. 320
Enrollment: A
4-year private
W: AIAW, EAIAW, MAIAW
W: Basketball, Crew, Cross Country, Field Hockey, Gymnastics, Lacrosse, Riding, Soccer, Softball, Squash, Swimming-Diving, Tennis, Volleyball

Snead State Junior College
Walnut Street

Boaz, AL 35957
M: (205) 593–5120
W: (205) 593–5120
Enrollment: A
2-year public funding
M: Alabama JCAC, NJCAA
W: Alabama JCAC, NJCAA
M: Baseball, Basketball
W: Basketball

Southampton College
Southampton, NY 11768
M: (516) 283–4000 X. 223
W: (516) 283–4000 X. 223
Enrollment: A
4-year private
M: ECAC, NCAA
W: ECAC
M: Cross Country, Golf, Lacrosse, Tennis, Basketball, Soccer
W: Volleyball

University of the South
Sewanee, TN 37375
M: (615) 598–5931
W: (615) 598–5931
Enrollment: A
4-year private
M: NCAA, CAC
W: AIAW
M: Baseball, Basketball, Cross Country, Football, Golf, Soccer, Swimming-Diving, Tennis, Track & Field, Wrestling
W: Basketball, Cross Country, Field Hockey, Swimming-Diving, Tennis, Volleyball

University of South Carolina
Columbia, SC 29208
M: (803) 777–5204
W: (803) 777–5257
Enrollment: C
4-year public funding
M: Independent
W: Independent
M: Baseball, Basketball, Cross Country, Football, Golf, Soccer, Swimming-Diving, Tennis, Track & Field
W: Basketball, Golf, Softball, Swimming-Diving, Tennis, Volleyball

University of South Alabama
307 University Boulevard
Mobile, AL 36688
M: (205) 460–7121
W: (205) 460–7121
Enrollment: C
4-year public funding
M: Sun Belt, NCAA
W: AAIAW
M: Baseball, Basketball, Cross Country, Golf, Soccer, Tennis, Track & Field
W: Basketball, Tennis, Volleyball

South Carolina State College
Orangeburg, SC 29115
M: (803) 536–7242
W: (803) 536–7242
Enrollment: B
4-year public funding
M: MEAC
W: AIAW
M: Basketball, Football, Golf, Swimming-Diving, Tennis, Track & Field, Wrestling
W: Basketball, Tennis, Track & Field, Volleyball

University of South Dakota
Springfield, SD 57062
M: (605) 369-2298
W: (605) 369-2298
Enrollment: A
4-year public funding
M: SDIA
W: AIAW
M: Baseball, Cross Country, Tennis, Track & Field, Basketball, Football, Wrestling
W: Cross Country, Softball, Tennis, Track & Field, Volleyball, Basketball

University of South Dakota
Vermillion, SD 57069
M: (605) 677-5338
W: (605) 677-5336
Enrollment: C
4-year public funding
M: NCAA
W: NCAA
M: Golf, Tennis, Baseball, Basketball, Cross Country, Football, Swimming-Diving, Track & Field
W: Golf, Tennis, Basketball, Cross Country, Softball, Swimming-Diving, Track & Field, Volleyball

South Dakota School of Mines and Technology
East Saint Jo Street
Rapid City, SD 57701
M: (605) 394-2351
W: (605) 394-2351
Enrollment: A
4-year public funding
M: SDIC
W: SDIC
M: Basketball, Cross Country, Football, Golf, Tennis, Track & Field
W: Basketball, Volleyball

Southeast Community College
10th and K Streets
Fairbury, NE 68352
M: (402) 729-6148
W: (402) 729-6148
Enrollment: A
2-year public funding
M: NCCAC, NJCAA
W: NCCAC, NJCAA
M: Cross Country, Tennis, Basketball, Golf, Track & Field
W: Cross Country, Tennis, Basketball, Golf, Softball, Track & Field, Volleyball

Southeastern Community College
West Burlington, IA 52655
M: (319) 752-2731 X. 70
W: (319) 752-2731 X. 71
Enrollment: A
2-year public funding
M: Eastern Iowa
W: Eastern Iowa
M: Bowling, Golf, Tennis, Baseball, Basketball
W: Bowling, Golf, Tennis, Basketball, Softball

Southeastern Louisiana University
North Hazel Street
Hammond, LA 70401
M: (504) 549-2253
W: (504) 549-2253
Enrollment: C
4-year public funding
M: Independent

W: Independent
M: Baseball, Basketball, Cross
   Country, Football, Golf,
   Tennis, Track & Field
W: Basketball, Tennis, Volleyball

Southeastern Oklahoma State University
Durant, OK 74701
M: (405) 924-0121
W: (405) 924-0121
Enrollment: B
4-year public funding
M: OICC, NAIA
W: NAIA
M: Golf, Track & Field, Baseball,
   Basketball, Football, Tennis
W: Basketball, Tennis, Track &
   Field, Volleyball

Southeastern University
501 Eye Street, SW
Washington, DC 20024
M: (202) 488-8162
W: (202) 488-8162
Enrollment: A
4-year private
M: NAIA
W: NAIA
M: Basketball, Soccer, Tennis
W: Basketball

Southeast Missouri State University
900 Normal
Cape Girardeau, MO 63701
M: (314) 651-2227
W: (314) 651-2227
Enrollment: C
4-year public funding
M: MIAA
W: MAIAW
M: Baseball, Basketball, Cross
   Country, Football, Swimming-
   Diving, Tennis, Track &
   Field, Wrestling
W: Basketball, Field Hockey,
   Gymnastics, Softball,
   Swimming-Diving, Tennis,
   Track & Field

Southern Arkansas University
Mangolia, AR 71753
M: (501) 234-5120 X. 223
W: (501) 234-5120 X. 223
Enrollment: A
4-year public funding
M: AIC
W: AWISA
M: Baseball, Basketball, Cross
   Country, Football, Golf,
   Swimming-Diving, Tennis,
   Track & Field
W: Basketball, Softball,
   Swimming-Diving, Tennis,
   Volleyball

Southern Baptist College
Walnut Ridge, AR 72476
M: (501) 866-6741
W: (501) 866-6741
Enrollment: A
2-year private
M: Arkansas JUCO
W: Arkansas JUCO
M: Baseball, Basketball
W: Basketball

University of Southern California
Los Angeles, CA 90007
M: (213) 743-2221
W: (213) 743-2221
Enrollment: C
4-year private
M: Pacific-10

W: WCAA
M: Crew, Sailing, Skiing, Soccer, Baseball, Basketball, Football, Golf, Gymnastics, Swimming-Diving, Tennis, Track & Field, Volleyball, Water Polo
W: Crew, Skiing, Basketball, Golf, Gymnastics, Tennis, Track & Field, Volleyball

Southern California College
55 Fair Drive
Costa Mesa, CA 92626
M: (714) 556–3610 X. 278
W: (714) 556–3610 X. 278
Enrollment: A
4-year private
M: NAIA
W: Independent
M: Baseball, Basketball, Soccer
W: Basketball, Volleyball

University of Southern Colorado
2200 North Bonforte Boulevard
Pueblo, CO 81001
M: (303) 549–2711
W: (303) 549–2660
Enrollment: C
4-year public funding
M: Rocky Mountain
W: Rocky Mountain
M: Golf, Tennis, Baseball, Basketball, Cross Country, Football, Track & Field
W: Tennis, Track & Field, Basketball, Gymnastics, Volleyball

Southern Connecticut State College
501 Crescent Street
New Haven, CT 06515
M: (203) 397–4377
W: (203) 397–4482
Enrollment: C
4-year public funding
M: NCAA, ECAC
W: EAIAW, AIAW
M: Baseball, Basketball, Cross Country, Football, Golf, Gymnastics, Soccer, Swimming-Diving, Tennis, Track & Field, Wrestling
W: Basketball, Cross Country, Field Hockey, Gymnastics, Softball, Swimming-Diving, Tennis, Track & Field, Volleyball

University of Southern Illinois
Carbondale, IL 62901
M: (618) 453–5311
W: (618) 536–5566
Enrollment: C
4-year public funding
M: Missouri Valley
W: AIAW
M: Baseball, Basketball, Cross Country, Football, Golf, Gymnastics, Swimming-Diving, Tennis, Track & Field, Wrestling
W: Badminton, Basketball, Cross Country, Field Hockey, Golf, Gymnastics, Softball, Swimming-Diving, Tennis, Track & Field, Volleyball

University of Southern Maine
Gorham, ME 04038
M: (207) 780–5430
W: (207) 780–5431
Enrollment: B
4-year public funding
M: NCAA, NAIA, WMAC

W: AIAW, EAIAW, MAIAW,
   WMAC
M: Baseball, Basketball, Cross
   Country, Golf, Soccer, Tennis
W: Cross Country, Softball,
   Tennis, Volleyball

**Southern Maine Vocational
Technical Institute**
South Portland, ME 04106
M: (207) 799-7303 X. 261
W: (207) 799-7303 X. 261
Enrollment: A
2-year public funding
M: MSTS, MSCC, NNESCC
W: MSTS, MSCC, NNESCC
M: Baseball, Basketball, Golf,
   Soccer, Softball, Volleyball,
   Cross Country
W: Basketball, Softball, Volleyball

Southern Methodist University
Dallas, TX 75275
M: (214) 692-2864
W: (214) 692-2864
Enrollment: C
4-year private
M: Southwest
W: TAIAW
M: Golf, Basketball, Cross
   Country, Football, Soccer,
   Swimming-Diving, Tennis,
   Track & Field
W: Basketball, Golf, Swimming-
   Diving, Tennis

Southern Oregon State College
Ashland, OR 97520
M: (503) 482-6236
W: (503) 482-6236
Enrollment: B
4-year private funding

M: Independent
W: Cascade
M: Soccer, Water Polo, Baseball,
   Basketball, Cross Country,
   Football, Swimming-Diving,
   Tennis, Track & Field,
   Wrestling
W: Basketball, Cross Country,
   Swimming-Diving, Tennis,
   Track & Field, Volleyball

Southern State Community College
P. O. Box 71
Sardinia, OH 45171
M: (513) 695-0751
W: (513) 695-0751
Enrollment: A
2-year public funding
M: Independent
W: Independent
M: Basketball, Golf, Volleyball
W: Basketball, Golf, Volleyball

**Southern Union State Junior
College**
Wadley, AL 36276
M: (205) 395-2211
W: (205) 395-2211
Enrollment: A
2-year public funding
M: Alabama JCAC
W: Alabama JCAC
M: Baseball, Basketball
W: Basketball

Southern University
6400 Press Drive
New Orleans, LA 70126
M: (504) 282-4401 X. 301
W: (504) 282-4401 X. 301
Enrollment: B
4-year public funding

M: Independent
W: Independent
M: Basketball, Track & Field
W: Track & Field

Southern University and Agricultural and Mechanical College
Baton Rouge, LA 70813
M: (504) 771-3170
W: (504) 771-3170
Enrollment: C
4-year public funding
M: Southwestern
W: Southwestern
M: Cross Country, Baseball, Basketball, Football, Golf, Tennis, Track & Field
W: Cross Country, Track & Field, Basketball, Volleyball

Southern Utah State College
Cedar City, UT 84720
M: (801) 586-4411 X. 283
W: (801) 586-4411 X. 283
Enrollment: A
4-year public funding
M: RMAC
W: RMAC
M: Baseball, Basketball, Cross Country, Football, Golf, Track & Field
W: Basketball, Gymnastics, Softball, Track & Field, Volleyball

University of South Florida
4202 East Fowler Avenue
Tampa, FL 33620
M: (813) 974-2125
W: (813) 974-2125
Enrollment: C

4-year public funding
M: Sun Belt
W: AIAW
M: Baseball, Basketball, Cross Country, Golf, Soccer, Swimming-Diving, Tennis
W: Basketball, Golf, Softball, Swimming-Diving, Tennis, Volleyball

Southwest Baptist College
Bolivas, MO 65613
M: (417) 326-5281
W: (417) 326-5281
Enrollment: A
4-year private
M: Independent
W: Independent
M: Bowling, Cross Country, Baseball, Basketball, Tennis
W: Basketball, Softball, Tennis, Volleyball

Southwestern at Memphis
2000 North Parkway
Memphis, TN 38112
M: (901) 274-1800
W: (901) 274-1800
Enrollment: A
4-year private
M: CAC
W: AIAW, TCWSF
M: Baseball, Basketball, Cross Country, Football, Golf, Soccer, Tennis, Track & Field
W: Basketball, Cross Country, Tennis, Track & Field, Volleyball

Southwestern College
Winfield, KS 67156
M: (316) 221-4150 X. 41

W: (316) 221–4150 X. 41
Enrollment: A
4-year private
M: KCAC
W: KCAC
M: Basketball, Cross Country,
  Football, Golf, Tennis, Track
  & Field
W: Basketball, Cross Country,
  Tennis, Track & Field,
  Volleyball

Southwestern Community College
Townline Road
Creston, IA 50801
M: (515) 782–7081
W: (515) 782–7081
Enrollment: A
2-year public funding
M: Iowa JUCO
W: Iowa JUCO
M: Baseball, Basketball
W: Basketball, Softball

**University of Southwestern
  Louisiana**
Lafayette, LA 70501
M: (318) 264–6310
W: (318) 264–6327
Enrollment: C
4-year public funding
M: Southland
W: LAIAW
M: Baseball, Basketball, Cross
  Country, Football, Golf,
  Tennis, Track & Field
W: Basketball, Tennis, Volleyball

Southwestern University
Georgetown, TX 78626
M: (512) 863–6511 X. 300
W: (512) 863–6511 X. 300

Enrollment: A
4-year private
M: Big State, NAIA
W: AIAW
M: Baseball, Basketball, Golf,
  Tennis
W: Basketball, Tennis, Volleyball

Southwest State University
Marshall, MN 56258
M: (507) 537–7271
W: (507) 537–7271
Enrollment: A
4-year public funding
M: NIC
W: Northern Sun
M: Cross Country, Track & Field,
  Wrestling, Baseball,
  Basketball, Football
W: Basketball, Cross Country,
  Softball, Swimming-Diving,
  Tennis, Track & Field,
  Volleyball

Southwest Texas State University
San Marcos, TX 78666
M: (512) 245–2114
W: (512) 245–2139
Enrollment: C
4-year public funding
M: Lone Star
W: AIAW
M: Basketball, Cross Country,
  Football, Golf, Tennis, Track
  & Field
W: Basketball, Cross Country,
  Gymnastics, Swimming-
  Diving, Tennis, Volleyball

**Spartanburg Methodist Junior
  College**
Spartanburg, SC 29301

M: (803) 576–3911
W: (803) 576–3911
Enrollment: A
2-year private
M: WCJCC
W: WCJCC
M: Bowling, Baseball, Basketball, Golf
W: Bowling, Basketball, Softball, Volleyball

Spring Arbor College
Spring Arbor, MI 49283
M: (517) 750–1200 X. 279
W: (517) 750–1200 X. 279
Enrollment: A
4-year private
M: Independent, NAIA
W: Independent, AIAW
M: Baseball, Basketball, Cross Country, Soccer, Tennis, Track & Field
W: Basketball, Cross Country, Softball, Track & Field, Volleyball

Spring Garden College
102 East Mermaid Lane
Chestnut Hill, PA 19118
M: (215) 242–3700
W: (215) 242–3700
Enrollment: A
4-year private
M: NAIA
W: PAIAW, NAIA
M: Cross Country, Golf, Tennis, Baseball, Basketball, Soccer
W: Softball, Basketball

Spring Hill College
Mobile, AL 36608
M: (205) 460–2346
W: (205) 460–2346
Enrollment: A
4-year private
M: SSC
W: AAIAW
M: Baseball, Basketball, Golf, Tennis
W: Basketball, Tennis

Stanford University
Stanford, CA 94305
M: (415) 497–4591
W: (415) 497–4591
Enrollment: C
4-year private
M: Pacific-10
W: Nor Cal
M: Baseball, Basketball, Cross Country, Fencing, Football, Golf, Gymnastics, Soccer, Swimming-Diving, Tennis, Track & Field, Volleyball, Water Polo
W: Basketball, Cross Country, Fencing, Field Hockey, Golf, Gymnastics, Swimming-Diving, Tennis, Track & Field, Volleyball

State Fair Community College
1900 Clarendon Road
Sedalia, MO 65301
M: (816) 826–9635
W: (816) 826–9635
Enrollment: A
2-year public funding
M: Mid-American
W: Mid-American
M: Soccer, Tennis, Baseball, Basketball, Golf
W: Tennis, Basketball, Golf, Volleyball

College of Staten Island
715 Ocean Terrace
Staten Island, NY 10301
M: (212) 390-7607
W: (212) 390-7607
Enrollment: C
4-year public funding
M: ECAC, NCAA, CUNYAC
W: AIAW
M: Baseball, Basketball, Soccer,
   Tennis
W: Softball, Tennis, Volleyball

Stephen F. Austin State University
Nacogdoches, TX 75961
M: (713) 569-2606
W: (713) 569-2605
Enrollment: C
4-year public funding
M: Lone Star
W: TAIAW, SWAIAW, AIAW
M: Basketball, Cross Country,
   Football, Golf, Tennis, Track
   & Field
W: Basketball, Softball, Tennis,
   Track & Field, Volleyball

Sterling College
Sterling, KS 67579
M: (316) 278-2173 X. 210
W: (316) 278-2173 X. 210
Enrollment: A
4-year private
W: KCAC
W: AIAW
M: Baseball, Basketball, Football,
   Tennis, Track & Field
W: Basketball, Softball, Tennis,
   Track & Field, Volleyball

Stetson University
DeLand, FL 32720
M: (904) 734-4121
W: (904) 734-4121
Enrollment: B
4-year private
M: Independent
W: Independent
M: Golf, Soccer, Tennis, Baseball,
   Basketball
W: Basketball, Softball, Tennis,
   Volleyball

University of Steubenville
Steubenville, OH 43952
M: (614) 283-3771 X. 252
W: (614) 283-3771 X. 337
Enrollment: A
4-year private
M: NAIA, Independent
W: Pennwood West
M: Basketball
W: Basketball

Stevens Institute of Technology
Castle Point Station
Hoboken, NJ 07030
M: (201) 420-5690
Enrollment: A
4-year private
M: IAC, NCAA, ECAC
M: Baseball, Basketball, Fencing,
   Lacrosse, Soccer, Squash,
   Wrestling

Stevens State Technology
Lancaster, PA 17603
M: (717) 397-2491
Enrollment: A
2-year public funding
M: Independent
M: Basketball, Cross Country,
   Football, Track & Field,
   Wrestling

Sul Ross State University
Alpine, TX 79830
M: (915) 837-8226
W: (915) 837-8226
Enrollment: B
4-year public funding
M: TIAA
W: TIAA
M: Basketball, Football, Golf, Tennis, Track & Field
W: Basketball, Golf, Tennis, Track & Field, Volleyball

Surry Community College
Dobson, NC 27017
M: (919) 386-8121
W: (919) 386-8121
Enrollment: A
2-year public funding
M: Western Tarheel
W: Western Tarheel
M: Basketball, Golf, Tennis
W: Basketball, Golf, Tennis

Susquehanna University
Selinsgrove, PA 17870
M: (717) 374-0101
W: (717) 374-0101
Enrollment: A
4-year private
M: NCAA, ECAC, MAC
W: EAIAW, MAC
M: Baseball, Basketball, Cross Country, Football, Golf, Soccer, Swimming-Diving, Tennis, Track & Field, Wrestling
W: Basketball, Field Hockey, Softball, Swimming-Diving, Tennis, Volleyball

Division III: all aid awarded on the basis of financial need.

Swarthmore College
Swarthmore, PA 19081
M: (215) 447-7218
W: (215) 447-7218
Enrollment: A
4-year private
M: MASCAC, NCAA
W: PAIAW, EAIAW, AIAW
M: Baseball, Basketball, Cross Country, Football, Golf, Lacrosse, Soccer, Swimming, Tennis, Track & Field, Wrestling
W: Badminton, Basketball, Field Hockey, Gymnastics, Lacrosse, Softball, Swimming, Tennis, Volleyball

Syracuse University
Syracuse, NY 13210
M: (315) 423-2384
W: (315) 423-2508
Enrollment: C
4-year private
M: Independent
W: AIAW, EAIAW, NSAIAW
M: <u>Basketball</u>, <u>Crew</u>, <u>Cross Country</u>, <u>Football</u>, <u>Gymnastics</u>, <u>Lacrosse</u>, <u>Soccer</u>, <u>Swimming-Diving</u>, <u>Track & Field</u>, <u>Wrestling</u>
W: <u>Basketball</u>, <u>Crew</u>, <u>Field Hockey</u>, <u>Swimming-Diving</u>, <u>Tennis</u>, <u>Volleyball</u>

Tabor College
Hillsboro, KS 67063
M: (316) 947-3121
W: (316) 947-3121
Enrollment: A
4-year private
M: KCAC, NAIA
W: KCAC, NAIA, AIAW

M: Baseball, Basketball, Football,
   Golf, Soccer, Tennis
W: Basketball, Softball, Tennis,
   Volleyball

Tacoma Community College
Tacoma, WA 98465
M: (206) 756–5097
W: (206) 756–5097
Enrollment: C
2-year public funding
M: AACC
W: AACC
M: Baseball, Basketball, Cross
   Country, Golf, Soccer, Track
   & Field
W: Basketball, Cross Country,
   Softball, Tennis, Track &
   Field, Volleyball

Scholarships are awarded to
   students from Washington,
   Oregon, Idaho, and British
   Columbia by conference rule.

University of Tampa
401 West Kennedy Boulevard
Tampa, FL 33606
M: (813) 253–8861 X. 287
W: (813) 253–8861 X. 287
Enrollment: A
4-year private
M: NCAA
W: AIAW
M: Crew, Cross Country, Golf,
   Riflery, Tennis, Baseball,
   Soccer, Swimming-Diving
W: Crew, Cross Country, Golf,
   Riflery, Tennis, Basketball,
   Swimming-Diving, Volleyball

Tarkio College
Tarkio, MO 64491
M: (816) 736–4131 X. 356
W: (816) 736–4131 X. 356
Enrollment: A
4-year private
M: HAAC, NAIA
W: HAAC, NAIA, AIAW
M: Basketball, Cross Country,
   Football, Track & Field
W: Basketball, Cross Country,
   Softball, Track & Field,
   Volleyball

Tarleton State University
Stephenville, TX 76401
M: (817) 968–9186
W: (817) 968–9186
Enrollment: B
4-year public funding
M: TIAA
W: TIAA
M: Basketball, Football, Golf,
   Track & Field
W: Basketball, Gymnastics, Track
   & Field, Volleyball

Taylor University
Upland, IN 46989
M: (317) 998–2751 X. 311
W: (317) 998–2751 X. 311
Enrollment: A
4-year private
M: Hoosier-Buckeye
W: IAIAW
M: Baseball, Basketball, Cross
   Country, Football, Golf,
   Tennis, Track & Field,
   Wrestling
W: Basketball, Field Hockey,
   Softball, Tennis, Track &
   Field, Volleyball

Temple University
Philadelphia PA 19122
M: (215) 787-7445
W: (215) 787-8736
Enrollment: C
4-year public funding
M: ECAC, ECC, NCAA
W: PAIAW, AIAW, EAIAW
M: Baseball, Basketball, Crew,
   Cross Country, Fencing,
   Football, Golf, Gymnastics,
   Soccer, Swimming-Diving,
   Tennis, Track & Field,
   Wrestling
W: Badminton, Basketball,
   Bowling, Cross Country,
   Fencing, Field Hockey,
   Gymnastics, Lacrosse,
   Softball, Swimming-Diving,
   Tennis, Track & Field,
   Volleyball

University of Tennessee
Knoxville, TN 37916
M: (615) 974-1212
W: (615) 974-4275
Enrollment: C
4-year public funding
M: SEC
W: SEC
M: Baseball, Basketball, Cross
   Country, Football, Golf,
   Swimming-Diving, Tennis,
   Track & Field, Wrestling
W: Basketball, Cross Country,
   Swimming-Diving, Tennis,
   Track & Field, Volleyball

University of Tennessee
Martin, TN 38237
M: (901) 587-7660
W: (901) 587-7680
Enrollment: C

4-year public funding
M: Gulf South
W: TCWSF, AIAW
M: Baseball, Basketball, Football,
   Tennis
W: Basketball, Tennis, Volleyball

Tennessee State University
Nashville, TN 37203
M: (615) 320-3596
W: (615) 320-3596
Enrollment: B
4-year public funding
M: Independent
W: AIAW
M: Baseball, Cross Country, Golf,
   Tennis, Basketball, Football,
   Swimming-Diving, Track &
   Field
W: Basketball, Track & Field

Tennessee Technological University
Cookeville, TN 38501
M: (615) 528-3214
W: (615) 528-3314
Enrollment: B
4-year public funding
M: Ohio Valley
W: Ohio Valley, TCWSF
M: Cross Country, Golf, Soccer,
   Tennis, Wrestling, Baseball,
   Basketball, Football, Riflery
W: Cross Country, Tennis,
   Basketball, Riflery, Volleyball

Tennessee Wesleyan College
Athens, TN 37303
M: (615) 745-6712
W: (615) 745-6712
Enrollment: A
4-year private
M: VSAC, NAIA

W: VSAC, NAIA
M: Baseball, Basketball, Soccer, Tennis
W: Basketball, Tennis

University of Texas
Arlington, TX 76019
M: (817) 273-2261
W: (817) 273-2261
Enrollment: C
4-year public funding
M: Southland
W: Independent
M: Fencing, Riflery, Tennis, Volleyball, Weightlifting, Baseball, Basketball, Cross Country, Football, Golf, Track & Field (indoor and outdoor)
W: Tennis, Basketball, Cross Country, Softball, Track & Field (indoor and outdoor), Volleyball

University of Texas
Austin, TX 78712
M: (512) 471-4602
W: (512) 471-7693
Enrollment: C
4-year public funding
M: Southwest
W: AIAW
M: Baseball, Basketball, Cross Country, Football, Golf, Swimming-Diving, Tennis, Track & Field
W: Basketball, Golf, Gymnastics, Swimming-Diving, Tennis, Track & Field, Volleyball

University of Texas
El Paso, TX 79968
M: (915) 747-5347
W: (915) 747-5722
Enrollment: C
4-year public funding
M: WAC
W: Intermountain
M: Baseball, Basketball, Cross Country, Football, Riflery, Track & Field
W: Basketball, Cross Country, Gymnastics, Track & Field, Volleyball

Texas A & I University
Kingsville, TX 78363
M: (512) 595-2411
W: (512) 595-2411
Enrollment: C
4-year public funding
M: Lone Star
W: TAIAW
M: Cross Country, Golf, Tennis, Basketball, Football, Track & Field
W: Basketball, Tennis, Track & Field, Volleyball

Texas Christian University
Fort Worth, TX 76129
M: (817) 921-7965
W: (817) 921-7965
Enrollment: C
4-year private
M: Southwest
W: AIAW
M: Baseball, Basketball, Cross Country, Football, Golf, Riflery, Soccer, Swimming-Diving, Tennis, Track & Field
W: Basketball, Golf, Gymnastics, Riflery, Swimming-Diving, Tennis, Track & Field

Texas Lutheran College
Seguin, TX 78155
M: (512) 379–4161
W: (512) 379–4161
Enrollment: A
4-year private
M: Big State, Independent
W: AIAW
M: Baseball, Basketball, Football, Golf, Tennis
W: Basketball, Cross Country, Tennis, Track & Field, Volleyball

University of Texas of the Permian Basin
Odessa, TX 79762
W: (915) 367-2136
Enrollment: A
4-year public funding
W: AIAW
W: Tennis

Texas Southern University
3201 Wheeler Street
Houston, TX 77004
M: (713) 527–7271
W: (713) 527–7271
Enrollment: C
4-year public funding
M: NAIA, NCAA, Southwestern
W: NAIA, Southwestern, AIAW
M: Baseball, Basketball, Cross Country, Football, Golf, Tennis, Track & Field
W: Basketball, Cross Country, Track & Field

Texas Tech University
Lubbock, TX 79409
M: (806) 742–3355
W: (806) 742–3360

Enrollment: C
4-year public funding
M: Southwest
W: AIAW
M: Baseball, Basketball, Cross Country, Football, Golf, Swimming-Diving, Tennis, Track & Field
W: Basketball, Cross Country, Golf, Swimming-Diving, Tennis, Track & Field

Texas Wesleyan College
Fort Worth, TX 76105
M: (817) 534–0251 X. 400
W: (817) 534–0251 X. 400
Enrollment: A
4-year private
M: NAIA, Texas Athletic
W: AIAW
M: Baseball, Basketball, Golf, Tennis
W: Basketball, Softball, Tennis, Volleyball

Texas Woman's University
Denton, TX 76204
W: (817) 387–7555
Enrollment: C
4-year public funding
W: AIAW, TAIAW, SWAIAW
W: Cross Country, Gymnastics, Swimming-Diving, Tennis, Basketball, Softball, Track & Field, Volleyball

Thiel College
Greenville, PA 16125
M: (412) 588–7700 X. 226
W: (412) 588–7700 X. 222
Enrollment: A

4-year private
M: PAC
W: WKC
M: Baseball, Basketball, Cross Country, Football, Golf, Tennis, Track & Field, Wrestling
W: Basketball, Softball, Tennis, Volleyball

Division III: all aid awarded on the basis of financial need.

Thomas College
West River Road
Waterville, ME 04901
M: (207) 873-0771 X. 41
W: (207) 873-0771 X. 41
Enrollment: A
4-year private
M: WMAC, NCAA, NAIA, ECAC
W: MAIAW
M: Baseball, Basketball, Golf, Soccer, Tennis
W: Basketball, Field Hockey, Golf, Softball, Tennis

Thomas More College
Fort Mitchell, KY 41017
M: (606) 341-5800
W: (606) 341-5800
Enrollment: A
4-year private
M: NCAA, NAIA
W: Independent
M: Baseball, Golf, Tennis, Basketball
W: Volleyball

Three Rivers Community College
507 Vine
Poplar Bluff, MO 63901
M: (314) 686-4101
W: (314) 686-4101
Enrollment: A
2-year public funding
M: MJCAC
W: MJCAC
M: Baseball, Basketball, Golf
W: Basketball, Tennis, Volleyball

Tiffen University
Tiffen, OH 44883
M: (419) 447-6442
W: (419) 447-6442
Enrollment: A
4-year private
M: Mid-Ohio
W: Independent
M: Baseball, Basketball, Golf
W: Softball, Volleyball

University of Toledo
2801 West Bancroft Street
Toledo, OH 43606
M: (419) 537-4184
W: (419) 537-4184
Enrollment: C
4-year public funding
M: Mid-American
W: AIAW
M: Soccer, Volleyball, Baseball, Basketball, Cross Country, Football, Golf, Swimming-Diving, Tennis, Track & Field, Volleyball, Wrestling
W: Basketball, Field Hockey, Softball, Tennis, Volleyball

Tougaloo College
Tougaloo, MI 39174
M: (601) 956-4941
W: (601) 956-4941

Enrollment: A
4-year private
M: NCAA, NAIA
W: NCAA, NAIA, AIAW
M: Basketball, Cross Country, Soccer, Tennis, Track & Field
W: Basketball, Cross Country, Tennis, Track & Field

Towson State University
Towson, MD 21204
M: (301) 321-2758
W: (301) 321-2758
Enrollment: C
4-year public funding
M: ECAC
W: EAIAW
M: Baseball, Basketball, Cross Country, Football, Golf, Gymnastics, Lacrosse, Soccer, Swimming-Diving, Tennis, Track & Field, Wrestling
W: Basketball, Field Hockey, Gymnastics, Lacrosse, Softball, Swimming-Diving, Tennis, Track & Field, Volleyball

Treasure Valley Community College
650 College Boulevard
Ontario, OR 97914
M: (503) 548-5448
W: (503) 548-5448
Enrollment: A
2-year public funding
M: WTCC
W: WTCC
M: Baseball, Basketball, Bowling, Cross Country, Golf, Soccer, Softball, Tennis, Wrestling
W: Basketball, Bowling, Softball, Tennis, Volleyball

Trenton Junior College
Trenton, MO 64683
M: (816) 359-3948
W: (816) 359-3948
Enrollment: A
2-year public funding
M: Mid-American
W: Mid-American
M: Basketball
W: Basketball

Trenton State College
Trenton, NJ 08625
M: (609) 771-2230
W: (609) 771-2230
Enrollment: C
4-year public funding
M: ECAC, NCAA, NJSCC
W: AIAW
M: Archery, Baseball, Basketball, Cross Country, Football, Golf, Gymnastics, Soccer, Tennis, Track & Field, Wrestling
W: Archery, Basketball, Field Hockey, Gymnastics, Lacrosse, Softball, Swimming-Diving, Tennis, Track & Field, Volleyball

Trinidad State Junior College
Trinidad, CO 81082
M: (303) 846-5510
W: (393) 846-5510
Enrollment: A
2-year public funding
M: Empire
W: Empire
M: Baseball, Basketball, Golf
W: Basketball

Trinity Bible Institute
Ellendale ND 58436
M: (701) 349-3372
W: (701) 349-3621 X. 36
Enrollment: A
4-year private
M: NICC
W: NICC
M: Basketball
W: Basketball

Trinity College
Hartford, CT 06106
M: (203) 527-3151 X. 217/370
Enrollment: A
4-year private
M: NESCAC
M: Baseball, Basketball, Crew, Cross Country, Fencing, Golf, Lacrosse, Soccer, Softball, Squash, Swimming-Diving, Tennis, Track & Field, Water Polo, Wrestling

Trinity University
715 Stadium Drive
San Antonio, TX 78284
M: (512) 736-8406
W: (512) 736-8406
Enrollment: B
4-year private
M: TIAA
W: AIAW
M: Baseball, Basketball, Bowling, Football, Golf, Riflery, Soccer, Track & Field, Tennis
W: Basketball, Bowling, Riflery, Soccer, Softball, Track & Field, Volleyball, Tennis

Tri-State University
Angola, IN 46703
M: (219) 665-3141 X. 267
W: (219) 665-3141 X. 267
Enrollment: A
4-year private
M: Mid-Central
W: Mid-Central
M: Baseball, Basketball, Cross Country, Fencing, Golf, Soccer, Tennis, Track & Field
W: Basketball, Fencing, Track & Field, Volleyball

Triton College
2000 North Fifth Avenue
River Grove, IL 60171
M: (312) 456-0300 X. 506
W: (312) 456-0300 X. 507
Enrollment: C
2-year public funding
M: NCCCC
W: NCCCC
M: Baseball, Basketball, Cross Country, Football, Golf, Soccer, Tennis, Track & Field, Wrestling
W: Basketball, Cross Country, Gymnastics, Softball, Tennis, Track & Field, Volleyball

Troy State University
Troy, AL 36081
M: (205) 566-3000 X. 480
W: (205) 566-3000 X. 480
Enrollment: C
4-year public funding
M: Gulf South
W: AAIAW
M: Badminton, Basketball, Cross Country, Football, Golf, Track & Field
W: Basketball, Golf, Track & Field, Volleyball

Truett-McConnell College
Cleveland, GA 30528
M: (404) 805-2137
W: (404) 865-2137
Enrollment: A
2-year private
M: GJCAA
W: GJCAA
M: Basketball, Tennis
W: Basketball, Softball, Tennis

Tufts University
Medford, MA 02155
M: (617) 628-5000 X. 247
Enrollment: B
4-year private
M: NESCAC
M: Baseball, Basketball, Crew, Cross Country, Football, Golf, Lacrosse, Sailing, Soccer, Squash, Swimming-Diving, Tennis, Track & Field

Tulane University
6401 Willow Street
New Orleans, LA 70118
M: (504) 865-4391
W: (504) 865-4798
Enrollment: C
4-year private
M: Metro
W: Metro
M: Cross Country, Golf, Track & Field, Baseball, Basketball, Football, Swimming-Diving, Tennis
W: Basketball, Swimming-Diving, Tennis, Volleyball

University of Tulsa
600 South College
Tulsa, OK 74104
M: (918) 592-6000 X. 321
W: (918) 592-6000 X. 321
Enrollment: C
4-year private
M: NCAA, Missouri Valley
W: AIAW
M: Basketball, Cross Country, Football, Golf, Soccer, Tennis, Track & Field
W: Basketball, Cross Country, Golf, Swimming-Diving, Tennis, Track & Field, Volleyball

Tunxis Community College
Farmington, CT 06032
M: (203) 677-7701 X. 41
W: (203) 677-7701 X. 57
Enrollment: B
2-year public funding
M: CCCAA, NJCAA
W: CCCAA, NJCAA
M: Baseball, Basketball, Cross Country, Golf, Tennis
W: Basketball, Cross Country, Softball, Tennis, Volleyball

Tuskegee Institute
Tuskegee, AL 36088
M: (205) 727-8849/8850
W: (205) 727-8855
Enrollment: B
4-year private
M: SIAC
W: SIAC
M: Baseball, Basketball, Cross Country, Football, Tennis, Track & Field
W: Basketball, Tennis, Track & Field, Volleyball

Umpqua Community College
Roseberg, OR 97470
M: (503) 440-4600
W: (503) 440-4600
Enrollment: A
2-year public funding
M: Baseball, Basketball, Cross Country, Golf, Tennis, Track & Field, Wrestling
W: Basketball, Cross Country, Tennis, Track & Field, Volleyball

Scholarships are restricted to in-district tuition only.

Union College
Barbourville, KY 40906
M: (606) 546-4151 X. 133
W: (606) 546-4151 X. 133
Enrollment: A
4-year private
M: KIAC
W: KWIAC
M: Baseball, Basketball, Cross Country, Golf, Soccer, Swimming-Diving, Tennis, Track & Field
W: Basketball, Swimming-Diving, Tennis, Volleyball

United Wesleyan College
1414 East Cedar Street
Allentown, PA 18103
M: (215) 439-8709
W: (215) 439-8709
Enrollment: A
4-year private
M: NACC
W: NACC
M: Baseball, Basketball, Soccer
W: Basketball, Softball, Volleyball

Upper Iowa University
Fayette, IA 52142
M: (319) 425-3311 X. 266/267
W: (319) 425-3311 X. 266/267
Enrollment: A
4-year private
M: IICC
W: IICC
M: Baseball, Basketball, Football, Golf, Tennis, Wrestling
W: Softball, Tennis, Volleyball

Upsala College
East Orange, NJ 07019
M: (201) 266-7227
W: (201) 266-7227
Enrollment: A
4-year private
M: Middle Atlantic
W: Middle Atlantic
M: Baseball, Basketball, Fencing, Football, Golf, Ice Hockey, Lacrosse, Soccer, Tennis, Track & Field, Wrestling
W: Basketball, Softball, Tennis, Volleyball

Division III: all aid awarded on the basis of financial need.

Urbana College
Urbana, OH 43078
M: (513) 652-1301 X. 345
W: (513) 652-1301 X. 346
Enrollment: A
4-year private
M: Mid-Ohio
W: Independent
M: Baseball, Basketball, Golf, Wrestling
W: Basketball, Softball, Volleyball

Ursinus College
Collegeville, PA 19426
M: (215) 489-4111 X. 251
W: (215) 489-4111 X. 251
Enrollment: A
4-year private
M: MAC, ECAC, NCAA
W: AIAW, EAIAW, PAIAW
M: Baseball, Basketball, Cross Country, Football, Golf, Gymnastics, Lacrosse, Soccer, Swimming-Diving, Tennis, Track & Field, Wrestling
W: Basketball, Field Hockey, Gymnastics, Lacrosse, Softball, Swimming-Diving, Tennis, Track & Field, Volleyball

University of Utah
Salt Lake City, UT 84112
M: (801) 581-8171
W: (801) 581-8171
Enrollment: C
4-year public funding
M: Western Athletic
W: AIAW
M: Baseball, Basketball, Cross Country, Football, Golf, Skiing, Swimming-Diving, Tennis, Track & Field
W: Basketball, Cross Country, Gymnastics, Skiing, Softball, Swimming-Diving, Tennis, Track & Field, Volleyball

Utah State University
Logan, UT 84381
M: (801) 750-1850
W: (801) 750-2060
Enrollment: C
4-year public funding
M: PCAA

W: AIAW
M: Basketball, Cross Country, Football, Golf, Indoor Track, Tennis, Track & Field, Wrestling
W: Basketball, Cross Country, Gymnastics, Indoor Track, Softball, Track & Field, Volleyball

Utica College of Syracuse University
Utica, NY 13502
M: (315) 792-3050
W: (315) 792-3052
Enrollment: A
4-year private
M: ECAC
W: ECAC
M: Golf, Baseball, Basketball, Swimming-Diving
W: Basketball, Swimming-Diving

Utica Junior College
Utica, MI 39175
M: (601) 885-6062
Enrollment: A
2-year public funding
M: MJCAC
M: Baseball, Basketball

Valparaiso University
Valparaiso, IN 46383
M: (219) 464-5232
W: (219) 464-5232
Enrollment: B
4-year private
M: Heartland, Independent
W: AIAW
M: Baseball, Basketball, Cross Country, Football, Golf, Swimming-Diving, Tennis,

Track & Field, Wrestling
W: Basketball, Field Hockey,
Gymnastics, Swimming-
Diving, Tennis, Volleyball

Vanderbilt University
Nashville, TN 37203
M: (615) 322–4727
W: (615) 322–2888
Enrollment: C
4-year private
M: Southeastern
W: AIAW
M: Cross Country, Golf, Soccer,
Swimming-Diving, Track &
Field, Baseball, Basketball,
Football, Tennis
W: Cross Country, Track & Field,
Volleyball, Basketball,
Swimming-Diving, Tennis

Ventura College
Ventura, CA 93003
M: (805) 642–3211 X. 381
W: (805) 642–3211 X. 388
Enrollment: C
2-year public funding
M: Western State
W: Western State
M: Baseball, Basketball, Cross
Country, Football, Golf,
Swimming-Diving, Tennis,
Track & Field, Water Polo,
Wrestling
W: Basketball, Cross Country,
Softball, Swimming-Diving,
Track & Field, Volleyball

Villanova University
Villanova, PA 19085
M: (215) 645–4110
W: (215) 645–4112
Enrollment: C
4-year private
M: Independent
W: Independent
M: Bowling, Crew, Fencing,
Football, Lacrosse, Sailing,
Soccer, Tennis, Water Polo,
Baseball, Basketball,
Swimming-Diving, Track &
Field
W: Bowling, Crew, Lacrosse,
Soccer, Tennis, Basketball,
Field Hockey, Swimming-
Diving, Track & Field,
Volleyball

University of Virginia
Charlottesville, VA 22903
M: (804) 924–3011
W: (804) 924–3011
Enrollment: C
4-year public funding
M: Atlantic Coast
W: Atlantic Coast
M: Fencing, Baseball, Basketball,
Cross Country, Football,
Golf, Lacrosse, Soccer,
Swimming-Diving, Tennis,
Track & Field, Wrestling
W: Volleyball, Basketball, Cross
Country, Field Hockey,
Lacrosse, Softball, Swimming-
Diving, Tennis, Track & Field

Virginia Commonwealth University
West Franklin Street
Richmond, VA 23284
M: (804) 257–1278
W: (804) 252–7127
Enrollment: C
4-year public funding
M: Sun Belt
W: AIAW

M: Cross Country, Baseball, Basketball, Golf, Soccer, Swimming-Diving, Tennis, Volleyball, Wrestling
W: Cross Country, Basketball, Field Hockey, Swimming-Diving, Tennis, Volleyball

Virginia Polytechnic Institute
Blacksburg, VA 24061
M: (703) 961–6726
W: (703) 961–6726
Enrollment: C
4-year public funding
M: Metro
W: Metro
M: Baseball, Basketball, Cross Country, Football, Golf, Soccer, Swimming-Diving, Tennis, Track & Field, Wrestling
W: Basketball, Field Hockey, Swimming-Diving, Tennis, Volleyball

Virginia State College
Petersburg, VA 23803
M: (804) 520–6231
W: (804) 520–6232
Enrollment: B
4-year public funding
M: CIAA, NAIA, NCAA
W: CIAA, NAIA
M: Basketball, Cross Country, Football, Golf, Track & Field
W: Softball, Basketball, Track & Field

Virginia Union University
1500 North Lombardy Street
Richmond, VA 23220
M: (919) 486–1314
W: (919) 486–1315
Enrollment: A
4-year private
M: CIAA, NCAA, NAIA
W: CIAA, NCAA, NAIA
M: Basketball, Cross Country, Football, Golf, Tennis, Track & Field
W: Basketball, Softball, Tennis, Track & Field, Volleyball

All aid for men and women is based on financial need.

Viterbo College
815 South 9th
La Crosse, WI 54601
M: (608) 784–0040 X. 357
W: (608) 784–0040 X. 357
Enrollment: A
4-year private
M: TRCC
W: Independent
M: Basketball, Soccer
W: Basketball, Track & Field

Wabash College
301 West Wabash Avenue
Crawfordsville, IN 47933
M: (317) 362–1400
Enrollment: A
4-year private
M: NCAA
M: Baseball, Basketball, Cross Country, Football, Golf, Soccer, Swimming-Diving, Tennis, Track & Field, Wrestling

Wagner College
631 Howard Avenue
Staten Island, NY 10301

M: (212) 390–3068/3088
Enrollment: A
4-year private
M: Independent
M: Football, Golf, Tennis,
   Baseball, Basketball, Cross
   Country, Track & Field,
   Wrestling

Wake Forest University
Winston-Salem, NC 27109
M: (919) 761–5640
W: (919) 761–5751
Enrollment: C
4-year private
M: Atlantic Coast
W: Atlantic Coast
M: Baseball, Basketball, Cross
   Country, Football, Golf,
   Soccer, Tennis, Track & Field
W: Basketball, Cross Country,
   Field Hockey, Golf, Tennis,
   Track & Field, Volleyball

Walsh College
2020 Easton Street
Canton, OH 44720
M: (216) 499–7090 X. 73
W: (216) 499–7090 X. 66
Enrollment: A
4-year private
M: Mid-Ohio, NAIA
W: Mid-Ohio, NAIA
M: Baseball, Basketball, Cross
   Country, Golf, Soccer,
   Swimming-Diving, Tennis,
   Track & Field
W: Basketball, Softball, Volleyball

Warner Pacific College
2219 SE 68th
Portland, OR 97215

M: (503) 775–4366
W: (503) 775–4366
Enrollment: A
4-year private
M: Independent
W: Independent
M: Basketball, Soccer, Tennis
W: Basketball, Tennis, Volleyball

Warren Wilson College
Swannanoa, NC 28778
M: (704) 298–3325
W: (704) 298–3325
Enrollment: A
4-year private
M: NLCAA
W: NLCAA
M: Baseball, Basketball, Cross
   Country, Soccer
W: Basketball, Cross Country,
   Softball

All students work fifteen hours per week for which they receive room and meals.

Washburn University
Topeka, KS 66621
M: (913) 295–6334
W: (913) 295–6300 X. 459
Enrollment: C
4-year public funding
M: CSIC
W: CSIC
M: Baseball, Golf, Tennis, Track
   & Field, Basketball, Football
W: Gymnastics, Softball, Tennis,
   Volleyball, Basketball

University of Washington
Seattle, WA 98195
M: (206) 543–2210

W: (206) 543–2279
Enrollment: C
4-year public funding
M: Pacific-10
W: AIAW
M: Baseball, Basketball, Cross Country, Football, Golf, Soccer, Swimming-Diving, Tennis, Track & Field
W: Basketball, Crew, Cross Country, Golf, Gymnastics, Squash, Swimming-Diving, Tennis, Track & Field

Washington and Lee University
Lexington, VA 24450
M: (703) 463–9111 X. 226
Enrollment: A
4-year private
M: ODAC
M: Baseball, Basketball, Cross Country, Football, Golf, Lacrosse, Soccer, Swimming-Diving, Tennis, Track & Field, Water Polo, Wrestling

Washington Bible College
6511 Princess Garden Parkway
Lanham, MD 20801
M: (301) 552–1400 X. 231
W: (301) 552–1400 X. 253
Enrollment: A
4-year private
M: NACC
W: NACC
M: Baseball, Basketball, Cross Country, Soccer
W: Basketball, Cross Country, Field Hockey, Softball, Volleyball

Washington State University
Pullman, WA 99163
M: (509) 335–4501
W: (509) 335–9571
Enrollment: C
4-year public funding
M: Pacific-10
W: NCWSA
M: Golf, Swimming-Diving, Water Polo, Basketball, Cross Country, Football, Gymnastics, Tennis, Track & Field, Wrestling
W: Basketball, Cross Country, Field Hockey, Gymnastics, Skiing, Swimming-Diving, Tennis, Track & Field, Volleyball

Washington University
St. Louis, MO 63130
M: (314) 889–5185
W: (314) 889–5185
Enrollment: B
4-year private
M: NCAA
W: AIAW
M: Baseball, Cross Country, Football, Golf, Soccer, Swimming-Diving, Tennis, Track & Field, Wrestling
W: Basketball, Cross Country, Swimming-Diving, Tennis, Track & Field, Volleyball

All aid for men and women is based on financial need.

Wayland Baptist College
1900 West 7th Street
Plainview, TX 79072
M: (806) 296–5521 X. 19
W: (806) 296–5521 X. 19

Enrollment: A
4-year private
M: TAC
W: AIAW
M: Tennis, Basketball, Cross
   Country, Track & Field
W: Basketball, Tennis

Waynesburg College
Waynesburg, PA 15370
M: (412) 627–8191
W: (412) 627–8191
Enrollment: A
4-year private
M: Independent, NAIA
W: Independent
M: Baseball, Golf, Tennis, Track
   & Field, Basketball, Football,
   Wrestling
W: Volleyball

Wayne State University
Detroit, MI 48202
M: (313) 577–4280
W: (313) 577–4280
Enrollment: C
4-year public funding
M: GLIAC
W: GLIAC
M: Baseball, Basketball, Crew,
   Cross Country, Fencing,
   Football, Golf, Swimming-
   Diving, Tennis, Track & Field
W: Basketball, Fencing, Softball,
   Tennis, Volleyball

Webber College
Babson Park, FL 33827
M: (813) 638–1431
W: (813) 638–1431
Enrollment: A
4-year private

M: Independent
W: Independent
M: Basketball, Tennis, Wrestling
W: Basketball, Tennis, Volleyball

Weber State College
3750 Harrison Boulevard
Ogden, UT 84403
M: (801) 626–6500
W: (801) 626–6500
Enrollment: C
4-year public funding
M: Big Sky
W: Intermountain
M: Basketball, Cross Country,
   Football, Golf, Tennis, Track
   & Field, Wrestling
W: Basketball, Cross Country,
   Golf, Softball, Tennis, Track
   & Field, Volleyball

Wenatchee Valley Junior College
1300 Fifth Street
Wenatchee, WA 98801
M: (509) 662–1651 X. 240
W: (509) 662–1651 X. 241
Enrollment: A
2-year public funding
M: AACC
W: AACC
M: Basketball, Football, Tennis,
   Track & Field
W: Basketball, Tennis, Track &
   Field

Scholarships are awarded to
students from Washington,
Oregon, Idaho, and British
Columbia by conference rule.

Wesleyan University
Middletown, CT 06457

M: (203) 347-9411 X. 554
W: (203) 347-9411 X. 554
Enrollment: A
4 year private
M: NCAA, ECAC, NESCAC
W: NESCAC, EAIAW, AIAW
M: Baseball, Basketball, Crew, Cross Country, Football, Golf, Ice Hockey, Lacrosse, Soccer, Squash, Swimming, Tennis, Track & Field
W: Basketball, Crew, Cross Country, Field Hockey, Lacrosse, Squash, Swimming, Tennis, Track & Field

West Chester State College
West Chester, PA 19380
M: (215) 436-3555/3556
W: (215) 436-2917
Enrollment: C
4-year public funding
M: East Coast
W: PAIAW
M: Basketball, Cross Country, Golf, Gymnastics, Tennis, Track & Field, Baseball, Football, Soccer, Swimming-Diving, Wrestling
W: Badminton, Basketball, Cross Country, Field Hockey, Gymnastics, Lacrosse, Softball, Swimming-Diving, Tennis, Track & Field, Volleyball

Western Carolina University
Cullowhee, NC 28723
M: (704) 227-7338
W: (704) 227-7338
Enrollment: C
4-year public funding
M: Southern

W: NCAIAW
M: Riflery, Soccer, Swimming-Diving, Tennis, Volleyball, Baseball, Basketball, Cross Country, Football, Golf, Track & Field
W: Riflery, Swimming-Diving, Tennis, Basketball, Gymnastics, Softball, Volleyball

Western Illinois University
Macomb, IL 61455
M: (309) 298-1106
W: (309) 298-1964
Enrollment: C
4-year public funding
M: Mid-Continent
W: AIAW
M: Baseball, Basketball, Cross Country, Football, Golf, Soccer, Swimming-Diving, Tennis, Track & Field, Wrestling
W: Badminton, Basketball, Cross Country, Field Hockey, Gymnastics, Softball, Swimming-Diving, Tennis, Track & Field, Volleyball

Western Kentucky University
College Heights
Bowling Green, KY 42101
M: (502) 745-3542
W: (502) 745-3542
Enrollment: C
4-year public funding
M: OVC
W: OVC, KWIC
M: Baseball, Basketball, Cross Country, Football, Golf, Riflery, Swimming-Diving, Tennis, Track & Field

W: Basketball, Cross Country, Golf, Gymnastics, Riflery, Tennis, Track & Field

Western Maryland College
Westminster, MD 21157
M: (301) 848–7000 X. 580
W: (301) 848–7000 X. 575
Enrollment: A
4-year private funding
M: Middle Atlantic
W: Middle Atlantic, Penn-Mar
M: Baseball, Basketball, Cross Country, Football, Golf, Lacrosse, Soccer, Swimming-Diving, Tennis, Track & Field, Wrestling
W: Basketball, Cross Country, Field Hockey, Lacrosse, Softball, Tennis, Track & Field, Volleyball

Western Michigan University
Kalamazoo, MI 49001
M: (616) 383–1930
W: (616) 383–1930
Enrollment: C
4-year public funding
M: Mid-American
W: Mid-American
M: Baseball, Basketball, Cross Country, Football, Golf, Gymnastics, Ice Hockey, Soccer, Swimming-Diving, Tennis, Track & Field, Wrestling
W: Basketball, Cross Country, Field Hockey, Gymnastics, Softball, Swimming-Diving, Tennis, Track & Field

Western Montana College
Dillon, MT 59725
M: (406) 683–7201
W: (406) 683–7201
Enrollment: A
4-year public
M: Frontier
W: Frontier
M: Basketball, Football, Track & Field, Wrestling
W: Basketball, Track & Field, Volleyball

Western New England College
1215 Wilbraham Road
Springfield, MA 01119
M: (413) 782–3111
W: (413) 782–3111
Enrollment: A
4-year private
M: NCAA, NAIA, ECAC, NEIBA
W: AIAW, EIAW, NAIAW
M: Baseball, Basketball, Bowling, Cross Country, Golf, Lacrosse, Skiing, Soccer, Tennis, Wrestling
W: Basketball, Bowling, Cross Country, Skiing, Softball, Tennis, Volleyball

Western Piedmont Community College
Morganton, NC 28655
M: (704) 437–8688 X. 217
Enrollment: A
2-year public funding
M: Independent
M: Golf, Tennis

Western State College of Colorado
Gunnison, CO 81230

M: (303) 943–3089
W: (303) 943–2169
Enrollment: B
M: Rocky Mountain
W: Rocky Mountain
4-year public funding
M: Baseball, Basketball, Cross Country, Football, Golf, Skiing, Swimming-Diving, Track & Field, Wrestling
W: Basketball, Gymnastics, Skiing, Softball, Swimming-Diving, Tennis, Volleyball

Western Washington University
516 High Street
Bellingham, WA 98225
M: (206) 676–3109
W: (206) 676–3109
Enrollment: C
4-year public funding
M: NAIA
W: AIAW
M: Baseball, Basketball, Crew, Cross Country, Football, Golf, Tennis, Track & Field, Wrestling
W: Basketball, Crew, Cross Country, Field Hockey, Tennis, Track & Field, Volleyball

All aid for men and women is based on financial need.

Westfield State College
Westfield, MA 01085
M: (413) 568–3311 X. 405
W: (413) 568–3311 X. 405
Enrollment: B
4-year public funding
M: NCAA, ECAC, MASCAC
W: NCAA, ECAC, MASCAC

M: Baseball, Basketball, Cross Country, Hockey, Lacrosse, Soccer, Tennis, Track & Field, Volleyball
W: Basketball, Field Hockey, Gymnastics, Soccer, Softball, Tennis, Track & Field, Volleyball

All aid for men and women is based on financial need.

West Georgia College
Carrollton, GA 30117
M: (404) 834–1357
W: (404) 834–1357
Enrollment: C
4-year public funding
M: South Atlanta, NCAA, NAIA
W: GAIAW
M: Football, Baseball, Basketball, Cross Country, Golf, Tennis, Track & Field
W: Basketball, Softball, Tennis, Volleyball

West Hills College
300 Cherry Lane
Coalinga, CA 93210
M: (209) 935–0801
W: (209) 935–0801
Enrollment: A
2-year public funding
M: Central Valley
W: Central Valley
M: Baseball, Basketball, Football, Tennis, Track & Field
W: Softball, Tennis, Track & Field, Volleyball

West Liberty State College
West Liberty, WV 26074

M: (304) 336–8082
W: (304) 336–8046
Enrollment: B
4-year public funding
M: WVIAC
W: WVIAA
M: Baseball, Basketball, Football, Golf, Tennis, Wrestling
W: Basketball, Softball, Tennis, Volleyball

West Los Angeles College
Culver City, CA 90230
M: (213) 836–7110
W: (213) 836–7110
Enrollment: B
2-year public funding
M: Western State
W: Western State
M: Baseball, Basketball, Cross Country, Football, Track & Field
W: Cross Country, Tennis, Track & Field, Volleyball

Westminster College
Fulton, MO 65251
M: (314) 642–3361 X. 301
Enrollment: A
4-year private
M: NAIA, Independent
M: Soccer, Baseball, Basketball, Cross Country, Golf, Tennis, Track & Field

Westmont College
Santa Barbara, CA 93108
M: (805) 969–9051 X. 257
W: (805) 969–9051 X. 257
Enrollment: A
4-year private
M: NAIA

W: AIAW
M: Baseball, Basketball, Cross Country, Soccer, Tennis, Track & Field
W: Cross Country, Soccer, Tennis, Volleyball

Westmoreland Community College
Youngwood, PA 15697
M: (412) 925–4000
W: (412) 925–4000
Enrollment: B
2-year public funding
M: Skyline
W: Skyline
M: Golf, Tennis
W: Tennis, Volleyball

West Texas State University
Canyon, TX 79016
M: (806) 656–2131
W: (806) 656–2131
Enrollment: C
4-year public funding
M: Missouri Valley
W: AIAW
M: Basketball, Cross Country, Football, Golf, Tennis, Track & Field
W: Basketball, Cross Country, Softball, Tennis, Track & Field, Volleyball

West Virginia State College
Institute, WV 25112
M: (304) 766–3165
W: (304) 766–3165
Enrollment: B
4-year public funding
M: WVIAC
W: WVIAA
M: Baseball, Basketball, Cross

Country, Football, Tennis,
  Track & Field
W: Basketball, Tennis, Track &
  Field

West Virginia University
Morgantown, WV 26506
M: (304) 293–5621
W: (304) 293–5621
Enrollment: C
4-year public funding
M: NCAA, EAA
W: AIAW
M: Baseball, Basketball, Cross
  Country, Football, Golf,
  Gymnastics, Riflery, Soccer,
  Swimming-Diving, Tennis,
  Track & Field (indoor and
  outdoor), Wrestling
W: Basketball, Cross Country,
  Gymnastics, Riflery, Softball,
  Swimming-Diving, Tennis,
  Track & Field (indoor and
  outdoor), Volleyball

West Virginia Wesleyan College
Buckhannon, WV 26201
M: (304) 473–8099
W: (304) 473–8099
Enrollment: A
4-year private
M: WVIAC
W: WVIAA
M: Baseball, Cross Country, Golf,
  Basketball, Football, Soccer,
  Tennis, Track & Field
W: Basketball, Field Hockey,
  Tennis, Track & Field

Wharton County Junior College
Wharton, TX 77488
M: (713) 532–4563
W: (713) 532–4563
Enrollment: A
2-year public funding
M: TJCAC, TJCFC, NJCAA
W: TJCAC, TJCFC, NJCAA
M: Baseball, Basketball, Cross
  Country, Football, Golf,
  Tennis, Track & Field
W: Basketball, Cross Country,
  Golf, Tennis, Track & Field,
  Volleyball

Wheaton College
Wheaton, IL 60187
M: (312) 266–5125
W: (312) 266–5125
Enrollment: A
4-year private
M: CCIW
W: AIAW
M: Baseball, Basketball, Cross
  Country, Football, Golf,
  Gymnastics, Soccer,
  Swimming-Diving, Tennis,
  Track & Field, Wrestling
W: Basketball, Field Hockey,
  Gymnastics, Softball,
  Swimming-Diving, Tennis,
  Track & Field, Volleyball

Wheaton College
Norton, MA 02766
W: (617) 285–7722 X. 364
Enrollment: A
4-year private
W: AIAW, EAIAW
W: Basketball, Fencing, Field
  Hockey, Lacrosse, Softball,
  Tennis, Volleyball

Wheeling College
315 Washington Avenue

Wheeling, WV 26003
M: (304) 243-2365
W: (304) 243-2365
Enrollment: A
4-year private
M: WVIAC, NAIA
W: WVIAA, AIAW
M: Basketball, Cross Country, Golf, Soccer, Tennis
W: Basketball, Softball, Tennis, Volleyball

Whitworth College
Spokane, WA 99251
M: (509) 466-3235
W: (509) 466-3235
Enrollment: A
4-year private
M: NAIA
W: AIAW
M: Baseball, Basketball, Cross Country, Football, Golf, Swimming-Diving, Tennis, Track & Field
W: Basketball, Cross Country, Swimming-Diving, Tennis, Track & Field, Volleyball

Wichita State University
Wichita, KS 67208
M: (316) 689-3265
Enrollment: C
4-year public funding
M: Missouri Valley
M: Baseball, Basketball, Cross Country, Football, Golf, Tennis, Track & Field

Wilberforce University
Wilberforce, OH 45384
M: (513) 376-2911 X. 287
W: (513) 376-2911 X. 287
Enrollment: A
4-year private
M: Independent
W: Independent
M: Basketball, Tennis, Volleyball
W: Basketball, Soccer, Tennis, Volleyball

Wiley College
Marshall, TX 75670
M: (214) 938-8341 X. 44
W: (214) 938-8341 X. 48
Enrollment: A
4-year private
M: IAC
W: IAC
M: Baseball, Basketball, Cross Country, Track & Field, Volleyball
W: Basketball, Cross Country, Softball, Track & Field, Volleyball

Wilkes College
Wilkes-Barre, PA 18703
M: (717) 824-4651
W: (717) 824-4651
Enrollment: A
4-year private
M: ECAC, MAC
W: ECAC, MAC, NPWIAA
M: Baseball, Basketball, Cross Country, Golf, Lacrosse, Soccer, Swimming-Diving, Tennis, Wrestling
W: Basketball, Cross Country, Field Hockey, Golf, Soccer, Softball, Swimming-Diving, Tennis, Volleyball

College of William and Mary
Williamsburg, VA 23185

M: (804) 229-3111
W: (804) 253-4750
Enrollment: B
4-year public funding
M: ECAC
W: AIAW
M: Fencing, Riflery, Baseball, Basketball, Cross Country, Football, Golf, Gymnastics, Lacrosse, Soccer, Swimming-Diving, Tennis, Track & Field, Wrestling
W: Badminton, Bowling, Fencing, Golf, Gymnastics, Riflery, Volleyball, Basketball, Field Hockey, Lacrosse, Swimming-Diving, Tennis, Track & Field

William Carey College
Tuscan Avenue
Hattiesburg, MI 39401
M: (601) 582-5051
W: (601) 582-5051
Enrollment: A
4-year private
M: Southern States
W: Southern States
M: Baseball, Basketball
W: Basketball, Softball

Williamette University
900 State Street
Salem, OR 97301
M: (503) 370-6424
W: (503) 370-6422
Enrollment: A
4-year private
M: Pacific Northwest, NAIA
W: AIAW
M: Baseball, Basketball, Cross Country, Football, Golf, Swimming-Diving, Tennis, Track & Field, Wrestling
W: Basketball, Cross Country, Softball, Swimming-Diving, Tennis, Track & Field, Volleyball

William Paterson College
300 Pompton Road
Wayne, NJ 07470
M: (201) 595-2100
W: (201) 595-2100
Enrollment: C
4-year public funding
M: NJSCAC
W: NJSCAC
M: Baseball, Basketball, Cross Country, Fencing, Football, Golf, Soccer, Swimming-Diving, Track & Field
W: Basketball, Fencing, Field Hockey, Gymnastics, Softball, Swimming-Diving, Tennis, Volleyball

William Penn College
Trueblood Avenue
Oskaloosa, IA 52577
M: (515) 673-8311
W: (515) 673-8311
Enrollment: A
4-year private
M: NCAA
W: AIAW
M: Baseball, Basketball, Cross Country, Football, Golf, Tennis, Track & Field, Wrestling
W: Basketball, Cross Country, Golf, Softball, Tennis, Track & Field, Volleyball

Division III: all aid awarded on the basis of financial need.

Williams College
Williamstown, MA 01267
M: (413) 597–2277
W: (413) 597–2277
Enrollment: A
4-year private
M: NCAA, ECAC, NESCAC, Little 3
W: ECAC, NESCAC
M: Baseball, Basketball, Crew, Cross Country, Football, Golf, Lacrosse, Skiing, Soccer, Squash, Swimming-Diving, Tennis, Track & Field, Wrestling
W: Basketball, Crew, Cross Country, Field Hockey, Lacrosse, Skiing, Soccer, Squash, Swimming-Diving, Tennis, Track & Field, Volleyball

All aid for men and women is based on financial need.

Williamsport Area Community College
Williamsport, PA 17701
M: (717) 326–3761
W: (717) 326–3761
Enrollment: A
2-year public funding
M: EPCCC
W: EPCCC
M: Basketball, Cross Country, Golf, Tennis, Wrestling
W: Basketball, Field Hockey, Golf, Tennis

Wilmington College
Wilmington, OH 45177
M: (513) 382–6661
W: (513) 382–6661
Enrollment: A
4-year private
M: Hoosier-Buckeye
W: AIAW
M: Baseball, Basketball, Cross Country, Football, Golf, Soccer, Tennis, Track & Field, Wrestling
W: Basketball, Softball, Tennis, Track & Field, Volleyball

Wilson College
Chambersburg, PA 17201
W: (717) 264–4141 X. 292
Enrollment: A
4-year private
W: EAIAW, Cen Penn
W: Basketball, Field Hockey, Gymnastics, Lacrosse, Tennis, Volleyball

Winona State College
Winona, MN 55987
M: (507) 457–2909
W: (507) 457–2908
Enrollment: C
4-year public funding
M: NIC, NAIA, NCAA
W: MAIAW, AAIAW, Northern Sun
M: <u>Baseball</u>, <u>Basketball</u>, <u>Cross Country</u>, <u>Football</u>, <u>Golf</u>, <u>Tennis</u>, <u>Track & Field</u>, <u>Wrestling</u>
W: <u>Basketball</u>, <u>Cross Country</u>, <u>Golf</u>, <u>Gymnastics</u>, <u>Softball</u>, <u>Tennis</u>, <u>Track & Field</u>, <u>Volleyball</u>

Winston-Salem State University
Winston-Salem, NC 27102
M: (919) 761–2108

W: (919) 761-2108
Enrollment: A
4-year public funding
M: CIAA
W: CIAA, NAIA
M: Basketball, Football, Golf, Tennis, Track & Field, Wrestling
W: Basketball, Softball, Volleyball

Winthrop College
Rock Hill, SC 29730
M: (803) 323-2129
W: (803) 323-2129
Enrollment: B
4-year public funding
M: NAIA
W: SCAIAW
M: Baseball, Basketball, Soccer, Tennis
W: Field Hockey, Basketball, Softball, Tennis, Volleyball

University of Wisconsin
Eau Claire, WI 54701
M: (715) 836-2427
W: (715) 836-2427
Enrollment: C
4-year public funding
M: WSUC
W: WWIAC
M: Baseball, Basketball, Cross Country, Football, Golf, Hockey, Swimming-Diving, Tennis, Track & Field, Wrestling
W: Basketball, Cross Country, Gymnastics, Swimming-Diving, Tennis, Track & Field, Volleyball

The Wisconsin State University Conference does not allow for athletic scholarships.

University of Wisconsin
2420 Nicolet Drive
Green Bay, WI 54302
M: (414) 465-2145
W: (414) 465-2145
Enrollment: B
4-year public funding
M: Independent
W: WWIAC
M: Cross Country, Golf, Sailing, Tennis, Basketball, Soccer
W: Cross Country, Field Hockey, Sailing, Tennis, Basketball, Swimming-Diving

University of Wisconsin
La Crosse, WI 54601
M: (608) 785-8616
W: (608) 785-8616
Enrollment: C
4-year public funding
M: WSUC
W: WWIAC
M: Baseball, Basketball, Cross Country, Football, Golf, Gymnastics, Swimming-Diving, Tennis, Track & Field, Wrestling
W: Badminton, Basketball, Cross Country, Field Hockey, Golf, Gymnastics, Swimming-Diving, Tennis, Track & Field, Volleyball

The Wisconsin State University Conference does not allow for athletic scholarships.

University of Wisconsin
Milwaukee, WI 53201
M: (414) 963-5151
W: (414) 963-5669
Enrollment: C
4-year public funding

M: NCAA
W: AIAW, WAIAW, WWIAC
M: Basketball, Cross Country, Golf, Swimming-Diving, Tennis, Track & Field, Soccer
W: Basketball, Cross Country, Field Hockey, Gymnastics, Swimming-Diving, Tennis, Track & Field, Volleyball

University of Wisconsin
800 Algoma Boulevard
Oshkosh, WI 54901
M: (414) 424-1034
W: (414) 424-1383
Enrollment: C
4-year public funding
M: WSUC
W: WWIAC
M: Baseball, Basketball, Cross Country, Football, Golf, Gymnastics, Riflery, Swimming-Diving, Tennis, Track & Field, Wrestling
W: Badminton, Basketball, Field Hockey, Gymnastics, Softball, Swimming-Diving, Tennis, Track & Field, Volleyball

The Wisconsin State University Conference does not allow for athletic scholarships.

University of Wisconsin
Platteville, WI 53818
M: (608) 342-1573
W: (608) 342-1573
Enrollment: B
4-year public funding
M: WSUC
W: WSUC
M: Baseball, Basketball, Cross Country, Football, Golf, Gymnastics, Soccer, Swimming-Diving, Tennis, Track & Field, Wrestling
W: Badminton, Gymnastics, Track & Field

The Wisconsin State University Conference does not allow for athletic scholarships.

University of Wisconsin
River Falls, WI 54022
M: (715) 425-3900
W: (715) 425-3900
Enrollment: B
4-year public funding
M: WSUC
W: WWIAC
M: Baseball, Basketball, Cross Country, Football, Golf, Ice Hockey, Swimming-Diving, Tennis, Track & Field, Wrestling
W: Basketball, Cross Country, Field Hockey, Gymnastics, Swimming-Diving, Tennis, Track & Field, Volleyball

The Wisconsin State University Conference does not allow for athletic scholarships.

University of Wisconsin
Stevens Point, WI 54481
M: (715) 346-3677
W: (715) 346-3677
Enrollment: C
4-year public funding
M: WSUC
W: WWIAC
M: Baseball, Basketball, Cross Country, Football, Golf, Swimming-Diving, Tennis, Track & Field, Wrestling

W: Basketball, Cross Country,
   Field Hockey, Golf, Softball,
   Swimming-Diving, Tennis,
   Track & Field, Volleyball

The Wisconsin State University
Conference does not allow for
athletic scholarships.

University of Wisconsin
Superior, WI 54880
M: (715) 392–8101 X. 371
W: (715) 392–8101 X. 371
Enrollment: A
4-year public funding
M: WSUC
W: WSUC
M: Baseball, Basketball, Football,
   Golf, Ice Hockey, Track &
   Field, Wrestling
W: Basketball, Gymnastics,
   Volleyball

The Wisconsin State University
Conference does not allow for
athletic scholarships.

University of Wisconsin
1500 University Drive
Waukesha, WI 53186
M: (414) 542–8825
W: (414) 542–8825
Enrollment: A
2-year public funding
M: WCC, WJCAA
W: WCC, WJCAA
M: Basketball, Cross Country,
   Fencing, Golf, Soccer, Tennis
W: Basketball, Cross Country,
   Fencing, Golf, Soccer,
   Softball, Tennis, Volleyball

University of Wisconsin
Marathon County
Wausau, WI 54401
M: (715) 845–9602
W: (715) 845–9602
Enrollment: A
2-year public funding
M: WCC
W: WCC
M: Basketball, Golf, Soccer,
   Tennis
W: Basketball, Golf, Soccer,
   Tennis, Volleyball

University of Wisconsin
Whitewater, WI 53190
M: (414) 472–4661
W: (414) 472–1649
Enrollment: C
4-year public funding
M: WSUC
W: WWIAC
M: Baseball, Basketball, Cross
   Country, Football, Golf,
   Gymnastics, Soccer,
   Swimming-Diving, Tennis,
   Track & Field, Wrestling
W: Basketball, Field Hockey,
   Golf, Gymnastics, Softball,
   Swimming-Diving, Tennis,
   Track & Field, Volleyball

The Wisconsin State University
Conference does not allow for
athletic scholarships.

Wofford College
Spartanburg, SC 29301
M: (803) 585–4821
W: (803) 585–4821
Enrollment: A
4-year private
M: NAIA, Independent

W: AIAW, Independent
M: Fencing, Riflery, Baseball, Basketball, Football, Soccer, Tennis
W: Basketball, Volleyball

Worcester State College
486 Chandler Street
Worcester, MA 01602
M: (617) 752–7700 X. 288
W: (617) 752–7700 X. 288
Enrollment: B
4-year public funding
M: MSCC
W: MSCC
M: Baseball, Basketball, Cross Country, Golf, Soccer, Tennis, Track & Field
W: Basketball, Cross Country, Field Hockey, Softball, Tennis, Track & Field, Volleyball

Worthington Community College
Worthington, MN 56187
M: (507) 372–2107
W: (507) 372–2107
Enrollment: A
2-year public funding
M: MCC
W: MCC
M: Baseball, Basketball, Football, Golf, Wrestling
W: Basketball, Golf, Softball, Volleyball

Wright State University
Dayton, OH 45431
M: (513) 873–2771
W: (513) 873–2771
Enrollment: C
4-year public funding
M: NCAA, Independent
W: AIAW, OAISW
M: Golf, Tennis, Baseball, Basketball, Cross Country, Soccer, Swimming-Diving, Wrestling
W: Softball, Tennis, Basketball, Swimming-Diving, Track & Field

University of Wyoming
Laramie, WY 82070
M: (307) 766–2292
W: (307) 766–3290
Enrollment: C
4-year public funding
M: Western Athletic
W: Intermountain
M: Riflery, Baseball, Basketball, Cross Country, Football, Golf, Skiing, Swimming-Diving, Track & Field, Wrestling
W: Basketball, Cross Country, Skiing, Softball, Swimming-Diving, Track & Field, Volleyball

Xavier University
Cincinnati, OH 45207
M: (513) 745–3416
W: (513) 745–3416
Enrollment: C
4-year private
M: Midwestern City
W: AIAW
M: Bowling, Riflery, Sailing, Swimming-Diving, Baseball, Basketball, Golf, Soccer, Tennis
W: Sailing, Swimming-Diving, Basketball, Tennis, Volleyball

Xavier University of Louisiana
7325 Pine Palmetto
New Orleans, LA 70125
M: (504) 486–7411 X. 305
W: (504) 486–7411 X. 305
Enrollment: A
4-year private
M: NAIA
W: AIAW
M: Basketball
W: Basketball

Yakima Valley Community College
Yakima, WA 98902
M: (509) 575-2393
W: (509) 575-2393
Enrollment: C
2-year public funding
M: AACC
W: AACC
M: Baseball, Basketball, Football, Tennis, Track & Field
W: Basketball, Tennis, Track & Field, Volleyball

Scholarships are awarded to students from Washington, Oregon, Idaho, and British Columbia by conference rule.

Yale University
New Haven, CT 06520
M: (203) 436-0805
W: (203) 436-0805
Enrollment: C
4-year private
M: Ivy League
W: Ivy League
M: Baseball, Basketball, Cross Country, Fencing, Football, Golf, Gymnastics, Ice Hockey, Lacrosse, Soccer, Squash, Swimming-Diving, Tennis, Track & Field, Volleyball, Water Polo, Wrestling
W: Basketball, Crew, Cross Country, Fencing, Field Hockey, Golf, Gymnastics, Lacrosse, Soccer, Softball, Squash, Swimming-Diving, Tennis, Track & Field, Volleyball

Yankton College
North Douglas
Yankton, SD 57078
M: (605) 665-3661 X. 127
W: (605) 665-3661 X. 127
Enrollment: A
4-year private
M: Tri State, SDIC
W: AIAW
M: Baseball, Basketball, Cross Country, Football, Tennis, Track & Field, Wrestling
W: Basketball, Cross Country, Golf, Softball, Tennis, Track & Field, Volleyball

York College
York, NE 68467
M: (402) 362-4441
W: (402) 362-4441
Enrollment: A
2-year private
M: PJCC, NJCAA
W: PJCC, NJCAA
M: Baseball, Basketball, Soccer, Tennis
W: Basketball, Tennis, Volleyball

Young Harris College
Young Harris, GA 30582
M: (404) 379-3236

Enrollment: A
2-year private
M: GJCAA
M: Tennis

Youngstown State University
410 Wick Avenue
Youngstown, OH 44555
M: (216) 742–3483
W: (216) 742–3483
Enrollment: C
4-year public funding
M: Mid-Continent
W: Independent
M: Riflery, Soccer, Baseball, Basketball, Football, Golf, Swimming-Diving, Tennis, Wrestling
W: Basketball, Field Hockey, Gymnastics, Softball, Swimming-Diving, Volleyball

Yuba Community College
Marysville, CA 95901
M: (916) 742–7351
W: (916) 742–7351
Enrollment: B
2-year public funding
M: Golden Valley
W: Golden Valley
M: Baseball, Basketball, Cross Country, Football, Tennis, Track & Field
W: Cross Country, Field Hockey, Softball, Tennis, Track & Field, Volleyball

PART III

Sport-by-Sport Index

GETTING STARTED

This section of the book contains a sport-by-sport listing, showing, in alphabetical order, all schools that play the sport. (Remember, this only lists participation; it does not in any way refer to scholarship opportunities.)

The left-hand column running down the page shows the school, while the right-hand column shows the state in which the school is located. If the school has a program in that sport for men, it will show a dagger (†). If there is a program for women, the listing will include an asterisk (*).

STATE ABBREVIATIONS

Alabama	AL	Maine	ME
Alaska	AK	Maryland	MD
Arizona	AZ	Massachusetts	MA
Arkansas	AR	Michigan	MI
California	CA	Minnesota	MN
Colorado	CO	Mississippi	MS
Connecticut	CT	Missouri	MO
Delaware	DE	Montana	MT
District of Columbia	DC	Nebraska	NE
Florida	FL	Nevada	NV
Georgia	GA	New Hampshire	NH
Hawaii	HI	New Jersey	NJ
Idaho	ID	New Mexico	NM
Illinois	IL	New York	NY
Indiana	IN	North Carolina	NC
Iowa	IA	North Dakota	ND
Kansas	KS	Ohio	OH
Kentucky	KY	Oklahoma	OK
Louisiana	LA	Oregon	OR

Pennsylvania	PA	Utah	UT
Puerto Rico	PR	Vermont	VT
Rhode Island	RI	Virginia	VA
South Carolina	SC	Washington	WA
South Dakota	SD	West Virginia	WV
Tennessee	TN	Wisconsin	WI
Texas	TX	Wyoming	WY

SPORT-BY-SPORT LISTING

ALPINE SKIING

Alaska, University of, at Anchorage†*	AK
Alfred University†*	NY
Amherst College†*	MA
Babson College†	MA
Bates College†*	ME
Boston College†*	MA
Bowdoin College†	ME
California, University of, at San Diego†	CA
Castleton State College†*	VT
Champlain College†*	VT
Colorado, University of†*	CO
Colorado College†*	CO
Colorado School of Mines†*	CO
Cornell University†*	NY
Dartmouth College†	NH
Denver, University of†*	CO
Franklin Pierce College†	NH
Harvard University†*	MA
Idaho, The College of†*	ID
Lake Superior State College†	MI
Lees-McRae College†*	NC
Lowell, University of†	MA
Lyndon State College†*	VT
Maine, University of†*	ME
Massachusetts, University of†*	MA
Massachusetts Institute of Technology†	MA
Middlebury College†*	VT
Montana State University†*	MT
New Hampshire College†*	NH
New Hampshire Technical Institute†*	NH
Northern Michigan University†	MI
Northland College†*	WI
Norwich University†*	VT
Pacific Lutheran University†*	WA
Paul Smith's College†*	NY
Plymouth State College†*	NH
Regis College†*	CO
Rockmont College†*	CO
St. Lawrence University†*	NY
St. Olaf College†*	MN
St. Peter's College†*	NJ
Syskiyous, College of the†*	CA
Southern California, University of†*	CA
Utah, University of†*	UT
Washington State University*	WA
Western New England College†*	MA
Western State College of Colorado†*	CO
Williams College†*	MA
Wyoming, University of†*	WY

ARCHERY

Albion College*	MI
Alma College*	MI
Arizona State University†*	AZ
Barnard College*	NY
Brevard Community College†*	FL
Brooklyn College of the City University of New York†*	NY
California State University, Long Beach†*	CA
Calvin College*	MI
Colorado Northwestern Community College†*	CO
Cottey College*	MO
Cypress College†*	CA

East Stroudsburg State College†*   PA
Glassboro State College†*   NJ
Hope College*   MI
James Madison University†*   VA
Jones County Junior College†*   MI
Lycoming College†*   PA
Palomar Community College†*   CA
Pima Community College†*   AZ
San Francisco, City College of*   CA
Trenton State College†*   NJ

BADMINTON

Albright College*   PA
Arizona State University†*   AZ
Ball State University*   IN
Baltimore Community College of†*   MD
California, University of, Los Angeles†*   CA
California, University of, San Diego†*   CA
California State University, Haywood†*   CA
California State University, Long Beach†*   CA
Carthage College*   WI
Centenary College*   NJ
Citrus College†*   CA
Eastern Illinois University*   IL
El Camino College†*   CA
Fresno State University*   CA
George Washington University*   DC
Illinois State University*   IL
La Verne College†   CA
Los Angeles Pierce Junior College*   CA
North Dakota, University of*   ND
Northern Illinois University*   IL
Pennsylvania, University of*   PA
San Francisco, City College of*   CA
San Francisco State University†*   CA
Southern Illinois, University of*   IL
Swarthmore College*   PA
Temple University*   PA
Troy State University†   AL
West Chester State College*   PA
Western Illinois University*   IL
William and Mary, College of*   VA
Wisconsin, University of, at La Crosse*   WI
Wisconsin, University of, at Oshkosh*   WI
Wisconsin, University of, at Platteville*   WI

BASEBALL

Adrian College†   MI
Akron, University of†   OH
Alabama, University of, at Birmingham†   AL
Alabama, University of, at University†   AL
Alabama Agricultural and Mechanical University†   AL
Alabama Christian Junior College†   AL
Alabama State University†   AL
Albany State College†   GA
Albion College†   MI
Albright College†   PA
Alcorn State University†   MS
Allegheny College†   PA
Allen County Community Junior College†   KS
Allentown College of St. Francis De Sales†   PA
Alma College†   MI
Alvin Junior College†   TX
American International College†   MA
American University, The†   DC
Amherst College†   MA
Anderson College†   IL
Angelina College†   TX
Anne Arundel Community College†   MD
Appalachian State University†   NC
Aquinas College†   MI
Arizona, University of†   AZ
Arizona Western College†   AZ
Arizona State University†   AZ
Arkansas, University of†   AR
Arkansas, University of, at Little Rock†   AR
Arkansas, University of, at Monticello†   AR
Arkansas State University†   AR
Arkansas Tech University†   AR
Armstrong State College†   GA
Ashland College†   OH
Assumption College†   MA
Athens State College†   AL
Atlantic Christian College†   NC
Auburn University, at Auburn†   AL
Augusta College†   GA
Augustana College†   IL
Augustana College†   SD
Aurora College†   IL
Azusa Pacific College†   CA
Babson College†   MA
Baker University†   KS
Ball State University†   IN

Baltimore, Community College of†	MD
Baltimore, University of†	MD
Baptist Bible College†	MO
Baptist Bible College†	PA
Baptist College at Charleston†	SC
Barton County Community College†	KS
Bates College†	ME
Baylor University†	TX
Beaver College†	PA
Belhaven College†	MS
Bellarmine College†	KY
Bellevue College†	NE
Belmont College†	TN
Bemidji State University†	MN
Benedictine College†	KS
Bentley College†	MA
Berea College†	KY
Bethany College†	KS
Bethel College†	MN
Bethune-Cookman College†	FL
Biola College†	CA
Biscayne College†	FL
Bishop College†	TX
Bismarck Junior College†	ND
Blinn College†	TX
Bluefield†	VA
Bluffton College†	OH
Boston College†	MA
Boston State College†	MA
Bowdoin College†	ME
Bowie State College†	MD
Bowling Green State University†	OH
Bradley University†	IL
Brandeis University†	MA
Brandywine College†	DE
Brevard Community College†	FL
Briar Cliff College†	IA
Bridgewater College†	VA
Bridgewater State College†	MA
Brigham Young University†	UT
Brooklyn College of the City University of New York†	NY
Brown University†	RI
Bryan College†	TN
Bryant College†	RI
Bucknell University†	PA
Butler County Community Junior College†	KS
Butler University†	IN
California, University of, at Davis†	CA
California, University of, at Irvine†	CA
California, University of, at Los Angeles†	CA
California, University of, at Riverside†	CA
California, University of, at San Diego†	CA
California, University of, at Santa Barbara†	CA
California Institute of Technology†	CA
California Polytechnic State University†	CA
California State College, at Sonoma†	CA
California State College, at Stanislaus†	CA
California State University, at Chico†	
California State University, at Fullerton†	CA
California State University, at Haywood†	CA
California State University, at Long Beach†	CA
Calvin College†	MI
Cameron University†	OK
Campbell College†	NC
Campbellsville College†	KY
Canisius College†	NY
Cape Cod Community College†	MA
Carl Sandburg College†	IL
Carroll College†	WI
Carson-Newman College†	TN
Carthage College†	WI
Castleton State College†	VT
Catawaba College†	NC
Centenary College†	LA
Central Arkansas, University of†	AR
Centralia College†	WA
Central Junior College†	KS
Central Michigan University†	MI
Central Missouri State University†	MO
Central State University†	OK
Centre College†	KY
Chadron State College†	NE
Chaminade University†	HI
Charleston, University of†	WV
Chattahoochee Valley Community College†	AL
Chicago, The University of†	IL
Chicago State University†	IL
Chowan College†	NC
Cincinnati, University of†	OH
Citadel, The†	SC
Citrus College†	CA
Clackamas Community College†	OR
Claremore College†	OK
Clarion State College†	PA
Clark College†	GA
Clark University†	MA
Clemson University†	SC
Cleveland State University†	OH

271

Coahoma Junior College†	MS
Coastal Carolina College†	SC
Cochise College†	AZ
Coe College†	IA
Coffeyville Community College†	KS
Colby College†	ME
Colgate University†	NY
Colorado College†	CO
Colorado Northwestern Community College†	CO
Colorado School of Mines†	CO
Colorado State University†	CO
Columbia University†	NY
Columbus College†	GA
Compton Community College†	CA
Concord College†	WV
Concordia College†	IL
Concordia College†	OR
Concordia College†	NE
Concordia College†	TX
Connecticut, University of†	CT
Connors State College†	OK
Contra Costa College†	CA
Copiah-Lincoln Junior College†	MS
Cornell College†	IA
Cornell University†	NY
Cosumnes River College†	CA
Covenant College†	TN
Cowley County Community College†	KS
Creighton University†	NE
Crowder College†	MO
Culver-Stockton College†	MO
Cumberland College†	KY
Cuyahoga Community College†	OH
Cuyahoga Community College, Metro Campus†	OH
C. W. Post College†	NY
Cypress College†	CA
Dartmouth College†	NH
David Lipscomb College†	TN
Davidson College†	NC
Delaware, University of†	DE
Delaware State College†	DE
Delaware Valley College†	PA
Delta State College†	MS
Denver, University of†	CO
Desert, College of the†	CA
Detroit, University of†	MI
Dickenson State College†	ND
District of Columbia, University of†	DC
Dominican College†	NY
Dubuque, University of†	IA
Duke University†	NC
Dundalk Community College†	MD
Duquesne University†	PA
Eastern College†	PA
Eastern Illinois University†	IL
Eastern Kentucky University†	KY
Eastern Michigan University†	MI
Eastern Nazarene College†	MA
Eastern Oklahoma State College†	OK
Eastern Utah, College of†	UT
East Carolina University†	NC
East Central Junior College†	MS
East Central University†	OK
East Stroudsburg State College†	PA
East Tennessee State University†	TN
Eckerd College†	FL
Edgewood College†	WI
Edinboro State College†	PA
Edmonds Community College†	WA
Eisenhower College†	NY
El Camino College†	CA
Elizabethtown College†	PA
Elmhurst College†	IL
Elon College†	NC
Emory and Henry College†	VA
Emporia State University†	KS
Erskine College†	SC
Essex Community College†	MD
Evansville, University of†	IN
Everett Community College†	WA
Fairleigh Dickinson University†	NJ
Fairmont State College†	WV
Fergus Falls Community College†	MN
Ferris State College†	MI
Ferrum College†	WA
Findlay College†	OH
Fitchburg State College†	MA
Flagler College†	FL
Florida, University of†	FL
Florida A. and M. University†	FL
Florida Atlantic University†	FL
Florida International University†	FL
Florida Junior College†	FL
Florida Southern College†	FL
Florida State University†	FL
Florida Technological University†	FL
Fordham University†	NY
Fort Hayes State College†	KS
Fort Steilacoom Community College†	WA
Fort Valley State College†	GA
Framingham State College†	MA
Francis Marion College†	SC
Franklin Pierce College†	NH
Freed-Hardeman College†	TN
Fresno State University†	CA
Friendship Junior College†	SC
Friends University†	KS
Frostburg State College†	MD
Furman University†	SC
Gadsden State Junior College†	AL
Gannon College†	PA
Gardner-Webb College†	NC

Garrett Community College†	MD
George Fox College†	OR
Georgetown University†	DC
George Washington University†	DC
Georgia, University of†	GA
Georgia College†	GA
Georgia Institute of Technology†	GA
Georgia Southern College†	GA
Georgia Southwestern College†	GA
Georgia State University†	GA
Gettysburg College†	PA
Glassboro State College†	NJ
Glen Oaks Community College†	MI
Golden Valley Lutheran College†	MN
Gonzaga University†	WA
Gordon Junior College†	GA
Grace College†	IN
Graceland College†	IA
Grand Canyon College†	AZ
Grand Rapids Baptist College†	MI
Grand Rapids Junior College†	MI
Grand Valley State College†	MI
Green River Community College†	WA
Greensville College†	IL
Grinnell College†	IA
Grove City College†	PA
Guilford College†	NC
Gustavus Adolphus College†	MN
Hagerstown Junior College†	MD
Hamilton College†	NY
Hamline University†	MN
Hannibal-LaGrange College†	MO
Hanover College†	IN
Harding University†	AR
Hardin-Simmons University†	TX
Hartford, University of†	CT
Harvard University†	MA
Hawaii, University of, at Hilo†	HI
Hawaii, University of, at Honolulu†	HI
Heidelberg College†	OH
Henderson State University†	OR
Herbert H. Lehman College†	NY
Hesston College†	KS
High Point College†	NC
Highland Community Junior College†	KS
Highland Park Community College†	MI
Hilbert College†	NY
Hillsborough Community College†	FL
Hillsdale College†	MI
Hiram College†	OH
Holy Cross College†	MA
Hope College†	MI
Houghton College†	NY
Housatonic Community College†	CT
Houston, University of†	TX
Humboldt State University†	CA
Hunter College†	NY
Huntington College†	IN
Husson College†	ME
Hutchinson Community Junior College†	KS
Illinois, University of, at Champaign†	IL
Illinois, University of, at Chicago Circle†	IL
Illinois Benedictine College†	IL
Illinois College†	IL
Illinois State University†	IL
Illinois Valley Community College†	IL
Illinois Wesleyan University†	IL
Indian Hills Community College†	IA
Indian River Community College†	FL
Indiana Central University†	IN
Indiana State University†	IN
Indiana University, at Bloomington†	IN
Indiana University of Pennsylvania†	PA
Indiana University-Perdue University, at Fort Wayne†	IN
Indiana University-Purdue University, at Indianapolis†	IN
Inver Hills College†	MN
Iowa, University of†	IA
Iowa Lakes Community College†	IA
Iowa State University†	IA
Iowa Wesleyan College†	IA
Ithaca College†	NY
Jacksonville State University†	AL
James Madison University†	VA
Jamestown College†	ND
Jarvis Christian College†	TX
Jefferson State Junior College†	AL
Jersey City State College†	NJ
John Carroll University†	OH
John C. Calhoun Community College†	AL
Jones County Junior College†	MS
Juniata College†	PA
Kalamazoo Valley Community College†	MI
Kankakee Community College†	IL
Kansas, University of†	KS
Kansas State University†	KS
Kean College of New Jersey†	NJ
Kearney State College†	NE
Kent State University†	OH
Kentucky, University of†	KY
Kentucky State University†	KY
Kentucky Wesleyan College†	KY
Kenyon College†	OH
King's College, The†	NY

Kirkwood Community College†	IA
Kishwaukee College†	IL
Kutztown State College†	PA
Lafayette College†	PA
Lamar University†	TX
Lambuth College†	TN
Lancaster Bible College†	PA
Lane Community College†	OR
La Salle College†	PA
La Verne College†	CA
Lawrence University†	WI
Le Moyne College†	NY
Lebanon Valley College†	PA
Lehigh University†	PA
Lenoir Community College†	NC
Lenoir-Rhyne College†	NC
Lewis and Clark Community College†	IL
Lewis University†	IL
Lewis-Clark State Colege†	ID
Liberty Baptist College†	VA
Lincoln Christian College†	IL
Lincoln Land Community College†	IT
Lincoln University†	MO
Lindenwood College, The†	MO
Linfield College†	OR
Livingston University†	AL
Lock Haven State College†	PA
Long Island University†	NY
Longwood College†	VA
Loras College†	IA
Los Angeles Baptist College†	CA
Los Angeles City College†	CA
Los Angeles Pierce Junior College†	CA
Los Angeles Southwest College†	CA
Louisiana College†	LA
Louisiana State University†	LA
Louisiana Tech University†	LA
Louisville, University of†	KY
Lowell, University of†	MA
Lower Columbia College†	WA
Loyola Marymount University†	CA
Lubbock Christian College†	TX
Luther College†	IA
Lynchburg College†	VA
Lyndon State College†	VT
Macalester College†	MN
McKendree College†	IL
McNeese State University†	LA
Maine, University of, at Farmington†	ME
Maine, University of, at Presque Isle†	ME
Malone College†	OH
Manchester College†	IN
Manhattan College†	NY
Mankato State University†	MN
Mansfield State College†	PA
Marian College†	IN
Marietta College†	OH
Marin, College of†	CA
Marion Military Institute†	AL
Mars Hill College†	NC
Marshall University†	WV
Marshall Town Community College†	IA
Martin College†	TN
Mary Hardin-Baylor College†	TX
Mary Holmes College†	MS
Maryland, University of, at Catonsville†	MD
Maryland, University of, at College Park†	MD
Maryville College†	TN
Massachusetts, University of†	MA
Massachusetts Institute of Technology†	MA
Massasoit Community College†	MA
Mattatuck Community College†	CT
Memphis State University†	TN
Menlo College†	CA
Mercer University†	GA
Mercer University, at Atlanta†	GA
Mercy College†	NY
Merrimack College†	MA
Metropolitan State College†	CO
Miami, University of†	FL
Miami University†	OH
Miami Dade Community College, New World Center†	FL
Miami Dade Community College, South Campus†	FL
Michigan, University of†	MI
Michigan Christian Junior College†	MI
Michigan State University†	MI
Middle Tennessee State University†	TN
Middlebury College†	VT
Midwest Christian College†	OK
Midwestern State University†	TX
Milligan College†	TN
Millikin University†	IL
Millsaps College†	MS
Milwaukee Area Technical College†	WI
Milwaukee School of Engineering†	WI
Mineral Area Junior College†	MO
Minnesota, University of, at Minneapolis†	MN
Minnesota, University of, at Morris†	MN
Mira Costa College†	CA
Mississippi College†	MS
Mississippi State University†	MS
Missouri, University of†	MO
Missouri, University of, at Rolla†	MO

Missouri, University of, at St. Louis†	MO
Missouri Baptist College†	MO
Missouri Southern State College†	MO
Missouri Valley College†	MO
Missouri Western College†	MO
Mitchell College†	CT
Monmouth College†	IL
Monmouth College†	NJ
Montclair State University†	NJ
Montevallo, University of†	AL
Moorhead State University†	MN
Moorpark College†	AR
Morehead State University†	KY
Morehouse College†	GA
Morningside College†	IA
Motlow State Community College†	TN
Mott Community College†	MN
Mount Olive Junior College†	NC
Mount St. Mary's College†	MD
Mount San Jacinto College†	CA
Muhlenberg College†	PA
Murray State University†	KY
Napa Community College†	CA
Nebraska, University of†	NE
Nebraska, University of, at Omaha†	NE
Nebraska Wesleyan University†	NE
Newberry College†	SC
New Hampshire College†	NH
New Hampshire Technological Institute†	NH
New Haven, University of†	CT
New Mexico Highlands University†	NM
New Orleans, University of†	LA
New York, State University College of, at Fredonia†	NY
New York, State University College of, at New Paltz†	NY
New York, State University College of, at Oneonta†	NY
New York, State University of, at Albany†	NY
New York, State University of, at Binghamton†	NY
New York, State University of, at Buffalo†	NY
New York Institute of Technology†	NY
Niagara University†	NY
Nicholls State University†	LA
Nichols College†	MA
Norfolk State College†	VA
North Adams State College†	MA
North Alabama, University of†	AL
North Carolina, University of, at Chapel Hill†	NC
North Carolina, University of, at Charlotte†	NC
North Carolina, University of, at Wilmington†	NC
North Carolina Agricultural and Technical State University†	NC
North Carolina State University†	NC
North Carolina Wesleyan College†	NC
North Central College†	IL
North Dakota, University of†	ND
North Dakota State University, at Bottineau†	ND
North Dakota State University, at Fargo†	ND
Northeastern Illinois University†	IL
Northeastern Oklahoma A and M College†	OK
Northeast Louisiana University†	LA
Northern Arizona University†	AZ
Northern Colorado, University of†	CO
Northern Illinois University†	IL
Northern Iowa, University of†	IA
Northern Kentucky University†	KY
Northern State College†	SD
North Greenville College†	SC
North Idaho College†	ID
Northland Community College†	MN
Northwestern College†	MN
Northwestern College†	WI
Northwestern State University†	LA
Northwestern University†	IL
Northwest Missouri State University†	MO
Northwest Nazarene College†	ID
Norwich University†	VT
Notre Dame, University of†	IN
Oakland City College†	IN
Oakland University†	MI
Oberlin College†	OH
Occidental College†	CA
Ohio Northern University†	OH
Ohio State University†	OH
Ohio Valley College†	WV
Ohio Wesleyan University†	OH
Oklahoma, University of†	OK
Oklahoma Baptist University†	OK
Oklahoma City University†	OK
Oklahoma State University†	OK
Old Dominion University†	VA
Olivet College†	MI
Olivet Nazarene College†	IL
Olney Central College†	IL
Oral Roberts University†	OK
Oregon, University of†	OR
Oregon State University†	OR
Oregon Technical Institute†	OR
Oscar Rose Junior College†	OK
Otero Junior College†	CO
Otterbein College†	OH

Ouachita Baptist College†	AR
Oxnard College†	CA
Ozarks, College of the†	AR
Ozarks, School of the†	MO
Pace University†	NY
Pacific, University of the†	CA
Pacific Lutheran University†	WA
Pacific University†	OR
Paducah Community College†	KY
Palm Beach Junior College†	FL
Palomar College†	CA
Pan American University†	TX
Paris Junior College†	TX
Park College†	MO
Parkland College†	IL
Pembroke State University†	NC
Pennsylvania, University of†	PA
Pennsylvania State University, at Altoona†	PA
Pennsylvania State University, at Beaver Campus†	PA
Pennsylvania State University, at McKeesport†	PA
Pennsylvania State University, at Middletown†	PA
Pennsylvania State University, at University Park†	PA
Pennsylvania State University (Behrend College)†	PA
Pensacola Junior College†	FL
Pepperdine University†	CA
Pfeiffer College†	NC
Philadelphia Community College†	PA
Phillips University†	OK
Pikeville College†	KY
Pima Community College†	AZ
Pittsburgh, University of†	PA
Pittsburgh, University of, at Johnstown†	PA
Plymouth State College†	NH
Point Loma College†	CA
Point Park College†	PA
Porterville College†	CA
Portland, University of†	OR
Portland State University†	OR
Pratt Community Junior College†	KS
Princeton University†	NJ
Principia College†	IL
Providence College†	RI
Purdue University, at West Lafayette†	IL
Quincy College†	IL
Quinnipiac College†	CT
Randolph-Macon College†	VA
Redlands, University of†	CA
Redwoods, College of the†	CA
Regis College†	CO
Rensselaer Polytechnic Institute†	NY
Rice University†	TX
Rider College†	NJ
Rio Grande College†	OH
Ripon College†	WI
Riverside City College†	CA
Robert Morris College†	PA
Rochester, University of†	NY
Rust College†	MS
Rutgers, State University of, at Camden†	NJ
Rutgers, State University of, at Newark†	NJ
Rutgers, State University of, at New Brunswick†	NJ
Sacred Heart University†	CT
Saginaw Valley College†	MI
St. Augustine's College†	NC
St. Bonaventure University†	NY
St. Clair County Community College†	MI
St. Cloud State University†	MN
St. Edwards University†	TX
St. Francis College†	NY
St. Francis, College of†	IL
St. Johns College†	KS
St. Johns University†	MN
St. Joseph College†	IN
St. Lawrence University†	NY
St. Leo College†	FL
St. Louis Community College†	MO
St. Louis University†	MO
St. Mary of the Plains College†	KS
St. Mary's College†	MN
St. Mary's College of California†	CA
St. Mary's University of Texas†	TX
St. Norbert College†	WY
St. Olaf College†	MN
St. Paul's College†	PA
St. Paul's College†	VA
St. Peter's College†	NJ
St. Thomas, College of†	MN
St. Vincent College†	PA
St. Xavier College†	IL
Salisbury State College†	MD
Sam Houston State University†	TX
San Diego, University of†	CA
San Diego State University†	CA
San Francisco, City College of†	CA
San Francisco, University of†	CA
San Francisco State University†	CA
San Jose State University†	CA
San Mateo, College of†	CA
Santa Ana College†	CA
Santa Barbara City Junior College†	CA
Santa Clara, University of†	CA
Scranton, University of†	PA
Seminole Community College†	FL
Seward County Community Junior College†	KS
Shaw College at Detroit†	MI

Shawnee College†	IL	Stanford University†	CA
Shelby State Community College†	TN	State Fair Community College†	MO
		Staten Island, College of†	NY
Shepherd College†	WV	Sterling College†	KS
Shorter College†	GA	Stetson University†	FL
Siena College†	NY	Stevens Institute of Technology†	NJ
Siena Heights College†	MI	Susquehanna University†	PA
Siskiyous, College of the†	CA	Swarthmore College†	PA
Skagit Valley College†	WA	Tabor College†	KS
Skyline College†	CA	Tacoma Community College†	WA
Slippery Rock State College†	PA	Tampa, University of†	FL
Snead State Junior College†	AL	Taylor University†	IN
South, University of the†	TN	Temple University†	PA
South Alabama, University of†	AL	Tennessee, University of†	TN
South Carolina, University of†	SC	Tennessee, University of, at Martin†	TN
South Dakota, University of, at Springfield†	SD	Tennessee State University†	TN
South Dakota, University of, at Vermillion†	SD	Tennessee Technological University†	TN
Southeastern Community College†	IA	Tennessee Wesleyan College†	TN
		Texas, University of†	TX
Southeastern Louisiana University†	LA	Texas, University of, at Arlington†	TX
Southeastern Oklahoma State University†	OK	Texas, The University of, at El Paso†	TX
Southeast Missouri State†	MO	Texas Christian University†	TX
Southern Arkansas University†	AR	Texas Lutheran College†	TX
Southern Baptist College†	AR	Texas Southern University†	TX
Southern California, University of†	CA	Texas Tech University†	TX
		Texas Wesleyan College†	TX
Southern California College†	CA	Thiel College†	PA
Southern Colorado, University of†	CO	Thomas College†	ME
		Thomas More College†	KY
Southern Connecticut State College†	CT	Three Rivers Community College†	MO
Southern Illinois University†	IL	Tiffin University†	OH
Southern Maine, University of†	ME	Toledo, University of†	OH
Southern Maine Vocational Technical Institute†	ME	Towson State University†	MD
		Treasure Valley Community College†	OR
Southern Oregon State College†	OR	Trenton State College†	NJ
Southern Union State Junior College†	AL	Trinidad State Junior College†	CO
		Trinity College†	CT
Southern University and Agricultural and Mechanical College†	LA	Trinity University†	TX
		Tri-State University†	IN
Southern Utah State College†	UT	Triton College†	IL
South Florida, The University of†	FL	Tufts University†	MA
		Tulane University†	LA
Southwest Baptist College†	MO	Tunxis Community College†	CT
Southwestern at Memphis†	TN	Tuskegee Institute†	AL
Southwestern Community College†	IA	Umpqua Community College†	OR
		Union College†	KY
Southwestern Louisiana, University of†	LA	United Wesleyan College†	PA
		Upper Iowa University†	IA
Southwestern University†	TX	Upsala College†	NJ
Southwest State University†	MN	Urbana College†	OH
Spartanburg Methodist College†	SC	Ursinus College†	PA
Spring Arbor College†	MI	Utah, University of†	UT
Spring Garden College†	PA	Utica College of Syracuse University†	NY
Spring Hill College†	AL		

Utica Junior College†	NY
Valparaiso University†	IN
Vanderbilt University†	TN
Ventura College†	CA
Villanova University†	PA
Virginia, University of†	VA
Virginia Commonwealth University†	VA
Virginia Polytechnic Institute†	VA
Wabash College†	IN
Wagner College†	NY
Wake Forest University†	NC
Walsh College†	OH
Warren Wilson College†	NC
Washburn University†	KS
Washington, University of†	WA
Washington and Lee University†	VA
Washington Bible College†	MD
Washington University †	MO
Waynesburg College†	PA
Wayne State University†	MI
Wesleyan College†	CT
West Chester State College†	PA
Western Carolina University†	NC
Western Illinois University†	IL
Western Kentucky University†	KY
Western Maryland College†	MD
Western Michigan University†	MI
Western New England College†	MA
Western State College of Colorado†	CO
Western Washington University†	WA
Westfield State College†	MA
West Georgia College†	GA
West Hills College†	CA
West Liberty State College†	WV
West Los Angeles College†	CA
Westminster College†	MO
Westmount College†	CA
West Virginia State College†	WV
West Virginia University†	WV
West Virginia Wesleyan College†	WV
Wharton County Junior College†	TX
Wheaton College†	IL
Whitworth College†	WA
Wichita State University†	KS
Wiley College†	TX
Wilkes College†	PA
Willamette University†	OR
William and Mary, College of†	VA
William Carey College†	MS
William Paterson College†	NJ
William Penn College†	IA
Williams College†	MA
Wilmington College†	OH
Winona State College†	MN
Winthrop College†	SC
Wisconsin, University of, at Eau Claire†	WI
Wisconsin, University of, at La Crosse†	WI
Wisconsin, University of, at Oshkosh†	WI
Wisconsin, University of, at Platteville†	WI
Wisconsin, University of, at River Falls†	WI
Wisconsin, University of, at Stevens Point†	WI
Wisconsin, University of, at Superior†	WI
Wisconsin, University of, at Whitewater†	WI
Wofford College†	SC
Worcester State College†	MA
Worthington Community College†	MN
Wright State University†	OH
Wyoming, University of†	WY
Xavier University†	OH
Yakima Valley College†	WA
Yale University†	CT
Yankton College†	SD
York College†	NE
Youngstown State University†	OH
Yuba College†	CA

BASKETBALL

Abilene Christian University†*	TX
Adams State College of Colorado†*	CO
Adrian College†*	MI
Akron, University of†*	OH
Alabama, University of, at Birmingham†*	AL
Alabama University of, at Huntsville†*	AL
Alabama, University of, at University†*	AL
Alabama Agricultural and Mechanical University†*	AL
Alabama Christian Junior College†*	AL
Alabama State University†*	AL
Alaska, University of, at Anchorage†*	AK
Alaska, University of, at Fairbanks†*	AK
Albany, Junior College of†*	NY
Albany State College†*	GA
Albion College†*	MI
Albright College†*	PA
Alcorn State University†*	MS
Alfred University†*	NY

Alice Lloyd College†*	KY	Barber-Scotia College†*	NC
Allegheny College†*	PA	Barnard College*	NY
Allen County Community Junior College†*	KS	Barton County Community College†*	KS
Allentown College of St. Francis De Sales†*	PA	Bates College†*	ME
Alma College†*	MI	Baylor University†*	TX
Alpena Community College†*	MI	Beaver College†*	PA
Alvin Junior College†	TX	Belhaven College†*	MS
American International College†*	MA	Bellarmine College†*	KY
		Bellevue College†	NE
American University, The†*	DC	Belmont College†*	TN
Amherst College†*	MA	Beloit College†*	WI
Anderson College†*	IN	Bemidji State University†*	MN
Anderson Junior College†*	SC	Benedictine College†*	KS
Angelina College†*	TX	Bennett College*	NC
Angelo State University†*	TX	Bentley College†*	MA
Anne Arundel Community College†*	MD	Berea College†*	KY
		Berry College†*	GA
Appalachian State University†	NC	Bethany College†*	KS
Aquinas College†*	MI	Bethany Lutheran College†*	MN
Arizona, University of†*	AZ	Bethel College†*	MN
Arizona State University†*	AZ	Bethune-Cookman College†*	FL
Arizona Western College†*	AZ	Biola College†*	CA
Arkansas, University of†*	AR	Biscayne College†	FL
Arkansas, University of, at Little Rock†*	AR	Bishop College†*	TX
		Bismarck Junior College†*	ND
Arkansas, University of, at Monticello†*	AR	Blackburn College†*	IL
		Blinn College†*	TX
Arkansas, University of, at Pine Bluff†*	AR	Blue Mountain College*	MS
		Bluefield College†	VA
Arkansas State University†*	AR	Bluefield State College†*	WV
Arkansas Tech University†*	AR	Bluffton College†*	OH
Armstrong State College†*	GA	Boise State University†*	ID
Asbury College†	KY	Boston College†*	MA
Asheville-Buncombe Technical Institute†*	NC	Boston State College†*	MA
		Boston University†*	MA
Ashland College†*	OH	Bowdoin College†	ME
Assumption College†*	MA	Bowie State College†*	MD
Athens State†*	AL	Bowling Green State University†*	OH
Atlanticaf1Chritian Collged*	NC		
Auburn University, at Auburn†*	AL	Bradley University†*	IL
Auburn University, at Montgomery†	AL	Brandeis University†*	MA
		Brandywine College†*	DE
Augusta College†*	GA	Brevard College†*	NC
Augustana College†*	IL	Brevard Community College†*	FL
Augustana College†*	SD	Briar Cliff College†*	IA
Aurora College†*	IL	Bridgewater College†*	VA
Averett College†*	VA	Bridgewater State College†*	MA
Azusa Pacific College†*	CA	Brigham Young University†*	UT
Babson College†*	MA	Brigham Young University†*	HI
Baker University†*	KS	Bristol College†	TN
Ball State University†*	IN	Brooklyn College of the City University of New York†*	NY
Baltimore, Community College of†*	MO		
		Brown University†*	RI
Baltimore, University of†	MD	Bryan College†*	TN
Baptist Bible College†	MO	Bryant College†*	RI
Baptist Bible College†*	PA	Bucknell University†*	PA
Baptist College, at Charleston†*	SC	Butler County Community Junior College†*	KS
Barat College*	IL		
		Butler University†*	IN

California, University of, at Davis†*	CA
California, University of, at Irvine†	CA
California, University of, at Los Angeles†*	CA
California, University of, at Riverside†*	CA
California, University of, at San Diego†*	CA
California, University of, at Santa Barbara†	CA
California Institute of Technology†	CA
California Polytechnic State University†*	CA
California State College, at Bakersfield†	CA
California State College, at Sonoma†*	CA
California State College, at Stanislaus†*	CA
California State University, at Chico†*	CA
California State University, at Fullerton†*	CA
California State University, at Haywood†*	CA
California State University, at Long Beach†*	CA
Calvary Bible College†*	MO
Calvin College†*	MI
Cameron University†*	OK
Campbell College†*	NC
Campbellsville College†*	KY
Canisius College†*	NY
Cape Cod Community College†*	MA
Carlow College*	PA
Carl Sandburg College†*	IL
Carroll College†*	MT
Carroll College†*	WI
Carson-Newman College†*	TN
Carthage College†*	WI
Casper College†*	WY
Castleton State College†*	VT
Catawaba College†*	NC
Cathedral College†	NY
Centenary College†*	LA
Central Arkansas, University of†*	AR
Centralia College†*	WA
Central Junior College†*	KS
Central Michigan University†*	MI
Central Missouri State University†*	MO
Central State University†*	OK
Centre College†*	KY
Chadron State College†*	NE
Chaminade University†	HI
Champlain College†	VT
Charleston, College of†*	SC
Charleston, University of†*	WV
Chatham College*	PA
Chattahoochee Valley Community College†*	AL
Chicago, The University of†*	IL
Chicago State University†	IL
Chowan College†*	NC
Christopher Newport College†*	VA
Cincinnati, University of†*	OH
Cincinnati Bible College†*	OH
Cisco Junior College†*	TX
Citadel, The†	SC
Citrus College†*	CA
Clackamas Community College†*	OR
Claremore College†*	OK
Clarion State College†*	PA
Clark College†*	GA
Clarke College*	IA
Clark University†*	MA
Clemson University†*	SC
Cleveland State University†*	OH
Coahoma Junior College†*	MS
Coastal Carolina College†*	SC
Coastal Carolina Community College†	NC
Cochise College†*	AZ
Coe College†*	IA
Coffeyville Community College†*	KS
Colby College†*	ME
Colgate University†*	NY
Colorado, University of†*	CO
Colorado College†*	CO
Colorado Northwestern Community College†*	CO
Colorado School of Mines†*	CO
Colorado State University†*	CO
Columbia Basin College†*	WA
Columbia Christian College†	OR
Columbia College*	SC
Columbia University†	NY
Columbus College†	GA
Compton Community College†*	CA
Concord College†*	WV
Concordia College†*	IL
Concordia College†*	OR
Concordia College†*	TX
Concordia College†*	MN
Concordia College†*	NE
Connecticut, University of†*	CT
Connors State College†*	OK
Contra Costa College†	CA
Converse College*	SC
Cooke County Junior College†*	TX
Copiah-Lincoln Junior College†*	MS
Cornell College†*	IA
Cornell University†*	NY
Cosumnes River College†	CA

Cottey College*	MO
Covenant College†*	TN
Cowley County Community College†*	KS
Creighton University†*	NE
Crowder College†*	MO
Culver-Stockton College†*	MO
Cumberland College†*	KY
Cuyahoga Community College†*	OH
Cuyahoga Community College, Metro Campus†*	OH
C. W. Post College†*	NY
Cypress College†*	CA
Daemen College†*	NY
Dakota Wesleyan University†*	SD
Dartmouth College†*	NY
David Lipscomb College†*	TN
Davidson College†*	NC
Dawson College†*	MT
Dayton, University of†*	OH
Daytona Beach Community College†	FL
De Kalb Community College (Central)†*	GA
Delaware, University of†*	DE
Delaware State College†*	DE
Delaware Valley College†*	PA
Delta State College†*	MS
Denver, University of†*	CO
DePauw University†*	IN
Desert, College of the†*	CA
Detroit, University of†*	MI
Dickenson State College†*	ND
Dillard University†*	LA
District of Columbia, University of*	DC
Doane College†*	NE
Dominican College†*	NY
Drew University†*	NJ
Drury College†	MO
Dubuque, University of†*	IA
Duke University†*	NC
Dundalk Community College†*	MD
Duquesne University†*	PA
D'Youville College†*	NY
East Carolina University†*	NC
East Central Junior College†*	MS
East Central University†*	OK
Eastern College†*	PA
Eastern Illinois University†*	IL
Eastern Kentucky University†*	KY
Eastern Michigan University†*	MI
Eastern Montana College†*	MT
Eastern Nazarene College†*	MA
Eastern Oklahoma State College†*	OK
Eastern Utah, College of†*	UT
Eastern Wyoming College†*	WY
East Stroudsburg State College†*	PA
East Tennessee State University†*	TN
East Texas State University†*	TX
Eckerd College†*	FL
Edgewood College†*	WI
Edinboro State College†*	PA
Edmonds Community College†*	WA
Edward Williams Junior College†	NJ
Eisenhower College†*	NY
El Camino College†*	CA
Elizabethtown College†*	PA
Elmhurst College†*	IL
Elmira College†*	NY
Elon College†*	NC
Emory and Henry College†*	VA
Emporia State University†*	KS
Erskine College†*	SC
Essex Community College†*	MD
Evansville, University of†*	IN
Everett Community College†*	WA
Fairleigh Dickinson University†*	NJ
Fairmont State College†*	WV
Fergus Falls Community College†*	MN
Ferris State College†	MI
Ferrum College†*	WA
Findlay College†*	OH
Flagler College†*	FL
Florida, University of†*	FL
Florida A. and M. Univeristy†*	FL
Florida International University*	FL
Florida Junior College†	FL
Florida Southern College†*	FL
Florida State University†*	FL
Florida Technological University†*	FL
Fontbonne College*	MO
Fordham University†*	NY
Fort Hayes State College†*	KS
Fort Steilacoom Community College†*	WA
Fort Valley State College†*	GA
Fort Wayne Bible College†*	IN
Framingham State College†	MA
Francis Marion College†	SC
Frank Phillips College†*	TX
Franklin Pierce College†*	NH
Freed-Hardeman College†*	TN
Fresno State University†*	CA
Friendship Junior College†*	SC
Friends University†*	KS
Frostburg State College†	MD
Furman University†*	SC
Gadsden State Junior College†*	AL
Gainesville Junior College†*	GA
Gannon College†*	PA
Gardner-Webb College†*	NC
Garrett Community College†*	MD
Gateway Technical Institute†*	WI
George Fox College†*	OR
Georgetown University†*	DC

George Washington University†*	DC	College†	FL
Georgia, University of†*	GA	Hillsdale College†*	MI
Georgia College†	GA	Hiram College†*	OH
Georgia Institute of Technology†*	GA	Hofstra University†*	NY
		Holy Cross College†*	MA
Georgian Court College*	NJ	Holy Family College†*	PA
Georgia Southern College†*	GA	Hood College*	MD
Georgia Southwestern College†*	GA	Hope College†*	MI
Georgia State University†*	GA	Houghton College†*	NY
Gettysburg College†*	PA	Housatonic Community College†*	CT
Glassboro State College†*	NJ		
Glen Oaks Community College†*	MI	Houston, University of†*	TX
		Houston Baptist University†	TX
Golden Valley Lutheran College†*	MN	Howard Payne University†*	TX
		Humboldt State University†*	CA
Gonzaga University†*	WA	Hunter College†*	NY
Gordon College†*	MA	Huntington College†*	IN
Gordon Junior College*	GA	Husson College†*	ME
Grace College†*	IN	Hutchinson Community Junior College†*	KS
Graceland College†*	IA		
Grand Canyon College†	AZ	Idaho, College of†	ID
Grand Rapids Baptist College†*	MI	Idaho, University of†*	ID
Grand Rapids Junior College†*	MI	Idaho State University†*	ID
Grand Valley State College†*	MI	Illinois, University of, at Champaign†*	IL
Great Falls, College of†*	MT		
Green River Community College†*	WA	Illinois, University of, at Chicago Circle†*	IL
Greensboro College†*	NC	Illinois Benedictine College†*	IL
Greensville College†*	IL	Illinois College†*	IL
Grinnell College†*	IA	Illinois State University†*	IL
Grove City College†*	PA	Illinois Valley Community College†*	IL
Guilford College†*	NC		
Gustavus Adolphus College†*	MN	Illinois Wesleyan University†*	IL
Hagerstown Junior College†*	MD	Indian Hills Community College†*	IA
Hamilton College†*	NY		
Hamline University†*	MN	Indian River Community College†*	FL
Hampton Institute†*	VA		
Hannibal-LaGrange College†	MO	Indiana Central University†*	IN
Hanover College†	IN	Indiana Institute of Technology†*	IN
Harding University†	AR		
Hardin-Simmons University†*	TX	Indiana State University†*	IN
Hartford, University of†*	CT	Indiana University, at Bloomington†*	IN
Harvard University†*	MA		
Hastings College†*	NE	Indiana University of Pennsylvania†*	PA
Hawaii, University of, at Hilo†	HI		
Hawaii, University of, at Honolulu†*	HI	Indiana University-Purdue University, at Fort Wayne†*	IN
Hawaii Pacific College†	HI	Indiana University-Purdue University, at Indianapolis†*	IN
Heidelberg College†*	OH		
Henderson State University†*	OR	Inver Hills College†*	MN
Hendrix College†	AR	Iowa, University of†*	IA
Herbert H. Lehman College†*	NY	Iowa Lakes Community College†*	IA
Hesston College†*	KS		
High Point College†*	NC	Iowa State University†*	IA
Highland Community Junior College†*	KS	Iowa Wesleyan College†*	IA
		Ithaca College†*	NY
Highland Park Community College†*	MI	Jacksonville State University†*	AL
		James Madison University†*	VA
Hilbert College†*	NY	Jamestown College†*	ND
Hillsborough Community		Jarvis Christian College†*	TX

Jefferson Davis Junior College†	MS
Jefferson State Junior College†	AL
Jersey City State College†*	NJ
John Carroll University†*	OH
John C. Calhoun Community College†*	AL
Johnson C. Smith University†*	NC
Jones County Junior College†*	MS
Jordan College†	MI
Josephenum College†	OH
Judson College*	AL
Juniata College†*	PA
Kalamazoo Valley Community College†*	MI
Kankakee Community College†*	IL
Kansas, University of†*	KS
Kansas State University†*	KS
Kansas Wesleyan College†*	KS
Kean College of New Jersey†*	NJ
Kearney State College†*	NE
Kent State University†*	OH
Kentucky, University of†*	KY
Kentucky State University†*	KY
Kentucky Wesleyan College†*	KY
Kenyon College†*	OH
King's College, The†*	NY
Kirkwood Community College†*	IA
Kishwaukee College†*	IL
Kutztown State College†*	PA
Lackawanna Junior College†*	PA
Lafayette College†*	PA
La Grange College†	GA
Lake Erie College*	OH
Lake Region Junior College†*	ND
Lake Superior State College†*	MI
Lamar University†*	TX
Lambuth College†*	TN
Lancaster Bible College†*	PA
Lander College†*	SC
Lane Community College†*	OR
Laredo Junior College†	TX
La Salle College†*	PA
La Verne College†*	CA
Lawrence University†*	WI
Le Moyne College†*	NY
Lebanon Valley College†*	PA
Lees McRae College†*	NC
Lehigh University†*	PA
Lenoir Community College†*	NC
Lenoir-Rhyne College†*	NC
Lewis and Clark Community College†*	IL
Lewis University†*	IL
Lewis-Clark State College†*	ID
Liberty Baptist College†*	VA
Lincoln Christian College†*	IL
Lincoln Land Community College†*	IL
Lincoln Trail College†*	IL
Lincoln University†*	MO
Lindenwood College, The†*	MO
Linfield College†*	OR
Livingstone College†*	NC
Livingston University†*	AL
Lock Haven State College†*	PA
Long Island University†*	NY
Longwood College†*	VA
Loras College†*	IA
Los Angeles Baptist College†*	CA
Los Angeles City College†	CA
Los Angeles Pierce Junior College†*	CA
Los Angeles Southwest College†	CA
Louisiana College†*	LA
Louisiana State University†*	LA
Louisiana Tech University†*	LA
Louisville, University of†*	KY
Lowell, University of†*	MA
Lower Columbia College†*	WA
Loyola Marymount University†*	CA
Lubbock Christian College†*	TX
Luther College†*	IA
Lycoming College†*	PA
Lynchburg College†*	VA
Lyndon State College†*	VT
Macalester College†*	MN
McKendree College†*	IL
McMurray College†*	TX
McNeese State University†*	LA
McPherson College†*	KS
Maine, University of, at Farmington†*	ME
Maine, University of, at Fort Kent†*	ME
Maine, University of, at Presque Isle†*	ME
Malone College†*	OH
Manchester College†	IN
Manhattan College†*	NY
Mankato State University†*	MN
Mansfield State College†*	PA
Marian College†*	IN
Marietta College†*	OH
Marin, College of†*	CA
Marist College†*	NY
Marquette University†*	WI
Mars Hill College†*	NC
Marshall University†*	WV
Marshall Town Community College†*	IA
Martin College†*	TN
Mary Baldwin College*	VA
Mary Hardin-Baylor College†*	TX
Mary Holmes College†*	MS
Mary Washington College†*	VA
Maryland, University of, at Catonsville†*	MD
Maryland, University of, at College Park†*	MD
Maryville College†*	TN

Marywood College*	PA
Massachusetts, University of†*	MA
Massachusetts Institute of Technology†	MA
Massasoit Community College†*	MA
Mattatuck Community College†*	CT
Medgar Evers College†	NY
Memphis State University†*	TN
Menlo College†	CA
Mercer University†*	GA
Mercy College†*	NY
Meredith College*	NC
Merrimack College†*	MA
Metropolitan State College*	CO
Miami, University of*	FL
Miami Christian College†*	FL
Miami University†*	OH
Miami University, at Middletown Campus†*	OH
Miami Dade Community College, New World Center†*	FL
Miami Dade Community College, South Campus†	FL
Michigan, University of†*	MI
Michigan Christian Junior College†*	MI
Michigan State University†*	MI
Mid-Plains Community College†*	NE
Mid-State Technical Institute†*	WI
Middle Tennessee State University†*	TN
Middlebury College†*	VT
Midwest Christian College†*	OK
Midwestern State University†*	TX
Miles Community College†*	MT
Milligan College†*	TN
Millikan University†	IL
Mills College*	CA
Millsaps College†*	MS
Milwaukee Area Technical College†*	WI
Milwaukee School of Engineering†	WI
Mineral Area Junior College†*	MO
Minnesota, University of, at Minneapolis†*	MN
Minnesota, University of, at Morris†*	MN
Minnesota, University of, Technical College†*	MN
Minnesota Bible College†	MN
Mira Costa College†*	CA
Mississippi College†*	MS
Mississippi State University†*	MS
Missouri, University of†*	MO
Missouri, University of, at Rolla†*	MO
Missouri, University of, at St. Louis†*	MO
Missouri Baptist College†	MO
Missouri Southern State College†*	MO
Missouri Valley College†*	MO
Missouri Western College†*	MO
Mitchell College†*	CT
Mitchell Community College†*	NC
Monmouth College†*	IL
Monmouth College†*	NJ
Montana, University of†*	MT
Montana State University†*	MT
Montana Tech†*	MT
Montclair State University†*	NJ
Montevallo, University of†*	AL
Moorhead State University†*	MN
Moorpark College†	AR
Morehead State University†*	KY
Morehouse College†*	GA
Morgan State University†*	MD
Morningside College†*	IA
Motlow State Community College†*	TN
Mott Community College†*	MN
Mount Ida Junior College*	MA
Mount Marty College†*	SD
Mount Olive Junior College†*	NC
Mount St. Mary's College†*	MD
Mount San Jacinto College†*	CA
Mount St. Joseph, College of*	OH
Mount Vernon College*	DC
Muhlenberg College†*	PA
Murray State University†*	KY
Muskegon Community College†*	MI
Napa Community College†	CA
National College†*	SD
Nazareth College†*	NY
Nebraska, University of†*	NE
Nebraska, University of, at Omaha†*	NE
Nebraska Wesleyan University†*	NE
Newberry College†*	SC
New Castle Business College†	PA
New Hampshire College†*	NH
New Hampshire Technological Institute†*	NH
New Haven, University of†*	CT
New Mexico Highlands University†*	NM
New Mexico Junior College†	NM
New Mexico Military Institute†	NM
New Orleans, University of†*	LA
New York, State University College of, Brockport†*	NY
New York, State University College of, Fredonia†*	NY
New York, State University College of, Genesco†*	NY
New York, State University College of, New Paltz†*	NY
New York, State University	

College of, Oneonta†*	NY
New York, State University College of, Oswego†*	NY
New York, State University College of, Plattsburgh†*	NY
New York, State University College of, Potsdam†*	NY
New York, State University College of, Purchase†*	NY
New York, State University of, at Albany†*	NY
New York, State University of, at Binghamton†*	NY
New York, State University of, at Buffalo†*	NY
New York, State University, College of Technology†*	NY
New York Institute of Technology†*	NY
Niagara University†*	NY
Nicholls State University†*	LA
Nichols College†*	MA
Norfolk State College†*	VA
North Adams State College†*	MA
North Alabama, University of†*	AL
North Carolina, University of, at Asheville†	NC
North Carolina, University of, at Chapel Hill†*	NC
North Carolina, University of, at Charlotte†*	NC
North Carolina, University of, at Greensboro†*	NC
North Carolina, University of, at Wilmington†*	NC
North Carolina Agricultural and Technical State University†*	NC
North Carolina State University†*	NC
North Carolina Wesleyan College†*	NC
North Central College†*	IL
North Dakota, University of†*	ND
North Dakota State University, at Bottineau†*	ND
North Dakota State University, at Fargo†*	ND
Northeastern Illinois University†*	IL
Northeastern Oklahoma A and M College†*	OK
Northeast Louisiana University†*	LA
Northeast Mississippi College†*	MS
Northern Arizona University†*	AZ
Northern Colorado, University of†*	CO
Northern Illinois University†*	IL
Northern Iowa, University of†*	IA
Northern Kentucky University†*	KY
Northern Michigan University†*	MI
Northern Montana College†*	MT
Northern State College†*	SD
North Georgia College†*	GA
North Greenville College†*	SC
North Harris County College†*	TX
North Idaho College†*	ID
North Land College†*	WI
Northland Community College†*	MN
North Texas State University†*	TX
Northwest Christian College†	OR
Northwest College†*	WA
Northwestern College†*	MN
Northwestern College†	WI
Northwestern State University†	LA
Northwestern University†*	IL
Northwest Missouri State University†*	MO
Northwest Nazarene College†*	ID
Norwich University†*	VT
Notre Dame, University of†*	IN
Notre Dame College*	MD
Oakland City College†*	IN
Oakland University†*	MI
Oakton Community College†	IL
Oberlin College†*	OH
Occidental College†*	CA
Ohio Northern University†	OH
Ohio State University†*	OH
Ohio University*	OH
Ohio Valley College†	WV
Ohio Wesleyan University†*	OH
Oklahoma, University of†*	OK
Oklahoma University of Science and Arts†*	OK
Oklahoma Baptist University†*	OK
Oklahoma City University†*	OK
Oklahoma State University†*	OK
Old Dominion University†*	VA
Olivet College†*	MI
Olivet Nazarene College†*	IL
Olney Central College†*	IL
Oral Roberts University†*	OK
Oregon, University of†*	OR
Oregon State University†*	OR
Oregon Technical Institute†*	OR
Oscar Rose Junior College†*	OK
Otero Junior College†*	CO
Ottawa University†*	KS
Otterbein Colege†*	OH
Ouachita Baptist College†*	AR
Oxnard College†	CA
Ozarks, College of the†*	AR
Ozarks, School of the†*	MO
Pace University†*	NY
Pacific, University of the†*	CA
Pacific Lutheran University†*	WA
Pacific University†*	OR
Paducah Community College†*	KY
Palm Beach Junior College†	FL

Palomar College†*	CA	Regis College†*	CO
Pan American University†*	TX	Rensselaer Polytechnic Institute†*	NY
Paris Junior College†*	TX	Rice University†*	TX
Park College†*	MO	Rider College†*	NJ
Parkland College†*	IL	Rio Grande College†*	OH
Paul Smith's College†*	NY	Ripon College†*	WI
Peace College*	NC	Riverside City College†*	CA
Pembroke State University†*	NC	Roanoke College†*	VA
Penn Valley Community College†	MO	Robert Morris College†*	PA
Pennsylvania, University of†*	PA	Robert Wesleyan College†*	NY
Pennsylvania State University, at Altoona†*	PA	Rochester, University of†*	NY
		Rockhurst College†*	MO
Pennsylvania State University, at Beaver Campus†*	PA	Rockmont College†*	CO
		Rollins College†*	FL
Pennsylvania State University, at DuBois†	PA	Rust College†*	MS
		Rutgers, State University of, at Camden†*	NJ
Pennsylvania State University, at McKeesport†	PA	Rutgers, State University of, at Newark†*	NJ
Pennsylvania State University, at University Park†*	PA	Rutgers, State University of, at New Brunswick†*	NJ
Pennsylvania State University (Behrend College)†*	PA	Sacred Heart University†*	CT
Pensacola Junior College†*	FL	Saginaw Valley College†*	MI
Pepperdine University†*	CA	St. Augustine's College†*	NC
Pfeiffer College†*	NC	St. Bonaventure University†*	NY
Philadelphia Community College†*	PA	St. Clair County Community College†*	MI
Phillips University†*	OK	St. Cloud State University†*	MN
Piedmont Bible College†	NC	St. Edwards University†*	TX
Pikeville College†*	KY	St. Francis College†*	NY
Pima Community College†*	AZ	St. Francis College of Pennsylvania†*	PA
Pittsburg State University†*	KS		
Pittsburgh, University of†*	PA	St. Francis, College of†*	IL
Pittsburgh, University of, at Johnstown†*	PA	St. John Fisher College†*	NY
		St. Johns College†*	KS
Plymouth State College†*	NH	St. Johns University†	MN
Point Loma College†*	CA	St. Joseph College†*	IN
Point Park College†*	PA	St. Joseph the Provider, College of†*	VT
Porterville College†	CA		
Portland, University of†*	OR	St. Lawrence University†*	NY
Portland State University†*	OR	St. Leo College†*	FL
Pratt Community Junior College†*	KS	St. Louis College of Pharmacy†	MO
		St. Louis Community College†*	MO
Pratt Institute†*	NY	St. Louis University†*	MO
Presbyterian College†*	SC	St. Mary, College of*	NE
Princeton University†*	NJ	St. Mary of the Plains College†*	KS
Principia College†*	IL	St. Mary's College†*	MN
Providence College†*	RI	St. Mary's College†	MI
Puerto Rico Agricultural and Mechanical University†*	PR	St. Mary's College of California†*	CA
Purdue University, at Calumet*	IL	St. Mary's University of Texas†*	TX
Purdue University, at West Lafayette†*	IL	St. Norbert College†*	WY
		St. Olaf College†*	MN
Quincyf17College†*	IL	St. Paul's College†*	VA
Quinnipiac College†*	CT	St. Peter's College†*	NJ
Radford College†*	VA	St. Scholastica, College of†*	MN
Randolph-Macon College†*	VA	St. Teresa, College of*	MN
Redlands, University of†*	CA	St. Thomas, College of†*	MN
Redwoods, College of the†*	CA	St. Vincent College†	PA

St. Xavier College †*	IL
Salisbury State College †*	MD
Sam Houston State University †*	TX
San Diego, University of †*	CA
San Diego State University †*	CA
San Francisco, City College of †	CA
San Francisco, University of †*	CA
San Francisco State University †*	CA
San Jose State University †*	CA
San Mateo, College of †*	CA
Santa Ana College †*	CA
Santa Barbara City Junior College †*	CA
Santa Clara, University of †*	CA
Schoolcraft College †*	MI
Schreiner College †*	TX
Scranton, University of †*	PA
Seminole Community College †*	FL
Sequoias, College of the †*	CA
Seward County Community Junior College †*	KS
Shaw College, at Detroit †*	MI
Shawnee College †*	IL
Shawnee State College †*	OH
Shelby State Community College †*	TN
Shepherd College †*	WV
Sheridan College †*	WY
Shorter College †*	GA
Siena College †*	NY
Siena Heights College †*	MI
Siskiyous, College of the †*	CA
Skagit Valley College †*	WA
Skidmore College †*	NY
Skyline College †*	CA
Slippery Rock State College †	PA
Smith College*	MA
Snead State Junior College †*	AL
South, University of the †*	TN
South Alabama, University of †*	AL
Southampton College †	NY
South Carolina, University of †*	SC
South Carolina State College †*	SC
South Dakota, University of, at Springfield †*	SD
South Dakota, University of, at Vermillion †*	SD
South Dakota School of Mines and Technology †*	SD
Southeast Community College †*	NE
Southeastern Community College †*	IA
Southeastern Louisiana University †*	LA
Southeastern Oklahoma State University †*	OK
Southeastern University †*	DC
Southeast Missouri State †*	MO
Southern Arkansas Uniersity †*	AR
Southern Baptist College †*	AR
Southern California, University of †*	CA
Southern California College †*	CA
Southern Colorado, University of †*	CO
Southern Connecticut State College †*	CT
Southern Illinois University †*	IL
Southern Maine University †	ME
Southern Maine Vocational Technical Institute †*	ME
Southern Methodist University †*	TX
Southern Oregon State College †*	OR
Southern State Community College †*	OH
Southern Union State Junior College †*	AL
Southern University †	LA
Southern University and Agricultural and Mechanical College †*	LA
Southern Utah State College †*	UT
South Florida, The University of †*	FL
Southwest Baptist College †*	MO
Southwestern at Memphis †*	TN
Southwestern College †*	KS
Southwestern Community College †*	IA
Southwestern Louisiana, University of †*	LA
Southwestern University †*	TX
Southwest State University †*	MN
Southwest Texas State University †*	TX
Spartanburg Methodist College †*	SC
Spring Arbor College †*	MI
Spring Garden College †*	PA
Spring Hill College †*	AL
Stanford University †*	CA
State Fair Community College †*	MO
Staten Island, College of †	NY
Stephen F. Austin State University †*	TX
Sterling College †*	KS
Stetson University †*	FL
Steubenville, University of †*	OH
Stevens Institute of Technology †	NJ
Stevens State Technology †	PA
Sul Ross State University †*	TX
Surry Community College †*	NC
Susquehanna University †*	PA
Swarthmore College †*	PA
Syracuse University †*	NY
Tabor College †*	KS
Tacoma Community College †*	WA
Tampa, University of*	FL
Tarkio College †*	MO

Tarleton State College†*	TX
Taylor University†*	IN
Temple University†*	PA
Tennessee, University of†*	TN
Tennessee, University of, at Martin†*	TN
Tennessee State University†*	TN
Tennessee Technological University†*	TN
Tennessee Wesleyan College†*	TN
Texas, University of†*	TX
Texas, University of, at Arlington†*	TX
Texas, The University of, at El Paso†*	TX
Texas A and I University†*	TX
Texas Christian University†*	TX
Texas Lutheran College†*	TX
Texas Southern University†*	TX
Texas Tech University†*	TX
Texas Wesleyan College†*	TX
Texas Woman's University*	TX
Thiel College†*	PA
Thomas College†*	ME
Thomas More College†	KY
Three Rivers Community College†*	MO
Tiffin University†	OH
Toledo, University of†*	OH
Tougaloo College†*	MS
Towson State University†*	MD
Treasure Valley Community College†*	OR
Trenton Junior College†*	MO
Trenton State College†*	NJ
Trinidad State Junior College†*	CO
Trinity Bible Institute†*	ND
Trinity College†	CT
Trinity University†*	TX
Tri-State University†*	IN
Triton College†*	IL
Troy State University†*	AL
Truett-McConnell College†*	GA
Tufts University†	MA
Tulane University†*	LA
Tulsa, University of†*	OK
Tunxis Community College†*	CT
Tuskegee Institute†*	AL
Umpqua Community College†*	OR
Union College†*	KY
United Wesleyan College†*	PA
Upper Iowa University†	IA
Upsala College†*	NJ
Urbana College†*	OH
Ursinus College†*	PA
Utah, University of†*	UT
Utah State University†*	UT
Utica College of Syracuse University†*	NY
Utica Junior College†	NY
Valparaiso University†*	IN
Vanderbilt University†*	TN
Ventura College†*	CA
Villanova University†*	PA
Virginia, University of†*	VA
Virginia Commonwealth University†*	VA
Virginia Polytechnic Institute†*	VA
Virginia State College†*	VA
Virginia Union University†*	VA
Viterboro College†*	WY
Wabash College†	IN
Wagner College†	NY
Wake Forest University†*	NC
Walsh College†*	OH
Warner Pacific College†*	OR
Warren Wilson College†*	NC
Washburn University†*	KS
Washington, University of†*	WA
Washington and Lee University†	VA
Washington Bible College†*	MD
Washington State University†*	WA
Washington University*	MO
Wayland Baptist College†*	TX
Waynesburg College†	PA
Wayne State University†*	MI
Webber College†*	FL
Weber State College†*	UT
Wenatchee Valley College†*	WA
Wesleyan College†*	CT
West Chester State College†*	PA
Western Carolina University†*	NC
Western Illinois University†*	IL
Western Kentucky University†*	KY
Western Maryland College†*	MD
Western Michigan University†*	MI
Western Montana College†*	MT
Western New England College†*	MA
Western State College of Colorado†*	CO
Western Washington University†*	WA
Westfield State College†*	MA
West Georgia College†*	GA
West Hills College†	CA
West Liberty State College†*	WV
West Los Angeles College†	CA
Westminster College†	MO
Westmount College†	CA
West Texas State University†*	TX
West Virginia State College†*	WV
West Virginia University†*	WV
West Virginia Wesleyan College†*	WV
Wharton County Junior College†*	TX
Wheaton College†*	IL
Wheaton College*	MA

Wheeling College†*	WV
Whitworth College†*	WA
Wichita State University†	KS
Wilberforce University†*	OH
Wiley College†*	TX
Wilkes College†*	PA
Willamette University†*	OR
William and Mary, College of†*	VA
William Carey College†*	MS
William Paterson College†*	NJ
William Penn College†*	IA
Williams College†*	MA
Williamsport Area Community College†*	PA
Wilmington College†*	OH
Wilson College*	PA
Winona State College†*	MN
Winston-Salem State University†*	NC
Winthrop College†*	SC
Wisconsin, University of, at Eau Claire†*	WI
Wisconsin, University of, at Green Bay†*	WI
Wisconsin, University of, at La Crosse†*	WI
Wisconsin, University of, at Marathon County†*	WI
Wisconsin, University of, at Milwaukee†*	WI
Wisconsin, University of, at Oshkosh†*	WI
Wisconsin, University of, at Platteville†	WI
Wisconsin, University of, at River Falls†*	WI
Wisconsin, University of, at Stevens Point†*	WI
Wisconsin, University of, at Superior†*	WI
Wisconsin, University of, at Waukesha†*	WI
Wisconsin, University of, at Whitewater†*	WI
Wofford College†*	SC
Worcester State College†*	MA
Worthington Community College†*	MN
Wright State University†*	OH
Wyoming, University of†*	WY
Xavier University†*	OH
Xavier University of Louisiana†*	LA
Yakima Valley College†*	WA
Yale University†*	CT
Yankton College†*	SD
York College†*	NE
Youngstown State University†*	OH
Yuba College†	CA

BOWLING

Albany, Junior College of†*	NY
Alpena Community College†	MI
Arkansas, University of†	AR
Armstrong State College†*	GA
Baker University†*	KS
Baltimore, Community College of†*	MD
Benedictine College†*	KS
Brooklyn College, City University of New York†	NY
Bryant College†	RI
Calvary Bible College†*	MO
Canisius College†*	NY
Cornell University*	NY
Cuyahoga Community College†*	OH
Cuyahoga Community College, Metro Campus†*	OH
Duquesne University†*	PA
D'Youville College†*	NY
Eisenhower College†*	NY
Elmira College†*	NY
Essex Community College†*	MD
Florida A and M University†*	FL
Fontbonne College*	MO
Gateway Technical Institute†*	WI
Gettysburg College†*	PA
Gustavus Adolphus College†*	MN
Harding University†	AR
Ithaca College*	NY
Lowell, University of†*	MA
Mid-State Technical Institute†*	WI
Milwaukee Area Technical College†*	WI
New York, State University College of, at Oswego*	NY
New York, State University of, at Buffalo*	NY
Northwest College†*	WA
Ohio Wesleyan University*	OH
Otterbein College*	OH
Pace University†	NY
Pacific University†*	OR
Pennsylvania State University, at Middletown†	PA
Pennsylvania State University, at University Park†*	PA
Rockhurst College†*	MO
Saginaw Valley College†	MI
St. Augustine's College†*	NC
St. Francis College†	NY
St. Louis Community College†*	MO
St. Peter's College†*	NJ
St. Vincent College†	PA
Southeastern Community College†*	IA

Southwest Baptist College†	MO
Spartanburg Methodist College†*	SC
Temple University*	PA
Treasure Valley Community College†*	OR
Trinity University†*	TX
Villanova University†*	PA
Western New England College†*	MA
William and Mary, College of*	VA
Xavier University†	OH

CREW

Alabama, University of, at Huntsville†*	AL
Amherst College†	MA
Assumption College†*	MA
Boston University†*	MA
Brown University†*	RI
California, University of, at Irvine†	CA
California, University of, at Los Angeles†*	CA
California, University of, at San Diego†*	CA
California State University, at Long Beach†	CA
Canisius College†	NY
Charleston, University of†	WV
Clark University†	MA
Columbia University†	NY
Connecticut College†*	CT
Cornell University†*	NY
Dartmouth College†	NH
District of Columbia, University of†	DC
Florida Institute of Technology†	FL
Georgetown University†*	DC
George Washington University†*	DC
Grand Rapids Baptist†	MI
Grand Valley State College†*	MI
Harvard University†*	MA
Holy Cross College†*	MA
Ithaca College†	NY
La Salle College†*	PA
Lowell, University of†*	MA
Loyola Marymount University†*	CA
Manhattan College†	NY
Marietta College†*	OH
Marist College†*	NY
Massachusetts Institute of Technology†	MA
Mills College*	CA
New York Institute of Technology†	NY
Oregon State University†*	OR
Pacific Lutheran University†*	WA
Pennsylvania, University of†*	PA
Princeton University†*	NJ
Rutgers University†*	NJ
St. Mary's College†*	CA
San Diego, University of†*	CA
Santa Clara, University of†*	CA
Simmons College*	MA
Skidmore College†*	NY
Smith College*	MA
Southern California, University of†*	CA
Syracuse University†*	NY
Tampa, University of†*	FL
Temple University†	PA
Trinity College†	CT
Tufts University†	MA
Villanova University†*	PA
Washington, University of*	WA
Wayne State University†	MI
Wesleyan University†*	CT
Western Washington University†*	WA
Williams College†*	MA
Yale University*	CT

CROSS COUNTRY

Abilene Christian University†*	TX
Adams State College of Colorado†*	CO
Adrian College†	MI
Akron, University of†	OH
Alabama, University of, at Birmingham†*	AL
Alabama, University of, at University†	AL
Alabama Agricultural and Mechanical University†*	AL
Alaska, University of, at Anchorage†*	AK
Alaska, University of, at Fairbanks†*	AK
Albany State College†	GA
Albion College†	MI
Albright College†	PA
Alcorn State University†*	MS
Allegheny College†*	PA
Allen County Community Junior College†*	KS
Allentown College of St. Francis De Sales†*	PA

Alma College†*	MI	Boston State College†*	MA
Amherst College†*	MA	Boston University†*	MA
Anderson College†	IA	Bowdoin College†	ME
Angelo State University†*	TX	Bowling Green State University†*	OH
Anne Arundel Community College†*	MD	Bradley University†	IL
Appalachian State University†	NC	Brandeis University†*	MA
Aquinas College†	MI	Brevard College†	NC
Arizona, University of†*	AZ	Brevard Community College†*	FL
Arizona State University†	AZ	Bridgewater College†	VA
Arkansas, University of†*	AR	Bridgewater State College†*	MA
Arkansas, University of, at Monticello†	AR	Brigham Young University†*	UT
		Brooklyn College of the City University of New York†*	NY
Arkansas State University†	AR	Brown University†*	RI
Arkansas Tech University†	AR	Bryan College†	TN
Armstrong State College†	GA	Bryant College†	RI
Asbury College†	KY	Bucknell University†*	PA
Asheville-Buncombe Technical Institute†*	NC	Butler County Community Junior College†*	KS
Ashland College†	OH	Butler University†	IN
Assumption College†*	MA	California, University of, at Davis†*	CA
Auburn University, at Auburn†*	AL		
Augusta College†	GA	California, University of, at Irvine†*	CA
Augustana College†*	IL		
Augustana College†*	SD	California, University of, at Los Angeles†*	CA
Averett College†	VA		
Azusa Pacific College†*	CA	California, University of, at Riverside†*	CA
Babson College†	MA		
Baker University†*	KS	California, University of, at San Diego†*	CA
Ball State University†*	IN		
Baltimore, Community College of†*	MD	California, University of, at Santa Barbara†	CA
Baltimore, University of†	MD	California Institute of Technology†*	CA
Baptist Bible College†	MO		
Baptist Bible College†*	PA	California Polytechnic State University†*	CA
Baptist College at Charleston†	SC		
Barnard College*	NY	California State College, at Bakersfield†*	CA
Barton County Community College†*	KS		
Bates College†*	ME	California State College, at Sonoma†*	CA
Baylor University†	TX		
Beaver College†*	PA	California State College, at Stanislaus†	CA
Bellarmine College†	KY		
Belmont College†	TN	California State University, at Chico†*	CA
Beloit College†*	WI		
Bemidji State University†	MN	California State University, at Fullerton†*	CA
Benedictine College†*	KS		
Bentley College†	MA	California State University, at Haywood†*	CA
Berea College†	KY		
Berry College†*	GA	California State University at Long Beach†*	CA
Bethany College†	KS		
Bethel College†*	MN	Calvary Bible College†*	MO
Bethune-Cookman College†	FL	Calvin College†	MI
Biola College†	CA	Campbell College†	NC
Biscayne College*	FL	Canisius College†	NY
Bismarck Junior College†*	ND	Carl Sandburg College†	IL
Bluffton College†*	OH	Carroll College†*	WI
Boise State University†*	ID	Carson-Newman College†	TN
Boston College†*	MA	Carthage College†	WI

Castleton State College†*	VT
Centenary College†	LA
Central Arkansas, University of†	AR
Central Junior College†*	KS
Central Michigan University†*	MI
Central Missouri State University†*	MO
Central State University†	OK
Centre College†	KY
Chadron State College†	NE
Chaminade University†	HI
Chicago, The University of†	IL
Chicago State University*	IL
Christopher Newport College†	VA
Cincinnati, University of†	OH
Citadel, The†	SC
Citrus College†*	CA
Clackamas Community College†*	OR
Clarion State College†*	PA
Clark College†	GA
Clark University†*	MA
Clemson University†*	SC
Cleveland State University†	OH
Coe College†*	IA
Colby College†*	ME
Colgate University†	NY
Colorado, University of†*	CO
Colorado School of Mines†	CO
Colorado State University†*	CO
Columbia University†	NY
Columbus College†	GA
Concordia College†	IL
Concordia College†*	NE
Connecticut, University of†*	CT
Connecticut College†*	CT
Cornell University†*	NY
Cosumnes River College†*	CA
Cottey College*	MO
Covenant College†	TN
Cumberland College†	KY
C. W. Post College†	NY
Cypress College†*	CA
Dakota Wesleyan University†*	SD
Dartmouth College†*	NH
David Lipscomb College†	TN
Davidson College†*	NC
Delaware, University of†*	DE
Delaware State College†*	DE
Delaware Valley College†*	PA
Delta State College†*	MS
DePauw University†	IN
Desert, College of the†*	CA
Detroit, University of†	MI
Dickenson State College†*	ND
District of Columbia, University of*	DC
Doane College†*	NE
Drew University†*	NJ
Dubuque, University of†*	IA
Duke University†	NC
Duquesne University†*	PA
Eastern College†	PA
Eastern Illinois University†*	IL
Eastern Kentucky University†*	KY
Eastern Michigan University†*	MI
Eastern Montana College†*	MT
Eastern Nazarene College†	MA
Eastern Oklahoma State College†*	OK
East Stroudsburg State College†	PA
East Tennessee State University†*	TN
Eckerd College†	FL
Edinboro State College†	PA
Eisenhower College†*	NY
El Camino College†*	CA
Emory and Henry College†	VA
Emory University†	GA
Emporia State University†*	KS
Essex Community College†*	MD
Evansville, University of†	IN
Everett Community College†*	WA
Fairleigh Dickinson University†	NJ
Fairmont State College†*	WV
Ferris State College†	MI
Ferrum College†	WA
Findlay College†	OH
Fitchburg State College†*	MA
Flagler College†	FL
Florida, University of†	FL
Florida A A. and M. University†*	FL
Florida International University†*	FL
Florida Junior College†*	FL
Florida Southern College†	FL
Florida State University†*	FL
Florida Technological University†*	FL
Fordham University†*	NY
Fort Hayes State†*	KS
Fort Valley State College†*	GA
Framingham State College†	MA
Francis Marion College†	SC
Franklin Pierce College†	NH
Freed-Hardeman College†*	TN
Fresno State University†	CA
Frostburg State College†	MD
Furman University†	SC
Gannon College†	PA
Gardner-Webb College†	NC
Gateway Technical Institute†*	WI
George Fox College†*	OR
Georgetown University†*	DC
Georgia, University of†*	GA
Georgia State University†*	GA
Gettysburg College†*	PA
Glassboro State College†*	NJ
Golden Valley Lutheran	

College†*	MN
Gonzaga Universtiy†*	WA
Gordon College†	MA
Grace College†	IN
Graceland College†	IA
Grand Rapids Junior College†	MI
Grand Valley State College†	MI
Green River Community College†*	WA
Greensville College†	IL
Grinnell College†*	IA
Grove City College†*	PA
Gustavus Adolphus College†*	MN
Hagerstown Junior College†	MD
Hamilton College†*	NY
Hamline University†*	MN
Hampton Institute†*	VA
Hanover College†	IN
Harding University†	AR
Hardin-Simmons University†*	TX
Harvard University†*	MA
Hastings College†	NE
Hawaii, University of, at Honolulu*	HI
Henderson State University†	OR
Hendrix College†	AR
Herbert Lehman College†*	NY
Highland Park Community College†*	MI
Hillsdale College†*	MI
Hiram College†*	OH
Holy Cross College†*	MA
Hope College†	MI
Houghton College†*	NY
Houston, University of†*	TX
Houston Baptist University†	TX
Howard Payne University†	TX
Humboldt State University†*	CA
Hunter College†*	NY
Huntington College†	IN
Hutchinson Community Junior College†	KS
Idaho, University of†*	ID
Idaho State University†*	ID
Illinois, University of, at Champaign†*	IL
Illinois, University of, at Chicago Circle†*	IL
Illinois Benedictine College†*	IL
Illinois State University†*	IL
Illinois Valley Community College†*	IL
Illinois Wesleyan University†	IL
Indiana Central University†	IN
Indiana State University†	IN
Indiana University, at Bloomington†*	IN
Indiana University of Pennsylvania†*	PA
Iowa, University of†*	IA
Iowa State University†*	IA
Ithaca College†	NY
Jacksonville State University†*	AL
James Madison University†*	VA
Jamestown College†*	ND
Jersey City State College†	NJ
John Carroll University†	OR
Johnson C. Smith University†	NC
Jordan College†*	MI
Josephenum College†	OH
Juniata College†*	PA
Kansas, University of†*	KS
Kansas State University†*	KS
Kansas Wesleyan College†*	KS
Kearney State College†*	NE
Kent State University†*	OH
Kentucky, University of†*	KY
Kenyon College†*	OH
King's College, The†	NY
Kutztown State College†*	PA
Lafayette College†*	PA
Lake Superior State College†	MI
Lamar University†*	TX
Lane Community College†*	OR
La Salle College†*	PA
La Verne College†	CA
Lawrence University†*	WI
Le Moyne College†	NY
Lebanon Valley College†	PA
Lehigh University†	PA
Lewis University†	IL
Liberty Baptist College†*	VA
Lincoln Land Community College†	IT
Lincoln University†	MO
Linfield College†*	OR
Livingstone College*	NC
Lock Haven State College†*	PA
Long Island University*	NY
Loras College†*	IA
Los Angeles Baptist College†*	CA
Los Angeles City College†	CA
Los Angeles Pierce Junior College†*	CA
Los Angeles Southwest College†*	CA
Louisiana State University†*	LA
Louisiana Tech University†	LA
Louisville, University of†*	KY
Lowell, University of†*	MA
Loyola Marymount University†*	CA
Luther College†*	IA
Lynchburg College†*	VA
Lyndon State College†*	VT
Macalester College†*	MN
McNeese State University†	LA
McPherson College†*	KS
Maine, University of, at Presque Isle†*	ME
Maine Maritime Academy†	ME

Malone College†	OH
Manchester College†	IN
Manhattan College†	NY
Mankato State University†*	MN
Mansfield State College†	PA
Marian College†	IN
Marietta College†*	OH
Marin, College of†*	CA
Marist College†	NY
Marquette University†*	WI
Mars Hill College†	NC
Marshall University†	WV
Maryland, University of, at Catonsville†*	MD
Maryland, University of, at College Park†*	MD
Mary Washington College†*	VA
Massachusetts, University of†*	MA
Massachusetts Institute of Technology†	MA
Mattatuck Community College†	CT
Medgar Evers College†*	NY
Memphis State University†*	TN
Menlo College†*	CA
Mercy College†	NY
Metropolitan State College†	CO
Miami-Dade Community College, New World Center†	FL
Miami University†	OH
Michigan, University of†*	MI
Michigan Christian Junior College†*	MI
Michigan State University†*	MI
Middlebury College†*	VT
Middle Tennessee State University†*	TN
Milligan College†	TN
Millikan University†	IL
Milwaukee Area Technical College†*	WI
Minnesota, University of, at Minneapolis†*	MN
Minnesota, University of, Technical College†*	MN
Mississippi College†*	MS
Mississippi State University†	MS
Missouri, University of†*	MO
Missouri, University of, at Rolla†	MO
Missouri, University of, at St. Louis†	MO
Monmouth College†	IL
Monmouth College†	NJ
Montana, University of†*	MT
Montana State University†	MT
Montclair State University†*	NJ
Moorhead State University†*	MN
Moorpark College†	AR
Morehead State University†*	KY
Morehouse College†	GA
Mount St. Mary's College†*	MD
Muhlenberg College†	PA
Murray State University†*	KY
Napa Community College†*	CA
Nazareth College†*	NY
Nebraska, University of†*	NE
Nebraska, University of, at Omaha*	NE
Nebraska Wesleyan University†*	NE
New Haven, University of†	CT
New Mexico Highlands University†	NM
New Mexico Junior College†	NM
New Orleans, University of†*	LA
New York, State University College of, at Fredonia†	NY
New York, State University College of, at Genesco†*	NY
New York, State University College of, at New Paltz†	NY
New York, State University College of, at Oneonta†*	NY
New York, State University College of, at Oswego†*	NY
New York, State University College of, at Plattsburgh†	NY
New York, State University College of, at Potsdam†	NY
New York, State University of, at Albany†*	NY
New York, State University of, at Binghamton†*	NY
New York, State University of, at Buffalo†	NY
Niagara University†*	NY
Nicholls State University†	LA
Norfolk State College†	VA
North Adams State College†*	MA
North Carolina, University of, at Chapel Hill†*	NC
North Carolina, University of, at Charlotte†	NC
North Carolina, University of, at Wilmington†*	NC
North Carolina Agricultural and Technical State University†	NC
North Carolina State University†*	NC
North Central College†*	IL
North Dakota, University of†*	ND
North Dakota State University, at Fargo†*	ND
Northeastern Illinois University†*	IL
Northeast Louisiana University†	LA
Northern Arizona University†*	AZ
Northern Colorado, University of†*	CO
Northern Illinois University†*	IL
Northern Iowa, University of†*	IA
Northern Kentucky University†	KY

Northern Michigan University†	MI	Principia College†	IL
Northern State College†	SD	Providence College†*	RI
North Idaho College†*	ID	Puerto Rico Agricultural and	
Northland Community College	MN	Mechanical University†*	PR
North Texas State University†*	TX	Purdue University, at West	
Northwestern College†	MN	Lafayette†*	IL
Northwestern College†	WI	Quinnipiac College†	CT
Northwestern University†*	IL	Radford College†*	VA
Northwest Missouri State		Redlands, University of†*	CA
University†*	MO	Redwoods, College of the†	CA
Northwest Nazarene College†*	ID	Rensselaer Polytechnic Institute†	NY
Norwich University†*	VT	Rice University†*	TX
Notre Dame, University of†	IN	Rider College†	NJ
Oakland University†	MI	Riverside City College†*	CA
Oakton Community College†*	IL	Roanoke College†*	VA
Oberlin College†*	OH	Robert Morris College†	PA
Occidental College†*	CA	Roberts Wesleyan College†*	NY
Ohio Northern University†	OH	Rochester, University of†	NY
Ohio State University†*	OH	Rollins College†	FL
Ohio University*	OH	Rust College†*	MS
Ohio Wesleyan University†	OH	Rutgers, State University of, at	
Oklahoma, University of*	OK	New Brunswick†*	NJ
Oklahoma State University†*	OK	Rutgers, State University of, at	
Old Dominion University†*	VA	Camden†*	NJ
Olivet College†	MI	Sacred Heart University†*	CT
Oral Roberts University†	OK	Saginaw Valley College†	MI
Oregon, University of†*	OR	St. Augustine's College†*	NC
Oregon State University†*	OR	St. Bonaventure University†	NY
Ottawa University†*	KS	St. Cloud State University†*	MN
Otterbein College†	OH	St. Francis College†	NY
Ouachita Baptist College†	AR	St. Francis College of	
Oxnard College†	CA	Pennsylvania†	PA
Ozarks, College of the†	AR	St. John Fisher College†	NY
Ozarks, School of the†	MO	St. Johns University†	MN
Pace University†	NY	St. Joseph College†	IN
Pacific Lutheran University†*	WA	St. Lawrence University†	NY
Pacific University†	OR	St. Leo College†*	FL
Paducah Community College†*	KY	St. Louis Community College†*	MO
Palomar College†*	CA	St. Louis University†*	MO
Pan American University†	TX	St. Mary's College†*	MN
Park College†*	MO	St. Mary's College of California†	CA
Parkland College†*	IL	St. Norbert College†	WI
Pembroke State University†	NC	St. Olaf College†*	MN
Pennsylvania, University of†*	PA	St. Paul's College†	VA
Pennsylvania State University, at		St. Peter's College†*	NJ
Middletown†	PA	St. Scholastica, College of†*	MN
Pennsylvania State University, at		St. Thomas, College of†*	MN
University Park†*	PA	St. Vincent College†	PA
Philadelphia Community		St. Xavier College†	IL
College†*	PA	Salisbury State College†	MD
Pima Community College†*	AZ	San Diego, University of†*	CA
Pittsburgh State University†*	KS	San Diego State University†	CA
Pittsburgh, University of†	PA	San Francisco, City College of†*	CA
Pittsburgh, University of, at		San Francisco, University of†*	CA
Johnstown†	PA	San Francisco State University†*	CA
Point Loma College†*	CA	San Jose State University†	CA
Porterville College†	CA	San Mateo, College of†*	CA
Portland, University of†	OR	Santa Ana College†*	CA
Pratt Institute†	NY	Santa Barbara City Junior	
Princeton University†*	NJ	College†*	CA

Santa Clara, University of†*	CA	Swarthmore College†	PA
Schoolcraft College†*	MI	Syracuse University†	NY
Scranton, University of†*	PA	Tacoma Community College†*	WA
Seminole Community College†	FL	Tampa, University of†*	FL
Sequoias, College of the†*	CA	Tarkto College†*	MO
Siena College†	NY	Taylor University†	IN
Siena Heights College†*	MI	Temple University†*	PA
Siskiyous, College of the†*	CA	Tennessee, University of†*	TN
Skagit Valley College†*	WA	Tennessee State University†	TN
Skyline College†*	CA	Tennessee Technological	
Slippery Rock State College†*	PA	University†*	TN
Smith College†	MA	Texas, The University of†	TX
South, University of the†*	TN	Texas, The University of, at	
South Alabama, University of†	AL	Arlington†*	TX
Southampton College†	NY	Texas, The University of, at El	
South Carolina, University of†	SC	Paso†*	TX
South Dakota, University of, at		Texas A and I University†	TX
Springfield†*	SD	Texas Christian University†	TX
South Dakota, University of, at		Texas Lutheran College*	TX
Vermillion†*	SD	Texas Southern University†*	TX
South Dakota School of Mines		Texas Tech University†*	TX
and Technology†	SD	Texas Woman's University*	TX
Southeast Community College†*	NE	Thiel College†	PA
Southeastern Louisiana		Toledo, University of†	OH
University†	LA	Tougaloo College†*	MS
Southeast Missouri State†	MO	Towson State University†	MD
Southern Arkansas University†	AR	Treasure Valley Community	
Southern Colorado, University		College†	OR
of†	CO	Trenton State College†	NJ
Southern Connecticut State		Trinity College†	CT
College†*	CT	Tri-State University†	IN
Southern Illinois University†*	IL	Triton College†*	IL
Southern Maine University†*	ME	Troy State University†	AL
Southern Maine Vocational		Tufts University†	MA
Technical Institute†	ME	Tulane University†	LA
Southern Methodist University†	TX	Tulsa, University of†*	OK
Southern Oregon State		Tunxis Community College†	CT
College†*	OR	Tuskegee Institute†	AL
Southern University and		Umpqua Community College†*	OR
Agricultural and Mechanical		Union College†	KY
College†*	LA	Ursinus College†	PA
Southern Utah State College†	UT	Utah, University of†*	UT
South Florida, The University		Utah State University†*	UT
of†	FL	Valparaiso University†	IN
Southwest Baptist College†	MO	Vanderbilt University†*	TX
Southwestern at Memphis†*	TN	Ventura College†*	CA
Southwestern College†*	KS	Virginia, University of†*	VA
Southwestern Louisiana,		Virginia Commonwealth	
University of†	LA	University†*	VA†
Southwest State University†*	MN	Virginia Polytechnic Institute†	VA
Southwest Texas State		Virginia State College†	VA
University†*	TX	Virginia Union University†	VA
Spring Arbor College†*	MI	Wabash College†	IN
Spring Garden College†	PA	Wagner College†	NY
Stanford University†*	CA	Wake Forest University†*	NC
Steven F. Austin State		Walsh College†	OH
University†	TX	Warren Wilson College†*	NC
Stevens State Technology†	PA	Washington, University of†*	WA
Susquehanna University†	PA	Washington and Lee University†	VA

Washington Bible College†*	MD
Washington State University†*	WA
Washington University†	MO
Wayland Baptist College†	TX
Wayne State University†	MI
Weber State College†*	UT
Wesleyan College†*	CT
West Chester State College†*	PA
Western Carolina University†	NC
Western Illinois University†*	IL
Western Kentucky University†*	KY
Western Maryland College†*	MD
Western Michigan University†*	MI
Western New England College†*	MA
Western State College of Colorado†	CO
Western Washington University†*	WA
Westfield State College†	MA
West Georgia College†	GA
West Los Angeles College†*	CA
Westminster College†	MO
Westmount College†*	CA
West Texas State University†*	TX
West Virginia State College†	WV
West Virginia University†*	WV
West Virginia Wesleyan College†	WV
Wharton County Junior College†*	TX
Wheaton College†	IL
Wheeling College†	WV
Whitworth College†*	WA
Wichita State University†	KS
Wiley College†*	TX
Wilkes College†*	PA
Willamette University†*	OR
William and Mary, College of†	VA
William Paterson College†	NJ
William Penn College†*	IA
Williams College†*	MA
Williamsport Area Community College†	PA
Wilmington College†	OH
Winona State College†*	MN
Wisconsin, University of, at Eau Claire†*	WI
Wisconsin, University of, at Green Bay†*	WI
Wisconsin, University of, at La Crosse†*	WI
Wisconsin, University of, at Milwaukee†*	WI
Wisconsin, University of, at Oshkosh†	WI
Wisconsin, University of, at Platteville†	WI
Wisconsin, University of, at River Falls†*	WI
Wisconsin, University of, at Stevens Point†*	WI
Wisconsin, University of, at Waukesha†*	WI
Wisconsin, University of, at Whitewater†	WI
Worcester State College†*	MA
Wright State University†	OH
Wyoming, University of†*	WY
Yale University†*	CT
Yankton College†*	SD
Yuba College†*	CA

CROSS COUNTRY SKIING

Alaska, University of, at Anchorage†*	AK
Alaska, University of, at Fairbanks†*	AK

DIVING

Rider College*	NJ

EQUESTRIAN

Beaver College†*	PA
Centenary College*	NJ
James Madison University†*	VA
Mary Baldwin College*	VA
Mary Washington College*	VA
St. Lawrence University†*	NY
Skidmore College†*	NY
Smith College*	MA

FENCING

Arkansas State University†	AR
Barnard College*	NY
Boston College*	MA
Brandeis University†*	MA

Brevard Community College†*	FL
Brooklyn College of the City University of New York†*	NY
California, University of, at Los Angeles†*	CA
California, University of, at San Diego†*	CA
California Institute of Technology†*	CA
California State College, at Fullerton†*	CA
California State College, at Sonoma†*	CA
California State University, at Long Beach†*	CA
Chicago, University of†	IL
Clemson University†*	SC
Cleveland State University†*	OH
Columbia University†	NY
Cornell University†*	NY
Detroit, University of†	MI
Drew University†*	NJ
Duke University†*	NC
Eisenhower College†*	NY
Elmira College†*	NY
Fairleigh Dickinson University*	NJ
Harvard University†*	MA
Hofstra University*	NY
Holy Cross College†*	MA
Hunter College†*	NY
Illinois, University of†	IL
Indiana University of Pennsylvania†*	PA
James Madison University*	VA
Jersey City State College†*	NJ
Lafayette College†*	PA
Lake Superior State College†*	MI
Lamar University†	TX
Lawrence University†*	WI
Lynchburg College*	VA
Mary Baldwin College*	VA
Maryland, University of†	MD
Massachusetts Institute of Technology†	MA
Michigan State University†	MI
Milwaukee Area Technical College†*	WI
Montclair State College*	NJ
New York, State University College of, at New Paltz†*	NY
New York, State University College of, at Oswego†*	NY
New York, State University College of, at Purchase†*	NY
North Carolina, University of†*	NC
North Carolina State University†*	NC
Northwestern University†*	IL
Notre Dame, University of†*	IN
Ohio State University†*	OH
Pace University†*	NY
Pennsylvania, University of†*	PA
Pennsylvania State University, at University Park†*	PA
Portland State University*	OR
Pratt Institute†*	NY
Princeton University†*	NJ
Rutgers University, at Newark†	NJ
Rutgers University, at New Brunswick†*	NJ
St. Augustine's College†*	NC
St. Peter's College†*	NJ
San Francisco, City College of†*	CA
San Francisco State University†*	CA
San Jose State University†*	CA
Stanford University†*	CA
Stevens Institute of Technology†*	NJ
Temple University†*	PA
Texas, University of, at Arlington†	TX
Trinity College†	CT
Tri-State University†*	IN
Upsala College†	NJ
Villanova University†	PA
Virginia, University of†	VA
Wayne State University†*	MI
Wheaton College*	MA
William and Mary, College of†*	VA
William Paterson College†*	NJ
Wisconsin, University of, at Waukesha†*	WI
Wofford College†	SC
Yale University†*	CT

FIELD HOCKEY

Adrian College*	MI
Albion College*	MI
Albright College*	PA
Alma College*	MI
American University, The*	DC
Amherst College*	MA
Anne Arundel Community College*	MD
Appalachian State University*	NC
Arizona, University of*	AZ
Asbury College*	KY
Ashland College*	OH
Assumption College*	MA
Averett College*	VA
Ball State University*	IN
Bates College*	ME
Beaver College*	PA
Bemidji State University*	MN
Bentley College*	MA

Berea College*	KY
Boise State University*	ID
Boston College*	MA
Boston University*	MA
Bowling Green State University*	OH
Brandywine College*	DE
Bridgewater College*	VA
Bridgewater State College*	MA
Brigham Young University*	UT
Brown University*	RI
Bucknell University*	PA
California, University of, at Davis*	CA
California, University of, at San Diego*	CA
California State University, at Chico*	CA
California State University, at Long Beach*	CA
Calvin College*	MI
Castleton State College*	VT
Catawaba College*	NC
Centenary College*	NJ
Central Michigan University*	MI
Central Missouri State University*	MO
Central State University*	OK
Centre College*	KY
Champlain College*	VT
Chatham College*	PA
Chicago, The University of*	IL
Clark University*	MA
Clemson University*	SC
Colby College*	ME
Colgate University*	NY
Colorado College*	CO
Colorado State University*	CO
Concordia College*	IL
Connecticut, University of*	CT
Connecticut College*	CT
Converse College*	SC
Cornell University*	NY
C. W. Post College*	NY
Dartmouth College*	NH
Davidson College*	NC
Delaware Valley College*	PA
Denver, University of*	CO
Duke University*	NC
East Carolina University*	NC
Eastern College*	PA
Eastern Illinois University*	IL
Eastern Kentucky University*	KY
Eastern Michigan University*	MI
East Stroudsburg State College*	PA
Elizabethtown College*	PA
Essex Community College*	MD
Fitchburg State College*	MA
Framingham State College*	MA
Franklin Pierce College*	NH
Frostburg State College*	MD
Furman University*	SC
Georgetown University*	DC
Gettysburg College*	PA
Glassboro State College*	NJ
Gordon College*	MA
Graceland College*	IA
Grand Valley State College*	MI
Grinnell College*	IA
Hamilton College*	NY
Hanover College*	IN
Harvard University*	MA
High Point College*	NC
Hiram College*	OH
Hofstra University*	NY
Holy Cross College*	MA
Hood College*	MD
Hope College*	MI
Houghton College*	NY
Idaho, University of*	ID
Idaho State University*	ID
Indiana University, at Bloomington*	IN
Indiana University of Pennsylvania*	PA
Iowa, University of*	IA
Iowa Wesleyan College*	IA
Ithaca College*	NY
James Madison University*	VA
Judson College*	AL
Kean College of New Jersey*	NJ
Kent State University*	OH
Kenyon College*	OH
King's College, The*	NY
Kutztown State College*	PA
Lafayette College*	PA
Lake Erie College*	OH
Lancaster Bible College*	PA
La Salle College*	PA
Lebanon Valley College*	PA
Lehigh University*	PA
Lock Haven State College*	PA
Longwood College*	VA
Louisville, University of*	KY
Lowell, University of*	MA
Luther College*	IA
Lycoming College*	PA
Lynchburg College*	VA
Lyndon State College*	VT
Maine, University of, at Farmington*	ME
Maine, University of, at Presque Isle*	ME
Mansfield State College*	PA
Marian College*	IN
Marietta College*	OH
Maryland, University of, at Catonsville*	MD
Maryland, University of, at College Park*	MD
Mary Washington College*	VA

Marywood College*	PA	Pfeiffer College*	NC
Massachusetts, University of*	MA	Pittsburgh, University of*	PA
Massachusetts Institute of Technology*	MA	Plymouth State College*	NH
		Princeton University*	NJ
Miami University*	OH	Principia College*	IL
Michigan, University of*	MI	Providence College*	RI
Michigan State University*	MI	Purdue University, at West Lafayette*	IL
Middlebury College*	VT		
Minnesota, University of, at Minneapolis*	MN	Randolph-Macon College*	VA
		Rensselaer Polytechnic Institute*	NY
Missouri, University of, at St. Louis*	MO	Rider College*	NJ
		Roanoke College*	VA
Mitchell College*	CT	Rochester, University of*	NY
Monmouth College*	NJ	Rutgers, State University of, at Camden*	NJ
Montclair State University*	NJ		
Moorhead State University*	MN	Rutgers, State University of, at New Brunswick*	NJ
Mount St. Mary's College*	MD		
Mount Vernon College*	DC	St. Bonaventure University*	NY
Muhlenberg College*	PA	St. Lawrence University*	NY
New Hampshire College*	NH	St. Louis University*	MO
New York, State University College of, at Brockport*	NY	Salisbury State College*	MD
		San Jose State University*	CA
New York, State University College of, at Oneonta*	NY	Scranton, University of*	PA
		Siena College*	NY
New York, State University College of, at Oswego*	NY	Skidmore College*	NY
		Slippery Rock State College*	PA
New York, State University College of, at Plattsburgh*	NY	Smith College*	MA
		South, University of the*	TN
New York, State University College of, at Potsdam*	NY	Southeast Missouri State*	MO
		Southern Connecticut State College*	CT
New York, State University of, at Buffalo*	NY		
		Southern Illinois University*	IL
Nichols College*	MA	Southwestern at Memphis*	TN
North Adams State College*	MA	Stanford University*	CA
North Carolina, University of, at Chapel Hill*	NC	Susquehanna University*	PA
		Swarthmore College*	PA
North Carolina, University of, at Greensboro*	NC	Syracuse University*	NY
		Taylor University*	IN
North Dakota, University of*	ND	Temple University*	PA
Northern Colorado, University of*	CO	Thomas College*	ME
		Toledo, University of*	OH
Northern Illinois University*	IL	Towson State University*	MD
Northern Iowa, University of*	IA	Trenton State College*	NJ
Northern Michigan University*	MI	Ursinus College*	PA
Northwestern University*	IL	Valparaiso University*	IN
Northwest Nazarene College*	ID	Villanova University*	PA
Norwich University*	VT	Virginia, University of*	VA
Notre Dame, University of*	IN	Virginia Commonwealth University*	VA
Oberlin College*	OH		
Ohio State University*	OH	Virginia Polytechnic Institute*	VA
Ohio University*	OH	Wake Forest University*	NC
Ohio Wesleyan University*	OH	Washington Bible College*	MD
Old Dominion University*	VA	Washington State University*	WA
Olivet College*	MI	Wesleyan College*	CT
Oregon, University of*	OR	West Chester State College*	PA
Pacific, University of the*	CA	Western Illinois University*	IL
Pacific Lutheran University*	WA	Western Maryland College*	MD
Palomar College*	CA	Western Michigan University*	MI
Pennsylvania, University of*	PA	Western Washington University*	WA
Pennsylvania State University, at University Park*	PA	Westfield State College*	MA
		West Virginia Wesleyan College*	WV

Wheaton College*	IL
Wheaton College*	MA
Wilkes College*	PA
William and Mary, College of*	VA
William Paterson College*	NJ
Williams College*	MA
Williamsport Area Community College*	PA
Wilson College*	PA
Winthrop College*	SC
Wisconsin, University of, at Green Bay*	WI
Wisconsin, University of, at La Crosse*	WI
Wisconsin, University of, at Milwaukee*	WI
Wisconsin, University of, at Oshkosh*	WI
Wisconsin, University of, at River Falls*	WI
Wisconsin, University of, at Stevens Point*	WI
Wisconsin, University of, at Whitewater*	WI
Worcester State College*	MA
Yale University*	CT
Youngstown State University*	OH
Yuba Community College*	CA

FOOTBALL

Abilene Christian University†	TX
Adams State College of Colorado†	CO
Adrian College†	MI
Akron, University of†	OH
Alabama, University of, at University†	AL
Alabama Agricultural and Mechanical University†	AL
Alabama State University†	AL
Albany State College†	GA
Albion College†	MI
Albright College†	PA
Alcorn State University†	MS
Alfred University†	NY
Allegheny College†	PA
Alma College†	MI
American International College†	MA
Anderson College†	IL
Angelo State University†	TX
Anne Arundel Community College†	MD
Appalachian State University†	NC
Arizona, University of†	AZ
Arizona State University†	AZ
Arizona Western College†	AZ
Arkansas, University of†	AR
Arkansas, University of, at Monticello†	AR
Arkansas, University of, at Pine Bluff†	AR
Arkansas State University†	AR
Arkansas Tech University†	AR
Ashland College†	OH
Assumption College†	MA
Auburn University, at Auburn†	AL
Augustana College†	IL
Augustana College†	SD
Azusa Pacific College†	CA
Baker University†	KS
Ball State University†	IN
Bates College†	ME
Baylor University†	TX
Beloit College†	WI
Bemidji State University†	MN
Benedictine College†	KS
Bethel College†	MN
Bethune-Cookman College†	FL
Bishop College†	TX
Bismarck Junior College†	ND
Blinn College†	TX
Bluefield State College†	WV
Bluffton College†	OH
Boise State University†	ID
Boston College†	MA
Boston State College†	MA
Boston University†	MA
Bowdoin College†	ME
Bowie State College†	MD
Bowling Green State University†	OH
Bridgewater College†	VA
Bridgewater State College†	MA
Brigham Young University†	UT
Brown University†	RI
Bucknell University†	PA
Butler County Community Junior College†	KS
Butler University†	IN
California, University of, at Davis†	CA
California, University of, at Los Angeles†	CA
California Institute of Technology†	CA
California Polytechnic State University†	CA
California State College, at Sonoma†	CA
California State University, at Chico†	CA
California State University, at Fullerton†	CA
California State University, at Haywood†	CA
California State University, at Long Beach†	CA
Cameron University†	OK

Canisius College†	NY	East Carolina University†	NC
Carroll College†	MT	East Central University†	OK
Carroll College†	WI	Eastern Illinois University†	IL
Carson-Newman College†	TN	Eastern Kentucky University†	KY
Carthage College†	WI	Eastern Michigan University†	MI
Catawaba College†	NC	Eastern Utah, College of†	UT
Central Arkansas, University of†	AR	East Stroudsburg State College†	PA
Central Michigan University†	MI	East Tennessee State University†	TN
Central Missouri State University†	MO	East Texas State University†	TX
		Edinboro State College†	PA
Central State University†	OK	El Camino College†	CA
Centre College†	KY	Elmhurst College†	IL
Chadron State College†	NE	Elon College†	NC
Chicago, The University of†	IL	Emory and Henry College†	VA
Chowan College†	NC	Emporia State University†	KS
Cincinnati, University of†	OH	Evansville, University of†	IN
Cisco Junior College†	TX	Fairmont State College†	WV
Citadel, The†	SC	Fergus Falls Community College†	MN
Citrus College†	CA		
Clarion State College†	PA	Ferris State College†	MI
Clark College†	GA	Ferrum College†	WA
Clemson University†	SC	Findlay College†	OH
Coahoma Junior College†	MS	Fitchburg State College†	MA
Coe College†	IA	Florida, University of†	FL
Coffeyville Community College†	KS	Florida A. and M. University†	FL
Colby College†	ME	Florida State University†	FL
Colorado, University of†	CO	Florida Technological University†	FL
Colorado College†	CO		
Colorado School of Mines†	CO	Fordham University†	NY
Colorado State University†	CO	Fort Hayes State†	KS
Columbia Basin College†	WA	Fort Valley State College†	GA
Columbia University†	NY	Framingham State College†	MA
Compton Community College†	CA	Fresno State University†	CA
Concord College†	WV	Friends University†	KS
Concordia College†	IL	Frostburg State College†	MD
Concordia College†	MN	Furman University†	SC
Concordia College†	NE	Gardner-Webb College†	NC
Connecticut, University of†	CT	Georgetown University†	DC
Contra Costa College†	CA	Georgia, University of†	GA
Copiah-Lincoln Junior College†	MS	Georgia Institute of Technology†	GA
Cornell College†	IA	Gettysburg College†	PA
Cornell University†	NY	Glassboro State College†	NJ
Cowley County Community College†	KS	Golden Valley Lutheran College†	MN
		Graceland College†	IA
Culver-Stockton College†	MO	Grand Rapids Junior College†	MI
C. W. Post College†	NY	Grand Valley State College†	MI
Dakota Wesleyan University†	SD	Grinnell College†	IA
Dartmouth College†	NH	Grove City College†	PA
Davidson College†	NC	Guilford College†	NC
Delaware, University of†	DE	Gustavus Adolphus College†	MN
Delaware State College†	DE	Hamilton College†	NY
Delaware Valley College†	PA	Hamline University†	MN
Delta State College†	MS	Hampton Institute†	VA
Desert, College of the†	CA	Hanover College†	IN
Dickinson State College†	ND	Harding University†	AR
District of Columbia, University of†	DC	Harvard University†	MA
		Hastings College†	NE
Doane College†	NE	Hawaii, University of, at Honolulu†	HI
Dubuque, University of†	IA		
Duke University†	NC	Heidelberg College†	OH
Duquesne University†	PA		

Henderson State University†	OR
Highland Community Junior College†	KS
Hillsdale College†	MI
Hiram College†	OH
Holy Cross College†	MA
Hope College†	MI
Houston, University of†	TX
Howard Payne University†	TX
Humboldt State University†	CA
Hutchinson Community Junior College†	KS
Idaho, University of†	ID
Idaho State University†	ID
Illinois, University of, at Champaign†	IL
Illinois Benedictine College†	IL
Illinois College†	IL
Illinois State University†	IL
Illinois Valley Community College†	IL
Illinois Wesleyan University†	IL
Indiana Central University†	IN
Indiana University, at Bloomington†	IN
Indiana University of Pennsylvania†	PA
Inver Hills College†	MN
Iowa, University of†	IA
Iowa Lakes Community College†	IA
Iowa State University†	IA
Iowa Wesleyan College†	IA
Ithaca College†	NY
Jacksonville State University†	AL
James Madison University†	VA
Jamestown College†	ND
Jersey City State College†	NJ
John Carroll University†	OH
Johnson C. Smith University†	NC
Jones County Junior College†	MS
Juniata College†	PA
Kansas, University of†	KS
Kansas State University†	KS
Kansas Wesleyan College†	KS
Kean College of New Jersey†	NJ
Kearney State College†	NE
Kent State University†	OH
Kentucky, University of†	KY
Kentucky State University†	KY
Kenyon College†	OH
Kutztown State College†	PA
Lafayette College†	PA
Lamar University†	TX
La Verne College†	CA
Lawrence University†	WI
Lebanon Valley College†	PA
Lees McRae College†	NC
Lehigh University†	PA
Lenoir-Rhyne College†	NC
Liberty Baptist College†	VA
Lincoln University†	MO
Linfield College†	OR
Livingstone College†	NC
Livingston University†	AL
Lock Haven State College†	PA
Loras College†	IA
Los Angeles City College†	CA
Los Angeles Pierce Junior College†	CA
Los Angeles Southwest College†	CA
Louisiana State University†	LA
Louisiana Tech University†	LA
Louisville, University of†	KY
Lowell, University of†	MA
Lubbock Christian College†	TX
Luther College†	IA
Lycoming College†	PA
Macalester College†	MN
McMurray College†	TX
McNeese State University†	LA
McPherson College†	KS
Maine Maritime Academy†	ME
Manchester College†	IN
Manhattan College†	NY
Mankato State University†	MN
Mansfield State College†	PA
Marietta College†	OH
Marin, College of†	CA
Marion Military Institute†	AL
Marist College†	NY
Marshall University†	WV
Mars Hill College†	NC
Maryland, University of, at College Park†	MD
Maryville College†	TN
Massachusetts, University of†	MA
Memphis State University†	TN
Menlo College†	CA
Miami, University of†	FL
Miami University†	OH
Michigan, University of†	MI
Michigan State University†	MI
Middlebury College†	VT
Middle Tennessee State University†	TN
Millikan University†	IL
Millsaps College†	MS
Minnesota, University of, at Minneapolis†	MN
Minnesota, University of, at Morris†	MN
Minnesota, University of, Technical College†	MN
Mira Costa College†	CA
Mississippi College†	MS
Mississippi State University†	MS
Missouri, University of†	MO
Missouri, University of, at Rolla†	MO
Missouri Southern State†	MO
Missouri Valley College†	MO
Missouri Western College†	MO
Monmouth College†	IL

Montana, University of†	MT	Northwestern State University†	LA
Montana State University†	MT	Northwestern University†	IL
Montana Tech†	MT	Northwest Missouri State University†	MO
Montclair State University†	NJ		
Moorhead State University†	MN	Norwich University†	VT
Moorpark College†	AR	Notre Dame, University of†	IN
Morehead State University†	KY	Oberlin College†	OH
Morehouse College†	GA	Occidental College†	CA
Morgan State University†	MD	Ohio Northern University†	OH
Morningside College†	IA	Ohio State University†	OH
Mount San Jacinto College†	CA	Ohio Wesleyan University†	OH
Muhlenberg College†	PA	Oklahoma, University of†	OK
Murray State University†	KY	Olivet College†	MI
Napa Community College†	CA	Olivet Nazarene College†	IL
Nebraska, University of†	NE	Oregon, University of†	OR
Nebraska, University of, at Omaha†	NE	Oregon State University†	OR
		Oregon Technical Institute†	OR
Nebraska Wesleyan University†	NE	Ottawa University†	KS
Newberry College†	SC	Otterbein College†	OH
New Haven, University of†	CT	Ouachita Baptist College†	AR
New Mexico Highlands University†	NM	Pace University†	NY
		Pacific, University of the†	CA
New Mexico Military Institute†	NM	Pacific Lutheran University†	WA
New York, State University College of, at Brockport†	NY	Pacific University†	OR
		Palomar College†	CA
New York, State University of, at Albany†	NY	Pennsylvania, University of†	PA
		Pennsylvania State University, at University Park†	PA
New York, State University of, at Buffalo†	NY		
		Pittsburg State University†	KS
New York Institute of Technology†	NY	Pittsburgh, University of†	PA
		Plymouth State College†	NH
Nicholls State University†	LA	Porterville College†	CA
Nichols College†	MA	Portland State University†	OR
Norfolk State College†	VA	Pratt Community Junior College†	KS
North Alabama, University of†	AL	Presbyterian College†	SC
North Carolina, University of, at Chapel Hill†	NC	Princeton University†	NJ
		Principia College†	IL
North Carolina Agricultural and Technical State University†	NC	Purdue University, at West Lafayette†	IL
		Randolph-Macon College†	VA
North Carolina State University†	NC	Redlands, University of†	CA
North Central College†	IL	Redwoods, College of the†	CA
North Dakota, University of†	ND	Rensselaer Polytechnic Institute†	NY
North Dakota State University, at Fargo†	ND	Rice University†	TX
		Ripon College†	WI
Northeastern Illinois University†	IL	Riverside City College†	CA
Northeastern Oklahoma A and M College†	OK	Rochester, University of†	NY
		Rutgers, State University of, at New Brunswick†	NJ
Northeast Louisiana University†	LA		
Northeast Mississippi College†	MS	Saginaw Valley College†	MI
Northern Arizona University†	AZ	St. Clair County Community College†	MI
Northern Colorado, University of†	CO		
		St. Francis College of Pennsylvania†	PA
Northern Illinois University†	IL		
Northern Iowa, University of†	IA	St. Johns University†	MN
Northern Michigan University†	MI	St. Joseph College†	IN
Northern State College†	SD	St. Lawrence University†	NY
North Georgia College†	GA	St. Leo College†	FL
Northland Community College†	MN	St. Mary of the Plains College†	KS
North Texas State University†	TX	St. Mary's College of California†	CA
Northwestern College†	MN	St. Norbert College†	WY
Northwestern College†	WI		

St. Olaf College†	MN
St. Paul's College†	VA
St. Peter's College†	NJ
St. Thomas, College of†	MN
Salisbury State College†	MD
Sam Houston State University†	TX
San Diego, University of†	CA
San Diego State University†	CA
San Francisco, City College of†	CA
San Francisco State University†	CA
San Jose State University†	CA
San Mateo, College of†	CA
Santa Ana College†	CA
Santa Barbara City Junior College†	CA
Santa Clara, University of†	CA
Sequoias, College of the†	CA
Shepherd College†	WV
Siena College†	NY
Siskiyous, College of the†	CA
Slippery Rock State College†	PA
South, University of the†	TN
South Carolina, University of†	SC
South Carolina State College†	SC
South Dakota University of, at Springfield†	SD
South Dakota, University of, at Vermillion†	SD
South Dakota School of Mines and Technology†	SD
Southeastern Louisiana University†	LA
Southeastern Oklahoma State University†	OK
Southeast Missouri State†	MO
Southern Arkansas University†	AR
Southern California, University of†	CA
Southern Colorado, University of†	CO
Southern Connecticut State College†	CT
Southern Illinois University†	IL
Southern Methodist University†	TX
Southern Oregon State College†	OR
Southern University and Agricultural and Mechanical College†	LA
Southern Utah State College†	UT
Southwestern at Memphis†	TN
Southwestern College†	KS
Southwestern Louisiana, University of†	LA
Southwest State University†	MN
Southwest Texas State University†	TX
Stanford University†	CA
Stephen F. Austin State University†	TX
Sterling College†	KS
Stevens State Technology†	PA
Sul Ross State University†	TX
Susquehanna University†	PA
Swarthmore College†	PA
Syracuse University†	NY
Tabor College†	KS
Tarkto College†	MO
Tarleton State College†	TX
Taylor University†	IN
Temple University†	PA
Tennessee, University of†	TN
Tennessee, University of, at Martin†	TN
Tennessee State University†	TN
Tennessee Technological University†	TN
Texas, The University of†	TX
Texas, The University of, at Arlington†	TX
Texas, The University of, at El Paso†	TX
Texas A and I University†	TX
Texas Christian University†	TX
Texas Lutheran College†	TX
Texas Southern University†	TX
Texas Tech University†	TX
Thiel College†	PA
Toledo, University of†	OH
Towson State University†	MD
Trenton State College†	NJ
Trinity University†	TX
Triton College†	IL
Troy State University†	AL
Tufts University†	MA
Tulane University†	LA
Tulsa, University of†	OK
Tuskegee Institute†	AL
Upper Iowa University†	IA
Upsala College†	NJ
Ursinus College†	PA
Utah, University of†	UT
Utah State University†	UT
Valparaiso University†	IN
Vanderbilt University†	TN
Ventura College†	CA
Villanova University†	PA
Virginia, University of†	VA
Virginia Polytechnic Institute†	VA
Virginia State College†	VA
Virginia Union University†	VA
Wabash College†	IN
Wagner College†	NY
Wake Forest University†	NC
Washburn University†	KS
Washington, University of†	WA
Washington and Lee University†	VA
Washington State University†	WA
Washington University†	MO
Waynesburg College†	PA
Wayne State University†	MI
Weber State College†	UT
Wenatchee Valley College†	WA

Wesleyan College†	CT
West Chester State College†	PA
Western Carolina University†	NC
Western Illinois University†	IL
Western Kentucky University†	KY
Western Maryland College†	MD
Western Michigan University†	MI
Western Montana College†	MT
Western State College of Colorado†	CO
Western Washington University†	WA
West Georgia College†	GA
West Hills College†	CA
West Liberty State College†	WV
West Los Angeles College†	CA
West Texas State University†	TX
West Virginia State College†	WV
West Virginia University†	WV
West Virginia Wesleyan College†	WV
Wharton County Junior College†	TX
Wheaton College†	IL
Whitworth College†	WA
Wichita State University†	KS
Willamette University†	OR
William and Mary, College of†	VA
William Paterson College†	NJ
William Penn College†	IA
Williams College†	MA
Wilmington College†	OH
Winona State College†	MN
Winston-Salem State University†	NC
Wisconsin, University of, at Eau Claire†	WI
Wisconsin, University of, at La Crosse†	WI
Wisconsin, University of, at Oshkosh†	WI
Wisconsin, University of, at Platteville†	WI
Wisconsin, University of, at River Falls†	WI
Wisconsin, University of, at Stevens Point†	WI
Wisconsin, University of, at Superior†	WI
Wisconsin, University of, at Whitewater†	WI
Wofford College†	SC
Worthington Community College†	MN
Wyoming, University of†	WY
Yakima Valley College†	WA
Yale University†	CT
Yankton College†	SD
Youngstown State University†	OH
Yuba College†	CA

GOLF

Abilene Christian University†	TX
Adams State College of Colorado†	CO
Adrian College†	MI
Akron, University of†	OH
Alabama, University of, at Birmingham†	AL
Alabama, University of, at University†*	AL
Alabama Agricultural and Mechanical University†*	AL
Albion College†	MI
Albright College†	PA
Alcorn State University†	MS
Allegheny College†	PA
Allen County Community Junior College†*	KS
Alma College†	MI
Alpena Community College†	MI
Alvin Junior College†	TX
American International College†	MA
American University, The†	DC
Amherst College†*	MA
Anderson College†	IL
Angelo State University†	TX
Anne Arundel Community College†	MD
Appalachian State University†*	NC
Aquinas College†	MI
Arizona, University of†*	AZ
Arizona State University†*	AZ
Arizona Western College†	AZ
Arkansas, University of†	AR
Arkansas, University of, at Little Rock†	AR
Arkansas, University of, at Monticello†	AR
Arkansas State University†	AR
Arkansas Tech University†	AR
Armstrong State College†	GA
Asbury College†	KY
Asheville-Buncombe Technical Institute†*	NC
Assumption College†	MA
Atlantic Christian College†	NC
Auburn University, at Auburn†*	AL
Augusta College†	GA
Augustana College†	IL
Augustana College†*	SD
Aurora College†	IL
Averett College†*	VA
Babson College†	MA
Baker University†	KS
Ball State University†*	IN
Baltimore, University of†	MD
Baptist Bible College†	MO

Baptist College at Charleston†	SC
Barton County Community College†*	KS
Bates College†	ME
Baylor University†	TX
Bellarmine College†	KY
Beloit College†*	WI
Bemidji State University†	MN
Benedictine College†	KS
Bentley College†	MA
Berea College†*	KY
Bethany College†*	KS
Bethel College†	MN
Bethune-Cookman College†	FL
Biscayne College†	FL
Bismarck Junior College†*	ND
Blackburn College†	IL
Bluefield State College†	WV
Bluffton College†*	OH
Boise State University†	ID
Boston College†*	MA
Bowdoin College†	ME
Bowling Green State University†*	OH
Bradley University†	IL
Brandywine College†	DE
Brevard College†	NC
Brevard Community College†	FL
Briar Cliff College†*	IA
Bridgewater College†	VA
Bridgewater State College†	MA
Brigham Young University†*	UT
Bristol College†	TN
Brooklyn College of the City University of New York†	NY
Brown University†	RI
Bryant College†	RI
Bucknell University†	PA
Butler County Community Junior College†	KS
Butler University†	IN
California, University of, at Davis†	CA
California, University of, at Irvine†	CA
California, University of, at Los Angeles†*	CA
California, University of, at Riverside†	CA
California, University of, at San Diego†	CA
California, University of, at Santa Barbara†	CA
California Institute of Technology†	CA
California State College, at Stanislaus†	CA
California State University, at Fullerton†*	CA
California State University, at Long Beach†*	CA
Calvary Bible College†	MO
Calvin College†	MI
Campbell College†	NC
Campbellsville†	KY
Canisius College†	NY
Carl Sandburg College†	IL
Carroll College†	WI
Carson-Newman College†	TN
Carthage College†	WI
Casper College†*	WY
Catawaba College†	NC
Centenary College†	LA
Central Arkansas, University of†	AR
Central Michigan University†*	MI
Central Missouri State University†	MO
Central State University†	OK
Centre College†	KY
Chadron State College†*	NE
Chaminade University†	HI
Charleston, College of†	SC
Chattahoochee Valley Community College†	AL
Chowan College†*	NC
Christopher Newport College†	VA
Cincinnati, University of†*	OH
Cisco Junior College†	TX
Citadel, The†	SC
Citrus College†	CA
Clackamas Community College†	OR
Claremore College†*	OK
Clarion State College†	PA
Clark University†*	MA
Clemson University†	SC
Cleveland State University†	OH
Coastal Carolina College†	SC
Coastal Carolina Community College†*	NC
Coe College†	IA
Coffeyville Community College†	KS
Colby College†	ME
Colgate University†	NY
Colorado, University of†	CO
Colorado College†*	CO
Colorado School of Mines†	CO
Colorado State University†*	CO
Columbia Basin College†	WA
Columbia University†	NY
Columbus College†	GA
Concord College†	WV
Concordia College†	MN
Concordia College†*	NE
Concordia College†	TX
Connecticut, University of†	CT
Contra Costa College†	CA
Copiah-Lincoln Junior College†*	MS
Cornell College†	IA
Cornell University†	NY
Cosumnes River College†	CA

Covenant College†	TN
Culver-Stockton College†	MO
Cumberland College†	KY
Cuyahoga Community College†	OH
C. W. Post College†	NY
Cypress College†	CA
Dartmouth College†	NH
David Lipscomb College†	TN
Davidson College†	NC
De Kalb Community College (Central)†	GA
Delaware, University of†	DE
Delaware State College†	DE
Delaware Valley College†	PA
Delta State College†	MS
DePauw University†	IN
Desert, College of the†	CA
Detroit, University of†	MI
Dickinson State College†	ND
District of Columbia, University of†*	DC
Doane College†	NE
Drury College†	MO
Dubuque, University of†	IA
Duke University†*	NC
Duquesne University†	PA
East Carolina University†	NC
East Central University†	OK
Eastern Illinois University†	IL
Eastern Kentucky University†	KY
Eastern Michigan Uniiversity†	MI
Eastern Montana College†*	MT
Eastern Oklahoma State College†*	OK
East Stroudsburg State College†	PA
East Tennessee State University†	TN
East Texas State University†	TX
Eckerd College†	FL
Eisenhower College†*	NY
El Camino College†	CA
Elmhurst College†	IL
Elmira College†	NY
Elon College†	NC
Emory and Henry College†	VA
Emporia State University†	KS
Erskine College†	SC
Essex Community College†	MD
Evansville, University of†*	IN
Everett Community College†	WA
Fairleigh Dickinson University†	NJ
Fairmont State College†	WV
Fergus Falls Community College†*	MN
Ferrum College†	WA
Findlay College†	OH
Flagler College†	FL
Florida, University of†*	FL
Florida A. and M. University†*	FL
Florida Atlantic University†*	FL
Florida International University†*	FL
Florida Junior College†	FL
Florida Southern College†	FL
Florida State University†*	FL
Florida Technological University†*	FL
Fort Hayes State†	KS
Franklin Pierce College†	NH
Freed-Hardeman College†	TN
Fresno State University†	CA
Friends University†	KS
Furman University†*	SC
Gadsden State Junior College†	AL
Gainesville Junior College†	GA
Gannon College†	PA
Gardner-Webb College†	NC
Gateway Technical Institute†	WI
Georgetown University†	DC
George Washington University†	DC
Georgia, University of†*	GA
Georgia Institute of Technology†	GA
Georgia Southern College†	GA
Georgia State University†*	GA
Gettysburg College†	PA
Glassboro State College†	NJ
Glen Oaks Community College†	MI
Gonzaga University†	WA
Grace College†	IN
Graceland College†	IA
Grand Canyon College†	AZ
Grand Rapids Junior College†	MI
Grand Valley State College†	MI
Green River Community College†*	WA
Greensboro College†	NC
Greensville College†	IL
Grinnell College†	IA
Grove City College†	PA
Guilford College†	NC
Gustavus Adolphus College†*	MN
Hagerstown Junior College†	MD
Hamilton College†	NY
Hannibal-LaGrange College†	MO
Hanover College†	IN
Harding University†	AR
Hardin-Simmons University†	TX
Hartford, University of†	CT
Harvard University†	MA
Hastings College†*	NE
Hawaii, University of, at Hilo†	HI
Hawaii, University of, at Honolulu†*	HI
Hawaii Pacific College†*	HI
Heidelberg College†	OH
Henderson State University†	OR
Hendrix College†	AR
High Point College†	NC
Hillsborough Community College†	FL
Hillsdale College†	MI

Hiram College†*	OH
Holy Cross College†	MA
Hope College†	MI
Housatonic Community College†*	CT
Houston, University of†	TX
Houston Baptist University†*	TX
Howard Payne University†	TX
Humboldt State University†	CA
Huntington College†	IN
Husson College†	ME
Hutchinson Community Junior College†	KS
Idaho, University of†*	ID
Idaho State University†	ID
Illinois, University of, at Champaign†*	IL
Illinois, University of, at Chicago Circle†	IL
Illinois Benedictine College†*	IL
Illinois College†	IL
Illinois State University†*	IL
Illinois Valley Community College†	IL
Illinois Wesleyan University†	IL
Indiana Central University†	IN
Indiana State University†	IN
Indiana University, at Bloomington†*	IN
Indiana University of Pennsylvania†	PA
Indian Hills Community College†*	IA
Inver Hills College†	MN
Iowa, University of†*	IA
Iowa Lakes Community College†	IA
Iowa State University†*	IA
Iowa Wesleyan College†	IA
Ithaca College†	NY
Jacksonville State University†	AL
James Madison University†*	VA
Jamestown College†	ND
Jefferson Davis Junior College†	MS
John Carroll University†	OH
Johf17C. Calhoun Community College†	AL
Johnson C. Smith University†	NC
Jones County Junior College†*	MS
Josephenum College†	OH
Juniata College†	PA
Kalamazoo Valley Community College†	MI
Kansas, University of†*	KS
Kansas State University†*	KS
Kean College of New Jersey†	NJ
Kent State University†	OH
Kentucky, University of†*	KY
Kentucky Wesleyan College†*	KY
Kenyon College†*	OH
Kishwaukee College†	IL
Kutztown State College†	PA
Lackawanna Junior College†	PA
Lafayette College†	PA
Lake Region Junior College†*	ND
Lamar University†*	TX
Laredo Junior College†	TX
La Salle College†	PA
La Verne College†	CA
Lawrence University†	WI
Lebanon Valley College†	PA
Le Moyne College†	NY
Lenoir Community College†	NC
Lenoir-Rhyne College†	NC
Lewis University†	IL
Lincoln Land Community College†	IL
Lincoln Trail College†	IL
Lincoln University†	MO
Lindenwood College, The†*	MO
Linfield College†	OH
Livingstone College†*	NC
Lock Haven State College†	PA
Longwood College†*	VA
Loras College†*	IA
Los Angeles Pierce Junior College†	CA
Louisiana State University†*	LA
Louisiana Tech University†	LA
Louisville, University of†	KY
Lowell, University of†	MA
Lower Columbia College†	WA
Loyola Marymount University†	CA
Luther College†	IA
Lycoming College†*	PA
Lynchburg College†	VA
Macalester College†	MN
McKendree College†	IL
McMurray College†*	TX
McNeese State University†	LA
McPherson College†	KS
Maine, University of, at Farmington†	ME
Maine Maritime Academy†	ME
Malone College†	OH
Manchester College†	IN
Manhattan College†	NY
Mankato State University†*	MN
Marian College†	IN
Marietta College†	OH
Marin, College of†	CA
Marion Military Institute†	AL
Marquette University†	WI
Marshalltown Community College†*	IA
Marshall University†*	WV
Martin College†*	TN
Mary Baldwin College*	VA
Mary Hardin-Baylor College†	TX
Maryland, University of, at College Park†	MD

Mary Washington College†*	VA	Napa Community College†	CA
Massachusetts, University of†*	MA	Nazareth College†*	NY
Massachusetts Institute of Technology†	MA	Nebraska, University of†*	NE
		Nebraska Wesleyan University†*	NE
Mattatuck Community College†*	CT	Newberry College†	SC
Memphis State University†*	TN	New Hampshire College†	NH
Menlo College†	CA	New Hampshire Technological Institute†	NH
Mercer University†	GA		
Mercy College†	NY	New Mexico Highlands University†*	NM
Meredith College*	NC		
Merrimack College†*	MA	New Mexico Junior College†	NM
Miami, University of†*	FL	New Mexico Military Institute†	NM
Miami-Dade Community College, New World Center†	FL	New Orleans, University of†	LA
		New York, State University College of, at New Paltz†	NY
Miami-Dade Community College, South Campus†	FL	New York, State University College of, at Oswego†	NY
Miami University†	OH		
Miami University, Middletown Campus†	OH	New York, State University College of, at Plattsburgh†	NY
Michigan, University of†*	MI	New York, State University College of, at Potsdam†	NY
Michigan State University†*	MI		
Middlebury College†	VT	New York, State University of, at Buffalo†	NY
Middle Tennessee State University†	TN		
		New York Institute of Technology†	NY
Mid-State Technical Institute†*	WI		
Millikan University†	IL	Niagara University†	NY
Milwaukee Area Technical College†	WI	Nicholls State University†	LA
		Nichols College†	MA
Milwaukee School of Engineering†	WI	North Adams State College†*	MA
		North Alabama, University of†	AL
Minnesota, University of, at Minneapolis†*	MN	North Carolina, University of, at Chapel Hill†*	NC
Minnesota, University of, at Morris†*	MN	North Carolina, University of, at Charlotte†	NC
Minnesota, University of, Technical College†	MN	North Carolina, University of, at Greensboro†*	NC
Minnesota Bible College†	MN	North Carolina, University of, at Wilmington†*	NC
Mississippi College†	MS		
Mississippi State University†*	MS	North Carolina Agricultural and Technical State University†	NC
Missouri, University of†*	MO		
Missouri, University of, at St. Louis†	MO	North Carolina State University†	NC
		North Carolina Wesleyan College†	NC
Missouri Southern State†	MO		
Missouri Valley College†	MO	North Central College†	IL
Missouri Western College†	MO	North Dakota, University of†*	ND
Mitchell Community College†*	NC	North Dakota State University, at Fargo†	ND
Monmouth College†	IL		
Montana University†	MT	Northeastern Illinois University†	IL
Montclair State University†	NJ	Northeastern Oklahoma A and M College†*	OK
Montevallo, University of†	AL		
Moorhead State University†*	MN	Northeast Louisiana University†	LA
Moorpark College†	AR	Northern Colorado, University of†*	CO
Morehead State University†	KY		
Morningside College†*	IA	Northern Illinois University†*	IL
Mott Community College†	MN	Northern Iowa, University of†*	IA
Mount Olive Junior College	NC	Northern Kentucky University†	KY
Mount St. Mary's College†*	MD	Northern State College†*	SD
Muhlenberg College†	PA	Northland Community College†*	MN
Murray State University†	KY	North Texas State University†*	TX
Muskegon Community College†	MI	Northwest College†	WA

Northwestern College†	MN	Purdue University, at West Lafayette†*	IL
Northwestern College†	WI	Quinnipiac College†	CT
Northwestern State University†	LA	Radford College†	VA
Northwestern University†	IL	Randolph-Macon College†	VA
Northwest Nazarene College†	ID	Redlands, University of†	CA
Notre Dame, University of†	IN	Redwoods, College of the†*	CA
Oakland University†*	MI	Regis College†	CO
Oakton Community College†	IL	Rensselaer Polytechnic Institute†	NY
Occidental College†	CA	Rice University†	TX
Ohio Northern University†	OH	Rider College†	NJ
Ohio State University†*	OH	Ripon College†	WI
Ohio Wesleyan University†	OH	Riverside City College†	CA
Oklahoma, University of†*	OK	Roanoke College†	VA
Oklahoma City University†	OK	Robert Morris College†	PA
Oklahoma State University†*	OK	Rochester, University of†	NY
Oklahoma University of Science and Arts†*	OK	Rollins College†*	FL
Old Dominion University†	VA	Rutgers, State University of, at Camden†	NJ
Olivet College†	MI	Rutgers, State University of, at Newark†	NJ
Olney Central College†	IL	Rutgers, State University of, at New Brunswick†*	NJ
Oral Roberts University†	OK	Sacred Heart University†	CT
Oregon, University of†*	OR	Saginaw Valley College†	MI
Oregon State University†*	OR	St. Augustine's College†*	NC
Otterbein College†	OH	St. Bonaventure University†	NY
Ouachita Baptist College†	AR	St. Clair County Community College†	MI
Oxford College of Emory University†*	GA	St. Cloud State University†*	MN
Pace University†	NY	St. Edward's University†	TX
Pacific, University of the†	CA	St. Francis, College of†	IL
Pacific Lutheran University†	WA	St. Francis College of Pennsylvania†	PA
Pacific University†	OR	St. John Fisher College†	NY
Paducah Community College†*	KY	St. Johns University†	MN
Palm Beach Junior College†*	FL	St. Joseph College†	IN
Palomar College†	CA	St. Leo College†	FL
Pan American University†	TX	St. Louis College of Pharmacy†	MO
Paris Junior College†	TX	St. Louis University†	MO
Parkland College†	IL	St. Mary of the Plains College†*	KS
Pembroke State University†	NC	St. Mary's College of California†	CA
Pennsylvania, University of†	PA	St. Mary's University of Texas†*	TX
Pennsylvania State University, at Beaver Campus†*	PA	St. Norbert College†*	WY
Pennsylvania State University, at University Park†*	PA	St. Olaf College†*	MN
Penn Valley Community College†	MO	St. Paul's College†	VA
Pfeiffer College†*	NC	St. Thomas, College of†*	MN
Pikeville College†*	KY	St. Vincent College†	PA
Pima Community College†	AZ	Salisbury State College†	MD
Pittsburgh, University of, at Johnstown†*	PA	Sam Houston State University†	TX
Plymouth State College†	NH	San Diego, University of†	CA
Point Loma College†	CA	San Diego State University†*	CA
Portland, University of†	OR	San Francisco, City College of†	CA
Portland State University†	OR	San Francisco, University of†	CA
Pratt Institute†	NY	San Francisco State University†*	CA
Presbyterian College†	SC	San Jose State University†*	CA
Princeton University*	NJ	San Mateo, College of†	CA
Principia College†	IL	Santa Ana College†	CA
Providence College†	RI	Santa Barbara City Junior College†	CA
Purdue University, at Calumet†	IL		

Santa Clara, University of†	CA
Schoolcraft College†	MI
Schreiner College†	TX
Scranton, University of†	PA
Sequoias, College of the†	CA
Shawnee College†*	IL
Shawnee State College†*	OH
Shelby State Community College†*	TN
Shepherd College†*	WV
Sheridan College†*	WY
Shorter College†	GA
Siena College†	NY
Siena Heights College†	MI
Skagit Valley College†*	WA
Skidmore College†*	NY
Slippery Rock State College†	PA
South, University of the†	TN
South Alabama, University of†	AL
Southampton College†	NY
South Carolina, University of†*	SC
South Carolina State College†	SC
South Dakota, University of, at Vermillion†*	SD
South Dakota School of Mines and Technology†	SD
Southeast Community College†*	NE
Southeastern Community College†*	IA
Southeastern Louisiana University†	LA
Southeastern Oklahoma State University†	OK
Southern Arkansas University†	AR
Southern California, University of†*	CA
Southern Colorado, University of†	CO
Southern Connecticut State College†	CT
Southern Illinois University†*	IL
Southern Maine, University of†	ME
Southern Maine Vocational Technical Institute†	ME
Southern Methodist University†*	TX
Southern State Community State College†*	OH
Southern University and Agricultural and Mechanical College†	LA
Southern Utah State College†	UT
South Florida, The University of†*	FL
Southwestern at Memphis†	TN
Southwestern College†	KS
Southwestern Louisiana, University of†	LA
Southwestern University†	TX
Southwest Texas State University†	TX
Spartanburg Methodist College†	SC
Spring Garden College†	PA
Spring Hill College†	AL
Stanford University†*	CA
State Fair Community College†*	MO
Stephen F. Austin State University†	TX
Stetson University†	FL
Sul Ross State University†*	TX
Surry Community College†*	NC
Susquehanna University†	PA
Swarthmore College†	PA
Tabor College†	KS
Tacoma Community College†	WA
Tampa, University of†*	FL
Tarleton State College†	TX
Taylor University†	TX
Taylor University†	IN
Temple University†	PA
Tennessee, University of†	TN
Tennessee State University†	TN
Tennessee Technological University†	TN
Texas, The University of†*	TX
Texas, The University of, at Arlington†	TX
Texas A and I University†	TX
Texas Christian University†*	TX
Texas Lutheran College†	TX
Texas Southern University†	TX
Texas Tech University†*	TX
Texas Wesleyan College†	TX
Thiel College†	PA
Thomas College†*	ME
Thomas More College†	KY
Three Rivers Community College†	MO
Tiffin University†	OH
Toledo, University of†	OH
Towson State University†	MD
Treasure Valley Community College†	OR
Trenton State College†	NJ
Trinidad State Junior College†	CO
Trinity College†	CT
Trinity University†	TX
Tri-State University†	IN
Triton College†	IL
Troy State University†*	AL
Tufts University†	MA
Tulane University†	LA
Tulsa, University of†*	OK
Tunxis Community College†	CT
Umpqua Community College†	OR
Union College†	KY
Upper Iowa University†	IA
Upsala College†	NJ
Urbana College†	OH
Ursinus College†	PA
Utah, University of†	UT

Utah State University†	UT
Utica College of Syracuse University†	NY
Valparaiso University†	IN
Vanderbilt University†	TN
Ventura College†	CA
Virginia, University of†	VA
Virginia Commonwealth University†	VA
Virginia Polytechnic Institute†	VA
Virginia State College†	VA
Virginia Union University†	VA
Wabash College†	IN
Wagner College†	NY
Wake Forest University†*	NC
Walsh College†	OH
Washburn University†	KS
Washington, University of†*	WA
Washington and Lee University†	VA
Washington State University†	WA
Washington University†	MO
Waynesburg College†	PA
Wayne State University†	MI
Weber State College†*	UT
Wesleyan College†	CT
West Chester State College†	PA
Western Carolina University†	NC
Western Illinois University†	IL
Western Kentucky University†*	KY
Western Maryland College†	MD
Western Michigan University†	MI
Western New England College†	MA
Western Piedmont Community College†	NC
Western State College of Colorado†	CO
Western Washington University†	WA
West Georgia College†	GA
West Liberty State College†	WV
Westminster College†	MO
Westmoreland Community College†	PA
West Texas State University†	TX
West Virginia University†	WV
West Virginia Wesleyan College†	WV
Wharton County Junior College†*	TX
Wheaton College†	IL
Wheeling College†	WV
Whitworth College†	WA
Wichita State University†	KS
Wilkes College†*	PA
Willamette University†	OR
William and Mary, College of†*	VA
William Paterson College†	NJ
William Penn College†*	IA
Williams College†	MA
Williamsport Area Community College†*	PA
Wilmington College†	OH
Winona State College†*	MN
Winston-Salem State University†	NC
Wisconsin, University of, at Eau Claire†	WI
Wisconsin, University of, at Green Bay†	WI
Wisconsin, University of, at La Crosse†*	WI
Wisconsin, University of, at Marathon County†*	WI
Wisconsin, University of, at Milwaukee†	WI
Wisconsin, University of, at Oshkosh†	WI
Wisconsin, University of, at Platteville†	WI
Wisconsin, University of, at Stevens Point†*	WI
Wisconsin, University of, at Superior†	WI
Wisconsin, University of, at Waukesha†*	WI
Wisconsin, University of, at Whitewater†*	WI
Worcester State College†	MA
Worthington Community College†*	MN
Wright State University†	OH
Wyoming, University of†	WY
Xavier University†	OH
Yale University†*	CT
Yankton College*	SD
Youngstown State University†	OH

GYMNASTICS

Adams State College of Colorado*	CO
Alabama, University of, at University*	AL
Arizona, University of†*	AZ
Arizona State University†*	AZ
Auburn University, at Auburn*	AL
Ball State University†*	IN
Bemidji State University*	MN
Boise State University*	ID
Boston State College*	MA
Bowling Green State University*	OH
Bridgewater State College*	MA
Brigham Young University†*	UT
Brown University*	RI
California, University of, at Davis†*	CA
California, University of, at Los Angeles†*	CA

California, University of, at Santa Barbara†*	CA	Champaign†*	IL
California Polytechnic State University*	CA	Illinois, University of, at Chicago Circle†*	IL
		Illinois State University†*	IL
California State College, at Sonoma†*	CA	Indiana University, at Bloomington†*	IN
California State University, at Chico†*	CA	Indiana University of Pennsylvania*	PA
California State University, at Fullerton†*	CA	Iowa, University of†*	IA
		Iowa State University†*	IA
California State University, at Haywood*	CA	Ithaca College*	NY
		Jacksonville State University†*	AL
California State University, at Long Beach†*	CA	James Madison University†*	VA
		Jarvis Christian College†*	TX
Canisius College*	NY	Jefferson State Junior College*	AL
Casper College*	WY	Jersey City State College*	NJ
Centenary College*	LA	Kean College of New Jersey*	NJ
Central Arkansas, University of*	AR	Kent State University*	OH
Central Michigan University†*	MI	Kentucky, University of*	KY
Central Missouri State University*	MO	King's College, The*	NY
		Kishwaukee College*	IL
Central State University*	OK	Lock Haven State College*	PA
Clarion State College*	PA	Long Island University†*	NY
Concordia College*	IL	Longwood College*	VA
Connecticut College*	CT	Los Angeles Pierce Junior College*	CA
Cornell University†*	NY		
Cottey College*	MO	Louisiana State University†*	LA
Dartmouth College†*	NH	Louisville, University of*	KY
Denver, University of†*	CO	Lowell, University of†	MA
Duke University*	NC	Maine, University of, at Farmington*	ME
East Carolina University*	NC		
Eastern Kentucky University†*	KY	Maine, University of, at Presque Isle*	ME
Eastern Michigan University†*	MI		
Eastern Montana College†*	MT	Mankato State University*	MN
Eastern Utah, College of*	UT	Maryland, University of, at Catonsville*	MD
East Stroudsburg State College†*	PA		
East Tennessee State University*	TN	Maryland, University of, at College Park*	MD
Edinboro State College*	PA		
El Camino College*	CA	Massachusetts, University of†*	MA
Emporia State University*	KS	Massachusetts Institute of Technology†	MA
Essex Community College†*	MD		
Florida, University of*	FL	Memphis State University†*	TN
Fort Hayes State†*	KS	Metropolitan State College†	CO
Fresno State University*	CA	Michigan, University of†*	MI
Frostburg State College†*	MD	Michigan State University†*	MI
Furman University*	SC	Minnesota, University of, at Minneapolis†*	MN
Georgetown University*	DC		
George Washington University*	DC	Missouri, University of*	MO
Georgia, University of†*	GA	Montana, University of*	MT
Georgia College*	GA	Montana State University*	MT
Georgia Institute of Technology†	GA	Montclair State University*	NJ
Glassboro State College†*	NJ	Moorhead State University*	MN
Gustavus Adolphus College*	MN	Morgan State University†*	MD
Hamline University*	MN	Napa Community College*	CA
Hofstra University*	NY	Nebraska, University of†*	NE
Houston Baptist University†	TX	New Mexico Junior College†	NM
Hunter College†*	NY	New York, State University College of, at Brockport*	NY
Idaho, College of the*	ID		
Illinois, University of, at		New York, State University	

College of, at New Paltz*	NY
New York, State University College of, at Oneonta†	NY
New York, State University of, at Albany*	NY
North Carolina, University of, at Chapel Hill*	NC
North Carolina State University†*	NC
North Dakota, University of†*	ND
North Dakota State University*	ND
Northeastern Illinois University*	IL
Northern Colorado, University of†*	CO
Northern Illinois University†*	IL
Northern Iowa, University of†*	IA
Northern Michigan University*	MI
Northwestern University*	IL
Norwich University†*	VT
Oakton Community College*	IL
Ohio State University†*	OH
Oklahoma, University of†*	OK
Oklahoma State University*	OK
Oral Roberts University*	OK
Oregon, University of†*	OR
Oregon State University*	OR
Pan American University†*	TX
Pennsylvania, University of†*	PA
Pennsylvania State University, at University Park†*	PA
Pittsburgh, University of†*	PA
Portland State University†*	OR
Princeton University†	NJ
Radford College*	VA
Rutgers, State University of, at New Brunswick*	NJ
St. Cloud State University†*	MN
St. Paul's College*	VA
San Diego State University*	CA
San Francisco, City College of*	CA
San Francisco State University*	CA
San Jose State University†*	CA
Schoolcraft College†	MI
Slippery Rock State College†*	PA
Smith College*	MA
Southeast Missouri State*	MO
Southern California, University of†*	CA
Southern Carolina, University of*	CO
Southern Connecticut State College†*	CT
Southern Illinois University†*	IL
Southern Utah State College*	UT
Southwest Texas State University*	TX
Stanford University†*	CA
Syracuse University†	NY
Tarleton State College*	TX
Temple University†*	PA
Texas, The University of*	TX
Texas, The University of, at El Paso*	TX
Texas Christian University*	TX
Texas Woman's University*	TX
Towson State University†*	MD
Trenton State College†*	NJ
Triton College*	IL
Ursinius College†*	PA
Utah, University of*	UT
Utah State University*	UT
Valparaiso University*	IN
Washburn University*	KS
Washington, University of*	WA
Washington State University†*	WA
West Chester State College†*	PA
Western Carolina University*	NC
Western Illinois University*	IL
Western Kentucky University*	KY
Western Michigan University†*	MI
Western State College of Colorado*	CO
Westfield State College*	MA
West Virginia University†*	WV
Wheaton College†*	IL
William and Mary, College of†*	VA
William Paterson College*	NJ
Wilson College*	PA
Winona State College*	MN
Wisconsin, University of, at Eau Claire*	WI
Wisconsin, University of, at La Crosse†*	WI
Wisconsin, University of, at Milwaukee*	WI
Wisconsin, University of, at Oshkosh†*	WI
Wisconsin, University of, at Platteville†*	WI
Wisconsin, University of, at River Falls*	WI
Wisconsin, University of, at Superior*	WI
Wisconsin, University of, at Whitewater†*	WI
Yale University†*	CT
Youngstown State University*	OH

HANDBALL

Jones County Junior College†*	MI
Memphis State University†*	TN
Ohio Northern University†*	OH
Pacific University†*	OR

ICE HOCKEY

Alaska, University of, at Anchorage†	AK
Alaska, University of, at Fairbanks†	AK
Amherst College†	MA
Babson College†	MA
Bemidji State University†	MN
Bentley College†	MA
Bethel College†	MN
Boston College†	MA
Boston State College†	MA
Boston University†	MA
Bowdoin College†	ME
Bridgewater State College†	MA
Brown University†	RI
Calvin College†	MI
Canisius College†	NY
Colby College†	ME
Colgate University†	NY
Colorado College†	CO
Cornell University†	NY
Denver, University of†	CO
Ferris State College†	MI
Framingham State College†	MA
Gordon College†	MA
Gustavus Adolphus College†	MN
Harvard University†	MA
Herbert H. Lehman College†	NY
Ithaca College†	NY
Kent State University†	OH
Lowell, University of†	MA
Mankato State University†	MN
Merrimack College†	MA
Michigan, University of†	MI
Michigan State University†	MI
Middlebury College†	VT
Minnesota, University of, at Minneapolis†	MN
New Hampshire College†	NH
New Haven, University of†	CT
New York, State University College of, at Oswego†	NY
New York, State University College of, at Plattsburgh†	NY
New York, State University College of, at Potsdam†	NY
Niagara University†	NY
North Dakota State University, at Bottineau†	ND
North Dakota State University, at Fargo†	ND
Northern Michigan University†	MI
Ohio State University†	OH
Plymouth State College†	NH
Princeton University†	NJ
Providence College†*	RI
St. Johns University†*	MN
St. Lawrence University†	NY
St. Mary's College†	MN
St. Olaf College†	MN
St. Scholastica, College of†	MN
Upsala College†	NJ
Wesleyan College†	CT
Western Michigan University†	MI
Westfield State College†	MA
Wisconsin, University of, at Eau Claire†	WI
Wisconsin, University of, at River Falls†	WI
Wisconsin, University of, at Superior†	WI
Yale University†	CT

INDOOR TRACK

Arkansas State University†	AR
Bethune-Cookman College†	FL
Idaho State University†	ID
Kent State University†*	OH
Kentucky, University of†*	KY
Lamar University†	TX
Montana, University of†*	MT
Northern Arizona University†*	AZ
Pennsylvania State University†*	PA
Texas, The University of, at Arlington†*	TX
Utah State University†*	UT
West Virginia University†*	WV

LACROSSE

Albion College†	MI
Alfred University†	NY
Amherst College†*	MA
Anne Arundel Community College†*	MD
Ashland College†	OH
Assumption College†	MA
Babson College†	MA
Ball State University*	IN
Baltimore, University of†	MD
Bates College†*	ME
Beaver College*	PA
Boston College†*	MA
Boston State College†	MA
Bowdoin College†	ME
Bowling Green State University*	OH
Brandeis University†	MA

316

Bridgewater College*	VA
Bridgewater State College*	MA
Brown University†*	RI
Bucknell University†*	PA
Castleton State College†*	VT
Centenary College*	NJ
Colby College†*	ME
Colgate University†*	NY
Colorado College†	CO
Colorado School of Mines†	CO
Connecticut, University of†	CT
Connecticut College†*	CT
Cornell University†*	NY
C. W. Post College†	NY
Dartmouth College†*	NH
Drew University†*	NJ
Duke University†*	NC
East Stroudsburg State College*	PA
Eisenhower College†	NY
Emory and Henry College†	VA
Essex Community College†*	MD
Fairleigh Dickinson University†	NJ
Frostburg State College*	MD
Georgetown University†*	DC
Gettysburg College†*	PA
Glassboro State College*	NJ
Guilford College†	NC
Hamilton College†*	NY
Hartford, University of†	CT
Harvard University†*	MA
Hofstra University†*	NY
Holy Cross College†*	MA
Ithaca College†*	NY
James Madison University*	VA
Kean College of New Jersey†	NJ
Kenyon College†*	OH
Kutztown State College†*	PA
Lafayette College†*	PA
Lebanon Valley College†*	PA
Lehigh University†*	PA
Lock Haven State College*	PA
Longwood College*	VA
Lowell, University of†	MA
Lynchburg College†*	VA
Lyndon State College†	VT
Marist College†	NY
Maryland, University of, at Catonsville†*	MD
Maryland, University of, at College Park†*	MD
Mary Washington College*	VA
Massachusetts, University of†*	MA
Massachusetts Institute of Technology†	MA
Merrimack College†	MA
Michigan State University†	MI
Middlebury College†*	VT
Montclair State University†*	NJ
Mount St. Mary's College†	MD
Mount Vernon College*	DC
New Hampshire College†	NH
New Haven, University of†	CT
New York, State University College of, at Genesco†	NY
New York, State University College of, at Oneonta†*	NY
New York, State University College of, at Oswego†	NY
New York, State University of, at Albany†	NY
North Carolina, University of, at Chapel Hill†	NC
North Carolina State University†	NC
Norwich University†	VT
Notre Dame College*	MD
Oberlin College†*	OH
Ohio State University†	OH
Ohio Wesleyan University†*	OH
Old Dominion University*	VA
Pennsylvania, University of†*	PA
Pennsylvania State University, at University Park†*	PA
Plymouth State College†*	NH
Princeton University†*	NJ
Providence College†*	RI
Radford College†	VA
Randolph-Macon College†*	VA
Rensselaer Polytechnic Institute†	NY
Roanoke College†*	VA
Rochester, University of†*	NY
Rutgers, State University of, at New Brunswick†*	NJ
St. Lawrence University†*	NY
Salisbury State College†*	MD
Siena College†	NY
Skidmore College†*	NY
Slippery Rock State College*	PA
Smith College*	MA
Southampton College†	NY
Stevens Institute of Technology†	NJ
Swarthmore College†*	PA
Syracuse University†	NY
Temple University*	PA
Towson State University†*	MD
Trenton State College*	NJ
Trinity College†	CT
Tufts University†	MA
Upsala College†	NJ
Ursinus College†*	PA
Villanova University†*	PA
Virginia, University of†*	VA
Washington and Lee University†*	VA
Wesleyan College†*	CT
West Chester State College†*	PA
Western Maryland College†*	MD
Western New England College†	MA
Westfield State College†	MA
Wheaton College*	MA
Wilkes College†	PA

William and Mary, College of†*   VA
Williams College†*   MA
Wilson College*   PA
Yale University†*   CT

MARTIAL ARTS

California, University of, at Riverside†*   CA
Los Angeles City College†   CA
Niagara University†*   NY
Puerto Rico Agricultural and Mechanical University†*   PR
Slippery Rock State College†*   PA

POLO

Skidmore College†   NY

POWER LIFTING

Louisiana Technical University†   LA

RACQUETBALL

Memphis State University†*   TN

RIFLERY

Akron, University of†   OH
Alaska, University of, at Anchorage†*   AK
Alaska, University of, at Fairbanks†*   AK
Appalachian State University†*   NC
Arkansas, University of†   AR
Brooklyn College of the City University of New York†   NY
California, University of, at Los Angeles†   CA
Canisius College†   NY
Citadel, The†   SC
Claremore College†   OK
Clarion State College†*   PA
Cornell College†   IA
Dartmouth College†   NH
Davidson College†*   NC
Dubuque, University of†*   IA
Eastern Kentucky University†*   KY
East Tennessee State University†*   TN
Furman University†   SC
Georgia, University of†*   GA
Gettysburg College†*   PA
Indiana University of Pennsylvania†   PA
John Carroll University†   OH
Kutztown State College†*   PA
Lake Superior State College†*   MI
La Salle College†   PA
Lehigh University†   PA
Louisiana Tech University†   LA
Marion Military Institute†   AL
Marshall University†*   WV
Massachusetts Institute of Technology†   MA
Mississippi State University†*   MS
Missouri, University of, at Rolla†   MO
Mount St. Mary's College†*   MD
Murray State University†*   KY
Nicholls State University†   LA
North Alabama, University of†   AL
North Carolina State University†*   NC
North Georgia College†*   GA
Northeast Louisiana University†   LA
Norwich University†*   VT
Ouachita Baptist College†   AR
Ohio State University†   OH
Pennsylvania State University, at University Park†*   PA
Presbyterian College†   SC
Rider College†*   NJ
St. Norbert College†*   WY
St. Paul's College†*   VA
Scranton, University of†*   PA
Tampa, University of†*   FL
Tennessee Technological University†*   TN
Texas, The University of†   TX
Texas Christian University†*   TX
Trinity University†*   TX
Western Carolina University†*   NC
Western Kentucky University†*   KY
West Virginia University†*   WV
William and Mary, College of†*   VA
Wisconsin, University of, at Oshkosh†   WI
Wofford College†   SC
Wyoming, University of†   WY

Xavier University† OH
Youngstown University† OH

RODEO

Chadron State College†* NE
Dawson Community College†* MT
National College†* SD
New Mexico Junior College† NM
Otero Junior College†* CO

RUGBY

Loyola Marymount University† CA
Niagara University† NY
Northwestern University† IL
St. Mary's College† CA

SAILING

Babson College† MA
Boston College†* MA
Boston University†* MA
Bowdoin College† ME
California, University of, at
 Irvine†* CA
California, University of, at San
 Diego†* CA
California State College, at
 Sonoma†* CA
Charleston, College of†* SC
Cleveland State University†* OH
Colby College†* ME
Cornell University†* NY
Dartmouth College†* NH
Davidson College†* NC
Eckerd College† FL
Franklin Pierce College† NH
Georgetown University†* DC
Harvard University†* MA
Hawaii, University of, at
 Honolulu† HI
Lamar University† TX
Maine Maritime Academy† ME
Massachusetts Institute of
 Technology† MA
Millikin University† IL
Ohio Wesleyan University†* OH
Old Dominion University† VA

Pennsylvania, University of†* PA
Princeton University* NJ
Simmons College* MA
Southern California, University
 of† CA
Tufts University† MA
Villanova University† PA
Wisconsin, University of, at
 Green Bay†* WI
Xavier University†* OH

SOCCER

Adrian College† MI
Akron, University of† OH
Alabama, University of, at
 Birmingham† AL
Alabama, University of, at
 Huntsville† AL
Niagara Agricultural and
 Mechanical University† AL
Albion College† MI
Albright College† PA
Alfred University†* NY
Allegheny College† PA
Allentown College of St. Francis
 De Sales† PA
Alma College† MI
American International College† MA
American University, The† DC
Amherst College†* MA
Anne Arundel Community
 College† MD
Appalachian State University† NC
Aquinas College† MI
Asbury College† KY
Ashland College† OH
Assumption College† MA
Atlantic Christian College† NC
Augusta College† GA
Augustana College† IL
Aurora College† IL
Averett College† VA
Azusa Pacific College† CA
Babson College† MA
Ball State University† IN
Baltimore, Community College
 of† MD
Baltimore, University of† MD
Baptist Bible College† MO
Baptist Bible College† PA
Baptist College at Charleston† SC
Barber-Scotia College†* NC
Bates College†* ME
Beaver College†* PA
Belhaven College† MS

319

Bellarmine College†	KY	Calvin College†	MI
Beloit College†	WI	Campbell College†	NC
Benedictine College†	KS	Canisius College†	NY
Bentley College†	MA	Castleton State College†*	VT
Berea College†	KY	Catawaba College†	NC
Berry College†	GA	Centenary College†	LA
Bethany Lutheran College†	MN	Central Junior College†	KS
Bethel College†	MN	Central Michigan University†	MI
Biola College†	CA	Centre College†	KY
Biscayne College†	FL	Champlain College†	VT
Blackburn College†	IL	Charleston, College of†	SC
Bluffton College†	OH	Charleston, University of†	WV
Boston College†*	MA	Chicago, The University of†	IL
Boston State College†	MA	Christopher Newport College†	VA
Boston University†	MA	Cincinnati, University of†	OH
Bowdoin College†	ME	Citadel, The†	SC
Bowling Green State University†	OH	Clackamas Community College†	OR
Brandeis University†*	MA	Claremore College†*	OK
Brandywine College†	DE	Clark University†	MA
Brevard College†	NC	Clemson University†	SC
Brevard Community College†*	FL	Cleveland State University†	OH
Bridgewater State College†	MA	Coastal Carolina College†	SC
Brigham Young University†	UT	Coastal Carolina Community	
Brooklyn College of the City		College†	NC
University of New York†	NY	Coe College†	IA
Brown University†*	RI	Colby College†*	ME
Bryan College†	TN	Colgate University†	NY
Bryant College†*	RI	Colorado College†*	CO
Bucknell University†	PA	Colorado School of Mines†	CO
Butler County Community Junior		Columbia Christian College†	OR
College	KS	Columbia University†	NY
California, University of, at		Columbus College†	GA
Davis†	CA	Concordia College†	MN
California, University of, at Los		Concordia College†	NE
Angeles†	CA	Concordia College†*	OR
California, University of, at		Connecticut, University of†*	CT
Riverside†	CA	Connecticut College†	CT
California, University of, at San		Contra Costa College†	CA
Diego†*	CA	Cornell University†*	NY
California, University of, at		Cosumnes River College†	CA
Santa Barbara†	CA	Covenant College†	TN
California Institute of		Creighton University†	NE
Technology†*	CA	Cumberland College†	KY
California Polytechnic State		Cuyahoga Community College†	OH
University†	CA	Cuyahoga Community College,	
California State College, at		Metro Campus†	OH
Bakersfield†	CA	C. W. Post College†	NY
California State College, at		Daemen College†	NY
Sonoma†	CA	Dartmouth College†*	NH
California State College, at		Davidson College†	NC
Stanislaus†	CA	De Kalb Community College	
California State University, at		(Central)†	GA
Chico†	CA	Delaware, University of†	DE
California State University, at		Delaware Valley College†	PA
Fullerton†	CA	Denver, University of†	CO
California State University, at		DePauw University†	IN
Haywood†	CA	Desert, College of the†*	CA
California State University, at		Detroit, University of†	MI
Long Beach†	CA	District of Columbia, University	
Calvary Bible College†	MO	of†	DC

Dominican College†	NY
Drew University†	NJ
Dubuque, University of†	IA
Duke University†	NC
Dundalk Community College†	MD
East Carolina University†	NC
Eastern College†	PA
Eastern Illinois University†	IL
Eastern Michigan University†	MI
Eastern Nazarene College†	MA
East Stroudsburg State College†	PA
Eckerd College†	FL
Edinboro State College†	PA
Edmonds Community College†	WA
Eisenhower College†	NY
El Camino College†	CA
Elizabethtown College†	PA
Elmira College†	NY
Elon College†	NC
Emory University†	GA
Erskine College†	SC
Essex Community College†	MD
Evansville, University of†	IN
Everett Community College†	WA
Fairleigh Dickinson University†	NJ
Findlay College†	OH
Fitchburg State College†	MA
Flagler College†	FL
Florida Atlantic University†	FL
Florida Institute of Technology†	FL
Florida International University†	FL
Florida Southern College†	FL
Florida Technological University†*	FL
Fordham University†	NY
Fort Steilacoom Community College†	WA
Fort Wayne Bible College†	IN
Framingham State College†	MA
Francis Marion College†	SC
Franklin Pierce College†	NH
Fresno State University†	CA
Frostburg State College†	MD
Furman University†	SC
Gannon College†	PA
George Fox College†	OR
Georgetown University†	DC
George Washington University†	DC
Georgia College†	GA
Georgia Southern College†	GA
Georgia State University†	GA
Gettysburg College†	PA
Glassboro State College†	NJ
Golden Valley Lutheran College†	MN
Gonzaga University†	WA
Gordon College†	MA
Grace College†	IN
Grand Rapids Baptist†	MI
Green River Community College†*	WA
Greensboro College†	NC
Greensville College†	IL
Grinnell College†	IA
Grove City College†	PA
Guilford College†	NC
Gustavus Adolphus College†	MN
Hamilton College†	NY
Hamline University†	MN
Hardin-Simmons University†	TX
Hartford, University of†	CT
Harvard University†*	MA
Heidelberg College†	OH
Hendrix College†	AR
Hesston College†	KS
High Point College†	NC
Hiram College†	OH
Hofstra University†	NY
Holy Cross College†	MA
Hope College†	MI
Houghton College†*	NY
Houston Baptist University†	TX
Humboldt State University†	CA
Hunter College†	NY
Huntington College†	IN
Husson College†	ME
Illinois, University of, at Chicago Circle†	IL
Illinois State University†	IL
Indiana Institute of Technology†	IN
Indiana State University†	IN
Indiana University, at Bloomington†	IN
Indiana University of Pennsylvania†	PA
Indiana University-Purdue University, at Fort Wayne†	IN
Ithaca College†	NY
James Madison University†	VA
Jersey City State College†	NJ
John Carroll University†	OH
Josephenum College†	OH
Juniata College†	PA
Kean College of New Jersey†	NJ
Kent State University†	OH
Kentucky Wesleyan College†	KY
Kenyon College†	OH
King's College, The†	NY
Kishwaukee College†	IL
Kutztown State College†	PA
Lafayette College†	PA
Lamar University†	TX
Lancaster Bible College†	PA
Lane Community College†	OR
La Salle College†	PA
La Verne College†	CA
Lawrence University†	WI
Lebanon Valley College†	PA
Lehigh University†	PA
Le Moyne College†	NY

Lewis and Clark Community College†	IL	College, New World Center†	FL
Lewis University†	IL	Miami-Dade Community College, South Campus†	FL
Liberty Baptist College†	VA	Miami University†	OH
Lincoln Christian College†	IL	Michigan State University†	MI
Lincoln Land Community College†	IL	Middlebury College†*	VT
		Midwestern State University†	TX
Lindenwood College, The†*	MO	Milligan College†	TN
Linfield College†*	OR	Milwaukee Area Technical College†	WI
Lock Haven State College†	PA		
Long Island University†	NY	Missouri, University of, at Rolla†	MO
Longwood College†	VA	Missouri, University of, at St. Louis†	MO
Los Angeles Baptist College†	CA		
Los Angeles City College†	CA	Missouri Baptist College†	MO
Los Angeles Pierce Junior College†	CA	Missouri Southern State†	MO
		Mitchell College†	CT
Louisiana Tech University†	LA	Monmouth College†	IL
Louisville, University of†	KY	Monmouth College†	NJ
Lowell, University of†	MA	Montclair State University†	NJ
Loyola Marymount University†	CA	Mount St. Mary's College†	MD
Lycoming College†	PA	Muhlenberg College†	PA
Lynchburg College†	VA	Nazareth College†	NY
Lyndon State College†*	VT	Newberry College†	SC
Macalester College†	MN	New Hampshire College†	NH
McKendree College†	IL	New Hampshire Technological Institute†	NH
Maine, University of, at Farmington†	ME		
		New Haven, University of†	CT
Maine, University of, at Fort Kent†	ME	New Orleans, University of†	LA
		New York, State University College of, at Brockport†	NY
Maine, University of, at Presque Isle†	ME		
		New York, State University College of, at Fredonia†	NY
Maine Maritime Academy†	ME		
Malone College†	OH	New York, State University College of, at Genesco†	NY
Manchester College†	IN		
Manhattan College†	NY	New York, State University College of, at New Paltz†	NY
Marian College†	IN		
Marietta College†	OH	New York, State University College of, at New Paltz†	NY
Marin, College of†	CA		
Marist College†	NY	New York, State University College of, at Oneonta†	NY
Marquette University†	WI		
Marshall University†	WV	New York, State University College of, at Oswego†	NY
Maryland, University of, at Catonsville†	MD		
		New York, State University College of, at Plattsburgh†*	NY
Maryland, University of, at College Park†	MD		
		New York, State University College of, at Potsdam†	NY
Maryville College†	TN		
Mary Washington College†	VA	New York State University College of, at Purchase†	NY
Massachusetts, University of†*	MA		
Massachusetts Institute of Technology†	MA	New York State University College of Technology†	NY
Massasoit Community College†	MA	New York, State University of, at Albany†	NY
Medgar Evers College†	NY		
Menlo College†	CA	New York, State University of, at Binghamton†	NY
Mercer University†	GA		
Mercer University at Atlanta†	GA	New York, State University of, at Buffalo†	NY
Mercy College†	NY		
Metropolitan State College†	CO	Niagara University†	NY
Miami, University of†	FL	Nichols College†	MA
Miami Christian College†	FL	North Adams State College†	MA
Miami-Dade Community		North Carolina, University of, at	

322

Asheville†	NC
North Carolina, University of, at Chapel Hill†*	NC
North Carolina, University of, at Charlotte†	NC
North Carolina, University of, at Greensboro†	NC
North Carolina, University of, at Wilmington†	NC
North Carolina State University†	NC
North Carolina Wesleyan College†	NC
North Central College†	IL
Northeast Louisiana University†	LA
Northern Illinois University†	IL
Northern Kentucky University†	KY
North Georgia College†	GA
Northland College†*	WI
North Texas State University†	TX
Northwest College†	WA
Northwestern College†	MN
Northwestern University†	IL
Northwest Nazarene College†	ID
Norwich University†	VT
Notre Dame, University of†	IN
Oakland City College*	IN
Oakland University†	MI
Oberlin College†	OH
Occidental College†	CA
Ohio Northern University†	OH
Ohio State University†	OH
Ohio Wesleyan University†	OH
Old Dominion University†	VA
Olivet College†	MI
Olivet Nazarene College†	IL
Ottawa University†	KS
Ouachita Baptist College†	AR
Oxford College of Emory University†	GA
Oxnard College†	CA
Pace University†	NY
Pacific, University of the†	CA
Pacific Lutheran University†*	WA
Pacific University†*	OR
Palomar College†	CA
Pan American University†	TX
Park College†	MO
Paul Smith College†	NY
Pembroke State University†	NC
Pennsylvania, University of†	PA
Pennsylvania State University, at Middletown†	PA
Pennsylvania State University, at University Park†	PA
Pennsylvania State University (Behrens College)†	PA
Pfeiffer College†	NC
Philadelphia Community College†	PA
Piedmont Bible College†	NC
Pittsburgh, University of†	PA
Pittsburgh, University of, at Johnstown†	PA
Plymouth State College†*	NH
Point Loma College†	CA
Portland, University of†	OR
Pratt Institute†	NY
Presbyterian College†	SC
Princeton University†*	NJ
Principia College†	IL
Providence College†	RI
Puerto Rico Agricultural and Mechanical University†*	PR
Purdue University, at Calumet†	IL
Quincy College†	IL
Quinnipiac College†	CT
Radford College†*	VA
Randolph-Macon College†	VA
Redlands, University of†	CA
Regis College†	CO
Rensselaer Polytechnic Institute†	NY
Rider College†	NJ
Ripon College†	WI
Roanoke College†	VA
Roberts Wesleyan College†	NY
Rochester, University of†*	NY
Rockhurst College†	MO
Rockmont College†	CO
Rollins College†	FL
Rutgers, State University of, at Camden†	NJ
Rutgers, State University of, at Newark†	NJ
Rutgers, State University of, at New Brunswick†	NJ
Sacred Heart University†	CT
St. Augustine's College†	NC
St. Bonaventure University†	NY
St. Francis College†	NY
St. John Fisher College†*	NY
St. Johns College†	KS
St. Johns University†	MN
St. Lawrence University†*	NY
St. Leo College†	FL
St. Louis Community College†	MO
St. Louis University†	MO
St. Mary's College†	MN
St. Mary's College of California†	CA
St. Mary's University of Texas†*	TX
St. Norbert College†	WY
St. Olaf College†*	MN
St. Peter's College†	NJ
St. Scholastica, College of†	MN
St. Thomas, College of†	MN
St. Vincent College†	PA
San Diego, University of†	CA
San Diego State University†	CA
San Francisco, City College of†	CA
San Francisco, University of†	CA
San Francisco State University†	CA

San Jose State University†	CA	Tufts University†	MA
Sangamon State University†	IL	Tulsa, University of†	OK
Santa Ana College†	CA	Union College†	KY
Santa Clara, University of†*	CA	United Wesleyan College†	PA
Schoolcraft College†	MI	Upsala College†	NJ
Scranton, University of†	PA	Ursinus College†	PA
Siena College†*	NY	Vanderbilt University†	TN
Siena Heights College†	MI	Villanova University†*	PA
Skagit Valley College†	WA	Virginia, University of†	VA
Skidmore College†*	NY	Virginia Commonwealth	
Skyline College†	CA	University†	VA
Slippery Rock State College†	PA	Virginia Polytechnic Institute†	VA
Smith College*	MA	Viterboro College†	WY
South, University of the†	TN	Wabash College†	IN
South Alabama, University of†	AL	Wake Forest University†	NC
Southampton College†	NY	Walsh College†	OH
South Carolina, University of†	SC	Warner Pacific College†	OR
Southeastern University†	DC	Warren Wilson College†	NC
Southern California, University		Washington, University of†	WA
of†	CA	Washington and Lee University†	VA
Southern California College†	CA	Washington Bible College†	MD
Southern Connecticut State		Washington University†	MO
College†	CT	Wesleyan College†	CT
Southern Maine, University of†	ME	West Chester State College†	PA
Southern Maine Vocational		Western Carolina University†	NC
Technical Institute†	ME	Western Illinois University†	IL
Southern Methodist University†	TX	Western Maryland College†	MD
Southern Oregon State College†	OR	Western Michigan University†	MI
South Florida, The University		Western New England College†	MA
of†	FL	Westfield State College†*	MA
Southwestern at Memphis†	TN	Westminster College†	MO
Spring Arbor College†	MI	Westmount College†*	CA
Spring Garden College†	PA	West Virginia University†	WV
Stanford University†	CA	West Virginia Wesleyan College†	WV
State Fair Community College†	MO	Wheaton College†	IL
Staten Island, College of†	NY	Wheeling College†	WV
Stetson University†	FL	Wilberforce University*	OH
Stevens Institute of Technology†	NJ	Wilkes College†*	PA
Susquehanna University†	PA	William and Mary, College of†*	VA
Swarthmore College†	PA	William Paterson College†	NJ
Syracuse University†	NY	Williams College†*	MA
Tabor College†	KS	Wilmington College†	OH
Tacoma Community College†	WA	Winthrop College†	SC
Tampa, University of†	FL	Wisconsin, University of, at	
Temple University†	PA	Green Bay†	WI
Tennessee Technological		Wisconsin, University of, at	
University†	TN	Marathon County†*	WI
Tennessee Wesleyan College†	TN	Wisconsin, University of, at	
Texas Christian University†	TX	Milwaukee†	WI
Thomas College†	ME	Wisconsin, University of, at	
Toledo, University of†	OH	Platteville†	WI
Tougaloo College†	MS	Wisconsin, University of, at	
Towson State University†	MD	Waukesha†*	WI
Treasure Valley Community		Wisconsin, University of, at	
College†	OR	Whitewater†	WI
Trenton State College†	NJ	Wofford College†	SC
Trinity College†	CT	Worcester State College†	MA
Trinity University†*	TX	Wright State University†	OH
Tri-State University†	IN	Xavier University†	OH
Triton College†	IL	Yale University†*	CT

York College†   NE
Youngstown State University†   OH

SQUASH

Amherst College†   MA
Babson College†   MA
Bowdoin College†   ME
Brown University*   RI
California, University of, at San
   Diego*   CA
Centre College*   KY
Colby College†*   ME
Cornell University†   NY
Dartmouth College†*   NH
Fordham University†   NY
George Washington University*   DC
Hamilton College†   NY
Harvard University†*   MA
Lehigh University†   PA
Lowell, University of†   MA
Massachusetts Institute of
   Technology†   MA
Middlebury College*   VT
Ohio Northern University†*   OR
Pennsylvania, University of†*   PA
Princeton University†*   NJ
Rochester, University of†   NY
Smith College*   MA
Stevens Institute of Technology†   NJ
Trinity College†   CT
Tufts University†   MA
Washington, University of*   WA
Wesleyan University†*   CT
Williams College†*   MA
Yale University†*   CT

SOFTBALL

Adams State College of
   Colorado*   CO
Adrian College*   MI
Akron, University of*   OH
Albright College*   PA
Allegheny College*   PA
Allentown College of St. Francis
   De Sales*   PA
Alma College*   MI
American International College*   MA
Anderson College*   IL
Angelo State University*   TX

Anne Arundel Community
   College*   MD
Appalachian State University*   NC
Aquinas College*   MI
Arizona State University*   AZ
Arizona Western College*   AZ
Armstrong State College*   GA
Ashland College*   OH
Assumption College*   MA
Atlantic Christian College*   NC
Auburn University, at Auburn*   AL
Augustana College*   IL
Augustana College*   SD
Aurora College*   IL
Averett College*   VA
Baker University*   KS
Ball State University*   IN
Baltimore, Community College
   of*   MD
Baptist Bible College*   PA
Barber-Scotia College*   NC
Bates College*   ME
Baylor University*   TX
Beaver College*   PA
Belhaven College*   MS
Bellarmine College*   KY
Bellevue College*   NE
Beloit College*   WI
Benedictine College*   KS
Bentley College*   MA
Berea College*   KY
Bethany College*   KS
Bethel College*   MN
Biola College*   CA
Blue Mountain College*   MS
Bluffton College*   OH
Bowie State College*   MD
Bowling Green State University*   OH
Bradley University*   IL
Brandeis University*   MA
Brandywine College*   DE
Brevard Community College*   FL
Briar Cliff College*   IA
Bridgewater State College*   MA
Brooklyn College of the City
   University of New York*   NY
Brown University*   RI
Bryan College*   TN
Bryant College*   RI
Bucknell University*   PA
Butler County Community Junior
   College*   KS
California, University of, at
   Davis*   CA
California, University of, at Los
   Angeles*   CA
California, University of, at
   Riverside*   CA
California, University of, at San
   Diego*   CA

California, University of, at Santa Barbara*	CA
California Polytechnic State University*	CA
California State College, at Sonoma*	CA
California State College, at Stanislaus*	CA
California State University, at Chico*	CA
California State University, at Fullerton*	CA
California State University, at Haywood*	CA
California State University, at Long Beach*	CA
Calvin College*	MI
Cameron University*	OK
Campbell College*	NC
Campbellsville College*	KY
Canisius College*	NY
Carl Sandburg College*	IL
Carthage College*	WI
Castleton State College*	VT
Catawaba College*	NC
Centenary College*	NJ
Central Junior College*	KS
Central Michigan University*	MI
Central Missouri State University*	MO
Central State University*	OK
Chadron State College*	NE
Champlain College*	VT
Charleston, University of*	WV
Chatham College*	PA
Chicago, The University of*	IL
Chicago State University*	IL
Chowan College*	NC
Cincinnati Bible College*	OH
Citrus College*	CA
Clarion State College*	PA
Clark University*	MA
Cleveland State University*	OH
Coahoma Junior College*	MS
Coastal Carolina Community College*	NC
Coe College*	IA
Colby College*	ME
Colgate University*	NY
Colorado College*	CO
Colorado Northwestern Community College*	CO
Colorado State University*	CO
Columbus College*	GA
Concord College*	WV
Concordia College*	IL
Concordia College*	MN
Concordia College*	NE
Concordia College*	OR
Connecticut, University of*	CT
Copiah-Lincoln Junior College*	MS
Cornell College*	IA
Cosumnes River College*	CA
Cottey College*	MO
Cowley County Community College*	KS
Creighton University*	NE
Crowder College*	MO
Culver-Stockton College*	MO
Cuyahoga Community College, Metro Campus*	OH
C. W. Post College*	NY
Cypress College*	CA
Daemen College*	NY
Dakota Wesleyan University*	SD
Delaware, University of*	DE
Delaware Valley College*	PA
Delta State College*	MS
DePauw University*	IN
Desert, College of the*	CA
Detroit, University of*	MI
District of Columbia, University of*	
Dominican College*	NY
Dubuque, University of*	IA
Dundalk Community College*	MD
East Carolina University*	NC
Eastern College*	PA
Eastern Illinois University*	IL
Eastern Michigan University*	MI
Eastern Nazarene College*	MA
Eastern Utah, College of*	UT
East Stroudsburg State College*	PA
Eckerd College*	FL
Edgewood College*	WI
Edinboro State College*	PA
Edmonds Community College*	WA
Eisenhower College*	NY
El Camino College*	CA
Elizabethtown College*	PA
Elmhurst College*	IL
Elmira College*	NY
Elon College*	NC
Emory and Henry College*	VA
Emporia State University*	KS
Erskine College*	SC
Essex Community College*	MD
Evansville, University of*	IN
Fairleigh Dickinson University*	NJ
Fergus Falls Community College*	MN
Ferris State College*	MI
Findlay College*	OH
Fitchburg State College*	MA
Flagler College*	FL
Florida, University of*	FL
Florida A. and M. University*	FL
Florida Atlantic University*	FL
Florida International University*	FL
Florida Junior College*	FL

Florida Southern College*	FL
Florida State University*	FL
Florida Technological University*	FL
Fontbonne College*	MO
Fort Hayes State*	KS
Framingham State College*	MA
Francis Marion College*	SC
Franklin Pierce College*	NH
Fresno State University*	CA
Friends University*	KS
Furman University*	SC
Gannon College*	PA
George Fox College*	OR
Georgia College*	GA
Georgian Court College*	NJ
Georgia Southern College*	GA
Georgia Southwestern College*	GA
Georgia State University*	GA
Gettysburg College*	PA
Glassboro State College*	NJ
Golden Valley Lutheran College*	MN
Gordon College*	MA
Grace College*	IN
Graceland College*	IA
Grand Rapids Baptist*	MI
Grand Rapids Junior College*	MI
Grand Valley State College*	MI
Green River Community College*	WA
Greensville College*	IL
Grinnell College*	IA
Grove City College*	PA
Guilford College*	NC
Gustavus Adolphus College*	MN
Hampton Institute*	VA
Hartford, University of*	CT
Harvard University*	MA
Herbert H. Lehman College*	NY
Hesston College*	KS
Highland Community Junior College*	KS
Hilbert College*	NY
Hillsborough Community College*	FL
Hillsdale College*	MI
Hiram College*	OR
Hofstra University*	NY
Holy Cross College*	MA
Holy Family College*	PA
Hope College*	MI
Houghton College*	NY
Housatonic Community College*	CT
Humboldt State University*	CA
Husson College*	ME
Idaho State University*	ID
Illinois, University of, at Chicago Circle*	IL
Illinois Benedictine College*	IL
Illinois College*	IL
Illinois State University*	IL
Illinois Valley Community College*	IL
Illinois Wesleyan University*	IL
Indiana Central University*	IN
Indiana State University*	IN
Indiana University, at Bloomington*	IN
Indiana University of Pennsylvania*	PA
Indiana University-Purdue University, at Indianapolis*	IN
Indian Hills Community College*	IA
Inver Hills College*	MN
Iowa, University of*	IA
Iowa Lakes Community College*	IA
Iowa State University*	IA
Iowa Wesleyan College*	IA
Ithaca College*	NY
Jacksonville State University*	AL
Jamestown College*	ND
Jarvis Christian College*	TX
Jefferson Davis Junior College*	MS
Jersey City State College*	NJ
Johnson C. Smith University*	NC
Juniata College*	PA
Kalamazoo Valley Community College*	MI
Kankakee Community College*	IL
Kansas, University of*	KS
Kansas State University*	KS
Kansas Wesleyan College*	KS
Kean College of New Jersey*	NJ
Kearney State College*	NE
Kent State University*	OH
Kentucky State University*	KY
Kentucky Wesleyan College*	KY
King's College, The*	NY
Kirkwood Community College*	IA
Kishwaukee College*	IL
Kutztown State College*	PA
Lafayette College*	PA
Lake Erie College*	OH
Lake Superior State College*	MI
Lancaster Bible College*	PA
La Salle College*	PA
La Verne College*	CA
Lawrence University*	WI
Lehigh University*	PA
Le Moyne College*	NY
Lenoir Community College*	NC
Lenoir-Rhyne College*	NC
Lewis University*	IL
Liberty Baptist College*	VA
Lincoln Christian College*	IL
Lincoln Land Community College*	IL
Lincoln Trail College*	IL
Lincoln University*	MO

Lindenwood College, The*	MO
Linfield College*	OR
Livingstone College*	NC
Livingston University*	AL
Lock Haven State College*	PA
Longwood College*	VA
Loras College*	IA
Los Angeles Baptist College*	CA
Los Angeles Pierce Junior College*	CA
Louisiana State University*	LA
Louisiana Tech University*	LA
Louisville, University of*	KY
Lowell, University of*	MA
Loyola Marymount University*	CA
Luther College*	IA
Lyndon State College*	VT
Macalester College*	MN
McKendree College*	IL
McNeese State University*	LA
Manhattan College*	NY
Mankato State University*	MN
Mansfield State College*	PA
Marietta College*	OH
Marin, College of*	CA
Marshalltown Community College*	IA
Mars Hill College*	NC
Marshall University*	WV
Martin College*	TN
Mary Holmes College*	MS
Maryville College*	TN
Marywood College*	PA
Massachusetts, University of*	MA
Massachusetts Institute of Technology*	MA
Massasoit Community College*	MA
Mattatuck Community College*	CT
Mercy College*	NY
Meredith College*	NC
Metropolitan State College*	CO
Miami, University of*	FL
Miami Christian College*	FL
Miami-Dade Community College, New World Center*	FL
Miami-Dade Community College, South Campus*	FL
Miami University*	OH
Michigan, University of*	MI
Michigan Christian Junior College*	MI
Michigan State University*	MI
Midwest Christian College*	OK
Milligan College*	TN
Milwaukee Area Technical College*	WI
Minnesota, University of, at Minneapolis*	MN
Minnesota, University of, Technical College*	MN
Minnesota Bible College*	MN
Mira Costa College*	CA
Mississippi College*	MS
Mississippi State University*	MS
Missouri, University of*	MO
Missouri, University of, at Rolla*	MO
Missouri, University of, at St. Louis*	MO
Missouri Baptist College*	MO
Missouri Southern State*	MO
Missouri Valley College*	MO
Missouri Western College*	MO
Mitchell College*	CT
Monmouth College*	IL
Monmouth College*	NJ
Montclair State University*	NJ
Moorhead State University*	MN
Morehead State University*	KY
Morningside College*	IA
Motlow State Community College*	TN
Mott Community College*	MN
Mount Ida Junior College*	MA
Mount Marty College*	SD
Mount Olive Junior College*	NC
Mount St. Mary's College*	MD
Muhlenberg College*	PA
Napa Community College*	CA
Nebraska, University of*	NE
Nebraska, University of, at Omaha*	NE
Nebraska Wesleyan University*	NE
Newberry College*	SC
New Hampshire College*	NH
New Hampshire Technological Institute*	NH
New Haven, University of*	CT
New Mexico Highlands University*	NM
New Orleans, University of*	LA
New York, State University College of, at Brockport*	NY
New York, State University College of, at Geneseo*	NY
New York, State University College of, at New Paltz*	NY
New York, State University College of, at Oneonta*	NY
New York, State University College of, at Oswego*	NY
New York, State University of, at Albany*	NY
New York, State University of, at Binghamton*	NY
New York, State University of, at Buffalo*	NY
New York, State University, College of Technology*	NY
New York Institute of Technology*	NY

Nicholls State University*	LA	Paducah Community College*	KY
Nichols College*	MA	Palm Beach Junior College*	FL
North Adams State College*	MA	Palomar College*	CA
North Carolina, University of, at Chapel Hill*	NC	Pan American University*	TX
		Parkland College*	IL
North Carolina, University of, at Charlotte*	NC	Paul Smith's College*	NY
		Pembroke State University*	NC
North Carolina, University of, at Greensboro*	NC	Pennsylvania, University of*	PA
		Pennsylvania State University, at Beaver Campus*	PA
North Carolina, University of, at Wilmington*	NC	Pennsylvania State University, at DuBois*	PA
North Carolina Agricultural and Technical State University*	NC	Pennsylvania State University, at McKeesport*	PA
North Carolina State University*	NC		
North Carolina Wesleyan College*	NC	Pennsylvania State University, at Middletown*	PA
North Central College*	IL	Pennsylvania State University, at University Park*	PA
North Dakota, University of*	ND		
North Dakota State University at Fargo*	ND	Pennsylvania State University (Behrend College)*	PA
Northeastern Illinois University*	IL	Pfeiffer College*	NC
Northeastern Oklahoma A and M College*	OK	Philadelphia Community College*	PA
Northeast Louisiana University*	LA	Pima Community College*	AZ
Northern Arizona University*	AZ	Pittsburg State University*	KS
Northern Colorado, University of*	CO	Plymouth State College*	NH
		Point Loma College*	CA
Northern Illinois University*	IL	Portland State University*	OR
Northern Iowa, University of*	IA	Princeton University*	NJ
Northern Kentucky University*	KY	Principia College*	IL
Northern State College*	SD	Providence College*	RI
North Georgia College*	GA	Puerto Rico Agricultural and Mechanical University*	PR
Northland Community College*	MN		
Northwestern College*	MN	Quincy College*	IL
Northwestern University*	IL	Quinnipiac College*	CT
Northwest Missouri State University*	MO	Redlands, University of*	CA
		Redwoods, College of the*	CA
Norwich University*	VT	Rensselaer Polytechnic Institute*	NY
Notre Dame College*	MD	Rider College*	NJ
Oakland University*	MI	Ripon College*	WI
Oakton Community College*	IL	Riverside City College*	CA
Ohio Northern University*	OH	Robert Morris College*	PA
Ohio State University*	OH	Roberts Wesleyan College*	NY
Ohio University*	OH	Rutgers, State University of, at Camden*	NJ
Ohio Wesleyan University*	OH		
Oklahoma, University of*	OK	Rutgers, State University of, at Newark*	NJ
Oklahoma Baptist University*	OK		
Oklahoma City University*	OK	Rutgers, State University of, at New Brunswick*	NJ
Oklahoma State University*	OK		
Olivet College*	MI	Sacred Heart University*	CT
Olivet Nazarene College*	IL	Saginaw Valley College*	MI
Olney Central College*	IL	St. Augustine's College*	NC
Oregon, University of*	OR	St. Bonaventure University*	NY
Oregon State University*	OR	St. Clair County Community College*	MI
Oregon Technical Institute*	OR		
Otterbein College*	OH	St. Cloud State University*	MN
Pace University*	NY	St. Francis, College of*	IL
Pacific, University of the*	CA	St. Johns College*	KS
Pacific Lutheran University*	WA	St. Joseph the Provider, College of*	VT
Pacific University*	OR		

St. Leo College*	FL
St. Louis Community College*	MO
St. Louis University*	MD
St. Mary, College of*	NE
St. Mary of the Plains College*	KS
St. Mary's College*	MN
St. Mary's College of California*	CA
St. Mary's University of Texas*	TX
St. Norbert College*	WY
St. Olaf College*	MN
St. Paul's College*	PA
St. Paul's College*	VA
St. Peter's College*	NJ
St. Teresa, College of*	MN
St. Thomas, College of*	MN
St. Xavier College*	IL
Salisbury State College*	MD
Sam Houston State University*	TX
San Diego, University of*	CA
San Diego State University*	CA
San Francisco, University of*	CA
San Francisco State University*	CA
San Mateo, College of*	CA
Santa Ana College*	CA
Santa Clara, University of*	CA
Scranton, University of*	PA
Seminole Community College*	FL
Sequoias, College of the*	CA
Shaw College at Detroit*	MI
Shawnee College*	IL
Shepherd College*	WV
Siena College*	NY
Siena Heights College*	MI
Siskiyous, College of the*	CA
Skagit Valley College*	WA
Skidmore College*	NY
Skyline College*	CA
Slippery Rock State College*	PA
Smith College*	MA
South Carolina, University of*	SC
South Dakota, University of, at Springfield*	SD
South Dakota, University of, at Vermillion*	SD
Southeast Community College*	NE
Southeastern Community College*	IA
Southeast Missouri State*	MO
Southern Arkansas University*	AR
Southern Connecticut State College*	CT
Southern Illinois University*	IL
Southern Maine, University of*	ME
Southern Maine Vocational Technical Institute*	ME
Southern Utah State College*	UT
South Florida, The University of†	FL
Southwest Baptist College*	MO
Southwestern Community College†	IA
Southwest State University†	MN
Spartanburg Methodist College†	SC
Spring Arbor College†	MI
Spring Garden College†	PA
Staten Island, College of*	NY
Stephen F. Austin State University†	TX
Sterling College*	KS
Stetson University*	FL
Susquehanna University*	PA
Swarthmore College*	PA
Tabor College*	KS
Tacoma Community College*	WA
Tarkto College*	MO
Taylor University*	IN
Temple University*	PA
Texas, The University of, at Arlington*	TX
Texas Wesleyan College*	TX
Texas Woman's University*	TX
Thiel College*	PA
Thomas College*	ME
Tiffin University*	OH
Toledo, University of*	OH
Towson State University*	MD
Treasure Valley Community College*	OR
Trenton State College*	NJ
Trinity University*	TX
Triton College*	IL
Truett McConnell College*	GA
Tunxis Community College*	CT
United Wesleyan College*	PA
Upper Iowa University*	IA
Upsala College*	NJ
Urbana College*	OH
Ursinus College*	PA
Utah, University of*	UT
Utah State University*	UT
Ventura College*	CA
Virginia, University of*	VA
Virginia State College*	VA
Virginia Union University*	VA
Walsh College*	OH
Warren Wilson College*	NC
Washburn University*	KS
Washington Bible College*	MD
Wayne State University*	MI
Weber State College*	UT
West Chester State College*	PA
Western Carolina University*	NC
Western Illinois University*	IL
Western Maryland College*	MD
Western Michigan University*	MI
Western New England College*	MA
Western State College of Colorado*	CO

Westfield State College*	MA	Anchorage†*	AK
West Georgia College*	GA	Albion College†*	MI
West Hills College*	CA	Alfred University†*	NY
West Liberty State College*	WV	Allegheny College†*	PA
West Texas State University†	TX	Alma College†*	MI
West Virginia University*	WV	American University, The†*	DC
Wheaton College*	IL	Amherst College†*	MA
Wheaton College*	MA	Anne Arundel Community College†*	MD
Wheeling College*	WV	Appalachian State University†*	NC
Wiley College*	TX	Arizona, University of†*	AZ
Wilkes College*	PA	Arizona State University†*	AZ
Willamette University*	OR	Arkansas, University of†*	AR
William Carey College*	MS	Arkansas, University of, at Little Rock†*	AR
William Paterson College*	NJ	Arkansas State University†	AR
William Penn College*	IA	Arkansas Tech University†	AR
Wilmington College*	OH	Ashland College†*	OR
Winona State College*	MN	Auburn University, at Auburn†*	AL
Winston-Salem State University*	NC	Augusta College†*	GA
Winthrop College*	SC	Augstaaollgeaf03†*	IL
Wisconsin, University of, at Oshkosh*	WI	Babson College†	MA
Wisconsin, University of, at Stevens Point*	WI	Ball State University†*	IN
Wisconsin, University of, at Waukesha*	WI	Barber-Scotia College†*	NC
		Barnard College*	NY
Wisconsin, University of, at Whitewater*	WI	Beloit College†*	WI
		Bemidji State University†*	MN
Worcester State College*	MA	Berea College†*	KY
Worthington Community College*	MN	Boston College†*	MA
		Boston University†*	MA
Wright State University*	OH	Bowdoin College†	ME
Wyoming, University of*	WY	Bowling Green State University†*	OH
Yale University*	CT	Bradley University†	IL
Yankton College*	SD	Brandeis University†	MA
Youngstown State University*	OH	Brevard Community College†*	FL
Yuba College*	CA	Bridgewater State College†*	MA
		Brigham Young University†*	UT
		Brooklyn College of the City University of New York†*	NY
		Brown University†*	RI
		Bucknell University†*	PA

SWIMMING

Kentucky, University of†	KY
Swarthmore College†*	PA
Wesleyan University†*	CT

SWIMMING-DIVING

		Butler University†*	IN
		California, University of, at Davis†*	CA
Adrian College†*	MI	California, University of, at Irvine†*	CA
Akron, University of†	OH	California, University of, at Los Angeles†*	CA
Alabama, University of, at University†*	AL	California, University of, at Riverside†*	CA
Alabama Agricultural and Mechanical University†*	AL	California, University of, at San Diego†*	CA
Alaska, University of, at		California, University of, at Santa Barbara†*	CA
		California Institute of Technology†*	CA
		California Polytechnic State University†*	CA

California State University, at Chico†*	CA
California State University, at Haywood†*	CA
California State University, at Long Beach†*	CA
Calvin College†*	MI
Canisius College†	NY
Carroll College†*	WI
Carthage College†*	WI
Cathedral College†	NY
Centenary College*	NJ
Central Arkansas, University of*	AR
Central Michigan University†*	MI
Central Missouri State University†*	MO
Centre College†	KY
Charleston, College of†*	SC
Chicago, The University of†*	IL
Chicago State University†	IL
Cincinnati, University of†*	OH
Citadel, The†	SC
Citrus College†*	CA
Clarion State College†*	PA
Clark University†*	MA
Clemson University†*	SC
Cleveland State University†*	OH
Coe College†*	IA
Colby College†*	ME
Colgate University†*	NY
Colorado College†*	CO
Colorado School of Mines†	CO
Colorado State University*	CO
Columbia University†	NY
Concordia College†*	NE
Connecticut, University of†*	CT
Connecticut College*	CT
Contra Costa College†	CA
Cornell University†*	NY
Cottey College*	MO
Cypress College†	CA
Dartmouth College†*	NH
Davidson College†	NC
Daytona Beach Community College†*	FL
Delaware, University of†*	DE
Denver, University of†*	CO
Drury College†	MO
Duke University†*	NC
Duquesne University†*	PA
East Carolina University†*	NC
Eastern Illinois University†*	IL
Eastern Kentucky University†*	KY
Eastern Michigan University†*	MI
East Stroudsburg State College†*	PA
Edgewood College*	WI
Edinboro State College†	PA
Eisenhower College†*	NY
El Camino College†*	CA
Elizabethtown College†*	PA
Elmira College†*	NY
Emory University†*	GA
Emporia State University*	KS
Essex Community College†*	MD
Evansville, University of†	IN
Fairmont State College†*	WV
Ferris State College†	MI
Ferrum College†	WA
Florida, University of†*	FL
Florida A. and M. University†*	FL
Florida State University†*	FL
Fordham University†*	NY
Fresno State University†*	CA
Frostburg State College†*	MD
Furman University†*	SC
Georgetown University†*	DC
George Washington University†*	DC
Georgia University of†*	GA
Georgia Institute of Technology†	GA
Georgia Southern College†*	GA
Georgia State University†*	GA
Gettysburg College†*	PA
Glassboro State College†*	NJ
Graceland College†*	IA
Grand Rapids Junior College†*	MI
Greensboro College†*	NC
Grinnell College†*	IA
Grove City College†	PA
Gustavus Adolphus College†*	MN
Hamilton College†*	NY
Hamline University†*	MN
Harding University†	AR
Harvard University†*	MA
Hawaii, University of, at Honolulu†*	HI
Heidelberg College†*	OH
Henderson State University†*	OR
Hendrix College†*	AR
Herbert H. Lehman College†*	NY
Highland Park Community College†*	MI
Hiram College†*	OR
Holy Cross College†*	MA
Hood College*	MD
Hope College†*	MI
Houston, University of†*	TX
Humboldt State University*	CA
Hunter College†*	NY
Idaho, University of†*	ID
Illinois, University of, at Champaign†*	IL
Illinois, University of, at Chicago Circle†*	IL
Illinois Benedictine College†*	IL
Illinois State University†*	IL
Indiana University, at Bloomington†*	IN
Indiana University of Pennsylvania†*	PA

Indian River Community College†*	FL
Iowa, University of†*	IA
Iowa State University†*	IA
Iowa Wesleyan College†*	IA
Ithaca College†*	NY
James Madison University†*	VA
Jersey City State College†*	NJ
John Carroll University†*	OH
Johnson C. Smith University†*	NC
Kansas, University of†*	KS
Kean College of New Jersey†*	NJ
Kearney State College*	NE
Kent State University†*	OH
Kenyon College†*	OH
Kutztown State College†	PA
Lafayette College†*	PA
Lamar University*	TX
La Salle College†*	PA
Lawrence University†*	WI
Lehigh University†*	PA
Linfield College†*	OR
Lock Haven State College*	PA
Long Island University†	NY
Loras College†*	IA
Los Angeles Pierce Junior College†*	CA
Louisiana State University†*	LA
Louisville, University of†	KY
Lowell, University of†*	MA
Loyola Marymount University†*	CA
Luther College†*	IA
Lycoming College†*	PA
Macalester College†*	MN
Manhattan College†	NY
Mankato State University†*	MN
Marin, College of†*	CA
Marist College†*	NY
Marshall University†	WV
Mary Baldwin College*	VA
Maryland, University of, at College Park†*	MD
Mary Washington College*	VA
Massachusetts, University of†*	MA
Massachusetts Institute of Technology†	MA
Menlo College†*	CA
Metropolitan State College†	CO
Miami, University of†*	FL
Miami-Dade Community College, South Campus†*	FL
Miami University†*	OH
Michigan, University of†*	MI
Michigan State University†*	MI
Middlebury College*	VT
Millikan University†	IL
Minnesota, University of, at Minneapolis†*	MN
Missouri, University of†*	MO
Missouri, University of, at Rolla†	MO
Missouri, University of, at St. Louis†*	MO
Monmouth College†*	IL
Monmouth College†*	NJ
Montana, University of*	MT
Montclair State University†*	NJ
Napa Community College†*	CA
Nazareth College†*	NY
Nebraska, University of†*	NE
New York, State University College of, at Brockport*	NY
New York, State University College of, at Fredonia†	NY
New York, State University College of, at Genesco†*	NY
New York, State University College of, at New Paltz†*	NY
New York, State University College of, at Oneonta*	NY
New York, State University College of, at Oswego*	NY
New York, State University College of, at Potsdam*	NY
New York, State University of, at Albany†*	NY
New York, State University of, at Binghamton†*	NY
New York, State University of, at Buffalo†*	NY
Niagara University†*	NY
North Carolina, University of, at Chapel Hill†*	NC
North Carolina, University of, at Greensboro†*	NC
North Carolina, University of, at Wilmington†*	NC
North Carolina State University†*	NC
North Central College†*	IL
North Dakota, University of†*	ND
North Dakota State University, at Fargo†	ND
Northeast Louisiana University†*	LA
Northern Colorado, University of†*	CO
Northern Illinois University†*	IL
Northern Iowa, University of†*	IA
Northern Michigan University*	MI
North Georgia College†*	GA
Northland College†*	WI
Northwestern University†*	IL
Norwich University†*	VT
Notre Dame, University of†*	IN
Notre Dame College*	MD
Oakland University†*	MI
Oberlin College†*	OH
Occidental College†*	CA
Ohio Northern University†*	OH
Ohio State University†*	OH

Ohio University*	OH
Ohio Wesleyan University†*	OH
Oklahoma, University of†*	OK
Old Dominion University†*	VA
Oregon, University of†*	OR
Oregon State University*	OR
Ouachita Baptist College†	AR
Ozarks, School of the*	MO
Pacific, University of the†*	CA
Pacific Lutheran University†*	WA
Pacific University†*	OR
Palomar College†*	CA
Pennsylvania, University of†*	PA
Pennsylvania State University, at University Park†*	PA
Pepperdine University†	CA
Pfeiffer College*	NC
Pittsburgh, University of†*	PA
Portland State University†*	OR
Princeton University†*	NJ
Principia College†*	IL
Puerto Rico Agricultural and Mechanial University af03†af03*	PR
Purdue University, at West Lafayette†*	IL
Redlands, University of†*	CA
Regis College†*	CO
Rensselaer Polytechnic Institute†	NY
Rice University†*	TX
Rider College†	NJ
Ripon College†*	WI
Riverside City College†*	CA
Roanoke College*	VA
Rochester, University of†*	NY
Rutgers, State University of, at New Brunswick†*	NJ
St. Bonaventure University†*	NY
St. Cloud State University†*	MN
St. Francis College†*	NY
St. Johns University†	MN
St. Lawrence University†*	NY
St. Louis Community College†*	MO
St. Louis University†*	MO
St. Olaf College†*	MN
St. Peter's College†*	NJ
St. Thomas, College of†*	MN
Salisbury State College†*	MD
San Diego, University of*	CA
San Diego State University†*	CA
San Francisco, City College of†*	CA
San Francisco State University†*	CA
San Jose State University†*	CA
Sequoias, College of the†*	CA
Shepherd College†*	WV
Skidmore College*	NY
Slippery Rock State College†*	PA
Smith College*	MA
South, University of the†*	TN
South Alabama, University of†*	AL
South Carolina State College†	SC
South Dakota, University of, at Vermillion†*	SD
Southeast Missouri State†*	MO
Southern Arkansas University†*	AR
Southern California, University of†	CA
Southern Connecticut State College†*	CT
Southern Illinois University†*	IL
Southern Methodist University†*	TX
Southern Oregon State College†*	OR
South Florida, The University of†*	FL
Southwest State University*	MN
Southwest Texas State University*	TX
Stanford University†*	CA
Susquehanna University†*	PA
Syracuse University†*	NY
Tampa, University of†*	FL
Temple University†*	PA
Tennessee, University of†*	TN
Tennessee State University†	TN
Texas, The University of†*	TX
Texas Christian University†*	TX
Texas Tech University†*	TX
Texas Woman's University*	TX
Toledo, University of†	OH
Towson State University†*	MD
Trenton State College*	NJ
Trinity College†	CT
Tufts University†	MA
Tulane University†*	LA
Tulsa, University of*	OK
Union College†*	KY
Ursinus College†*	PA
Utah, University of†*	UT
Utica College of Syracuse University†*	NY
Valparaiso University†*	IN
Vanderbilt University†*	TN
Ventura College†*	CA
Villanova University†*	PA
Virginia, University of†*	VA
Virginia Commonwealth University†*	VA
Virginia Polytechnic Institute†*	VA
Wabash College†	IN
Walsh College†	OH
Washington, University of†*	WA
Washington and Lee University†	VA
Washington State University†*	WA
Washington University†*	MO
Wayne State University†	MI
West Chester State College†*	PA
Western Carolina University†*	NC
Western Illinois University†*	IL
Western Kentucky University†	KY
Western Maryland College†	MD

Western Michigan University†*	MI
Western State College of Colorado†*	CO
West Virginia University†*	WV
Wheaton College†*	IL
Whitworth College†*	WA
Wilkes College†*	PA
Willamette University†*	OR
William and Mary, College of†*	VA
William Paterson College†*	NJ
Williams College†*	MA
Wisconsin, University of, at Eau Claire†*	WI
Wisconsin, University of, at Green Bay*	WI
Wisconsin, University of, at La Crosse†*	WI
Wisconsin, University of, at Milwaukee†*	WI
Wisconsin, University of, at Oshkosh†*	WI
Wisconsin, University of, at Platteville†	WI
Wisconsin, University of, at River Falls†*	WI
Wisconsin, University of, at Stevens Point†*	WI
Wisconsin, University of, at Whitewater†*	WI
Wright State University†*	OH
Wyoming, University of†*	WY
Xavier University†*	OH
Yale University†*	CT
Youngstown State University†*	OH

SYNCHRONIZED SWIMMING

Arizona, University of*	AZ
Converse College*	SC
Michigan, University of*	MI
New York, State University College of, at Genesco*	NY
Ohio State University*	OH

TENNIS

Abilene Christian University†*	TX
Adams State College of Colorado†	CO
Adrian College†*	MI
Akron, University of*	OH
Alabama, University of, at Birmingham†*	AL
Alabama, University of, at Huntsville*	AL
Alabama, University of, at University†*	AL
Alabama Agricultural and Mechanical University†*	AL
Alabama Christian Junior College†*	AL
Alabama State University†*	AL
Albany State College†*	GA
Albion College†*	MI
Albright College†*	PA
Alcorn State University†*	MS
Alfred University†*	NY
Allegheny College†*	PA
Allen County Community Junior College†*	KS
Allentown College of St. Francis De Sales†*	PA
Alma College†*	MI
Alvin Junior College†*	TX
American International College†	MA
American University, The†*	DC
Amherst College†*	MA
Anderson College†*	IL
Anderson Junior College†*	SC
Angelina College†*	TX
Angelo State University†*	TX
Anne Arundel Community College†*	MD
Appalachian State University†*	NC
Aquinas College†*	MI
Arizona, University of†*	AZ
Arizona State University†*	AZ
Arizona Western College†*	AZ
Arkansas, University of†*	AR
Arkansas, University of, at Little Rock†*	AR
Arkansas, University of, at Monticello†*	AR
Arkansas, University of, at Pine Bluff†	AR
Arkansas State University†*	AR
Arkansas Tech University†*	AR
Armstrong State College†*	GA
Asbury College*	KY
Asheville-Buncombe Technical Institute†*	NC
Ashland College*	OH
Assumption College†*	MA
Atlantic Christian College†*	NC
Auburn University, at Auburn†*	AL
Auburn University, at Montgomery†	AL
Augusta College†*	GA
Augustana College†*	IL
Augustana College†*	SD
Aurora College†*	IL

Averett College†*	VA	Bucknell University†*	PA
Azusa Pacific College†	CA	Butler County Community Junior	
Babson College*	MA	College†*	KS
Baker University†*	KS	Butler University†*	IN
Ball State University†*	IN	California, University of, at	
Baltimore, Community College		Davis†*	CA
of†*	MD	California, University of, at	
Baltimore, University of†	MD	Irvine†*	CA
Baptist Bible College†*	PA	California, University of, at Los	
Baptist College at Charleston†*	SC	Angeles†*	CA
Barber-Scotia College†*	NC	California, University of, at	
Barnard College*	NY	Riverside†*	CA
Barton County Community		California, University of, at San	
College†*	KS	Diego†*	CA
Bates College†*	ME	California, University of, at	
Baylor University†*	TX	Santa Barbara†*	CA
Beaver College†*	PA	California Institute of	
Belhaven College†	MS	Technology†	CA
Bellarmine College†	KY	California Polytechnic State	
Belmont College†*	TN	University†*	CA
Beloit College†*	WI	California State College, at	
Bemidji State University†*	MN	Bakersfield†*	CA
Benedictine College†*	KS	California State College, at	
Bentley College†*	MA	Sonoma†*	CA
Berea College†*	KY	California State College, at	
Berry College†*	GA	Stanislaus†*	CA
Bethany College†*	KS	California State University, at	
Bethany Lutheran College†*	MN	Chico*	CA
Bethel College†*	MN	California State University, at	
Bethune-Cookman College†	FL	Fullerton†*	CA
Biola College†*	CA	California State University, at	
Biscayne College†*	FL	Haywood†*	CA
Bismarck Junior College†*	ND	California State University, at	
Blackburn College†*	IL	Long Beach†*	CA
Blinn College†*	TX	Calvary Bible College†*	MO
Bluffton College†*	OH	Calvin College†*	MI
Boise State University†*	ID	Cameron University*	OK
Boston College†*	MA	Campbell College†*	NC
Boston State College*	MA	Campbellsville College†*	KY
Boston University†*	MA	Canisius College†*	NY
Bowdoin College†	ME	Cape Cod Community College†*	MA
Bowie State College†*	MD	Carlow College*	PA
Bowling Green State		Carl Sandburg College†	IL
University†*	OH	Carroll College†*	WI
Bradley University†*	IL	Carson-Newman College†*	TN
Brandeis University†*	MA	Carthage College†*	WI
Brandywine College†*	DE	Casper College†*	WY
Brevard College†*	NC	Castleton State College†*	VT
Brevard Community College†*	FL	Catawaba College†*	NC
Briar Cliff College†	IA	Centenary College†*	LA
Bridgewater College†*	VA	Centenary College*	NJ
Bridgewater State College†*	MA	Central Arkansas, University	
Brigham Young University†*	HI	of†*	AR
Brigham Young University†*	UT	Centralia College†*	WA
Bristol College†	TN	Central Junior Colege†*	KS
Brooklyn College of the City		Central Michigan University†*	MI
University of New York†*	NY	Central Missouri State	
Brown University†*	RI	University†*	MO
Bryan College†*	TN	Central State University†*	OK
Bryant College†*	RI	Centre College†*	KY

Chadron State College†*	NE
Chaminade University†*	HI
Charleston, College of†*	SC
Charleston, University of†*	WV
Chatham College*	PA
Chattahoochee Valley Community College†*	AL
Chicago, The University of†*	IL
Chicago, State University†	IL
Chowan College†*	NC
Christopher Newport College†*	VA
Cincinnati, University of†*	OH
Citadel, The†	SC
Citrus College†*	CA
Clackamas Community College†*	OR
Claremore College†*	OK
Clarion State College*	PA
Clark College†*	GA
Clark University†*	MA
Clemson University†*	SC
Cleveland State University†*	OH
Coastal Carolina College†*	SC
Coastal Carolina Community College†*	NC
Coe College†*	IA
Coffeyville Community College†*	KS
Colby College†*	ME
Colgate University†*	NY
Colorado, University of†*	CO
Colorado College†*	CO
Colorado School of Mines†	CO
Colorado State University†*	CO
Columbia Basin College†*	WA
Columbia Christian College†*	OR
Columbia College*	SC
Columbia University†	NY
Columbus College†*	GA
Compton Community College†*	CA
Concord College†*	WV
Concordia College†*	IL
Concordia College†*	MN
Concordia College†*	NE
Concordia College†*	OR
Concordia College†*	TX
Connecticut, University of†*	CT
Connecticut College†*	CT
Connors State College†*	OK
Contra Costa College†	CA
Converse College*	SC
Cooke County Junior College†*	TX
Copiah-Lincoln Junior College†*	MS
Cornell University†*	NY
Cosumnes River College†*	CA
Cowley County Community College†	KS
Creighton University†*	NE
Culver-Stockton College*	MO
Cumberland College†	KY
Cuyahoga Community College†*	OH
C. W. Post College†*	NY
Cypress College†*	CA
Dakota Wesleyan University†	SD
Dartmouth College†*	NH
David Lipscomb College†*	TN
Davidson College†*	NC
Daytona Beach Community College†*	FL
De Kalb Community College (Central)†*	GA
Delaware, University of†*	DE
Delta State College†*	MS
Denver, University of†*	CO
DePauw University†*	IN
Desert, College of the†*	CA
Detroit, University of†	MI
Dickinson State College†*	ND
District of Columbia, University of†*	DC
Doane College†*	NE
Drew University†*	NJ
Drury College†*	MO
Dubuque, University of†	IA
Duke University†*	NC
Dundalk Community College†*	MD
Duquesne University†*	PA
D'Youville College†*	NY
East Carolina University†*	NC
East Central Junior College†*	MS
East Central University†*	OK
Eastern College†*	PA
Eastern Illinois University†*	IL
Eastern Kentucky University†*	KY
Eastern Michigan University†*	MI
Eastern Montana College†*	MT
Eastern Nazarene College†*	MA
Eastern Oklahoma State College†*	OK
Eastern Utah, College of†	UT
Eastern Wyoming College†*	WY
East Stroudsburg State College†*	PA
East Tennessee State University†*	TN
East Texas State University†*	TX
Eckerd College†*	FL
Edinboro State College†*	PA
Eisenhower College†*	NY
El Camino College†*	CA
Elizabethtown College†*	PA
Elmhurst College†*	IL
Elmira College†*	NY
Elon College†*	NC
Emory and Henry College†*	VA
Emory University†*	GA
Emporia State University†*	KS
Erskine College†*	SC
Essex Community College†*	MD
Evansville, University of†*	IN
Everett Community College†*	WA

Fairleigh Dickinson University†*	NJ
Fairmont State College†*	WV
Fergus Falls Community College†*	MN
Ferris State College†*	MI
Ferrum College†*	WA
Findlay College†*	OH
Fitchburg State College†*	MA
Flagler College†*	FL
Florida, University of†*	FL
Florida A. and M. University†*	FL
Florida Atlantic University†*	FL
Florida International University†*	FL
Florida Junior College†*	FL
Florida Southern College†*	FL
Florida State University†*	FL
Florida Technological University†*	FL
Fontbonne College*	MO
Fordham University†*	NY
Fort Hayes State†*	KS
Fort Steilacoom Community College†*	WA
Fort Valley State College†	GA
Fort Wayne Bible College†	IN
Framingham State College†*	MA
Francis Marion College†*	SC
Franklin Pierce College†	NH
Freed-Hardeman College†*	TN
Fresno State University†*	CA
Friends University†*	KS
Frostburg State College†*	MD
Furman University†*	SC
Gadsden State Junior College†	AL
Gainesville Junior College†*	GA
Gannon College†*	PA
Gardner-Webb College†*	NC
Gateway Technical Institute†*	WI
Georgetown Univerisity†*	DC
George Washington University†*	DC
Georgia College†	GA
Georgia Institute of Technology†	GA
Georgia Southern College†*	GA
Georgia Southwestern College†*	GA
Georgia State University†*	GA
Gettysburg College†*	PA
Glassboro State College†*	NJ
Gonzaga University†*	WA
Gordon College†*	MA
Grace College†	IN
Graceland College†*	IA
Grand Canyon College†*	AZ
Grand Rapids Baptist†	MI
Grand Rapids Junior College†*	MI
Grand Valley State College†*	MI
Green River Community College†*	WA
Greensboro College†*	NC
Greensville College†*	IL
Grinnell College†*	IA
Grove City College†*	PA
Guilford College†*	NC
Gustavus Adolphus College†*	MN
Hamilton College†	NY
Hamline University†*	MN
Hampton Institute†	VA
Hanover College†*	IN
Harding University†	AR
Hardin-Simmons University†*	TX
Hartford, University of†*	CT
Harvard University†*	MA
Hastings College†*	NE
Hawaii, University of, at Hilo†*	HI
Hawaii, University of, at Honolulu†*	HI
Heidelberg College†*	OH
Henderson State University†*	OR
Hendrix College†*	AR
Herbert H. Lehman College†*	NY
Highland Park Community College†	MI
High Point College†*	NC
Hillsborough Community College*	FL
Hillsdale College†*	MI
Hiram College†*	OH
Holy Cross College†*	MA
Hood College*	MD
Hope College†*	MI
Houghton College†*	NY
Houston, University of†*	TX
Houston Baptist University†*	TX
Humboldt State University*	CA
Hunter College†*	NY
Huntington College†*	IN
Hutchinson Community Junior College†*	KS
Idaho, College of†*	ID
Idaho, University of†*	ID
Idaho State University†*	ID
Illinois, University of, at Champaign†*	IL
Illinois, University of, at Chicago Circle†*	IL
Illinois Benedictine College†	IL
Illinois College†*	IL
Illinois State University†*	IL
Illinois Valley Community College†*	IL
Illinois Wesleyan University†*	IL
Indiana Central University†*	IN
Indiana State University†*	IN
Indiana University, at Bloomington†*	IN
Indiana University of Pennsylvania†*	PA
Indiana University-Purdue University, at Fort Wayne†*	IN
Indiana University-Purdue	

University, at Indianapolis†	IN
Indian River Community College†*	FL
Inver Hills College†*	MN
Iowa, University of†*	IA
Iowa State University†*	IA
Iowa Wesleyan College†*	IA
Ithaca College†*	NY
Jacksonville State University†*	AL
James Madison University†*	VA
Jamestown College†*	ND
Jefferson Davis Junior College†*	MS
Jefferson State Junior College†*	AL
Jersey City State College†*	NJ
John Carroll University†*	OH
John C. Calhoun Community College†*	AL
Johnson C. Smith University†	NC
Jones County Junior College†*	MS
Josephenum College†	OH
Judson College*	AL
Juniata College†*	PA
Kalamazoo Valley Community College†*	MI
Kansas, University of†*	KS
Kansas State University†*	KS
Kean College of New Jersey†*	NJ
Kearney State College†*	NE
Kent State University†*	OH
Kentucky, University of†*	KY
Kentucky State University†	KY
Kentucky Wesleyan College†*	KY
Kenyon College†*	OH
King's College, The†*	NY
Kutztown State College†*	PA
Lackawanna Junior College†*	PA
Lafayette College†*	PA
Lake Erie College*	OH
Lake Region Junior College†*	ND
Lake Superior State College†*	MI
Lamar University†*	TX
Lambuth College†*	TN
Lancaster Bible College†*	PA
Lander College†*	SC
Lane Community College†*	OR
Laredo Junior College†*	TX
La Salle College†*	PA
La Verne College†*	CA
Lawrence University†*	WI
Lebanon Valley College†	PA
Lees-McRae College†*	NC
Lehigh University†	PA
Le Moyne College†*	NY
Lenoir-Rhyne College†*	NC
Lewis and Clark Community College†*	IL
Lewis University†*	IL
Lewis-Clark State College†*	ID
Lincoln Land Community College†*	IT
Lincoln Trail College†	IL
Lindenwood College, The†*	MO
Linfield College†*	OR
Livingstone College†*	NC
Livingston University†	AL
Lock Haven State College†*	PA
Long Island University†*	NY
Longwood College†*	VA
Loras College†*	IA
Los Angeles City College†	CA
Los Angeles Pierce Junior College†*	CA
Los Angeles Southwest College†	CA
Louisiana College†*	LA
Louisiana State University†	LA
Louisiana Tech University†*	LA
Louisville, University of†*	KY
Lowell, University of†*	MA
Lower Columbia College*	WA
Loyola Marymount University†*	CA
Lubbock Christian College†*	TX
Luther College†*	IA
Lycoming College†*	PA
Lynchburg College†*	VA
Lyndon State College†	VT
Macalester College†*	MN
McMurray College†*	TX
McNeese State University†*	LA
McPherson College†*	KS
Maine, University of, at Presque Isle*	ME
Malone College†*	OH
Manchester College†	IN
Manhattan College†	NY
Mankato State University†*	MN
Marian College†	IN
Marietta College†*	OH
Marin, College of†*	CA
Marion Military Institute†	AL
Marist College†*	NY
Marquette University†*	WI
Marshalltown Community College†*	IA
Marshall University†*	WV
Mars Hill College†*	NC
Martin College†*	TN
Mary Hardin-Baylor College†*	TX
Maryland, University of, at Catonsville†*	MD
Maryland, University of, at College Park†*	MD
Maryville College†*	TN
Mary Washington College†*	VA
Marywood College*	PA
Massachusetts, University of†*	MA
Massachusetts Institute of Technology†	MA
Massasoit Community College†*	MA
Mattatuck Community College†*	CT
Memphis State University†*	TN

Menlo College†*	CA
Mercer University†*	GA
Mercy College*	NY
Meredith College*	NC
Merrimack College†*	MA
Metropolitan State College†*	CO
Miami, University of†*	FL
Miami Christian College†	FL
Miami-Dade Community College, New World Center†*	FL
Miami-Dade Community College, South Campus†*	FL
Miami University†*	OH
Miami University, Middletown Campus†*	OH
Michigan, University of†*	MI
Michigan Christian Junior College†*	MI
Michigan State University†*	MI
Middlebury College†*	VT
Middle Tennessee State University†*	TN
Mid-State Technical Institute†*	WI
Midwestern State University†*	TX
Milligan College†*	TN
Millikan University†	IL
Mills College*	CA
Millsaps College†*	MS
Milwaukee Area Technical College†*	WI
Mineral Area Junior College†*	MO
Minnesota, University of, at Minneapolis†*	MN
Minnesota, University of, at Morris†*	MN
Minnesota Bible College†	MN
Mira Costa College†*	CA
Mississippi College†*	MS
Mississippi State University†*	MS
Missouri, University of†*	MO
Missouri, University of, at Rolla†*	MO
Missouri, University of, at St. Louis†*	MO
Missouri Southern State College†*	MO
Missouri Valley College†	MO
Missouri Western College†*	MO
Mitchell College†*	CT
Mitchell Community College†*	NC
Monmouth College†*	IL
Montana, University of†*	MT
Montana State University†*	MT
Montclair State University†*	NJ
Montevallo, University of†*	AL
Moorhead State University†*	MN
Moorpark College†	AR
Morehead State University†*	KY
Morehouse College†	GA
Mount Ida Junior College*	MA
Mount Olive Junior College†	NC
Mount St. Joseph, College of*	OH
Mount St. Mary's College†*	MD
Mount San Jacinto College†*	CA
Mount Vernon College*	DC
Muhlenberg College†*	PA
Murray State University†*	KY
Muskegon Community College*	MI
Napa Community College†*	CA
Nazareth College†*	NY
Nebraska, University of†*	NE
Nebraska Wesleyan University†*	NE
Newberry College†*	SC
New Hampshire College†*	NH
New Hampshire Technological Institute†*	NH
New Haven, University of†*	CT
New Mexico Highlands University*	NM
New Mexico Military Institute†	NM
New Orleans, University of†*	LA
New York, State University College of, at Fredonia†*	NY
New York, State University College of, at New Paltz†*	NY
New York, State University College of, at Oneonta†*	NY
New York, State University College of, at Oswego†	NY
New York, State University College of, at Plattsburgh†*	NY
New York, State University College of, at Potsdam†*	NY
New York, State University College of, at Purchase†*	NY
New York, State University of, at Albany†*	NY
New York, State University of, at Binghamton†*	NY
New York, State University of, at Buffalo*	NY
New York Institute of Technology†	NY
Niagara University†*	NY
Nicholls State University†*	LA
Nichols College†	MA
North Adams State College†*	MA
North Alabama, University of†*	AL
North Carolina, University of, at Asheville†	NC
North Carolina, University of, at Chapel Hill†*	NC
North Carolina, University of, at Charlotte†*	NC
North Carolina, University of, at Greensboro†*	NC
North Carolina, University of, at Wilmington†*	NC
North Carolina Agricultural and	

Technical State University†*	NC
North Carolina State University†*	NC
North Carolina Wesleyan College†	NC
North Central College†*	IL
North Dakota, University of†*	ND
North Dakota State University, at Fargo†*	ND
Northeastern Illinois University†*	IL
Northeastern Oklahoma A and M College†*	OK
Northeast Louisiana University†*	LA
Northern Arizona University†*	AZ
Northern Colorado, University of†*	CO
Northern Illinois University†*	IL
Northern Iowa, University of†*	IA
Northern Kentucky University†*	KY
Northern Michigan University†	MI
Northern State College†*	SD
North Georgia College†*	GA
North Greenville College†	SC
North Harris County College†*	TX
North Idaho College†*	ID
Northland Community College†*	MN
North Texas State University†*	TX
Northwest College†*	WA
Northwestern College†	MN
Northwestern College†	WI
Northwestern State University†	LA
Northwestern University†*	IL
Northwest Missouri State University*	MO
Northwest Nazarene College†*	ID
Notre Dame, University of†*	IN
Notre Dame College*	MD
Oakland City College†*	IN
Oakland University†*	MI
Oakton Community College†*	IL
Oberlin College†*	OH
Occidental College†*	CA
Ohio Northern University†*	OH
Ohio State University†*	OH
Ohio University*	OH
Ohio Valley College†*	WV
Ohio Wesleyan University†*	OH
Oklahoma, University of†*	OK
Oklahoma, University of Science and Arts†*	OK
Oklahoma Baptist University†	OK
Oklahoma City University†*	OK
Oklahoma State University†*	OK
Old Dominion University†*	VA
Olivet College†*	MI
Olivet Nazarene College†*	IL
Olney Central College†*	IL
Oral Roberts University†*	OK
Oregon, University of†*	OR
Oregon State University*	OR
Oscar Rose Junior College†*	OK
Ottawa University†	KS
Otterbein College†*	OH
Ouachita Baptist College†	AR
Oxford College of Emory University†*	GA
Oxnard College†	CA
Ozarks, College of the†	AR
Pace University†*	NY
Pacific, University of the†*	CA
Pacific Lutheran University†*	WA
Pacific University†*	OR
Paducah Community College†*	KY
Palm Beach Junior College†*	FL
Palomar College†*	CA
Pan American University†	TX
Paris Junior College†*	TX
Park College*	MO
Peace College*	NC
Pembroke State University†*	NC
Pennsylvania, University of†*	PA
Pennsylvania State University, at Altoona†*	PA
Pennsylvania State University, at University Park†*	PA
Pennsylvania State University (Behrend College)†*	PA
Pepperdine University†*	CA
Pfeiffer College†*	NC
Philadelphia Community College†*	PA
Phillips University†	OK
Pikeville College†*	KY
Pima Community College†*	AZ
Pittsburgh, University of†*	PA
Plymouth State College†*	NH
Point Loma College†*	CA
Porterville College†	CA
Portland, University of†*	OR
Portland State University*	OR
Pratt Institute†*	NY
Presbyterian College†*	SC
Princeton University†*	NJ
Principia College†*	IL
Providence College†*	RI
Puerto Rico Agricultural and Mechanical University†*	PR
Purdue University, at West Lafayette†*	IL
Quincy College†*	IL
Quinnipiac College†*	CT
Radford College†*	VA
Randolph-Macon College†*	VA
Redlands, University of†*	CA
Redwoods, College of the†*	CA
Regis College†*	CO
Rensselaer Polytechnic Institute†*	NY

Rice University†*	TX
Rider College†	NJ
Ripon College†*	WI
Riverside City College†*	CA
Roanoke College†*	VA
Robert Morris College†*	PA
Roberts Wesleyan College†	NY
Rochester, University of†*	NY
Rockhurst College†*	MO
Rollins College†*	FL
Rust College†*	MS
Rutgers, State University of, at Camden†*	NJ
Rutgers, State University of, at Newark†*	NJ
Rutgers, State University of, at New Brunswick*	NJ
Saginaw Valley College*	MI
St. Augustine's College†*	NC
St. Bonaventure University†*	NY
St. Clair County Community College†	MI
St. Cloud State University†*	MN
St. Edward's University†*	TX
St. Francis, College of†*	IL
St. Francis College†	NY
St. Francis College of Pennsylvania†*	PA
St. John Fisher College†*	NY
St. Johns University*	MN
St. Joseph College†*	IN
St. Lawrence University†*	NY
St. Leo College†*	FL
St. Louis College of Pharmacy†*	MO
St. Louis Community College†*	MO
St. Louis University†*	MO
St. Mary of the Plains College†*	KS
St. Mary's College†*	MN
St. Mary's College of California†*	CA
St. Mary's University of Texas†*	TX
St. Norbert College†*	WI
St. Olaf College†*	MN
St. Paul's College†*	VA
St. Peter's College†*	NJ
St. Scholastica, College of†*	MN
St. Teresa, College of*	MN
St. Thomas, College of†*	MN
St. Vincent College†	PA
Salisbury State College†*	MD
Sam Houston State University†*	TX
San Diego, University of†*	CA
San Diego State University†*	CA
San Francisco, City College of†*	CA
San Francisco, University of†*	CA
San Francisco State University*	CA
Sangamon State University†*	IL
San Jose State University†*	CA
San Mateo, College of*	CA
Santa Ana College†*	CA
Santa Barbara City Junior College†*	CA
Santa Clara, University of†*	CA
Schoolcraft College†*	MI
Schreiner College†*	TX
Scranton, University of†*	PA
Seminole Community College†*	FL
Sequoias, College of the†*	CA
Shawnee State College†*	OH
Shelby State Community College†*	TN
Shepherd College†*	WV
Sheridan College†*	WY
Shorter College†*	GA
Siena College†*	NY
Siena Heights College†*	MI
Simmons College*	MA
Siskiyous, College of the†*	CA
Skagit Valley College†	WA
Skidmore College†*	NY
Skyline College†	CA
Slippery Rock State College†*	PA
Smith College*	MA
South, University of the†*	TN
South Alabama, University of†*	AL
Southampton College†	NY
South Carolina, University of*	SC
South Carolina State College†*	SC
South Dakota, University of, at Springfield†*	SD
South Dakota, University of, at Vermillion†*	SD
South Dakota School of Mines and Technology†	SD
Southeast Community College†*	NE
Southeastern Community College†*	IA
Southeastern Louisiana University†*	LA
Southeastern Oklahoma State University†*	OK
Southeastern University†	DC
Southeast Missouri State†*	MO
Southern Arkansas University†*	AR
Southern California, University of†*	CA
Southern Colorado, University of†*	CO
Southern Connecticut State College†*	CT
Southern Illinois University†*	IL
Southern Maine, University of†*	ME
Southern Methodist University†*	TX
Southern Oregon State College†*	OR
Southern University and Agricultural and Mechanical College†	LA
South Florida, The University of†*	FL

Southwest Baptist College†*	MO
Southwestern at Memphis†*	TN
Southwest College†*	KS
Southwestern Louisiana, University of†*	LA
Southwestern University†*	TX
Southwest State University*	MN
Southwest Texas State University†*	TX
Spring Arbor College†	MI
Spring Garden College†	PA
Spring Hill College†*	AL
Stanford University†*	CA
State Fair Community College†*	MO
Staten Island, College of†*	NY
Stephen F. Austin State University†*	TX
Sterling College†*	KS
Stetson University†*	FL
Sul Ross State University†*	TX
Surry Community College†*	NC
Susquehanna University†*	PA
Swarthmore College†*	PA
Syracuse University*	NY
Tabor College†*	KS
Tacoma Community College*	WA
Tampa, University of†*	FL
Taylor University†*	IN
Temple University†*	PA
Tennessee, University of†*	TN
Tennessee, University of, at Martin†*	TN
Tennessee State University†	TN
Tennessee Technological University†*	TN
Tennessee Wesleyan College†*	TN
Texas, The University of†*	TX
Texas, The University of, at Arlington†*	TX
Texas, The University of, The Permian Basin*	TX
Texas A and I University†*	TX
Texas Christian University†*	TX
Texas Lutheran College†*	TX
Texas Southern University†	TX
Texas Tech University†*	TX
Texas Wesleyan College†*	TX
Texas Woman's University*	TX
Thiel College†*	PA
Thomas College†*	ME
Thomas More College†	KY
Three Rivers Community College*	MO
Toledo, University of†*	OH
Tougaloo College†*	MS
Towson State University†*	MD
Treasure Valley Community College†*	OR
Trenton State College†*	NJ
Trinity College†	CT
Trinity University†*	TX
Tri-State University†	IN
Triton College†*	IL
Truett-McConnell College†*	GA
Tufts University†	MA
Tulane University†*	LA
Tulsa, University of†*	OK
Tunxis Community College†*	CT
Tuskegee Institute†*	AL
Umpqua Community College†*	OR
Union College†*	KY
Upper Iowa University†*	IA
Upsala College†*	NJ
Ursinus College†*	PA
Utah, University of†*	UT
Utah State University†	UT
Valparaiso University†*	IN
Vanderbilt University†*	TN
Ventura College†	CA
Villanova University†*	PA
Virginia, University of†*	VA
Virginia Commonwealth University†*	VA
Virginia Polytechnic Institute†*	VA
Virginia Union University†*	VA
Wabash College†	IN
Wagner College†	NY
Wake Forest University†*	NC
Walsh College†	OH
Warner Pacific College†*	OR
Washburn University†*	KS
Washington, University of†*	WA
Washington and Lee University†	VA
Washington State University†*	WA
Washington University†*	MO
Wayland Baptist College†*	TX
Waynesburg College†	PA
Wayne State University†*	MI
Webber College†*	FL
Weber State College†*	UT
Wenatchee Valley College†*	WA
Wesleyan College†*	CT
West Chester State College†*	PA
Western Carolina University†*	NC
Western Illinois University†*	IL
Western Kentucky University†*	KY
Western Maryland College†*	MD
Western Michigan University†*	MI
Western New England College†*	MA
Western Piedmont Community College†	NC
Western State College of Colorado*	CO
Western Washington University†*	WA
Westfield State College†*	MA
West Georgia College†*	GA
West Hills College†*	CA
West Liberty State College†*	WV
West Los Angeles College*	CA

Westminster College†	MO
Westmount College†*	CA
Westmoreland Community College†*	PA
West Texas State University†*	TX
West Virginia State College†*	WV
West Virginia University†*	WV
West Virginia Wesleyan College†*	WV
Wharton County Junior College†*	TX
Wheaton College†*	IL
Wheaton College*	MA
Wheeling College†*	WV
Whitworth College†*	WA
Wichita State University†	KS
Wilberforce University†*	OH
Wilkes College†*	PA
Willamette University†*	OR
William and Mary, College of†*	VA
William Paterson College*	NJ
William Penn College†*	IA
Williams College†*	MA
Williamsport Area Community College†*	PA
Wilmington College†*	OH
Wilson College*	PA
Winona State College†*	MN
Winston-Salem State University†	NC
Winthrop College†*	SC
Wisconsin, University of, at Eau Claire†*	WI
Wisconsin, University of, at Green Bay†*	WI
Wisconsin, University of, at La Crosse†*	WI
Wisconsin, University of, at Marathon County†*	WI
Wisconsin, University of, at Milwaukee†*	WI
Wisconsin, University of, at Oshkosh†*	WI
Wisconsin, University of, at Platteville†	WI
Wisconsin, University of, at River Falls†*	WI
Wisconsin, University of, at Stevens Point†*	WI
Wisconsin, University of, at Waukesha†*	WI
Wisconsin, University of, at Whitewater†*	WI
Wofford College†	SC
Worcester State College†*	MA
Wright State University†*	OH
Xavier University†*	OH
Yakima Valley College†*	WA
Yale University†*	CT
Yankton College†*	SD
York College†*	NE
Young Harris College†	GA
Youngstown State University†	OH
Yuba College†*	CA

TRACK & FIELD

Abilene Christian University†*	TX
Adams State College of Colorado†*	CO
Adrian College†*	MI
Akron, University of†	OH
Alabama, University of, at University†*	AL
Alabama Agricultural and Mechanical University†*	AL
Alabama State University†*	AL
Albany State College†*	GA
Albion College†*	MI
Albright College†*	PA
Alcorn State University†*	MS
Alfred University†*	NY
Allegheny College†*	PA
Allen County Community Junior College†*	KS
Alma College†*	MI
Amherst College†*	MA
Anderson College†*	IL
Angelo State University†*	TX
Anne Arundel Community College†*	MD
Appalachian State University†*	NC
Aquinas College†*	MI
Arizona, University of†*	AZ
Arizona State University†*	AZ
Arkansas, University of†*	AR
Arkansas, University of, at Monticello†	AR
Arkansas, University of, at Pine Bluff†	AR
Arkansas State University†	AR
Arkansas Tech University†	AR
Asbury College†*	KY
Ashland College†*	OH
Assumption College†*	MA
Atlantic Christian College†	NC
Auburn University, at Auburn†*	AL
Augustana College†*	IL
Augustana College†*	SD
Averett College†	VA
Azusa Pacific College†*	CA
Baker University†*	KS
Ball State University†*	IN
Baltimore, Community College of†*	MD
Baptist Bible College†*	PA
Baptist College at Charleston†*	SC

Barber-Scotia College†*	NC
Barnard College*	NY
Barton County Community College†*	KS
Bates College†*	ME
Baylor University†*	TX
Beaver College†*	PA
Bellarmine College†	KY
Beloit College†*	WI
Bemidji State University†*	MN
Benedictine College†*	KS
Bentley College†	MA
Berea Colle†*	KY
Berry College†*	GA
Bethany College†*	KS
Bethel College†*	MN
Bethune-Cookman College†*	FL
Biola College†	CA
Bishop College†*	TX
Bismarck Junior College†*	ND
Blackburn College†*	IL
Blinn College†	TX
Bluffton College†*	OH
Boise State University†*	ID
Boston College†*	MA
Boston University†*	MA
Bowdoin College†	ME
Bowie State College†*	MD
Bowling Green State University†*	OH
Bradley University†*	IL
Brandeis University†*	MA
Brevard College†	NC
Brevard Community College†*	FL
Bridgewater College†	VA
Bridgewater State College†*	MA
Brigham Young University†*	UT
Brooklyn College of the City University of New York†*	NY
Brown University†*	RI
Bryant College†*	RI
Bucknell University†*	PA
Butler County Community Junior College†*	KS
Butler University†	IN
California, University of, at Davis†*	CA
California, University of, at Los Angeles†*	CA
California, University of, at Riverside†*	CA
California, University of, at San Diego†*	CA
California, University of, at Santa Barbara†*	CA
California Institute of Technology†*	CA
California Polytechnic State University†*	CA
California State College, at Bakersfield†*	CA
California State College, at Sonoma†*	CA
California State College, at Stanislaus†*	CA
California State University, at Chico†*	CA
California State University, at Fullerton†*	CA
California State University, at Haywood†*	CA
California State University, at Long Beach†*	CA
Calvin College†*	MI
Campbell College†	NC
Canisius College†	NY
Carroll College†*	WI
Carson-Newman†	TN
Carthage College†*	WI
Catawaba College†	NC
Central Arkansas, University of†	AR
Central Junior College†*	KS
Central Michigan University†*	MI
Central Missouri State University†*	MO
Central State University†*	OK
Centre College†*	KY
Chadron State College†*	NE
Chaminade University†	HI
Chicago, The University of†*	IL
Chicago State University*	IL
Christopher Newport College†	VA
Cincinnati, University of†	OH
Cincinnati Bible College†	OH
Citadel, The†	SC
Citrus College†*	CA
Clackamas Community College†*	OR
Clarion State College†*	PA
Clark College†*	GA
Clark University†*	MA
Clemson University†	SC
Cleveland State University†*	OH
Coahoma Junior College†	MS
Coe College†*	IA
Coffeyville Community College†*	KS
Colby College†*	ME
Colgate University†	NY
Colorado, University of†*	CO
Colorado College†*	CO
Colorado School of Mines†	CO
Colorado State University†*	CO
Columbia University†	NY
Compton Community College†*	CA
Concord College†*	WV
Concordia College†*	IL
Concordia College*	MN
Concordia College†*	NE
Connecticut, University of†*	CT

Contra Costa College†	CA
Copiah-Lincoln Junior College†	MS
Cornell College†*	IA
Cornell University†*	NY
Cosumnes River College†*	CA
Cottey College*	MO
Cumberland College†	KY
Cuyahoga Community College, Metro Campus†*	OH
C. W. Post College†	NY
Cypress College†*	CA
Dakota Wesleyan University†*	SD
Dartmouth College†	NH
David Lipscomb College†	TN
Davidson College†*	NC
De Kalb Community College (Central)†*	GA
Delaware, University of†*	DE
Delaware State College†*	DE
Delaware Valley College†	PA
Delta State College†	MS
DePauw University†	IN
Desert, College of the†*	CA
Dickinson State College†*	ND
District of Columbia, University of†*	DC
Doane College†*	NE
Dubuque, University of†*	IA
Duke University†	NC
East Carolina University†*	NC
East Central University†	OK
Eastern Illinois University†*	IL
Eastern Kentucky University†*	KY
Eastern Michigan University†*	MI
Eastern Montana College†*	MT
Eastern Oklahoma State College†*	OK
Eastern Utah, College of†	UT
Eastern Wyoming College†*	WY
East Stroudsburg State College†*	PA
East Tennessee State University†*	TN
East Texas State University†*	TX
Eckerd College*	FL
Edinboro State College†*	PA
Eisenhower College†*	NY
El Camino College†*	CA
Elizabethtown College†*	PA
Elmhurst College†	IL
Elon College†	NC
Emory and Henry College†*	VA
Emporia State University†*	KS
Essex Community College†*	MD
Evansville, University of†*	IN
Everett Community College†*	WA
Fairleigh Dickinson University†	NJ
Fairmont State College†*	WV
Fergus Falls Community College†	MN
Ferris State College†	MI
Ferrum College†	WA
Findlay College†*	OH
Fitchburg State College†*	MA
Florida, University of†*	FL
Florida A. and M. University†*	FL
Florida Junior College†*	FL
Florida State University†*	FL
Fordham University†*	NY
Fort Hayes State†*	KS
Fort Valley State College†*	GA
Francis Marion College†	SC
Fresno State University†	CA
Friendship Junior College*	SC
Friends University†*	KS
Frostburg State College†*	MD
Gardner-Webb College†	NC
George Fox College†*	OR
Georgetown University†*	DC
Georgia, University of†*	GA
Georgia Institute of Technology†	GA
Georgia Southwestern College†	GA
Gettysburg College†	PA
Glassboro State College†*	NJ
Golden Valley Lutheran College†*	MN
Gordon Junior College†	GA
Grace College†	IN
Graceland College†*	IA
Grand Rapids Baptist College†	MI
Grand Rapids Junior College†	MI
Grand Valley State College†	MI
Green River Community College†*	WA
Greensville College†*	IL
Grinnell College†*	IA
Grove City College†	PA
Gustavus Adolphus College†*	MN
Hagerstown Junior College†	MD
Hamilton College†*	NY
Hamline University†*	MN
Hampton Institute†*	VA
Hanover College†	IN
Harding University†	AR
Harvard University†*	MA
Hastings College†*	NE
Hawaii, University of, at Honolulu*	HI
Heidelberg College†*	OH
Henderson State University†	OR
Hendrix College†	AR
Herbert H. Lehman College†*	NY
High Point College†	NC
Highland Community Junior College†*	KS
Highland Park Community College†*	MI
Hillsadale College†*	MI
Hiram College†*	OH
Holy Cross College†*	MA
Hope College†*	MI

346

Houghton College†*	NY
Houston, University of†*	TX
Houston Baptist University†	TX
Howard Payne University†	TX
Humboldt State University†*	CA
Hunter College†*	NY
Huntington College†*	IN
Hutchinson Community Junior College†*	KS
Idaho, University of†*	ID
Idaho State University†*	ID
Illinois, University of, at Champaign†*	IL
Illinois, University of, at Chicago Circle†*	IL
Illinois Benedictine College†*	IL
Illinois College†*	IL
Illinois State University†*	IL
Illinois Valley Community College†*	IL
Illinois Wesleyan University†*	IL
Indiana Central University†*	IN
Indiana University, at Bloomington†*	IN
Indiana University of Pennsylvania†*	PA
Indiana University-Purdue University, at Fort Wayne*	IN
Iowa, University of†*	IA
Iowa State University†*	IA
Iowa Wesleyan College†*	IA
Ithaca College†*	NY
Jacksonville State University*	AL
James Madison University†*	VA
Jamestown College†*	ND
Jarvis Christian College†*	TX
Jefferson State Junior College†	AL
Jersey City State College†	NJ
John Carroll University†	OH
Johnson C. Smith University†*	NC
Jones County Junior College†*	MS
Juniata College†	PA
Kansas, University of†*	KS
Kansas State University†*	KS
Kansas Wesleyan College†*	KS
Kearney State College†*	NE
Kent State University†*	OH
Kentucky, University of†*	KY
Kentucky State University†	KY
Kenyon College†*	OH
King's College, The†	NY
Kutztown State College†*	PA
Lafayette College†	PA
Lake Region Junior College†*	ND
Lamar University†*	TX
Lane Community College†*	OR
Laredo Junior College†	TX
La Salle College†*	PA
La Verne College†*	CA
Lawrence University†*	WI
Lebanon Valley College†	PA
Lees-McRae College†	NC
Lehigh University†	PA
Lenoir-Rhyne College†	NC
Liberty Baptist College†*	VA
Lincoln Land Community College†	IL
Lincoln University†*	MO
Linfield College†*	OR
Livingstone College†*	NC
Lock Haven State College†*	PA
Long Island University*	NY
Loras College†*	IA
Los Angeles City College†	CA
Los Angeles Pierce Junior College†*	CA
Los Angeles Southwest College†*	CA
Louisiana State University†*	LA
Louisiana Tech University†	LA
Louisville, University of†*	KY
Lowell, University of†*	MA
Luther College†*	IA
Lycoming College†*	PA
Lynchburg College†*	VA
Macalester College†*	MN
McMurray College†*	TX
McNeese State University†	LA
McPherson College†*	KS
Malone College†*	OH
Manchester College†	IN
Manhattan College†	NY
Mankato State University†*	MN
Mansfield State College†	PA
Marian College†*	IN
Marietta College†*	OH
Marin, College of†*	CA
Marist College†*	NY
Marquette University†*	WI
Marshall University†*	WV
Mars Hill College†*	NC
Mary Holmes College†*	MS
Maryland, University of, at Catonsville†*	MD
Maryland, University of, at College Park†*	MD
Maryville College†	TN
Mary Washington College†*	VA
Massachusetts, University of†*	MA
Massachusetts Institute of Technology†	MA
Medgar Evers College†*	NY
Memphis State University†*	TN
Menlo College†*	CA
Mercer University at Atlanta*	GA
Metropolitan State College†	CO
Miami University†*	OH
Michigan, University of†*	MI
Michigan State University†*	MI
Middlebury College†*	VT

Middle Tennessee State University†*	TN	New York Institute of Technology†*	NY
Milligan College†	TN	Niagara University†*	NY
Millikan University†	IL	Nicholls State University†	LA
Milwaukee Area Technical College†*	WI	Nichols College†*	MA
		Norfolk State College†	VA
Minnesota, University of, at Minneapolis†*	MN	North Carolina, University of, at Chapel Hill†*	NC
Minnesota, University of, at Morris†*	MN	North Carolina Agricultural and Technical State University†*	NC
Minnesota, University of, Technical College†*	MN	North Carolina State University†*	NC
Mira Costa College†*	CA	North Carolina Wesleyan College*	NC
Mississippi College†*	MS		
Mississippi State University†	MS	North Central College†*	IL
Missouri, University of†*	MO	North Dakota, University of†*	ND
Missouri, University of, at Rolla†	MO	North Dakota State University, at Bottineau*	ND
Missouri Southern State*	MO		
Missouri Valley College†*	MO	North Dakota State University, at Fargo†*	ND
Monmouth College†	IL		
Monmouth College†	NJ	Northeastern Oklahoma A and M College†*	OK
Montana, University of†*	MT		
Montana State University†*	MT	Northeast Louisiana University†*	LA
Montclair State University†*	NJ		
Moorhead State University†*	MN	Northern Arizona University†*	AZ
Moorpark College†	AR	Northern Colorado, University of†*	CO
Morehead State University†*	KY		
Morehouse College†	GA	Northern Illinois University†*	IL
Morgan State University†*	MD	Northern Iowa, University of†*	IA
Morningside College†	IA	Northern Montana College†*	MT
Mount St. Joseph, College of*	OH	Northern State College†*	SD
Mount St. Mary's College†*	MD	North Georgia College†*	GA
Muhlenberg College†	PA	North Idaho College†*	ID
Murray State University†*	KY	North Texas State University†*	TX
Napa Community College†*	CA	Northwestern College†	MN
Nebraska, University of†*	NE	Northwestern College†	WI
Nebraska, University of, at Omaha†*	NE	Northwestern State University†	LA
		Northwestern University†*	IL
Nebraska Wesleyan University†*	NE	Northwest Missouri State University†*	MO
New Haven, University of†	CT		
New Mexico Junior College†	NM	Northwest Nazarene College†*	ID
New York, State University College of, at Brockport†*	NY	Norwich University†	VT
		Notre Dame, University of†	IN
New York, State University College of, at Fredonia†*	NY	Oakton Community College†	IL
		Oberlin College†*	OH
New York, State University College of, at Genesco†*	NY	Occidental College†*	CA
		Ohio Northern University†*	OH
New York, State University College of, at New Paltz†*	NY	Ohio State University†*	OH
		Ohio University*	OH
New York, State University College of, at Oswego†*	NY	Ohio Wesleyan University†*	OH
		Oklahoma, University of†*	OK
New York, State University College of, at Plattsburgh†	NY	Oklahoma Baptist University†	OK
		Oklahoma State University†*	OK
New York, State University College of, at Potsdam†	NY	Old Dominion University†*	VA
		Olivet College†	MI
New York, State University of, at Albany†*	NY	Olivet Nazarene College†	IL
		Oral Roberts University†	OK
New York, State University of, at Binghamton†*	NY	Oregon, University of†*	OR
		Oregon State University†*	OR
New York, State University of, at Buffalo†*	NY	Ottawa University†*	KS
		Otterbein College†*	OH

Ouachita Baptist College†	AR
Oxnard College†	CA
Ozarks, College of the†	AR
Ozarks, School of the†*	MO
Pacific Lutheran University†*	WA
Pacific University†*	OR
Palomar College†*	CA
Pan American University†	TX
Park College†*	MO
Parkland College†*	IL
Pembroke State University†	NC
Pennsylvania, University of†*	PA
Pennsylvania State University, at University Park†*	PA
Philadelphia Community College†*	PA
Pima Community College†*	AZ
Pittsburg State University†*	KS
Pittsburgh, University of†*	PA
Pittsburgh, University of, at Johnstown†	PA
Point Loma College†*	CA
Porterville College†	CA
Portland, University of†*	OR
Pratt Community Junior College†*	KS
Pratt Institute†*	NY
Presbyterian College†*	SC
Princeton University†	NJ
Principia College†*	IL
Providence College†	RI
Puerto Rico Agricultural and Mechanical University†*	PR
Purdue, University, at West Lafayette†*	IL
Redlands, University of†*	CA
Redwoods, College of the†*	CA
Rensselaer Polytechnic Institute†	NY
Rice University†*	TX
Rider College†	NJ
Rio Grande College†*	OH
Ripon College†*	WI
Riverside City College†*	CA
Roanoke College†*	VA
Roberts Wesleyan College†*	NY
Rochester, University of†*	NY
Rust College†*	MS
Rutgers, State University of, at Camden†	NJ
Rutgers, State University of, at New Brunswick†*	NJ
Saginaw Valley College†*	MI
St. Augustine's College†*	NC
St. Bonaventure University†	NY
St. Cloud State University†*	MN
St. John Fisher College†*	NY
St. Johns University†	MN
St. Joseph College†*	IN
St. Lawrence University†	NY
St. Louis Community College†*	MO
St. Louis University†*	MO
St. Norbert College†*	WY
St. Olaf College†*	MN
St. Paul's College†*	VA
St. Peter's College†	NJ
St. Scholastica, College of†*	MN
St. Thomas, College of†*	MN
Salisbury State College†*	MD
Sam Houston State University†*	TX
San Diego State University†*	CA
San Francisco, City College of†*	CA
San Francisco State University†*	CA
San Jose State University†	CA
San Mateo, College of†*	CA
Santa Ana College†*	CA
Santa Barbara City Junior College†*	CA
Seminole Community College†	FL
Sequoias, College of the†*	CA
Seward County Community Junior College†*	KS
Shaw College at Detroit†*	MI
Siena College†*	NY
Siena Heights College†*	MI
Syskiyous, College of the†*	CA
Skagit Valley College†*	WA
Skyline College†*	CA
Slippery Rock State College†*	PA
South, University of the†	TN
South Alabama, University of†	AL
South Carolina, University of†	SC
South Carolina State College†*	SC
South Dakota, University of, at Springfield†*	SD
South Dakota, University of, at Vermillion†*	SD
South Dakota School of Mines and Technology†	SD
Southeast Community College†*	NE
Southeastern Louisiana University†	LA
Southeastern Oklahoma State University†*	OK
Southeast Missouri State†*	MO
Southern Arkansas University†	AR
Southern California, University of†*	CA
Southern Colorado, University of†*	CO
Southern Connecticut State College†*	CT
Southern Illinois University†*	IL
Southern Methodist University†	TX
Southern Oregon State College†*	OR
Southern University†*	LA
Southern University and Agricultural and Mechanical College†*	LA
Southern Utah State College†*	UT
Southwestern at Memphis†*	TN
Southwestern College†*	KS

Southwestern Louisiana, University of†	LA
Southwest State University†*	MN
Southwest Texas State University†	TX
Spring Arbor College†*	MI
Stanford University†*	CA
Stephen F. Austin State University†*	TX
Sterling College†*	KS
Stevens State Technology†	PA
Sul Ross State University†*	TX
Susquehanna University†	PA
Swarthmore College†	PA
Syracuse University†	NY
Tacoma Community College†*	WA
Tarkio College†*	MO
Tarleton State College†*	TX
Taylor University†*	IN
Temple University†*	PA
Tennessee, University of†*	TN
Tennessee State University†*	TN
Texas, The University of†*	TX
Texas, The University of, at Arlington†*	TX
Texas, The University of, at El Paso†*	TX
Texas A and I University†*	TX
Texas Christian University†*	TX
Texas Lutheran College*	TX
Texas Southern University†*	TX
Texas Tech University†*	TX
Texas Woman's University*	TX
Thiel College†	PA
Toledo, University of†	OH
Tougaloo College†*	MS
Towson State University†*	MD
Trenton State College†*	NJ
Trinity College†	CT
Trinity University†*	TX
Tri-State University†*	IN
Triton College†*	IL
Troy State University†*	AL
Tufts University†	MA
Tulane University†	LA
Tulsa, University of†*	OK
Tuskegee Institute†*	AL
Umpqua Community College†*	OR
Union College†	KY
Upsala College†	NJ
Ursinus College†*	PA
Utah, University of†*	UT
Utah State University†*	UT
Valparaiso University†	IN
Vanderbilt University†*	TN
Ventura College†*	CA
Villanova University†*	PA
Virginia, University of†*	VA
Virginia Polytechnic Institute†	VA
Virginia State College†*	VA
Virginia Union University†*	VA
Viterboro College*	WY
Wabash College†	IN
Wagner College†	NY
Wake Forest University†*	NC
Walsh College†	OH
Washburn University†	KS
Washington, University of†*	WA
Washington and Lee University†	VA
Washington State University†*	WA
Washington University†*	MO
Wayland Baptist College†	TX
Waynesburg College†	PA
Wayne State University†	MI
Weber State College†*	UT
Wenatchee Valley College†*	WA
Wesleyan College†*	CT
West Chester State College†*	PA
Western Carolina University†	NC
Western Illinois University†*	IL
Western Kentucky University†*	KY
Western Maryland College†*	MD
Western Michigan University†*	MI
Western Montana College†*	MT
Western State College of Colorado†	CO
Western Washington University†*	WA
Westfield State College†*	MA
West Georgia College†	GA
West Hills College†*	CA
West Los Angeles College†*	CA
Westminster College†	MO
Westmount College†	CA
West Texas State University†*	TX
West Virginia State College†*	WV
West Virginia University†*	WV
West Virginia Wesleyan College†*	WV
Wharton County Junior College†*	TX
Wheaton College†*	IL
Whitworth College†*	WA
Wichita State University†	KS
Wiley College†*	TX
Willamette University†*	OR
William and Mary, College of†*	VA
William Paterson College†	NJ
William Penn College†*	IA
Williams College†*	MA
Wilmington College†*	OH
Winona State College†*	MN
Winston-Salem State University†	NC
Wisconsin, University of, at Eau Claire†*	WI
Wisconsin, University of, at La Crosse†*	WI
Wisconsin, University of, at Milwaukee†*	WI
Wisconsin, University of, at	

Oshkosh†*	WI
Wisconsin, University of, at Platteville†*	WI
Wisconsin, University of, at River Falls†*	WI
Wisconsin, University of, at Stevens Point†*	WI
Wisconsin, University of, at Superior†	WI
Wisconsin, University of, at Whitewater†*	WI
Worcester State College†*	MA
Wright State University*	OH
Wyoming, University of†*	WY
Yakima Valley College†*	WA
Yale University†*	CT
Yankton College†*	SD
Yuba College†*	CA

ULTIMATE FRISBEE

New York, State University College of, at Purchase†	NY

VOLLEYBALL

Abilene Christian University*	TX
Adams State College of Colorado*	CO
Adrian College*	MI
Akron, University of*	OH
Alabama, University of, at Birmingham*	AL
Alabama, University of, at University*	AL
Alabama Agricultural and Mechanical University*	AL
Alabama State University*	AL
Alaska, University of, at Anchorage*	AK
Alaska, University of, at Fairbanks*	AK
Albany, Junior College of†*	NY
Albion College*	MI
Albright College*	PA
Alfred University*	NY
Allegheny College†*	PA
Allen County Community Junior College*	KS
Allentown College of St. Francis De Sales*	PA
Alma College*	MI
Alvin Junior College*	TX
American International College*	MA
American University, The*	DC
Angelo State University*	TX
Appalachian State University*	NC
Aquinas College*	MI
Arizona, University of*	AZ
Arizona State University†*	AZ
Arizona Western College*	AZ
Arkansas, University of, at Little Rock*	AR
Arkansas, University of, at Pine Bluff*	AR
Arkansas State University†*	AR
Aransas Tech University*	AR
Asbury College*	KY
Ashland College*	OH
Assumption College*	MA
Atlantic Christian College*	NC
Auburn University, at Auburn*	AL
Augusta College*	GA
Augustana College*	IL
Augustana College*	SD
Aurora College*	IL
Azusa Pacific College*	CA
Babson College*	MA
Baker University*	KS
Ball State University†*	IN
Baltimore, Community College of*	MD
Baptist Bible College*	PA
Baptist College, at Charleston*	SC
Barat College*	IL
Barber-Scotia College†*	NC
Barnard College*	NY
Barton County Community College*	KS
Bates College*	ME
Baylor University*	TX
Bellarmine College*	KY
Bellevue College*	NE
Beloit College*	WI
Bemidji State University*	MN
Benedictine College*	KS
Bennett College*	NC
Berea College*	KY
Bethany College*	KS
Bethany Lutheran College*	MN
Bethel College*	MN
Biola College*	CA
Bishop College†*	TX
Bismarck Junior College*	ND
Blackburn College*	IL
Bluefield College*	VA
Bluffton College*	OH
Boise State University*	ID
Boston College*	MA
Boston State College†	MA
Bowie State College*	MD
Bowling Green State University*	OH

Bradley University*	IL
Brandeis University*	MA
Brandywine College*	DE
Brevard College*	NC
Brevard Community College*	FL
Briar Cliff College*	IA
Bridgewater College†*	VA
Bridgewater State College*	MA
Brigham Young University*	UT
Brigham Young University†*	HI
Brooklyn College of the City University of New York*	NY
Brown University*	RI
Bryan College*	TN
Bryant College†*	RI
Bucknell University*	PA
Butler County Community Junior College*	KS
Butler University*	IN
California, University of, at Davis*	CA
California, University of, at Irvine*	CA
California, University of, at Los Angeles†*	CA
California, University of, at Riverside†*	CA
California, University of, at San Diego†*	CA
California, University of, at Santa Barbara†*	CA
California Institute of Technology*	CA
California Polytechnic State University†*	CA
California State College, at Bakersfield*	CA
California State College, at Sonoma*	CA
California State College, at Stanislaus*	CA
California State University, at Chico*	CA
California State University, at Fullerton*	CA
California State University, at Haywood*	CA
California State University, at Long Beach†*	CA
Calvary Bible College*	MO
Calvin College*	MI
Cameron University*	OK
Canisius College*	NY
Carlow College*	PA
Carl Sandburg College*	IL
Carroll College*	MT
Carroll College*	WI
Carson-Newman College*	TN
Carthage College*	WI
Casper College*	WY
Catawaba College*	NC
Centenary College*	NJ
Central Arkansas, University of*	AR
Centralia College*	WA
Central Junior College*	KS
Central Michigan University*	MI
Central Missouri State University*	MO
Central State University*	OK
Chadron State College*	NE
Charleston, College of*	SC
Charleston, University of*	WV
Chatham College*	PA
Chicago, The University of*	IL
Chicago State University*	IL
Chowan College*	NC
Christopher Newport College*	VA
Cincinnati, University of†*	OH
Cincinnati Bible College*	OH
Citrus College*	CA
Clackamas Community College*	OR
Clarion State College*	PA
Clarke College*	IA
Clark University*	MA
Clemson University*	SC
Cleveland State University*	OH
Coastal Carolina College*	SC
Cochise College*	AZ
Coe College*	IA
Coffeyville Community College*	KS
Colgate University*	NY
Colorado College†*	CO
Colorado Northwestern Community College*	CO
Colorado School of Mines*	CO
Colorado State University*	CO
Columbia Basin College*	WA
Columbia Christian College*	OR
Columbia College*	SC
Columbus College*	GA
Concord College*	WV
Concordia College*	IL
Concordia College*	MN
Concordia College*	NE
Concordia College*	OR
Concordia College*	TX
Connecticut, University of*	CT
Connecticut College*	CT
Converse College*	SC
Cornell College*	IA
Cornell University*	NY
Cosumnes River College*	CA
Cottey College*	MO
Covenant College*	TN
Cowley County Community College*	KS
Creighton University*	NE
Culver-Stockton College*	MO
Cuyahoga Community College*	OH
Cuyahoga Community College,	

Metro Campus*	OH
C. W. Post College*	NY
Cypress College*	CA
Dakota Wesleyan University*	SD
Dayton, University of*	OH
Daytona Beach Community College*	FL
Delaware, University of*	DE
Delaware Valley College*	PA
DePauw University*	IN
Desert, College of the†*	CA
Dickinson State College*	ND
District of Columbia, University of†*	DC
Doane College*	NE
Dominican College*	NY
Drury College*	MO
Dubuque, University of*	IA
Duke University*	NC
Dundalk Community College*	MD
Duquesne University*	PA
D'Youville College*	NY
East Carolina University*	NC
East Central Junior College*	MS
Eastern College*	PA
Eastern Illinois University*	IL
Eastern Kentucky University*	KY
Eastern Michigan University*	MI
Eastern Montana College*	MT
Eastern Nazarene College*	MA
Eastern Utah, College of*	UT
Eastern Wyoming College*	WY
East Stroudsburg State College†*	PA
East Texas State University*	TX
Edinboro State College*	PA
Edmonds Community College*	WA
Eisenhower College*	NY
El Camino College†*	CA
Elizabethtown College*	PA
Elmhurst College*	IL
Elmira College*	NY
Elon College*	NC
Emory and Henry College*	VA
Emporia State University*	KS
Erskine College*	SC
Essex Community College*	MD
Everett Community College*	WA
Fairleigh Dickinson University*	NJ
Fairmont State College*	WV
Fergus Falls Community College*	MN
Ferris State College*	MI
Ferrum College*	WA
Findlay College*	OH
Fitchburg State College*	MA
Flagler College*	FL
Florida A. and M. University*	FL
Florida International University*	FL
Florida Junior College*	FL
Florida Southern College*	FL
Florida State University*	FL
Florida Technological University*	FL
Fontbonne College*	MO
Fordham University*	NY
Fort Hayes State*	KS
Fort Steilacoom Community College*	WA
Fort Wayne Bible College*	IN
Framingham State College*	MA
Francis Marion College*	SC
Franklin Pierce College*	NH
Fresno State University*	CA
Friends University*	KS
Furman University†*	SC
Gannon College*	PA
Gardner-Webb College*	NC
Garrett Community College*	MD
Gateway Technical Institute*	WI
George Fox College*	OR
Georgetown University*	DC
George Washington University*	DC
Georgia, University of*	GA
Georgian Court College*	NJ
Gettysburg College*	PA
Glassboro State College*	NJ
Glen Oaks Community College*	MI
Golden Valley Lutheran College*	MN
Gonzaga University*	WA
Gordon College*	MA
Grace College*	IN
Graceland College†*	IA
Grand Canyon College*	AZ
Grand Rapids Baptist College*	MI
Grand Rapids Junior College*	MI
Grand Valley State College*	MI
Green River Community College*	WA
Greensboro College*	NC
Greensville College*	IL
Grinnell College*	IA
Grove City College*	PA
Guilford College*	NC
Gustavus Adolphus College*	MN
Hagerstown Junior College*	MD
Hamline University*	MN
Hampton Institute*	VA
Hanover College*	IN
Hardin-Simmons University*	TX
Hartford, University of*	CT
Harvard University†	MA
Hastings College*	NE
Hawaii, University of, at Hilo*	HI
Hawaii, University of, at Honolulu†*	HI
Hawaii Pacific College†*	HI
Heidelberg College*	OH
Henderson State University*	OR
Hendrix College*	AR

Herbert H. Lehman College*	NY	Kalamazoo Valley Community College*	MI
Hesston College*	KS	Kankakee Community College*	IL
Highland Community Junior College*	KS	Kansas, University of*	KS
High Point College*	NC	Kansas State University*	KS
Hilbert College*	NY	Kansas Wesleyan College*	KS
Hillsborough Community College*	FL	Kean College of New Jersey*	NJ
Hillsdale College*	MI	Kearney State College*	NE
Hiram College*	OH	Kent State University*	OH
Hofstra University*	NY	Kentucky, University of*	KY
Holy Cross College*	MA	Kentucky State University*	KY
Hood College*	MD	Kentucky Wesleyan College*	KY
Hope College*	MI	Kenyon College*	OH
Houghton College*	NY	King's College, The*	NY
Houston, University of*	TX	Kishwaukee College*	IL
Howard Payne University*	TX	Kutztown State College*	PA
Humboldt State University*	CA	Lackawanna Junior College*	PA
Huntington College*	IN	Lafayette College*	PA
Husson College*	ME	Lake Erie College*	OH
Hutchinson Community Junior College*	KS	Lake Superior State College*	MI
Idaho, College of*	ID	Lamar University†*	TX
Idaho, University of*	ID	Lambuth College*	TN
Idaho State University*	ID	Lander College*	SC
Illinois, University of, at Champaign*	IL	Lane Community College*	OR
Illinois, University of, at Chicago Circle*	IL	Laredo Junior College*	TX
Illinois Benedictine College*	IL	La Salle College*	PA
Illinois College*	IL	La Verne College†*	CA
Illinois State University*	IL	Lawrence University*	WI
Illinois Valley Community College*	IL	Lees-McRae College*	NC
Illinois Wesleyan University*	IL	Lehigh University*	PA
Indiana Central University*	IN	Le Moyne College*	NY
Indiana Institute of Technology*	IN	Lenoir-Rhyne College*	NC
Indiana State University*	IN	Lewis and Clark Community College*	IL
Indiana University of Pennsylvania*	PA	Lewis University*	IL
Indiana University-Purdue University, at Fort Wayne†*	IN	Lewis-Clark State College*	ID
Indiana University-Purdue University, at Indianapolis*	IN	Liberty Baptist College*	VA
Indian River Community College*	FL	Lincoln Christian College*	IL
Inver Hills College*	MN	Lincoln Land Community College*	IL
Iowa, University of*	IA	Lincoln Trail College*	IL
Iowa Lakes Community College*	IA	Lincoln University*	MO
Iowa State University*	IA	Lindenwood College, The*	MO
Iowa Wesleyan College*	IA	Linfield College*	OR
Ithaca College*	NY	Livingstone College*	NC
Jacksonville State University*	AL	Livingston University*	AL
James Madison University*	VA	Longwood College*	VA
Jamestown College*	ND	Loras College*	IA
Jarvis Christian College†*	TX	Los Angeles Baptist College*	CA
John Carroll University*	OH	Los Angeles Pierce Junior College†*	CA
Judson College*	AL	Los Angeles Southwest College*	CA
Juniata College*	PA	Louisiana State University*	LA
		Louisiana Tech University†	LA
		Louisville, University of*	KY
		Lowell, University of*	MA
		Lower Columbia College*	WA
		Loyola Marymount University†*	CA
		Lubbock Christian College*	TX

354

Luther College*	IA
Lynchburg College*	VA
Macalester College*	MN
McKendree College*	IL
McMurray College*	TX
McNeese State University*	LA
McPherson College*	KS
Maine, University of, at Farmington*	ME
Maine, University of, at Fort Kent*	ME
Maine, University of, at Presque Isle*	ME
Malone College*	OH
Manchester College*	IN
Manhattan College*	NY
Mankato State University*	MN
Marian College*	IN
Marietta College*	OH
Marin, College of*	CA
Marist College*	NY
Marquette University*	WI
Marshall University*	WV
Mars Hill College*	NC
Mary Hardin-Baylor College*	TX
Maryland, University of, at Catonsville*	MD
Maryland, University of, at College Park*	MD
Maryville College*	TN
Mary Washington College*	VA
Massachusetts Institute of Technology*	MA
Mattatuck Community College*	CT
Medgar Evers College*	NY
Memphis State University*	TN
Menlo College†*	CA
Mercy College*	NY
Meredith College*	NC
Metropolitan State College*	CO
Miami, University of*	FL
Miami Christian College*	FL
Miami-Dade Community College, New World Center*	FL
Miami-Dade Community College, South Campus	FL
Miami University†*	OH
Miami University, Middletown Campus*	OH
Michigan, University of*	MI
Michigan State University*	MI
Middle Tennessee State University*	TN
Mid-Plains Community College*	NE
Mid-State Technical Institute*	WI
Midwestern State University*	TX
Milligan College*	TN
Millikan University†	IL
Mills College*	CA
Milwaukee Area Technical College*	WI
Milwaukee School of Engineering*	WI
Mineral Area Junior College*	MO
Minnesota, University of, at Minneapolis*	MN
Minnesota, University of, at Morris*	MN
Minnesota, University of, Technical College*	MN
Minnesota Bible College†*	MN
Mira Costa College*	CA
Mississippi State University*	MS
Missouri, University of*	MO
Missouri, University of, at St. Louis*	MO
Missouri Baptist College*	MO
Missouri Southern State College*	MO
Missouri Valley College*	MO
Missouri Western College*	MO
Monmouth College*	IL
Montana, University of*	MT
Montana State University*	MT
Montana Tech*	MT
Montevallo, University of*	AL
Moorhead State University*	MN
Mooorpark College†	AR
Morehead State University*	KY
Morgan State University*	MD
Morningside College*	IA
Mott Community College*	MN
Mount Ida Junior College*	MA
Mount Marty College*	SD
Mount St. Joseph, College of*	OH
Mount San Jacinto College*	CA
Muhlenberg College*	PA
Murray State University*	KY
Mustegon Community College*	MI
Napa Community College*	CA
National College*	SD
Nazareth College*	NY
Nebraska, University of*	NE
Nebraska, University of, at Omaha*	NE
Nebraska Wesleyan University*	NE
Newberry College*	SC
New Hampshire College*	NH
New Hampshire Technological Institute†*	NH
New Haven, University of*	CT
New Mexico Highlands University*	NM
New Orleans, University of*	LA
New York, State University College of, at Brockport*	NY
New York, State University College of, at Fredonia*	NY
New York, State University	

New York, State University College of, at New Paltz†*	NY
New York, State University College of, at Oneonta*	NY
New York, State University College of, at Oswego*	NY
New York, State University College of, at Plattsburgh*	NY
New York, State University College of, at Potsdam*	NY
New York, State University of, at Binghamton*	NY
New York, State University of, at Buffalo*	NY
New York Institute of Technology*	NY
Niagara University*	NY
Nicholls State University*	LA
North Adams State College*	MA
North Alabama, University of*	AL
North Carolina, University of, at Chapel Hill*	NC
North Carolina, University of, at Charlotte*	NC
North Carolina, University of, at Greensboro†*	NC
North Carolina, University of, at Wilmington*	NC
North Carolina Agricultural and Technical State University*	NC
North Carolina State University*	NC
North Central College*	IL
North Dakota, University of*	ND
North Dakota State University, at Bottineau*	ND
North Dakota State University, at Fargo*	ND
Northeastern Illinois University*	IL
Northeast Louisiana University*	LA
Northern Arizona University*	AZ
Northern Colorado, University of*	CO
Northern Illinois University*	IL
Northern Iowa, University of*	IA
Northern Kentucky University*	KY
Northern Michigan University*	MI
Northern Montana College*	MT
Northern State College*	SD
North Georgia College†*	GA
North Greenville College*	SC
North Idaho College*	ID
Northland College*	WI
Northland Community College*	MN
North Texas State University*	TX
Northwest Christian College*	OR
Northwest College*	WA
Northwestern College*	MN
Northwestern University*	IL
Northwest Missouri State University*	MO
Notre Dame, University of*	IN
Notre Dame College*	MD
Oakland City College*	IN
Oakland University*	MI
Oakton Community College*	IL
Oberlin College*	OH
Occidental College*	CA
Ohio Northern University*	OH
Ohio State University†*	OH
Ohio Wesleyan University*	OH
Oklahoma, University of*	OK
Oklahoma Baptist University*	OK
Oklahoma City University*	OK
Oklahoma State University*	OK
Olivet College*	MI
Olivet Nazarene College*	IL
Olney Central College*	IL
Oral Roberts University*	OK
Oregon, University of*	OR
Oregon State University*	OR
Oregon Technical Institute*	OR
Otero Junior College*	CO
Ottawa University*	KS
Otterbein College*	OH
Ouachita Baptist College*	AR
Oxnard College†	CA
Ozarks, School of the*	MO
Pace University*	NY
Pacific, University of the*	CA
Pacific Lutheran University*	WA
Pacific University*	OR
Palm Beach Junior College*	FL
Palomar College*	CA
Pan American University*	TX
Park College†*	MO
Parkland College*	IL
Paul Smith's College*	NY
Pembroke State University*	NC
Pennsylvania, University of†*	PA
Pennsylvania State University, at Altoona*	PA
Pennsylvania State University, at Beaver Campus*	PA
Pennsylvania State University, at DuBois*	PA
Pennsylvania State University, at McKeesport*	PA
Pennsylvania State University, at Middletown*	PA
Pennsylvania State University, at University Park†*	PA
Pennsylvania State University (Behrend College)*	PA
Penn Valley Community College*	MO
Pensacola Junior College*	FL
Pepperdine University†*	CA
Philadelphia Community College*	PA
Piedmont Bible College*	NC
Pima Community College*	AZ

Pittsburgh, University of†*	PA
Point Loma College*	CA
Porterville College*	CA
Portland, University of*	OR
Portland State University*	OR
Pratt Community Junior College*	KS
Pratt Institute*	NY
Presbyterian College*	SC
Princeton University†*	NJ
Principia College*	IL
Providence College†*	RI
Puerto Rico Agricultural and Mechanical University†	PR
Purdue University, at Calumet*	IL
Purdue University, at West Lafayette*	IL
Quincy College*	IL
Radford College*	VA
Redlands, University of*	CA
Redwoods, College of the*	CA
Regis College*	CO
Rice University*	TX
Rider College*	NJ
Rio Grande College*	OH
Ripon College*	WI
Riverside City College*	CA
Roanoke College*	VA
Robert Morris College*	PA
Roberts Wesleyan College*	NY
Rochester, University of*	NY
Rockhurst College*	MO
Rollins College*	FL
Rutgers, State University of, at Newark†*	NJ
Rutgers, State University of, at New Brunswick*	NJ
Sacred Heart University†*	CT
Saginaw Valley College*	MI
St. Augustine's College†*	NC
St. Cloud State University*	MN
St. Edward's University*	TX
St. Francis College*	NY
St. Francis College of Pennsylvania*	PA
St. Francis, College of*	IL
St. John Fisher College*	NY
St. Johns College*	KS
St. Joseph College*	IN
St. Joseph the Provider, College of*	VT
St. Lawrence University*	NY
St. Leo College*	FL
St. Louis Community College*	MO
St. Louis University*	MO
St. Mary, College of*	NE
St. Mary of the Plains College*	KS
St. Mary's College*	MN
St. Mary's College of California*	CA
St. Mary's University of Texas*	TX
St. Olaf College*	MN
St. Paul's College*	VA
St. Scholastica, College of*	MN
St. Teresa, College of*	MN
St. Thomas, College of*	MN
St. Xavier College*	IL
Salisbury State College*	MD
Sam Houston State University*	TX
San Diego, University of*	CA
San Diego State University†*	CA
San Francisco, City College of*	CA
San Francisco, University of*	CA
San Francisco State University*	CA
San Jose State University*	CA
San Mateo, College of*	CA
Santa Barbara City Junior College†*	CA
Santa Clara, University of†*	CA
Schoolcraft College*	MI
Scranton, University of*	PA
Seminole Community College*	FL
Sequoias, College of the*	CA
Seward County Community Junior College†*	KS
Shawnee College*	IL
Shawnee State College†*	OH
Shepherd College*	WV
Sheridan College*	WY
Siena College*	NY
Simmons College*	MA
Siskiyous, College of the*	CA
Skagit Valley College*	WA
Skidmore College†*	NY
Skyline College*	CA
Slippery Rock State College*	PA
Smith College*	MA
South, University of the*	TN
South Alabama, University of*	AL
Southampton College*	NY
South Carolina, University of*	SC
South Carolina State College*	SC
South Dakota, University of, at Springfield*	SD
South Dakota, University of, at Vermillion*	SD
South Dakota School of Mines and Technology*	SD
Southeast Community College*	NE
Southeastern Louisiana University*	LA
Southeastern Oklahoma State University*	OK
Southern Arkansas University*	AR
Southern California, University of†*	CA
Southern California College*	CA
Southern Colorado, University of*	CO
Southern Connecticut State College*	CT
Southern Illinois University*	IL

Southern Maine, University of*	ME
Southern Maine Vocational Technical Institute†*	ME
Southern Oregon State College*	OR
Southern State Community State College†*	OH
Southern University and Agricultural and Mechanical College*	LA
Southern Utah State College*	UT
South Florida, The University of*	FL
Southwest Baptist College*	MO
Southwestern at Memphis*	TN
Southwestern College*	KS
Southwestern Louisiana, University of*	LA
Southwestern University*	TX
Southwest State University*	MN
Southwest Texas State University*	TX
Spartanburg Methodist College*	SC
Spring Arbor College*	MI
Stanford University†*	CA
State Fair Community College*	MO
Staten Island, College of*	NY
Stephen F. Austin State University*	TX
Sterling College*	KS
Stetson University*	FL
Sul Ross State University*	TX
Susquehanna University*	PA
Swarthmore College*	PA
Syracuse University*	NY
Tabor College*	KS
Tacoma Community College*	WA
Tampa, University of*	FL
Tarkio College*	MO
Tarleton State College*	TX
Taylor University*	IN
Temple University*	PA
Tennessee, University of*	TN
Tennessee, University of, at Martin*	TN
Tennessee Technological University*	TN
Texas, The University of*	TX
Texas, The University of, at Arlington†*	TX
Texas, The University of, at El Paso*	TX
Texas A and I University*	TX
Texas Lutheran College*	TX
Texas Wesleyan College*	TX
Texas Woman's University*	TX
Thiel College*	PA
Thomas More College*	KY
Three Rivers Community College*	MO
Tiffin University*	OH
Toledo, University of†*	OH
Towson State University*	MD
Treasure Valley Community College*	OR
Trenton State College*	NJ
Trinity University*	TX
Tri-State University*	IN
Triton College*	IL
Troy State University*	AL
Tulane University*	LA
Tulsa, University of*	OK
Tunxis Community College*	CT
Tuskegee Institute*	AL
Umpqua Community College*	OR
Union College*	KY
United Wesleyan College*	PA
Upper Iowa University*	IA
Upsala College*	NJ
Urbana College*	OH
Ursinus College*	PA
Utah, University of*	UT
Utah State University*	UT
Valparaiso University*	IN
Vanderbilt University*	TN
Ventura College*	CA
Villanova University*	PA
Virginia, University of*	VA
Virginia Commonwealth University†*	VA
Virginia Polytechnic Institute*	VA
Virginia Union University*	VA
Wake Forest University*	NC
Walsh College*	OH
Warner Pacific College*	OR
Washburn University*	KS
Washington Bible College*	MD
Washington State University*	WA
Washington University*	MO
Waynesburg College*	PA
Wayne State University*	MI
Webber College*	FL
Weber State College*	UT
West Chester State College*	PA
Western Carolina University†*	NC
Western Illinois University*	IL
Western Maryland College*	MD
Western Montana College*	MT
Western New England College*	MA
Western State College of Colorado*	CO
Western Washington University*	WA
Westfield State College†*	MA
West Georgia College*	GA
West Hills College*	CA
West Liberty State College*	WV
West Los Angeles College*	CA
Westmount College*	CA
West Texas State University*	TX
West Virginia University*	WV
Westmoreland Community	

College*	PA
Wharton County Junior College*	TX
Wheaton College*	IL
Wheaton College*	MA
Wheeling College*	WV
Whitworth College*	WA
Wilberforce University†*	OH
Wiley College†*	TX
Wilkes College*	PA
Willamette University*	OR
William and Mary, College of*	VA
William Paterson College*	NJ
William Penn College*	IA
Williams College*	MA
Wilmington College*	OH
Wilson College*	PA
Winona State College*	MN
Winston-Salem State University*	NC
Winthrop College*	SC
Wisconsin, University of, at Eau Claire*	WI
Wisconsin, University of, at La Crosse*	WI
Wisconsin, University of, at Marathon County*	WI
Wisconsin, University of, at Milwaukee*	WI
Wisconsin, University of, at Oshkosh*	WI
Wisconsin, University of, at River Falls*	WI
Wisconsin, University of, at Stevens Point*	WI
Wisconsin, University of, at Superior*	WI
Wisconsin, University of, at Waukesha*	WI
Wisconsin, University of, at Whitewater*	WI
Wofford College*	SC
Worcester State College*	MA
Worthington Community College*	MN
Wyoming, University of*	WY
Xavier University*	OH
Yakima Valley College*	WA
Yale University†*	CT
Yankton College*	SD
York College*	NE
Youngstown State University*	OH
Yuba College*	CA

WATER POLO

Arkansas, University of, at Little Rock†	AR
Brown University†	RI
Bucknell University†	PA
California, University of, at Davis†	CA
California, University of, at Irvine†	CA
California, University of, at Los Angeles†	CA
California, University of, at Riverside†	CA
California, University of, at San Diego†	CA
California, University of, at Santa Barbara†	CA
California Institute of Technology†	CA
California Polytechnic State University†	CA
California State University, at Fullerton†	CA
California State University, at Haywood†	CA
California State University, at Long Beach†	CA
Citrus College†	CA
Cleveland State University†	OH
Contra Costa College†	CA
Cornell University†	NY
Cypress College†	CA
Dartmouth College†*	NH
El Camino College†	CA
Fordham University†	NY
Fresno State University†	CA
Georgia Southern College†	GA
Harvard University†	MA
Hendrix College†	AR
Jacksonville State University†	AL
Kentucky, University of†	KY
Loras College†	IA
Los Angeles Pierce Junior College†	CA
Loyola Marymount University†	CA
Marin, College of†*	CA
Massachusetts Institute of Technology†	MA
Monmouth College†	NJ
New York, State University College of, at Oswego†	NY
Northwestern University†	IL
Occidental College†	CA
Ohio Northern University†*	OH
Pacific, University of the†	CA
Pacific Lutheran University†	CA
Palomar Community College†	CA
Pepperdine University†	CA
Portland State University†	OR
Principia College†	IL
Puerto Rico Agricultural and Mechanical University†	PR
Redlands, University of†*	CA

Riverside City College†	CA
San Francisco State University†	CA
San Jose State University†	CA
Santa Ana College†	CA
Santa Clara, University of†	CA
Sequoias, College of the†	CA
Southern California, University of†	CA
Southern Oregon State College†	OR
Stanford University†	CA
Trinity College†	CT
Ventura College†	CA
Villanova University†	PA
Washington and Lee University†	VA
Washington State University†	WA
Yale University†	CT

WATER SKIING

Eckerd College†	FL
Rollins College†*	FL

WEIGHTLIFTING

Memphis State University†	TN
Puerto Rico Agricultural and Mechanical University†	PR
Texas, The University of, at Arlington†	TX

WRESTLING

Adams State College of Colorado†	CO
Adrian College†	MI
Akron, University of†	OH
Albright College†	PA
Allegheny College†	PA
Alma College†	MI
American University, The†	DC
Amherst College†	MA
Anderson College†	IL
Anne Arundel Community College†	MD
Appalachian State University†	NC
Arizona State University†	AZ
Arizona Western College†	AZ
Ashland College†	OH
Auburn University, at Auburn†	AL
Augustana College†	IL
Augustana College†	SD
Aurora College†	IL
Ball State University†	IN
Baptist Bible College†	MO
Barber-Scotia College†	NC
Bemidji State University†	MN
Bethany Lutheran College†	MN
Bethel College†	MN
Biola College†	CA
Bismarck Junior College†	ND
Boise State University†	ID
Boston State College†	MA
Boston University†	MA
Bowdoin College†	ME
Bowling Green State University†	OH
Brevard Community College†	FL
Bridgewater State College†	MA
Brigham Young University†	UT
Brooklyn College of the City University of New York†	NY
Brown University†	RI
Bucknell University†	PA
California, University of, at Davis†	CA
California Institute of Technology†	CA
California Polytechnic State University†	CA
California State College, at Bakersfield†	CA
California State College, at Stanislaus†	CA
California State University, at Chico†	CA
California State University, at Fullerton†	CA
California State University, at Long Beach†	CA
Calvin College†	MI
Campbell College†	NC
Carroll College†	WI
Carson-Newman College†	TN
Carthage College†	WI
Catawaba College†	NC
Central Michigan University†	MI
Central Missouri State University†	MO
Central State University†	OK
Chadron State College†	NE
Chicago, The University of†	IL
Chicago State University†	IL
Chowan College†	NC
Citadel, The†	SC
Clackamas Community College†	OR
Clarion State College†	PA
Clemson University†	SC
Cleveland State University†	OH
Coe College†	IA
Colgate University†	NY

Colorado Northwestern Community College†	CO
Colorado School of Mines†	CO
Colorado State University†	CO
Columbia Basin College†	WA
Columbia University†	NY
Concordia College†	IL
Concordia College†	MN
Cornell University†	NY
Crowder College†	MO
Cuyahoga Community College†	OH
Cuyahoga Community College, Metro Campus†	OH
C. W. Post College†	NY
Cypress College†	CA
Davidson College†	NC
Delaware, University of†	DE
Delaware State College†	DE
Delaware Valley College†	PA
Dickinson State College†	ND
Dubuque, University of†	IA
Duke University†	NC
East Carolina University†	NC
Eastern Illinois University†	IL
Eastern Michigan University†	MI
Eastern Utah, College of†	UT
East Stroudsburg State College†	PA
Edinboro State College†	PA
El Camino College†	CA
Elizabethtown College†	PA
Elmhurst College†	IL
Elon College†	NC
Evansville, University of†	IN
Fairleigh Dickinson University†	NJ
Ferris State College†	MI
Findlay College†	OH
Florida International University†	FL
Florida Technological University†	FL
Fort Hayes State†	KS
Fresno State University†	CA
Furman University†	SC
George Washington University†	DC
Georgia Institute of Technology†	GA
Gettysburg College†	PA
Glassboro State College†	NJ
Golden Valley Lutheran College†	MN
Graceland College†	IA
Grand Rapids Baptist College†	MI
Grand Rapids Junior College†	MI
Grand Valley State College†	MI
Grinnell College†	IA
Gustavus Adolphus College†	MN
Hamline University†	MN
Hampton Institute†	VA
Hanover College†	IN
Hartford, University of†	CT
Harvard University†	MA
Heidelberg College†	OH
Hiram College†	OH
Hofstra University†	NY
Holy Cross College†	MA
Hope College†	MI
Houghton College	NY
Humboldt State University†	CA
Hunter College†	NY
Huntington College†	IN
Idaho State University†	ID
Illinois, University of, at Champaign†	IL
Illinois College†	IL
Illinois State University†	IL
Illinois Wesleyan University†	IL
Indiana Central University†	IN
Indiana University, at Bloomington†	IN
Indiana University of Pennsylvania†	PA
Iowa, University of†	IA
Iowa State University†	IA
Ithaca College†	NY
James Madison University†	VA
Jamestown College†	ND
John Carroll University†	OH
Juniata College†	PA
Kean College of New Jersey†	NJ
Kearney State College†	NE
Kent State University†	OH
Kentucky, University of†	KY
King's College, The†	NY
Kutztown State College†	PA
Lafayette College†	PA
Lake Superior State College†	MI
Lancaster Bible College†	PA
Lane Community College†	OR
La Salle College†	PA
La Verne College†	CA
Lawrence University†	WI
Lebanon Valley College†	PA
Lehigh University†	PA
Liberty Baptist College†	VA
Lincoln University†	MO
Linfield College†	OH
Livingstone College†	NC
Lock Haven State College†	PA
Longwood College†	VA
Los Angeles Pierce Junior College†	CA
Louisiana State University†	LA
Lowell, University of†	MA
Luther College†	IA
Lycoming College†	PA
Lynchburg College†	VA
Maine, University of, at Presque Isle†	ME
Malone College†	OH
Manchester College†	IN
Manhattan College†	NY
Mankato State University†	MN

Mansfield State College†	PA
Marquette University†	WI
Marshall University†	WV
Maryland, University of, at College Park†	MD
Massachusetts, University of†	MA
Massachusetts Institute of Technology†	MA
Miami University†	OH
Michigan, University of†	MI
Michigan State University†	MI
Millikan University†	IL
Mills College	CA
Minnesota, University of, at Minneapolis†	MN
Minnesota, University of, at Morris†	MN
Minnesota, University of, Technical College†	MN
Missouri, University of†	MO
Missouri, University of, at Rolla†	MO
Missouri, University of, at St. Louis†	MO
Monmouth College†	IL
Montana, University of†	MT
Montana State University†	MT
Montclair State University†	NJ
Moorhead State University†	MN
Moorpark College†	AR
Morgan State University†	MD
Muhlenberg College†	PA
Mustegon Community College†	MI
Nebraska, University of†	NE
Nebraska, University of, at Omaha†	NE
Nebraska Wesleyan University†	NE
New Mexico Highlands University†	NM
New York, State University College of, at Brockport†	NY
New York, State University College of, at Oneonta†	NY
New York, State University College of, at Oswego†	NY
New York, State University of, at Albany†	NY
New York, State University of, at Binghamton†	NY
New York, State University of, at Buffalo†	NY
Norfolk State College†	VA
North Adams State College	MA
North Carolina, University of, at Chapel Hill†	NC
North Carolina Agricultural and Technical State University†	NC
North Carolina State University†	NC
North Central College†	IL
North Dakota, University of†	ND
North Dakota State University, at Fargo†	ND
Northeastern Oklahoma A and M College†	OK
Northern Arizona University†	AZ
Northern Colorado, University of†	CO
Northern Illinois University†	IL
Northern Iowa, University of†	IA
Northern Michigan University†	MI
Northern Montana College†	MT
Northern State College†	SD
North Idaho College†	ID
Northland College†	WI
Northwestern College†	MN
Northwestern College†	WI
Northwestern University†	IL
Northwest Missouri State University†	MO
Northwest Nazarene College†	ID
Norwich University†	VT
Notre Dame, University of†	IN
Oakland University†	MI
Oakton Community College†	IL
Ohio Northern University†	OR
Ohio State University†	OH
Ohio Wesleyan University†	OH
Oklahoma, University of†	OK
Oklahoma State University†	OK
Old Dominion University†	VA
Olivet Nazarene College†	IL
Oregon, University of†	OR
Oregon Institute of Technology†	OR
Oregon State University†	OR
Oscar Rose Junior College†	OK
Pacific Lutheran University†	WA
Pacific University†	OR
Palomar College†	CA
Paul Smith's College†	NY
Pembroke State University†	NC
Pennsylvania, University of†	PA
Pennsylvania State University, at Altoona†	PA
Pennsylvania State University, at University Park†	PA
Pfeiffer College†	NC
Pima Community College†	AZ
Pittsburgh, University of†	PA
Pittsburgh, University of, at Johnstown†	PA
Plymouth State College†	NH
Porterville College†	CA
Portland State University†	OR
Princeton University†	NJ
Puerto Rico Agricultural and Mechanical University†	PR
Purdue University, at West Lafayette†	IL
Redlands, University of†	CA
Redwoods, College of the†	CA
Rensselaer Polytechnic Institute†	NY

Rider College†	NJ
Ripon College†	WI
Rutgers, State University of, at Camden†	NJ
Rutgers, State University of, at Newark†	NJ
Rutgers, State University of, at New Brunswick†	NJ
Saginaw Valley College†	MI
St. Cloud State University†	MN
St. John Fisher College†	NY
St. Johns University†	MN
St. Lawrence University†	NY
St. Mary's College†	MN
St. Olaf College†	MN
St. Thomas, College of†	MN
Salisbury State College†	MD
San Francisco State University†	CA
San Jose State University†	CA
San Mateo, College of†	CA
Santa Ana College†	CA
Scranton, University of†	PA
Sequoias, College of the†	CA
Siena Heights College†	MI
Skyline College†	CA
Slippery Rock State College†	PA
South, University of the†	TN
South Carolina State College†	SC
South Dakota University, at Springfield†	SD
Southeast Missouri State University†	MO
Southern Connecticut State College†	CT
Southern Illinois University†	IL
Southern Oregon State College†	OR
Southwest State University†	MN
Stevens Institute of Technology†	NJ
Stevens State Technology†	PA
Susquehanna University†	PA
Swarthmore College†	PA
Syracuse University†	NY
Taylor University†	IN
Temple University†	PA
Tennessee, University of†	TN
Tennessee Technological University†	TN
Thiel College†	PA
Toledo, University of†	OH
Towson State University†	MD
Treasure Valley Community College†	OR
Trenton State College†	NJ
Trinity College†	CT
Triton College†	IL
Umpqua Community College†	OR
Upper Iowa University†	IA
Upsala College†	NJ
Urbana College†	OH
Ursinus College†	PA
Utah State University†	UT
Valparaiso University†	IN
Ventura College†	CA
Virginia, University of†	VA
Virginia Commonwealth University†	VA
Virginia Polytechnic Institute†	VA
Wabash College†	IN
Wagner College†	NY
Washington and Lee University†	VA
Washington State University†	MO
Waynesburg College†	PA
Webber College†	FL
Weber State College†	UT
West Chester State College†	PA
Western Illinois University†	IL
Western Maryland College†	MD
Western Michigan University†	MI
Western Montana College†	MT
Western New England College†	MA
Western State College of Colorado†	CO
Western Washington University†	WA
West Liberty State College†	WV
West Virginia State College†	WV
West Virginia University†	WV
Wheaton College†	IL
Wilkes College†	PA
Willamette University†	OR
William and Mary, College of†	VA
William Penn College†	IA
Williams College†	MA
Williamsport Area Community College†	PA
Wilmington College†	OH
Winona State College†	MN
Winston-Salem State University†	NC
Wisconsin, University of, at Eau Claire†	WI
Wisconsin, University of, at La Crosse†	WI
Wisconsin, University of, at Oshkosh†	WI
Wisconsin, University of, at Platteville†	WI
Wisconsin, University of, at River Falls†	WI
Wisconsin, University of, at Stevens Point†	WI
Wisconsin, University of, at Superior†	WI
Wisconsin, University of, at Whitewater†	WI
Worthington Community College†	MN
Wright State University†	OH
Wyoming, University of†	WY
Yale University†	CT
Yankton College†	SD
Youngstown State University†	OH

LIBRARY OF DAVIDSON COLLEGE

Books on regular loan may be checked out for **two weeks**. Books must be presented at the Circulation Desk in order to be renewed.

A fine is charged after date due.

books are subject to special regulations at the